CAMBRIDGE L]

Books of en

MW00775401

Archaeology

The discovery of material remains from the recent or the ancient past has always been a source of fascination, but the development of archaeology as an academic discipline which interpreted such finds is relatively recent. It was the work of Winckelmann at Pompeii in the 1760s which first revealed the potential of systematic excavation to scholars and the wider public. Pioneering figures of the nineteenth century such as Schliemann, Layard and Petrie transformed archaeology from a search for ancient artifacts, by means as crude as using gunpowder to break into a tomb, to a science which drew from a wide range of disciplines - ancient languages and literature, geology, chemistry, social history - to increase our understanding of human life and society in the remote past.

History of Ancient Pottery

The Egyptologist Samuel Birch (1813–85) began to study Chinese at school, and obtained his first post at the British Museum cataloguing Chinese coins. He maintained his interest in Chinese civilisation throughout his life, but also collaborated with C.T. Newton on a catalogue of Greek and Etruscan vases, and with Sir Henry Rawlinson on cuneiform inscriptions, while also specialising in the examination and cataloguing of the Museum's growing collection of Egyptian papyri and other artefacts. Birch describes this two-volume, highly illustrated work on ancient pottery, published in 1858, as filling a perceived need: 'A work has long been required which should embody the general history of the fictile art of the ancients.' Volume 2 continues to examine Greek pottery, including the work of named or identified individual craftsmen, moving to Etruscan and Roman wares, with a short final section on 'Celtic, Teutonic, and Scandinavian pottery'.

Cambridge University Press has long been a pioneer in the reissuing of out-of-print titles from its own backlist, producing digital reprints of books that are still sought after by scholars and students but could not be reprinted economically using traditional technology. The Cambridge Library Collection extends this activity to a wider range of books which are still of importance to researchers and professionals, either for the source material they contain, or as landmarks in the history of their academic discipline.

Drawing from the world-renowned collections in the Cambridge University Library and other partner libraries, and guided by the advice of experts in each subject area, Cambridge University Press is using state-of-the-art scanning machines in its own Printing House to capture the content of each book selected for inclusion. The files are processed to give a consistently clear, crisp image, and the books finished to the high quality standard for which the Press is recognised around the world. The latest print-on-demand technology ensures that the books will remain available indefinitely, and that orders for single or multiple copies can quickly be supplied.

The Cambridge Library Collection brings back to life books of enduring scholarly value (including out-of-copyright works originally issued by other publishers) across a wide range of disciplines in the humanities and social sciences and in science and technology.

History of Ancient Pottery

VOLUME 2:
GREEK, ETRUSCAN, AND ROMAN

SAMUEL BIRCH

CAMBRIDGE
UNIVERSITY PRESS

CAMBRIDGE
UNIVERSITY PRESS

University Printing House, Cambridge, CB2 8BS, United Kingdom

Cambridge University Press is part of the University of Cambridge.

It furthers the University's mission by disseminating knowledge in the pursuit of
education, learning and research at the highest international levels of excellence.

www.cambridge.org
Information on this title: www.cambridge.org/9781108081917

© in this compilation Cambridge University Press 2015

This edition first published 1858
This digitally printed version 2015

ISBN 978-1-108-08191-7 Paperback

This book reproduces the text of the original edition. The content and language reflect
the beliefs, practices and terminology of their time, and have not been updated.

Cambridge University Press wishes to make clear that the book, unless originally published
by Cambridge, is not being republished by, in association or collaboration with,
or with the endorsement or approval of, the original publisher or its successors in title.

The original edition of this book contains a number of colour plates,
which have been reproduced in black and white. Colour versions of these
images can be found online at www.cambridge.org/9781108081917

HISTORY

OF

ANCIENT POTTERY.

ATHENIAN PRIZE VASE (FROM NEAR BENGAZI).

HISTORY

OF

ANCIENT POTTERY.

BY SAMUEL BIRCH, F.S.A.

IN TWO VOLS.—VOL. II.

GREEK, ETRUSCAN, AND ROMAN.

ILLUSTRATED WITH COLOURED PLATES AND NUMEROUS ENGRAVINGS.

LONDON:

JOHN MURRAY, ALBEMARLE STREET.

1858.

CONTENTS OF VOLUME II.

PART II.

GREEK POTTERY.

(Continued.)

CHAPTER VII.

CHAPTER VIII.

CHAPTER IX.

CHAPTER X.

PART III.

ETRUSCAN POTTERY.

CHAPTER I.

PART IV.

ROMAN POTTERY.

CHAPTER I.

CHAPTER II.

PART V.

—◆—

CELTIC, TEUTONIC, AND SCANDINAVIAN POTTERY.

CHAPTER I.

LIST OF ILLUSTRATIONS TO VOL. II.

COLOURED PLATES.

* From Mr. Dennis's well-known work "The Cities and Cemeteries of Etruria," from which are also taken No. 155, and No. 111 of Vol. I. A few cuts of Vol. I. are also from Sir G. Wilkinson's "Manners and Customs of the Ancient Egyptians," and Mr. Layard's "Nineveh and its Babylon."

ERRATA IN VOL. II.

— ◆ —

Page 20, line 8, for "Erectheus," read "Erechtheus."

,, 21, line 8, for "Callirhoe," read "Callirrhoe."

,, 27, note 4, for "and," read "und."

,, 28, last line but one, before "artist," insert "the."

,, 40, line 20, for "διυο," read "δυοι."

,, 41, for "No. 126," read "No. 138."

,, 46, line 1, for "Gycnus," read "Cycnus." Line 4, for "Archecles," read "Archicles."

,, 50, line 6, for "is," read "are."

,, 51, note 7, line 3, for "and," read "und."

,, 60, note 3, for "introni," read "intorno i."

,, 67, note 2, for "Fittilii, read "Fittili."

,, 94, note 5, for "αμφιπολος," read "ἀμφίπολος."

,, 96, note 6, for "Nab," read "Nub."

,, 101, note 1, for "Isodorus," read "Isidorus."

,, 122, note 2, for "Gerherd," read "Gerhard."

,, 123, note 1, for "for," read "fur."

,, 132, for "Kuntsblatt," read "Kunstblatt."

,, 136, line 7, for "citharædi," read "citharœdi."

,, 154, line 9, for "gynacœum," read "gynæceum."

,, 174, note 2, for "Leyde," read "Leyden."

,, 177, note 3, for "Ashit," read "Ashik."

,, 218, line 23, for "scarabœi," read "scarabæi."

,, 246, line 22, read "freedmen or of slaves."

,, 297, line 15, for "sacilla," read "sacella."

,, 303, line 11, for "rabbit," read "rabbet."

,, 312, note 5, for "Pæn," read "Poen."

,, 330, line 5, before "burnt," insert "be."

,, 382, note 4, for "T," read "R."

PART II.

—◆—

GREEK POTTERY.

CHAPTER VII.

Glazed vases continued—Ornaments—Their nature and use—The Mæander—
Chequered bands—The fret or herring-bone—Annulets—Egg and tongue
ornament—Scales or feathers—The helix—Antefixal ornament—Wreaths—
Petals — Vine branches — Acanthus leaves — Flowers — Arrangement —
Sources from which the vase-painters copied—Inscriptions—Form of the
letters—Position—Dialects—Orthography—Different kinds of inscriptions:
painted inscriptions ; names of figures and objects. — Addresses—
Artists' names—Potters' names—Laudatory inscriptions—Unintelligible
inscriptions—Memoranda.

SUBORDINATE to the subjects in point of archæological
interest, but intimately interwoven with them, are the
ornaments which helped to relieve and embellish the
representations on pictures, and, so to speak, to frame
them. Numerous vases, indeed, are decorated with ornaments only, whilst many smaller ones are entirely black,
from which circumstance they were nicknamed " Libyes "
or " Moors." The ware of Nola is richest in vàses of
this class ; and amphoræ, hydriæ, stamnoi, cylices, phialæ,
pyxides, and lamps, of this unornamented description, are

found in the Campanian sepulchres.   Others have only
the simplest kind of ornaments, consisting of plain bands
or zones passing round their body and feet.   A very
common decoration is two bands or zones concentric to
the axis of the foot of the vase.   This is, however, found
only on the black vases of the best period.   Other vases,
both of the earliest and later classes, are painted with
ornaments, consisting of wreaths of laurel, myrtle, or
ivy, *helices*, egg and tongue borders, mæanders, waves or
the cymation moulding, chequers, guilloche, spirals, dentals, and petals.   These are artistically disposed upon
them according to certain rules of great symmetry and
taste ; and that the artist prided himself upon his talent
in this way is certain, from some vase-painters having
attached their names to vases only decorated with ornaments.   On the whole, there is a poverty in the variety
of ornaments employed, very different from the fruitful
caprices of the Teutonic races, amongst whom, from
religious motives, ornaments were often employed in pre-
ference to representations of the human form.   It is on
the earliest vases that ornament is most employed : as the
art developes itself, it is gradually lessened, till at the best
period it almost disappears.   But on the later efforts of
the potters it again rises like a noxious weed diminishing
the intent of, and ultimately superseding the subjects.   It
must be borne in mind that originally the ornament was
either the normal mode of representing certain things
extraneous to the subject, or a symbol introduced into
it.   Hence in the arrangement of ornaments different
principles were called into play.   The wreaths and bands
of artificial ornaments or *helices*, appear for instance to be

imitations of the crowns and fillets which it was the custom of the Greeks to tie round the vase at festive entertainments, whilst the *helix* at the handles seems to have represented the flowers attached to that part of the vase. Mæanders, ovolos, and astragals, on the other hand, were either architectural adaptations to the vase or accompaniments of subjects originally selected from the different members of buildings, such as the pediments, metopes, and friezes. Other ornaments were conventional, or symbols to denote particular conditions or places, which originally they defined, and were subsequently retained from habit. Thus the cymation or wave moulding, represented the sea or marine compositions, the mæander a river on the land, and a fleurette (fig. 30) the carpet of nature on which the figures walked. The ornaments, indeed, exhibit great monotony, and are repetitions of a type not diversified like the arabesque ; but they are distinguished by an airy lightness and an extreme simplicity which harmonise exquisitely with the human forms with which they are associated. They are well adapted to the shape and colour of the vases, and afford great relief to the subject depicted. We will now proceed to consider them in detail.

The mæander ornament differs very considerably on the various vases on which it is found. On the early fawn-coloured ones it predominates generally in the simplest forms like those depicted in figures 1, 2.

The pattern (fig. 3), indeed, a more complex variety, sometimes occurs. It occupies the most prominent places of the vases, as the neck, body, handles, and other parts.

On those with yellow grounds, in the rare instances in

which it appears, it is employed for bands round the neck
(fig. 4) ; whilst on vases of a more advanced style of
art it reappears in a more complete and connected form,
intermingled with flowers, and represents the ground upon
which the animals walk (fig 5).

At the foot of the amphoræ with black figures, the
ornament appears in the form represented in fig. 5.
This type is finally superseded by one resembling that
represented by fig. 3.   On the early vases with yellow
grounds, it consists of three, four, or five mæanders, with
a flower at the end, treated in a very conventional style,
generally as a square with diagonals, sometimes with
pellets in the sections (fig. 7), while at other times it resembles a quadrangular fort (fig. 6).   On some of the late
Apulian vases, on which this style of ornament first
appears, the flower is treated as a cross on a black back-
ground, bearing some resemblance to a Maltese cross
(fig. 8).   In the last style of all it appears as a square
divided at right angles, with pellets, and is probably
intended for a flower with four spots (fig 7).

Chequered panels, disposed either horizontally or vertically, are extensively used on the fawn-coloured vases, and
on those with yellow grounds (fig. 10, 11).   They also
appear on the vase of Capua, already cited, on vases with
black figures, and on the shoulders of *lecythi* [1] (fig. 12).

The fret or herring-bone (fig. 13) is of common occurrence on vases of the oldest style, disposed in horizontal or
vertical bands, either in a single or triple line.   It occurs
rarely on vases of the style called Phœnician, and still more
so on vases with black figures.   A remarkable employment

[1] See V. L. ii. xlix. l. 61.

of this ornament occurs on the early *hydriæ* with black figures, on which it is used as a boundary to the picture, and being knotted at the points of union, forms a reticulated pattern (fig.29).

On the earlier vases bands of annulets (fig. 14) occur, as on the foot of a vase in the British Museum.[1] This ornament does not appear on vases of the later styles.

Egg and tongue (fig. 15) ornaments are employed on vases of all periods. On the earlier ones they are much elongated, and principally appear on the shoulder of the vase. They are never placed below the handles, but are sometimes found at the place of insertion. On the hydria, or water vase, this ornament occurs between the frieze and body, its position on vases of a later style, where it sometimes divides the subjects. It is introduced with graceful effect at the lip. This ornament is of the Ionic order.

Another ornament imitated overlapping scales or feathers like the *opus pavonaceum* in tile work. It occurs only on vases of the early Doric style. Many examples occur on vases found at Nola.[2]

The development of the *helix* or ornament of the antefixæ is very remarkable ; on early vases of the intermediate style between the Phœnician and early Greek, it assumes the shape of a mere bud (fig. 16). On the cups with small figures it developes itself (fig. 17) from the handle on a single stem either with the petals closed or detached, and curling upon a spiral stem, like the leaf of a creeping plant. On the oldest vases, when it is employed in a bud, it sometimes assumes an abnormal appearance.

[1] No. 2559. [2] B. M. 397.

The *helix* is also extensively employed as a frieze or scroll on many hydriæ and vases both of the earlier and later styles. When it appears alone it resembles the leaf of an aquatic plant, with seven petals ; but in combination, it follows the scroll (fig. 18), like the leaf of a creeping plant, the points of which are either in one direction, or half of them one way and half the other (fig. 19), or alternately upright and pendent. This ornament is often intermingled with spurs and other portions of plants. On the earlier vases with red figures it forms a rich ornament when intermingled with other emblems—being then often disposed in red bands, on which it is coloured black. Sometimes it is seen as a frieze, with a kind of flower like the hyacinth interposed, in which it represents as it were the foliage to the flower (fig. 20), often treated in this way. On the neck of the later Nolan amphoræ, and on vases of the fine style with red figures, this ornament (fig 21) becomes more floral and picturesque, and fills up the whole space of the neck. The accompanying form of the leaf (fig. 22), which is seen in a wreath or collar of a vase of Etruscan style, bears so much resemblance to the antefixal ornament that it may be an early development of it. On the neck of some of the late *crateres* with red figures it is elegantly disposed in an oblique manner (fig. 23). It continued in use till the latest period of the fictile art—but on the vases of the style of the Basilicata and St. Agata dei Goti, it has more petals, becomes more splay, and the spiral tendrils are often altogether omitted (fig. 31). It is profusely employed, and generally in combination with the flower.

One of the earliest ornaments on the vases is a composite form of the antefixal ornament [1] called *helices*, intermingled with flowers. A very old arrangement is to place the flower and leaf alternately (fig. 24), by making an ornament, each part of which has a leaf at one end and flower at the other, so as to convey the idea of a double row of leaves and alternate flowers united by a broad band.

On the early Bacchic amphoræ with black figures this is the prevalent and most important ornament ; arranged generally, however, as a double wreath, the antefixal ornaments inversely to each other, and also the flowers, which are connected by a twisted cord or chain. On a vase made by Nicosthenes, this ornament assumes with its flowers a remarkable shape.

This *helix* or antefixal ornament is the same as that which appears in the Doric entablatures, but the ovolo, or egg and tongue, belongs to the Ionic order. Both are found united upon early vases with red figures. The combinations of helices and flowers at the handles of the Bacchic amphoræ will give an idea of the elegant appearance of this ornament.

A light and elegant arrangement of the helix is displayed on the necks of certain lecythi.[2]

The flower intermingled with these ornaments has been supposed by some writers to be that of the clematis cirrosa,[3] to which plant some varieties of the form of the antefixal ornament have also been referred.

On some of the Bacchic amphoræ of the later style the flowers are more elegantly turned, and their shape

---

[1] Various ideas have been put forth with regard to this ornament. See Annali, 1843, pp. 380, 384.

[2] For a vase entirely ornamented with helices, see V. L. ii. 41.

[3] Hogg, Trans. Roy. Soc. Lit., New Series, ii. p. 179, and foll.

approaches to its appearance on the red vases, the
antefixal ornament having a trefoil.

A very common ornament of the necks of amphoræ
and other vases is a wreath of interlaced flowers and
buds (fig. 28). Such wreaths often occur on vases of the
old style or that called Egyptian.

On vases of the transition style the flower gradually
becomes more like a bud and less enclosed. The manner
in which it appears mixed up with the antefixal ornament
has been shown in the preceding examples. This ornament is seen on the shoulders of the amphoræ called
Tyrrhenian, and on the feet of the Bacchic ones with the
points turned up. On the later vases it entirely disappears.
It is uncertain what flower it is intended to represent.
Some persons take it to be the hyacinth.

Ivy wreaths (fig. 25) appear on some of the pale vases
of the Etruscan style, and on some of the fine vases from
Athens ; and on the necks of some of the *lecythi* with
black figures. Sometimes the leaves only are seen, intermixed with the helix ornament.

On the *hydriæ*, or water vases, the boundary lines of
the pictures are sometimes formed by upright festoons of
ivy wreaths (fig. 26), which are also seen arranged vertically round the lips, and undulating with the contours of
the handles of the so-called Tyrrhenian amphoræ ; re-
lieving by their light and graceful contrast the sombre
monotony of the body of the vase.

On the necks of the *calpides*, and later vases of the
fine red ware, this ornament becomes more graceful and
the stems of the foliage more entwined (fig. 27), while
flowers or berries are introduced.

ORNAMENTS OF VASES.

On the late *celebæ*, or craters with columnar handles of the style of the Basilicata, the whole neck of the vases is often occupied by an ivy wreath in black upon a red ground, having as many flowers or berries as leaves.

The feet of the early vases, and of most of the *hydriæ* and *amphoræ*, are ornamented with the representation of petals of flowers in black upon a red ground. In some instances this ornament is doubled.

Vine branches appear only on the later vases. Such an ornament will be seen on an *ascos* of pale yellow clay with brown figures, in the British Museum.

In the same class of vases acanthus leaves are found grouped in a floral style, with antefixal ornaments at their sides. In the centre generally appears a full-faced head either of Aphrodite or Victory.

On these vases the floral ornaments become more elegant and architectural. The accompanying example (fig. 28), will show how the convolvulus was represented at this period. Sometimes there appears a small low flower rising from the earth—probably the asphodel. On some vases the floral ornaments assume the form of the architectural scroll, and are imitated from friezes or other members.

GROUPING OF ORNAMENTS.

Nor is the manner in which these ornaments are grouped on the early vases less instructive. The *hydriæ* constantly has its frieze, or upper picture, surmounted by the egg and tongue ornament.[1] The picture on the body is separated by a band,[2] mæander,[3] single or double [4] chequer,[5] or net ; [6] the sides are banded by ivy wreaths,[7] or bands of the *helix* ; [8] while the lower zone has interlaced buds,[9] the *helix*,[10] or a frieze of animals,[11] about $1\frac{3}{4}$ in. broad ; all which, however, are wanting in some examples.[12] The bases are always decorated with petals,[13] and the rest of the body is generally black ; yet some *hydriæ* have red lips,[14] and others the feet either half or entirely red.[15] The inner half of the handle, and sometimes the whole, is generally red, while at the place of insertion of the long handle is a modelled head.

The old *craters*, with columnar handles, have the floral ornament round the lip, the ovolo ornament round the edges, and the ivy leaves at the sides, which in the later vases of the style of St. Agata dei Goti occupy almost the whole of the neck.

On the craters, or the so called *oxybapha*, the lips are

[1] B. M., 454.
[2] B. M., 485.
[3] B. M., 468.
[4] B. M., 476.
[5] B. M., 486.
[6] B. M., 467.
[7] B. M., 486.
[8] B. M., 487.
[9] B. M., 464.
[10] B. M., 468.
[11] B. M., 485.
[12] B. M., 458.
[13] B. M., 468.
[14] B. M., 480.
[15] B. M., 470.

usually ornamented with a wreath of myrtle or olive, or else with the band of oblique antefixal ornaments. On those of the best style and finish, the lips and places of insertion of the handles have the ovolo.

The *œnochoœ*, or jugs, with black figures of the earliest style, have an ovolo round the neck, or sometimes an antefixal ornament. The pictures are generally banded with ivy wreaths.

On the Bacchic *hydriæ*, the monotony of the predominant mass of red colour is broken up by the profusion of ornaments. The frieze, for example, for the most part consists of the floral ornament, with the points generally upwards, but sometimes downwards ; or else of the ovolo fringe or border. The same ornament and the mæander is generally repeated below, and sometimes with a band of animals. On the neck are usually disposed the double antefixal and floral ornaments. At the feet are the petals.[1]

On the *lecythus*, the upper and lower parts of the picture are commonly ornamented with a mæander border, while the neck is either decorated with a series of rays or petals, or else with antefixal or *helix* ornaments, disposed in an inverted frieze. The band round the foot is usually left of the colour of the clay.

The rare *hydriæ*, with red figures, have their friezes enriched at the sides with bands of the *helix* or antefixal ornament, and their pictures are bounded by a *helix* wreath or by a reticulated ornament. The *calpides*, or later *hydriæ*, which have no frieze, have their lips and the lower part of their subject bordered with an egg and

[1] Brit. Mus. Vases, No. 546,-70,-71,-65,-97.

tongue ornament, and sometimes with antefixal ornaments and mæanders. Wreaths of ivy, myrtle, or laurel, are tastefully disposed round the neck.[1]

On Panathenaic and Bacchic amphoræ the arrangement is as follows :—

PANATHENAIC AMPHORA.

1. Double antefixal
2. Ovolo
3. Subject
4. Petals

} B. M., 571.

BACCHIC AMPHORÆ.

1. Double antefixal
2. Ovolo
3. Frieze
4. Mæanders
5. Lotus flowers
6. Subject
7. Mæanders
8. Petals

} B. M., 549, 555.[2]

SOURCES OF SUBJECTS.

We will now proceed to consider the different works of art from which the vase painter may have derived some of his ideas. These works were ever present to his eye in great number and variety, and he reproduced them in accordance with the spirit of his age, without making servile imitations ; for vase-paintings cannot be considered as mere mechanical copies, scarcely any two of them being alike. The treatment of the subjects generally resembles that observed in the mural paintings of the oldest sepulchres.

[1] See the vases, B. M., 716–20.
[2] For the details of a late amphora, cf. T. V. (I.), 40-41.

The fresco paintings of the *stoæ*, or porticos, and of the *leschæ*, or ancient picture galleries, must have been most instructive to artists, as well as the votive pictures of the principal shrines. On the oldest vases, however, may be decidedly traced an architectural manner, derived from the contemplation of metopes, friezes, and pediments. Some of the very oldest vases having numerous bands, or zones, of subjects, suggest the idea of their being copies from celebrated pieces of sculpture, such as the chest of Cypselus, or the throne of Bathycles at Amyclæ. The subjects on the later vases of the fine style recall to mind the descriptions of the pictures of Polygnotus ; whilst in those of the decadence the treatment resembles that adopted by Zeuxis, Apelles, and other artists of the Rhodian school, such as Nicias, from whose works they may have been copied. Yet it is almost impossible to identify vase-paintings with any particular works of anti-quity, although it is evident from Pausanias that their subjects were to be found in all the principal shrines of Greece. Few, however, present such entire compositions as occupied the time of the greatest painters. The greater part contain only portions of subjects, although some striking examples show that the whole argument of an Epos was sometimes painted. Hence their importance both to the study of ancient painting and to the recon-struction of the lost arguments of the Cyclic and other writers ; for, as in the so-called Raffaele ware, may be traced the arguments of the Scriptures and of Ovid ; so in the Greek vases may be found the subjects of the *Cypria*, and the *Nostoi*, and of the lost tragedies of the Athenian dramatists, together with traces of Comedies of

all styles, and even Allegories derived from the philosophical
schools, all of which had successively engaged the pencils of
the most celebrated artists.   That these vases were copies
from pictures or sculptures, is maintained by one of the
most acute connoisseurs, who cites the celebrated vase at
Naples of the last night of Troy, as an evident copy of
a frieze or picture, and the procession on a Vulcian cup
as taken from a sculpture.   But it is impossible, at the
same time, not to admit that, in so vast a number, there
are some, if not many, subjects which were invented by
the vase painters.   These are detected by the corrections
of the master's hand, and by the composition, with its
accompanying ornaments being adjusted to the character of
the vase.   Such works are supposed to be the production
of the vase painters, Archicles, Xenocles, Panthæus, Sosias,
and Epictetus.[1]

INSCRIPTIONS—DATE.

The inscriptions which occur on vases are limited to
those produced at the middle period of the art.   On the
earliest vases they are not found at all ; on those with
pale straw-coloured grounds they are of rare occurrence ;
on vases with black figures and red ground, they are often
seen ; and on these with red figures they are constant
accompaniments, and continue to be so till the decadence
of the art, as seen in the ware of the Basilicata and
Southern Italy, when inscriptions again become comparatively scarce.   Some of the last inscriptions are in the
Oscan and Latin language, showing the influence and

[1] Annali, 1830, p. 244.

domination of the Romans in Campania. The inscriptions
follow the laws of palæography of the period in which
they occur. The oldest inscriptions are those of the following vases : the Corinthian vase of Dodwell, with the
hunt of the boar of Calydon ; a cup of the maker Tleson,
with the same subject, and the nuptial dance of Ariadne ;
the vase of the Hamilton collection, found at Capua ; a vase
with the subject of the Geryon ; the so-called François
vase at Florence ; another with the combat over the body
of Achilles ; and a cup, on which is seen Arcesilaus, King
of Cyrene. Of these, the Dodwell vase has been supposed
by some archæologists to be of the seventh century B. C.
None, however, date earlier than Olympiad XXX. = B. C.
660, when writing is known to have been used in Greece.
The date of the Arcesilaus vase cannot be prior to
Olympiad XLVII-LI., when the first of the Battiads ruled at
Cyrene, nor much later than the LXXX. Olympiad = B. C.
458, when the fourth of the line was in power.[1]

The inscriptions are disposed in the *boustrophedon*
manner. B is used for E, M for Σ, X for Λ, C for Γ, ☐ for
the aspirate, ⊕ for Θ in a case where the T is not used,
Ϙ for K, ⅀ for I, R for P. At a later period the letters
which are more cursive are not distinguishable, except by
the context. Thus A ◇ O ▷ are confounded, and the ◇
often resembles them ; Λ and V are alike, so are Γ and
Π, M and Σ ; v is much like L, Λ itself is written L,
Σ like Ϛ, Υ as V. The aspirated letters ⊕ and +, the
invention of which was attributed to Palamedes, are
found on vases of the second class. The form which
subsequently became H is used for ⊦. The four letters

[1] Thiersch., l. c., s. 77.

Z Ψ H Ω, said to be invented by Simonides, are only found on later vases, Ψ being represented by Π Σ, H by E, and Ω by O. Ξ erroneously attributed to Palamedes, is represented by ΚΣ, or Χ ; but all these double letters are found on the later vases.[1] As compared with coins, ⊗ appears on the earlier coins of Athens, struck before the Persian war, 日 on the helmet of Hiero I., Ol. LXXV.-VIII. B.C. 474-467, and on the ancient Bœotian coins, erroneously assigned to Thebes. The M for Σ occurs on coins of Posidonia and Sybaris, struck about the seventh century B.C. ; ξ for I on those of the first-mentioned city ; Χ for the E, resembling the Etruscan B on uncertain coins of Campania ; H for the aspirate is seen on the coins of Himera, and in the names of the Bœotarchs about the fifth century B.C., and the ⌅ on the currency of the Thespiæ.[2] No numismatic examples are known of T for Θ, or of Π for Φ, ΚΣ for Ξ, or ΠΣ for Ψ ; but Q is the usual initial of the name of Corinth[3] on its oldest coins, and Γ for Γ on the later one of Phæstus in Crete ; all which proves the high antiquity of the potter's art, and that it was far older than the currency. Considerable light is thrown upon the relative age and the local fabrics of the vases by the forms of the letters seen on the vases of different styles. The letters on the vases of the Archaic Greek style resemble those of the oldest inscriptions found at Corcyra, and show their Doric character by the use of the koph.[4] This agrees with their probable Corinthian origin, their art, and oriental types of certain figures. The words,

---

[1] Gerhard, Rapp. Volc., p. 68.
[2] Kramer, ueber den Styl und die Herkunft, s. 54.
[3] Annali, 1837.

[4] Jahn, Beschreibung der Vasensammlung zu München, 8vo. Münch. 1854. Einleit, s. cxlvii.

however, with which they are inscribed are sometimes
Æolic,[1] and the antiquity of the alphabet undetermined.
The alphabet obtained from examining the letters on the
style transitional from this to that with black figures,
which is for the most part Doric, as evinced by the presence
of the *digamma* and the *koph*, is found in words not of the
Doric dialect. Its age is also not certain.[2] The letters on
the vases with black figures of the old style are those of
the oldest Attic alphabet, which was in use about Olympiad LXXX., and the words on these vases, although sometimes abnormal, are generally Attic. On the vases of
black figures of the later style the letters are those of the
Attic alphabet current about six Olympiads later.[3] The
letters on vases with red figures of the strong style are
nearly identical in form and epoch; while on the vases
of the fine style are found the letters of the Attic
alphabet which was admitted into official employment in
the second year of the XCIV. Olympiad, in the memorable
archonship of Eucleides,[4] after which the alphabet under-
went no change. The use of the *digamma*, however, is
continued on Doric vases, both of this and even of a
later age.

ARRANGEMENT.

There is no rule for the position or the presence of the
inscriptions on vases.[5] In some instances the field or
ground of the figures is completely covered, in others they
do not appear at all. The general position is governed

[1] As ΣΔΕVΣ for ΖΕVΣ, on a vase in the Campana Collection.
[2] Jahn, l. c., cxlix.
[3] Jahn, l. c., clxix.
[4] Jahn. l. c., cxvii.
[5] Gerhard, l. c, 69.

by the figures to which they refer; but they are also found on the figures themselves, and often upon objects, such as fountains, shields, discs, and even the legs of figures,[1] or on the handles, borders, and feet of the vases. Sometimes they are written from left to right, at other times from right to left, and often, especially upon the old vases, perpendicularly to the vase, but not, except on the Panathenaic amphoræ from the Cyrenaica, in that order called by the Greeks κιονιδὸν, or vertically as to themselves. *Boustrophedon* inscriptions are not uncommon, and sentences are often divided into two; as, HO ΠΑΙΣ, "*the boy,*" on one side of a vase, ΚΑΛΟΣ, "*is handsome,*" on the other. Even names are sometimes thus divided, as, ΑΝΔΡΟ on one side, and ΜΑΧΕ on the other side of a celebrated vase, for the name *Andromache.* This chiefly occurs on the older vases, as when the art reached its culmination more care was taken.

DIALECTS.

Inscriptions occur in all the three dialects, principally, however, in Ionic Greek, as ΑΝΤΙΟΠΕΙΑ for Antiope, ΑΘΕΝΑΙΑ for Pallas Athene, ΗΕΡΑΚΛΕΕΣ for Hercules; and sometimes the contractions, as, ΚΑΜΟΙ for ΚΑΙ ΕΜΟΙ, ΜΕΝΕΛΕΟΣ[2] and ΙΟΛΕΟΣ,[3] ΧΑΤΕΡΟΣ for ΚΑΙ ΕΤΕΡΟΣ. Vases with Doric inscriptions, which are comparatively rare, principally come from south Italy and Sicily. Such forms as ΗΑΡΑ, for Hera or Juno, ΑΩΣ ΚΑΛΕ,[4] for Aurora,

---

[1] Cf., the one on the thigh of a youth; and the name of the artist on the diadem or beard of a figure; A. Z., 1844, s. 317.

[2] G. A. V., ccxxvii.

[3] G. A. V., cxlviii.

[4] M. A. U. M., vi.

ΤΑΛΕΙΑ for ΘΑΛΕΙΑ, the name of the Muse,[1] and ΑΣΠΕΡΙΑΣ
for the Hesperidæ.[2] ΧΡΗΣΑΝ ΜΟΙ ΤΑΝ ΣΦΑΙΡΑΝ, "give
me the Ball." The Æolic digamma is prefixed to such
names as ϜΕΡΑΚΛΕΣ and ϜϒΨΙΠϒΛΗ ;[3] and is found in
the middle of others, such as, ΑΙϜΑΣ and ΣΙΣΙϜΟΣ,[4] and
Æolic forms are found, as ΣΔϒΣ for ΖΕϒΣ. The
old form of the aorist, with the final Ν, generally occurs,
as, ΕΓΡΑΦΣΕΝ and ΕΠΟΙΕΣΕΝ, although its use is not
constant. The derivation of Ψ and Ξ from ΦΣ and ΚΣ
is shown by such words as, ΕΓΡΑΦΣΕΝ[5] and ΕΚΣΕΚΙΑΣ.
The old diphthong ΟΕ for ΟΙ, as ΚΡΟΕΣΟΣ for ΚΡΟΙΣΟΣ,
and the Archaic Ο for Οϒ, as ΝΕΑΡΧΟ instead of ΝΕΑΡΧΟϒ,
are found on vases of the earliest period ; or, ΕΙ for Ι, as
ΕΙΟΛΕΟΣ for ΙΟΛΕΟΣ (Iolaus).[6] The aspirate is also
applied to words in which at present it does not appear,
as, ΗΙΑΚΧΟΣ[7] for ΙΑΚΧΟΣ, and ΗΑΦΡΟΔΙΤΕ for ΑΦΡΟ-
ΔΙΤΕ. The Ν instead of the Γ before Κ, as, ΑΝΧΙΠΟΣ[8]
for ΑΓΚΙΠΠΟΣ, or for Μ, as ΟΛϒΝΠΙΟΔΩΡΟΣ[9] for ΟΛϒΜ-
ΠΙΟΔΩΡΟΣ. Double letters are represented at all epochs
by single ones, as, ΗΙΠΟΔΑΜΕΙΑ for ΗΙΠΠΟΔΑΜΕΙΑ,
ΗΙΠΟΚΡΑΤΕΣ for ΗΙΠΠΟΚΡΑΤΕΣ, ΠΕΡΟΦΑΤΑ for ΠΕΡΟ-
ΦΑΤΤΑ ;[10] but the Σ is often reduplicated, on vases of
late style, as, ΟΡΕΣΣΤΕΣ for ΟΡΕΣΤΕΣ,[11] ΚΑΣΣΤΩΡ for
ΚΑΣΤΟΡ,[12] ΓΙΕΣΣΘΕ for ΠΙΕΣΘΕ.[13] Letters are often
omitted, as, ΛΑΠΟΣ for ΛΑΜΠΟΣ, in the name of one of

[1] A. Z., 1848, s. 247.
[2] Millin., Dub. Maison. I. iii. ;
D'Hancarville, i. 27 ; iii. 194 ; Passeri,
i. 4.
[3] Kramer, ibid. ; M. A. U. M., xii.
[4] G. A. V., clv.
[5] Gerhard, Rapp. Volc., p. 67. 68.
[6] M. I., lxxxix.

[7] Gerhard,l. c.,p. 690, Braun. Annali.
[8] Cat. Dur., p. 98, No. 296; Birch,
Class. Mus. 1848, p. 298.
[9] Gerhard, l. c., p. 169, n. 641.
[10] Birch, Class. Mus., l. c.
[11] B. A. B., 1007.
[12] Gerhard, Vase de Meidias.
[13] Gerhard, Rapp. Volc., p. 69.

the horses of Aurora; ΤΥΤΑΡΕΟΣ for ΤΥΝΔΑΡΕΥΣ, the father of Helen; ΘΕΡΥΤΑΙ[1] for ΘΕΡΥΕΤΑΙ, "is taken;" ΘΕΣΥΣ for ΘΕΣΕΥΣ;[2] ΚΑΛΙΡΕ ΚΡΕΝΕ for ΚΑΛΛΙΡΟΗ ΚΡΗΝΗ, the fountain of Callirhoe; ΣΑΠΟ for ΣΑΠΦΟ,[3] the poetess; ΧΑΝΘΟΣ for ΞΑΝΘΟΣ,[4] the name of a horse. The Λ on the old vases is always single, as, ΑΠΟΛΟΝΟΣ[5] for ΑΠΟΛΛΩΝΟΣ. So also, ΒΟΡΑΣ for ΒΟΡΕΑΣ; ΟΡΕΙΘΥΑ, for Oreithyia; ΕΡΕΧΣΕΣ, for Erectheus; ΚΕΚΡΟΣ, for Cecrops;[6] ΗΕΜΕΣ, for Hermes.[7]

PAINTED INSCRIPTIONS.

Inscriptions are divisible into two classes,—those painted and those incised.

I. Painted inscriptions, which are the most conspicuous, are generally small in size, the letters being ⅛ inch high. They are in black varnish on vases with black or maroon figures; on vases of the earliest style, with red figures, they are in crimson upon the black back-ground, or else in black varnish upon some of the red portions; on the later vases with red figures they are in white. In the last style they are engraved with a pointed tool through the glaze into the paste itself. They are divisible into the following subordinate classes :—

NAMES OF FIGURES.

No particular law seems to have guided the artist as to the insertion of the names of the figures represented on

---

[1] Gerhard, A. V., ccxxxviii.
[2] Cf., Gerhard, A. V., clviii. clxiii.
[3] Mill. Anc. Uned. Mon., pl. xxxiii.
[4] G. A. V., cxci.

[5] G. A. V., xx.
[6] C. C., p. 57, n. 105.
[7] B. A. B., 849.

his vase. The greater number of vases are without them ; yet it would appear that vases of the very finest class were thus inscribed at all periods. The design of them was to acquaint the public with the story represented. Sometimes not only every figure is accompanied with its name, but even the dogs, horses, and inanimate objects, such as ΒΟΜΟΣ,[1] or altar, where Priam is killed ; ΚΑΛΙΡΕ ΚΡΕΝΕ,[2] or fountain of Callirhoe ; ΗΕΔΡΑ,[3] or "the throne" of Priam ; ΛΥΚΟΣ,[4] the altar of Apollo Lycius ; and the ΗΥΔΡΙΑ,[5] or water-pitcher, which Polyxena let fall in her flight from Achilles ; ΛΥΡΛ, "the lyre," over that held by Ariadne in her hands, at the death of the Minotaur ; ΗΥΣ, "the sow," over "the Calydonian boar ;"[6] and ΔΗΜΟΣΙΑ, the "public" baths, on a laver.[7] These names are generally in the nominative, as, ΖΕΥΣ,[8] Jupiter ; ΗΕΡΜΕΣ,[9] Hermes : but occasionally in the oblique case, as, ΑΠΟΛΟΝΟΣ,[10] of Apollo ; ΠΟΣΕΙΔΟΝΟΣ, of Neptune ; ΑΦΡΟΔΙΤΕΣ,[11] of Aphrodite ; the word ΕΙΔΩΛΟΝ, "figure," or ΑΓΑΛΜΑ, "image," being understood. In a few instances from dramatic subjects expressions such as, ΕΙΔΩΛΟΝ ΛΗΤΟΥΣ, "the shade of Leto," show the origin of the genitive.[12] ΠΥΡΡΟΣ, Pyrrhus; ΑΓΑΜΕ[ΜΝΩΝ],[13] "Agamemnon;" ΙΔΑΣ, "Idas;"[14] occur over the sepulchres of these heroes. These names are sometimes accompanied with epithets, such as, ΗΕΚΤΟΡ ΚΑΛΟΣ,[15] "Hector the

[1] Gerhard. An. 1831, 183, 741.
[2] Bröndsted, Descr. of 32 Vases, p. 56.
[3] François Vase.
[4] G. A. V., ccxxv.
[5] François Vase.
[6] Gerhard, A. V., ccxxxvi.
[7] T., i. 58.
[8] G. A. V., iv.
[9] B. M., 567.
[10] G. A. V., xxi.; Gerhard, A. V., ccxxxvii.
[11] L. D., iii. xv.
[12] A. Z., 1852, s. 164.
[13] M. V. G., xiv.
[14] T., iv. 59.
[15] G. A. V., clxxxix.

handsome;" ΠΡΙΑΜΟΣ ΗΟ ΠΟΛΙΟΣ, "the hoary Priam ;"[1] ΣΙΛΑΝΟΣ ΤΕΡΠΩΝ, " Silenus rejoicing :"[2] or with a demonstrative pronoun, as, ΣΦΙΧΣ ΗΕΔΕ, "this is the Sphinx ;"[3] ΜΕΝΕΣΘΕΥΣ ΗΟΔΕ, "this is Menestheus."[4] In some instances the name is replaced by a periphrase or by a synonym : as ΗΑΛΙΟΣ ΓΕΡΟΝ,[5] " the old man of the sea," instead of Nereus ; ΤΑΥΡΟΣ ΦΟΡΒΑΣ and ΑΛΙΑΔΗΣ,[6] "the feeding" and "sea-going bull" over Jupiter metamorphosed into a bull, and carrying Europa; ΠΑΝΟΨ, " all eyes," instead of " Argos ;" ΧΡΥΣΗ ΦΙΛΟΜΗΔΗ, or "golden smiler," for " Venus ;"[7] ΔΙΟΣ ΠΑΙΣ, "the son of Zeus," for " Hercules ;"[8] ΔΑΣΤΑΣ ΗΜΙ,[9] "I am a pirate " on a dolphin ; ΑΙΔΟΣ, " Modesty," instead of Leto ; ΑΛΚΙΣ, instead of Cupid;[10] ΔΙΟΣ ΦΩΣ, " the light of Zeus," for Diana or Dionysos ;[11] ΔΕΞΑΜΕΝΟΣ, "the receiver," instead of Nessus.[12] Some of the later vases have the titles of the subjects, especially the dramatic ones, whence the pictures were derived ; as the ΠΑΤΡΟΚΛΙΑ, or funeral poem about Patroclus ;[13] ΚΡΕΟΝΤΕΙΑ, " the affairs of Creon ; "[14] ΤΡΩΩΝ ΙΕΡΕΑ, "the sacred places of Troy,"[15] on a subject representing the ill-usage of Cassandra ; ΝΑΞΙΩΝ, " the Naxians," on a vase representing Ariadne and Dionysos at Naxos ;[16] and the supposed ΧΕΙΡΟΝΕΙΑ.[17] Even on the older vases are found

[1] G. A. V., l. c. clxxviii.
[2] G. A. V.,l. c. ; cc. 135.
[3] G. A. V., ccxxxv.
[4] G. E. V., xiii.
[5] G. A. V., cxxii. cxxiii.
[6] G. A. V., xc.
[7] V. F., cclvi. ; B. A. N., iii. 51; Ann., v. 149.
[8] M. A. U. M., xxxviii., 92.
[9] A. Z., 1852, 165, for ΛΗΣΤΗΣ ΗΜΙ;

M. A. I., xii.
[10] C. M., 58 ; M. V. G., xiv.
[11] M. A. I., i.
[12] Mus. Borb., v. x.
[13] G. A. V., ccxxvii.
[14] A. Z., 1847, taf. iii. ; M. I., clii.
[15] V. L., ii. xxiv.
[16] M. A. U. M., xxvi.
[17] Micali, Storia, ciii. i., pp. 101, 163 ; C. C., 24.

the inscriptions ΣΤΑΔΙΟΝ ΑΝΔΡΟΝ ΝΙΚΕ, "the victory of men in the stadium," over a foot-race of men; ΠΕΝΤΑΘΛΟΝ, for the Pentathlon;[1] ΗΟΔΟΙ ΑΘΕ[ΝΑΙΑΙ], Athenian roads.[2]

SPEECHES.

Besides the names of figures and objects, there are several inscriptions containing the addresses or speeches of the figures represented, like the labels affixed to the figures of saints in the Middle Ages. These vary in length and purport, but in most cases they are extracts from poems, or expressions well-known at the period, but which are now obscure, or have perished in the wreck of Hellenic literature. They are distributed over the early vases of the black or hard style, and often appear on vases of the Archaic style, with red figures ; but they are very rare on vases of the earliest and of the latest styles. They are often colloquies. Thus, on a vase on which the contest of Heracles and Cycnus is depicted, the hero and his opponent exclaim, ΚΑΘΙΕ, "lay down," ΚΕΟΜΑΙ, "I am ready." In a boxing-match, is ΠΑΤΣΑΙ,[3] "cease." Ulysses says to his dog, ΜΗ ΑΙΤΑΙΗΣ,[4] "do not ask ;" Silenus, gloating over the wine, exclaims, ΗΔΤΣ ΟΙΝΟΣ,[5] "the wine is sweet," or, ΚΑΛΕ ΟΠΟΣ ΠΙΕΣΘΕ, "it is so good, that you may drink it."[6] On a vase representing a man standing and singing to an auletris, the song is ΟΔΕ ΛΩΤΩ ΣΤΤΡΙΣΟΙ, "Let him play to the flute."[7] Silenus, who swings a Bacchante, says, ΕΝ ΑΔΕΙΑ ΑΝΗ, "rise at

---

[1] C. C., p. 93, n. 146.
[2] C. C., p. 100, 159.
[3] Gerhard, Rapp. Volc., p. 79, 778.
[4] ΜΕΛΙΤΑΙΕ ΟΡΟΙ, B., 1851, p. 58.
[5] G. A. V.

[6] Gerhard, Rapp. Volc., p. 187, no. 780.
[7] B., 1829, p. 143; A. Z., 1852, s. 414.

pleasure."[1] In the scene of the capture of Silenus, one of the attendants exclaims, ΘΕΡΥΤΑΙ ΣΙΛΕΝΟΣ ΟΡΕΙΟΣ, "the mountain-haunting Silenus is captured!"[2] The Greek who lights the pyre of Crœsus exclaims, ΕΥΘΥΜΟ, "farewell!"[3] The old Tyndareus exclaims, ΧΑΙΡΕ ΘΕΣΕΥ, "hail, oh Theseus!"[4] and the females, ΕΙΔΟΣΘΕΜΕΝ, "it is known." ΧΑΙΡΕ, "hail!" often occurs in such a manner as to show that it emanates from the mouth of figures, although it is frequently an address from the potter. ΕΛΑ ΕΛΑ,[5] "drive, drive!" is placed in the mouth of a charioteer; and ΠΟΛΥΜΕΝΕ ΝΙΚΑΣ,[6] "thou conquerest, oh Polymenos!" in that of another. A *paidotribes* says to one of his pupils, ΑΠΟΔΟΣ ΤΟ ΔΙΑΜΕΡΟΝ, "pay me my day's salary."[7] On another vase, if correctly transcribed, may possibly be read a gnomic sentence, ΣΟΛΟΝ ΟΧΛΟΚΝΟΙΔΟΝ ΚΑΛΟΣ ΙΣΟΛΑΟΣ.[8] A cock crows, ΠΡΟΣΑΓΟΡΕΥΟ, "how d'ye do."[9] A herald or brabeus announces, ΗΙΠΟΣ ΔΥΝΕΙΚΕΤΥ ΝΙΚΑ, "the horse of Dysneiketes conquers."[10] Œdipus, interpreting the enigma of the Sphinx, says, ΚΑΙ ΤΡΙ Π[ΟΥΝ], "which has three feet."[11] On a vase having a representation of olive-gathering, the proprietor of the grounds—perhaps the merchant and sage, Thales, — says, in the Doric dialect, and in Iambic trimeter catalectic verse, Ο ΖΕΥ ΠΑΤΕΡ ΑΙΘΕ ΠΛΟΥΣΙΟΣ ΓΕΝΟ[ΙΜΑΝ], "Oh, father Jove, may I be rich!" a prayer responded to on the

[1] B., 1851, p. 185.
[2] G. A. V., ccxxxviii.
[3] Mon. i. Pl., liv.-lv.; Tr. R. Soc., Lib. 4to, ii., 1834, p. 28.
[4] G. A. V., clviii.
[5] St.; Rap. Volc., p. 78.
[6] Ibid.
[7] Stackelberg, Die Graeber, tav. xii. 3.
[8] Stackelberg. Ibid. xxiv.
[9] G. T. C., xxiv.
[10] Class. Mus., 1849, p. 296; B. M.
[11] M. G., ii. ii. lxxx. 1 b.; Arg. Phœn. Eurip., &c.; Aristid. Pan.. p. 193-245; Brunck. Anal., ii. 321.

reverse by the representation of a liberal harvest, and the reply, ΗΕΔΕ ΜΑΝ ΗΕΔΕ ΠΛΕΟΝ ΠΑΡΑΒΕΒΗΚΕΝ,[1] "See, it is already more than enough." On another vase, on which are depicted youths and old men beholding the return of the swallow in Spring, the following colloquy occurs[2]— ΙΔΟ ΧΕΛΙΔΟΝ, "behold the swallow;" ΝΕ ΤΟΝ ΗΕΡΑΚΛΕΑ, "by Hercules," ΑΥΤΕΙ, "it twitters;" ΕΑΡ ΗΕΔΕ, "it is already Spring,"—which is spoken, apparently in a metrical manner, by a company of men. On a terminal figure, or stêle, at which a winged youth plays at ball with Danaids, is the speech, ΧΡΗΣΑΝ ΜΟΙ ΤΑΝ ΣΦ[Α]ΙΡΑΝ—

"Send me the ball."[3]

On another vase, ΜΕ ΑΙΤΑΙΕ, "do not ask," is the supposed reply to a beggar, who says, ΙΟΡΟΡΟΙ, an unintelligible word, reading the same both backwards and forwards.[4]

POTTERS' ADDRESSES.

In order to enhance their ware in the estimation of the public, the potters painted on their vases, at an early period of the art, certain expressions addressed to the purchaser or spectator. One of the most usual is ΧΑΙΡΕ "hail!"[5] to which is sometimes added ΧΑΙΡΕ ΚΑΙ ΠΙΕΙ, "hail, and quaff,"[6] ΧΑΙΡΕ ΚΑΙ ΠΙΕΙ ΕΥ, "hail, and drink well;"[7] or ΧΑΙΡΕ ΚΑΙ ΠΙΕΙ ΤΕΝΔΕ, "hail and drink this [cup]."[8] ΝΑΙΧΙ, "just so."[9] On one remarkable vase was supposed

[1] M., 1837, tav., xliv. B.; Ritschl. Annali., ix., 1837, p. 183. Hermann Zeitschr. Alterthumw., 1837, no. 103, p. 854, 855 ; Bull., 1840, p. 48.
[2] M., ii. xxiv.
[3] Millingen, Anc. Unedit. Mon., Pl. xii., p. 30 ; Birch, Classic Mus., 1849, p. 302 ; Kramer, ueber den Styl., s. 183;

Neapels Antik. Bild. Z., vii. Schr. 2, 1-174 ; Mus. Borb., iii. xii.
[4] An., 1852, Pl. τ.
[5] G. A. V., iii. p. 150.
[6] M. G. II., lxvi. 3 b.
[7] De Beugnot. Cat., p. 68, n. 75.
[8] B. A. B., 1594.
[9] C. C., 147.

to be found ΟΥ ΠΑΝΤΟΣ ΕΣΤΙ ΚΟΡΙΝΘΟΣ, "every one cannot go to Corinth," [1] a familiar erotic proverb. The Athenian prize vases are inscribed ΤΟΝ ΑΘΕΝΕΘΕΝ ΑΘΛΟΝ ["I am] a prize from Athens," [2] to which is sometimes added ΕΜΙ, "I am." This inscription is also found in the abridged form, ΑΘΕΝΕΘΕΝ. [3] Sometimes the address was to some particular individual, as ΔΕΜΟΣΤΡΑΤΕ ΧΑΙΡΕ, "Hail, oh Demostratus." [4]

INSCRIBED OBJECTS.

Inscriptions upon representations of objects are much rarer than any of the kinds just mentioned, and, in cases where they appear, seem to have existed on the object represented. Some few are those found on stêles, or funeral tablets, as ΤΡΩΙΛΟΣ, [5] on the stêle of the youthful Troilos, lamented by his sisters ; ΑΓΑΜΕΜΝΟΝ, [6] on that of the King of Men ; ΟΡΕΣΤΑΣ [7] on that of his "fury-haunted son ;" ΙΔΑΣ, on that of Idas. [8] The most remarkable of these is an elegiac distich, inscribed upon the stêle of Œdipus, a copy of that recorded by Eustathius, from the poem called the Peplos, or "Shawl," written by Aristotle—

ΝΩΤΩ ΜΕΝ ΜΑΛΑΧΗΝ ΚΑΙ ΠΟΛΥΡΙΖΟΝ ΑΣΦΟΔΗΛΟΝ
ΚΟΛΠΩ ΟΙΔΙΠΟΔΑΝ ΛΑΙΟΥ ΥΙΟΝ ΕΧΩ. [9]

"On my back is grass and spreading-rooted asphodel :
In my bosom I contain Œdipus the son of Laius."

On the base of a statue of Pallas Athene is the unintel-

---

[1] On the cup of Aurora and Tithonos, Braun in Bull., 1848, p. 41, reads, ΠΑΝΤΟΞΕΝΑ ΚΑΛΑ ΚΟΡΙΝΘΟΙ ; both readings are doubtful.
[2] Millingen, Anc. Uned. Mon., Pl. i.;
[3] Thiersch. l. c., s. 68.
[4] G. A. V., xxii. i. s. 82, 83.

[5] Millingen, V. G., Pl. xvii.
[6] M. V G., xiv.
[7] Vase, B. M. 1559.
[8] I. S. V. T., xxxi. xxxvi.
[9] Millingen, Anc. Un. Mon. Vases, Pl. xxxvi. Mus. Borb., ix. xxix.

ligible inscription ΚΟΦΥΣΤ,[1] while ΔΗΜΟΣΙΑ,[1] "Public"[2] [baths] appear on a laver. Certain bucklers used for the armed race, the *hoplites dromos*, bear the inscription ΑΘΕ,[3] either to show that they belonged to Pallas Athene, or that they were Athenian. The often-repeated expression ΚΑΛΟΣ, "beautiful," appears on lavers, discs, a wineskin held by Silenus, and other objects; and on a column is inscribed ΗΟ ΠΑΙΣ ΚΑΛΟΣ ΝΑΙΧΙ,[4] "the boy is handsome forsooth;" while the inscription ΛΑΧΕΣ ΚΑΛΟΣ,[5] "Laches is handsome!" inscribed down the thigh of a statue, recalls to mind the expression, "Pantarces is beautiful," which Phidias slily incised on the finger of his Olympian Zeus at Elis, and the numerous apostrophes which covered the walls of the Ceramicus, and other edifices of Greece.

Other inscriptions are such as were taken from pedestals, and one remarkable example, reading ΑΚΑΜΑΝΤΙΣ ΕΝΙΚΑ ΦΥΛΕ, "the tribe of Akamantis has conquered," is on the base of a tripod dedicated by that tribe for a victory in some choragic festival.[6] ΔΙΟΣ, "the altar of Jove," occurs on that of the Olympian god at Elis, at which Pelops and Œnomaus are depicted taking the oath. On the supposed tessera, or ticket of hospitality, in the hands of a figure representing Jason, is ΣΙΣΙΦΟΣ.[7]

NAMES OF ARTISTS.

The artists who designed and painted the subjects of the vases often placed their names upon their finest

---

[1] Millingen, Anc. Un. Mon., i.Pl. 29.　Mus. xiii. 6.
[2] T., i. 58.　　　　　　　　　　　　[5] Ibid.
[3] Cat. Dur., 674.　　　　　　　　　[6] Panofka, Mus. Blac., i.
[4] Gerhard, Vasen. and Trinksch. Kgl·　[7] Ann., 1848, p. 162.

productions, accompanied with the words ΕΓΡΑΦΣΕΝ,
ΕΓΡΑΣΦΕΝ, ΕΓΡΑΨΕΝ, or ΕΓΡΑΦΕ; which words, from
their preceding the formula, ΚΑΠΟΕΣΕΜΕ, "and made
me," show that the painter ranked higher and was more
esteemed than the potter ; unless, indeed, they were placed
in this order with the view of forming a kind of Iambic
trimeter. Sometimes the artist's name alone is placed on a
vase ; at other times it occurs with those of the potter and of
the figures represented ; and is accompanied with speeches,
and addresses to youths. None of the older artists used
the imperfect, ΕΓΡΑΦΕ, " was painting," which was that
adopted by the followers of the later Athenian school, in
order modestly to affect that their most elaborate labours
were yet unfinished, but always the more decided aorist,
indicating completeness. These inscriptions do not occur on
the early vases, attributed to the Doric and Ionic potteries,
but commence with the vases with black figures, and terminate with those of the style of the decadence. Some
of the earliest artists appear to have used a kind of Iambic
verse, as :—

ΕΚΣΕΧΙΑΣ ΕΓΡΑΦΣΕ ΚΑΠΟΕΣΕΜΕ

Εξη̄|χῐᾱs|ἔγρᾰψ | ἔ κᾱ | πὄη̄s | ἔ με

Ĕxēcĭās ĭt wās whŏ mādĕ ānd pāintĕd mē.

In the next chapter, describing the principal artists
and their works, a further account will be given of the
artists.

An attempt has been made to connect the choice of
subjects on vases bearing artist's name, with allusions to the
name of the artist ; [1] but the connection, if it exists, is too

---

[1] Panofka, Abh. d. k. Akad. d. Wissenschaften, 4to, Berl., 1848, s. 153, 241.

vague to assist the interpretation of them.   It is possible
that such secret allusions may have been occasionally
intended, but the subjects of vases inscribed with the
names of artists are comparatively unimportant, and sometimes merely ornamental.

NAMES OF POTTERS.

A few vases have the potter's name inscribed upon them,
accompanied by the expression ΕΠΟΙΕΣΕΝ, "made," or
ΜΕΠΟΙΕΣΕΝ, "made me," which is rarely, if ever,
replaced by the ΕΠΟΕΙ, "was making," of the later
school of artists.   A rarer form of inscription is the word
ΕΡΓΟΝ, "work," instead of ΕΠΟΙΕΣΕΝ.   The potter always
wrote his name in the nominative, generally simply as
ΝΙΚΟΣΘΕΝΕΣ ΕΠΟΙΕΣΕΝ, "Nicosthenes made," me or
it.   To this he sometimes added the name of his father,
either to distinguish himself from rivals of the same name,
or because his father was in repute.   Thus Tleson, a celebrated maker of *cylices*, or cups, uses the phrase ΤΛΕΣΟΝ
ΗΟ ΝΕΑΡΧΟ ΕΠΟΙΕΣΕΝ, "Tleson, son of Nearchus,"
made it; while Eucheros, another potter, employed the
form ΗΟΡΓΟΤΙΜΟ ΗΥΙΥΣ ΕΥΧΕΡΟΣ ΕΠΟΙΕΣΕΝ "the son
of Ergotimus, Eucheros, made it."   ΕΡΓΟΝ, of course, has
the genitive ; as ΣΤΑΤΙΟ(Υ) ΕΡΓΟΝ, "the work of Statius."
These inscriptions are generally placed in prominent
positions, where they could readily be seen by purchasers.
In this respect the potters only imitated the painters,
sculptors, and architects, who inscribed their names
on some part of their works, and even clandestinely introduced them inside their statues.   The potter, who was

evidently exposed to an active competition, prided himself upon the fineness of his ware, and the elegance of the shapes which he produced. The vases with straw-coloured grounds have no potters' names, which first appear on vases of the old style, with pale red grounds, and are most common upon cups. They continued to be placed upon vases till the latest period, but with decreasing frequency. The art, in its decay, ceased to be either honourable or profitable.

Like the artist, the potter arranged his inscriptions often in a kind of Iambic trimeter, and the final N, which is a poetic form, shows that he had an eye to a little doggerel, as in the inscription—

ΗΟΡΓΟΤΙΜΟ ΗΥΙΥΣ ΕΥΧΕΡΟΣ ΕΠΟΙΕΣΕΝ

Ἐργὅ|τῑμὅυ|ὕιὅs|Εῦχἐρὅs|ἔπὅι|ῆσἔν

Eucheros, son of Ergotimus, [this vessel] made

in which, in frolicsome or sarcastic Iambi, some potter addresses his purchasers. In another, the following forms the end of a choriambic asclepiad.

ΗΟΣ ΟΥΔΕ ΠΟΤ ΕΥΦΡΟΝΙΟΣ

ὥσ|ού δἔ πὅτ|Εὔφρὅνῐ|ος

Such never made Euphronios.

NAMES OF YOUTHS.

An account of the potters and their labours, derived from the inscriptions, will be found in the next chapter. Besides the names of the principal figures, and of the artists and potters, a third name, either male or female, accompanied with the adjective ΚΑΛΟΣ,[1] or ΚΑΛΗ,[2] "the

---

[1] G. A. V., cxcv. cxcvi.; M. G., ii. lxxxv. 2, a; V. C. xxx. x.   [2] G. A. V., lxxix. lxxxi.

noble, beautiful or lovely, is found on several vases; which epithet is also sometimes found without any name. The archæologists who first studied the subject, imagined that these were laudatory inscriptions of the works of the potters. On many vases is HO ΠΑΙΣ ΚΑΛΟΣ, "the boy is handsome;"[1] sometimes with a repetition of ΚΑLΟΣ,[2] with certain anomalies, as HO ΠΑΙΣ ΚΑΛΕ,[3] or HE ΠΑΙΣ ΚΑΛΕ,[4] sometimes abridged to HO ΠΑΙΣ, "the boy;"[5] or ΠΑΙΣ,[6] or even with ΚΑΛΟΣ ΝΑΙΧΙ ΚΑΛΟΣ, "handsome—handsome forsooth."[7] The name, however, of some youth is generally understood, and in some instances expressed, as ΔΟΡΟΘΕΟΣ HO ΠΑΙΣ ΚΑΛΟΣ HO ΠΑΙΣ ΚΑΛΟΣ, "Dorotheos—the boy is handsome—the boy is handsome."[8] One remarkable cup has, interlaced with the foliage painted upon it, ΚΑΛΟΣ ΝΙΚΟΛΑΟΣ ΔΟΡΟΘΕΟΣ ΚΑΛΟΣ ΚΑΜΟΙ ΔΟΚΕΙ ΝΑΙ ΧΑΤΕΡΟΣ ΠΑΙΣ-ΚΑΛΟΣ ΜΕΜΝΟΝ ΚΑΜΟΙ ΚΑΛΟΣ ΦΙΛΟΣ. "Nicolaus is handsome, Dorotheos is handsome, seems to me that the one and the other is handsome. Memnon to me is handsome and dear."[9] A lecythus has ΟΠΙΣΘΕ ΜΕ ΚΑΙ ΕΥΠΟΛΕΣ ΕΙ ΚΑΛΟΣ, "behind (after) me even thou Eupoles art noble."[10] Once is found ΟΙΟΣ ΠΑΙΣ, "what a boy."[11]

The most usual form, however, is a proper name, accompanied with ΚΑΛΟΣ, as ΟΝΕΤΟΡΙΔΕΣ ΚΑΛΟΣ, "Onetorides is beautiful;" ΣΤΡΟΙΒΟΣ ΚΑΛΟΣ, "Stroibos

---

[1] M. G., ii. lxx. 1, a, b; G. A. V., ccxxix. lvii. lxxvi. 1 a; M. G. ii. lxix. 1 a; G. A. V., ccxxix.; V. D. C. xxii.; M. G. ii. clxii. 1 b; G. A. V., cxciii.
[2] V. D. C., xxxi. 1; M. G. ii. lxxxii. 2 a.
[3] M. G., ii. lxxxii. 2 b; V. G. xxii.
[4] M. G., ii. lxxxv. 2 b.
[5] M. G., ii. lxx. lxxi. 4 b.; G. A. V., ccxix.-cxxx.
[6] M. G., ii. lxxi. 4 a.
[7] B., 1851, 68.
[8] G. A. V., cii.
[9] An. 1833, 236-237; Mon. i. xxxix.
[10] Campana Collection.
[11] Vase at Naples; M. A. U. M. xxxviii. 92.

is beautiful ; " for which, on later vases, is substituted the form Ο ΚΑΛΟΣ, "the . beautiful," as ΝΙΚΟΔΗΜΟΣ Ο ΚΑΛΟΣ, "the noble Nicodemos." [1] One youth, indeed, Hippocritos, is called ΗΙΠΟΚΡΙΤΟΣ ΚΑΛΙΣΤΟΣ, " Hippocritos is the most handsome." [2]

NAMES OF FEMALES.

Besides the names of youths, those of females, either brides, beauties, or hetairæ, are found, accompanied with the expression ΚΑΛΕ, as ΟΙΝΑΝΘΕ ΚΑΛΕ " Œnanthe is lovely !" [3] Often, however, the names of females are accompanied with those of men. The most elliptical form is ΚΑΛΟΣ, " he is handsome ; " ΚΑΛΕ, " she is fair !" [4] One vase of the Canino collection had ΛΥΣΙΠΙΔΕΣ ΚΑΛΟΣ ΡΟΔΟΝ ΚΑΛΕ, " Lysippides is beautiful, Rodon is fair," apparently a kind of epithalamium. Before a lyrist is written on one vase, ΚΑΛΕ ΔΟΚΕΣ, [5] " thou seemest fair." This, however, might be part of the song. Of the nature of an Agonistic inscription is that cited by M. Böckh, reading ΚΕΛΗΤΙ ΔΑΜΟΚΛΕΙΔΑΣ. [6] " Damocleidas (was victor) in the horse race," which throws much light on the use of ΚΑΛΟΣ in the others already cited.

The import of these inscriptions has excited much controversy, for while some have taken them to be the names of the possessors of the vases, [7] others have considered that they were those of the persons for whom the vase was

---

[1] G. A. V. clv. Cf. ; Panofka, l. c.
[2] G. A. V., lxi.-lxii.
[3] G. A. V., cli.
[4] G. A. V., lxxxi.
[5] Mus. Borb., iii. xii.

[6] M. Böckh. in the Bull., 1832, p. 95 ; Walpole, Memoirs, p. 332 ; Böckh. Corp. Inscr. Græc.. no. 33.
[7] Panofka, Eigennamen mit καλος, s. 1 ; Gerhard, Annali. 1831. p. 81.

made, or to whom it was sent as a present,[1] or those of youths and maidens beloved or admired by the potter.[2] This last hypothesis is supported by the fact of lovers writing the name of the beloved object upon the walls of the Ceramicus.[3] In allusion to this, the same epithet of "handsome, or beautiful," is applied sarcastically by Aristophanes to the Demos, Pyrilampous,[4] and the same poet, speaking of the Thracian, Sitalcas, as a devoted admirer of Athens, describes him as writing upon the wall "the beautiful," or "handsome Athenians."[5] "He is an exceedingly good friend to Athens," says the poet, "and loves it so exceedingly, that often he scrawls upon the walls, 'The Athenians are beautiful!'" Females were repeatedly called "the fair,"[6] and their names inscribed on walls. Even dogs found their devoted masters, who called them καλὸς on their sepulchral monuments.[7] The case, however, most in point for the artists of antiquity, is that of Phidias inscribing the name of Pantarces, in the case already mentioned.[8] According to this hypothesis, where the word καλὸς is found alone, the name was intended to be supplied, as in a blank formula,[9] which, however, appears doubtful. It is generally supposed, indeed, that the word is intended to express the personal beauty of the individual named,[10] although it is by no

---

[1] Millingen, Peint. d. Vases Grec., fol. Romæ, 1813, p. iii., p. xi.

[2] Mazocchi, Tab. Heracl., 138; Böttiger, Vasengem., iii. 20.

[3] Suidas, voce, ὁ δεῖνα καλος ; Schol. Aristoph. Acharn., 143; Eustath. ii. p. 633.

[4] Aristoph. Vesp., 97, 98.

[5] Acharn., 143.

[6] Aristænet. i. 10 ; Lucian, Amor., c. 16 ; Xenoph. Eph., i. 2.

[7] Theophrast., Toup on Suid., Oxon., 1790, t. ii. p. 129.

[8] Clemens, Alex., p. 33 ; Arnob. adv. Gent., vi., p. 199 ; Greg. Nazien., xviii.; Pausan., v. 11.

[9] Visconti, Mus. Pio. Clem. V.; tav. xiii., p. 25, n. f.

[10] Müller, Götting. gelehrte Anzeigen, 134, 135; St., d. 25, Aug., 1831 s. 1331-1334.

means improbable that it was applied to those who
excelled in the games of the youths in the Stadium. These
names, which no doubt were the popular ones of the day,
were adopted by the potter, in order to induce the
admiring public to purchase objects which recalled their
idols to mind ; and the prominent manner in which the
names are placed upon the vases, shows that they were
not less essential than the subjects to their sale. The
influence which the beauty of boys, and the charms of
beautiful and accomplished women, exercised over the
Greek mind [1] is quite sufficient to account for the use of
the epithet, without supposing that it resulted from the
admiration of the potter. Above seventy names of men,
and about ten names of women, have been found with this
epithet, besides those of several deities. These names are
all Greek, many of them traceable to Athenian families ;
and as the vases bearing them were found amidst the
Etruscan sepulchres of Vulci and of Northern Italy, the
Campanian tombs of Nola, and in Southern Italy and
Sicily, it is plain that they could not have been those of
the possessors or donors.[2] A most ingenious attempt has
been made by M. Panofka to trace a connection between
the subjects of vases and the names which appear
upon them. Bearing in mind the apparent remoteness
of the allusions in the odes of Pindar to the victors
celebrated, and in the Greek choruses to the plot of the
drama, it is possible that such allusions may be intended,
although, whether the connection can be always satis-

---

[1] Bergk. Allgemeine Literatur Zei-
tung, n. 132, Juni, 1846, s. 1049-
52.

[2] Th. Bergk., loc. cit.; Panofka,
Eigennamen, s. 84-85.

factorily traced, is open to doubt.[1] A list of the names of persons mentioned, taken from M. Panofka's dissertation, is appended. (Appendix, No. I.)

UNINTELLIGIBLE INSCRIPTIONS.

A considerable number of vases are covered with inscriptions,[2] the meaning of which is quite unintelligible, although the letters can be distinctly read. This is not peculiar to vases found in Italy, but is of common occurrence on those of Greece itself. Nor can it be charged to the ignorance or barbarism of the potter, as such inscriptions are often found intermingled with others in good Greek. In some few cases these inscriptions can be traced to forgeries, as for instance of the names of potters; while in others a certain resemblance is observable between the illegible inscriptions, and the more correctly written names of the figures represented. Some few also may be intended for the sounds of animals, especially where there is a repetition of the same syllable placed near them, such as,

ΧΕΧΕΥΔΚΤΕΧΕΧΕΧϘϜΧΕΧϘϜΦϜΧΦΕΧΕ
ΚΥΕΧΕΥΛΚΚϙϜΥϜΧΕΛΔΧϜΧΕΧΧΚΧΕΛΑ

like the twittering and gibbering of the birds in the "Birds" of Aristophanes. Some few, perhaps, are vulgarisms, or owing to the abnormal state of the language

[1] This subject has been discussed at considerable length by M. Panofka, Die Griechischen Eigennamen mit ΚΑΛΟΣ, 4to, Berlin, 1850; Abhand. d. K. Akademie der Wissenschaften, 1849, p. 89-191; Thiersch. ueber die hellenischen bemalten Vasen, 4to, Munich, 44.

[2] Gerhard, Rapp. Volc. p. 173, n. 668.

at that time.[1] But many, especially those which are a series of words commencing with the same letters, and which often consist of agglomerations of consonants with few vowels, are the mere images of words, written down only to show that an inscription is intended.[2] Others may be meant for the imperfect words uttered by excited persons, such as drunkards[3] and revellers. Several of these unintelligible inscriptions occur on the early cups, such as, ENXIXNOIXITOIXNE', or ENIXIXOXIXINEIT, ΧΠΣΕΑΙΝ‥ ΚΝΣ.[5] Some of them have lately been conjectured to be a kind of cipher.[6] These inscriptions are found on vases of the earlier style with black figures, and occasionally on those with red; and they continue till the time of the later vases of Nola,[7] and of Apulia,[8] when names were incised by possessors; the names of the potters Andocides and Hieron occur in this manner on two vases.

II.—INCISED INSCRIPTIONS.

The second class of inscriptions is those which are engraved on the vases. Sometimes they have been incised before the vase was sent to the furnace, at other times after it was baked. On the vases of the later style the names of figures and objects are executed in this manner, the letters being incised through the black glaze on the red clay of the vase. On the older ones they

---

[1] Gerhard, Rapp. Volc., p. 71., who supposes the artists wished to give an appearance of great antiquity to their vases.

[2] Ibid., p. 173, n. 670; G. A. V., cxxiv. clxv.

[3] Cf., the expression, ΕΛΕΟΠ, ΕΛΕ-ΔΕΜ, with the word, ΚΟΜΑΡΧΟΣ,

Gerhard, A. V., clxxxviii.

[4] B. M., 678; C. D., 335.

[5] C. D. 335; B. M., 667-8.

[6] B. A. B., 1599.

[7] De Witte, Penelope, Annali, 1841, p. 264, pl. i.

[8] De Witte, Annali, 1841, 268.

have generally been incised before the vases were consigned to the furnace. They are found distributed in
different places, as the handles, border, feet, and especially
at the bottom of the vase under the foot ; having been
written when the vase stood upon its mouth, or on the
detached foot before it was united. Those on the body
of the vase relate either to the figures represented, or else
have the name of the possessor of the vase, or of the
person for whose ashes it was used. Some few, however,
relate to the potters.[1] A vase in the Museum at Naples[2]
has incised upon its neck the name of Charminos, son
of Theophamides—XAPMINOC ΘΕΟΦΑΜΙΔΑ ΚΩΙΟC—a
native of Cos, and came from Carthage. A *hydria*, or
pitcher, from Berenice, has in like manner the name of
Aristarchos son of Ariston.[3] Such formulæ are not
uncommon, as ΔΙΟΝΥΣΙΟΥ Α ΛΑΚΥΘΟΣ ΤΟΥ ΜΑΤΑΛΟΥ
" (I am) the *lecythus* of Dionysius, the son of Matalus ;"[4]
—ΤΡΕΜΙΟ ΕΜΙ, " I belong to Tromios ;" ΚΑΡΟΝΟΣ ΕΜΙ,
" I belong to Charon;"[5] ΣΟΣΤΡΑΤΟ ΕΜΙ, " I belong
to Sostratos ;"[6] ΤΑΤΑΙΗΣ ΕΙΜΙ ΛΗΚΥΘΟΣ ΟΣ ΔΑΝ ΜΕ
ΚΛΕΨ[Η] ΘΥΦΛΟΣ ΕΣΤΟ, " I am the *lecythus* of Tataies,
and may whoever steals me be struck blind."[7] On a vase
in the Museum of Naples is ΝΙΚΑ ΗΕΡΑΚΛΗΣ, "Heracles
conquers," but it is doubtful whether it is antique.[8] In one
instance a scratched inscription, reading ΗΕΜΙΚΟΤΥΛΙΟΝ,
indicated the capacity of a vase with two small handles,

---

[1] As that of Hieron. Bull., 1832,
p. 114.
[2] M. B., iv. 5. 1; Neapels. Ant.
Bild., s. 548.
[3] Formerly in Mr. Bidwell's Collection, Arch. Zeit., 1846, p. 216.

[4] B.,1830, p. 153; A., 1831, D.
[5] Raoul Rochette, Journ. des Sav.,
1830. p. 118.
[6] Ibid.
[7] B. Arch. Nap., tom. ii. tav. i., fig. i.
[8] Inghirami, S. V. T., xlii.

found at Corfû ; another of these inscriptions,[1] ΛΥΔΙΑ
ΜΕΖΩ ΚΕ ΛΕΠΑΣΤΙΔΕΣ ΚΖ, supposed to refer to
the capacity of some vase, holding 25 lydians
and 27 lepastides ; under another[2] ΙΧΘΥΑ, "dishes for
fish."[3]

On the foot of a crater from Girgenti is the word
ΧΑΡΙΤΩΝ, Chariton, probably a proper name.[4]

The most interesting inscriptions, however, are those on
the feet of the vases of the earlier style, of which a
considerable number have been discovered. They are
very difficult to decipher, being chiefly contracted forms
of words, and often monograms, or agglomerations of
letters and ciphers. The greater portion are consequently unintelligible, and probably were understood
only by the potter or his workman. Many of them,
however, are evidently memorandums made by the workman, about the number of vases in the batch ; and others
those of the merchant, respecting the price to be paid.
Such are the abridgments as ΥΕ[5] ΗΥΔ, ΗΥΔΡΙ Ηυδρια,[6] or
in a fuller form ΗΥΔΡΙΑΣ ΛΗΚ or ΛΗΚΥ ληκυθος,[7] ΟΞΥ for
ΟΞΥΒΑΦΑ,[8] oxybapha, another kind of vase, ΧΥΤΡΙ, for
" pots." The examination of these inscriptions under the
feet of vases leads to some curious results as to prices. On
one in the Louvre is :

[1] Arch. Zeit., 1846, s. 371.
[2] A. Z. 1848, s. 248.
[3] Collections of these will be found
in Pr. de Canino, Mus. Etr.; Gerhard,
Neuerworb. Ant. Denk. 8vo., Berlin,
1836, Taf. ii. ; Cat. Greek and Etr.
Vases in Brit. Mus., pl. A. and B.
[4] Millingen, Vases de Coghill, pl. xi.
The word also means " of the Graces."
i.e. " the crater of the Graces."

[5] M. E., 212.
[6] M. E., xxxvii., 1650.
[7] Panofka, Recherches, p. 8.
[8] Panofka, l. c.; Letronne, Journ.
des Sav. 1837, p. 750; Nouvelles Annales, i., p. 497 ; Journal des Sav., 1849,
p. 427; Böckh. Staatsh. i., p. 451;
Jahn. Bericht., d. k. Sachs. Gesellsch.,
. 8vo., Feb. 1854, p. 37.

ΚΡΑΤΕΡΕΣ : ΠΙ
TIME ; ⊢⊢⊢⊢ΟΞΙΔΕΣ : ΠΙΙΙ
ΒΑΦΕΑ : ΔΔ⊢Ι.

That is,[1]

Six crateres
value 4 drachmæ : 8 oxides.
20 baphea. 1 drachmæ . 1 obolos.

On another vase was inscribed[2]—

ΚΡΑΤΕΡΕΣ Π ΟΞΙΔΕΣ ΔΔΔΤΙΘ
ΟΞΥΒΑΦΑ ΔΙΙΙ
5 craters, 40 oxides, value 8 drachmæ
13 oxybapha . . .

Δ . ΚΥΑΘΕΑ
10 Cyathea (for Cyathoi).[3]

ΑΡΥΣΙΔΗ
30 arysides, or "ladles,"

VΡΙΑΣ ΙΙΙΙ (for Ηυδριας)
make " 4 hydriæ."

It is supposed that these inscriptions were placed on
the feet of vases while being turned for the potter, and
before they were united with the vase.[4]

	Present value of money about
1 Cylix cost 1 drachma	= 3 shillings.
1 Crater cost 4 obolos	= 2 shillings.
1 Lecythus cost 1 obolos	= 6 pence.
1 Small pot cost ½ obolos	= 3 pence.
1 Saucer (βαφιον) cost ⅓ obolos	= 2 pence.

[1] Letronne, sur les noms tracés à
la pointe; Nouvelles Annales, 1836,
p. 492.
[2] Ibid., 502.
[3] Ibid., 502, 503.
[4] Ibid., 506.

The following were the prices of *lecythi*, or oil-flasks :—

ΛHKΥ : ΛΛ : ΛH 20 lecythi are worth 27 drachmæ⎫
ΛHKΥ : IΓ : IA 13 „ „ 11 „ ⎬ or obols.[1]
ΛHKΥ : KΘ : ΛH 29 „ „ 27 „ ⎭

This was probably reckoned by obols, for according
to Aristophanes,[2] an obolos would purchase a very fine
lecythus, while an earthenware cask, or *cadus* (καδὸς), cost
3 drachmæ.[3] In an inscription published by Böckh,[4] one
Cephisophon values his *cylix*, or cup, at one drachma.
On another small vase at Berlin is—

ΔΔΔII : TIMH · Ͱ Ͱ ΙΠΙC.
32 vases value 2 dr. 4½ oboli.

Π.ΕΛΠΟΙ · ΔΔΔ.
5 elpi, value 30 drachme, or 1 elpos = 6 dr.[5]

Π · ΚΑΔΙΑ.
5 cadi = 12 dr. or 1 cados = 2⅖ dr.

The two annexed engravings will illustrate the nature
of these inscriptions completely. The first, which is at
the base of a small two-handled vase, called *pelike*, found
at Nola,[6] reads Δραχμαι δυο τιμη οβολοι τεσσαρες και ημισυ,—
"two drachmæ, value four oboli and a half,"—which is
supposed to refer to the value of this by no means fine vase.
The second is evidently a memorandum, beginning, XVTPIA
KΓ,[6] "Twenty-three pots,"—δραχμαις τριακοντα επτα, "thirty-

[1] Jahn. l. c. p. 37, 38.
[2] Ranæ, 1267.
[3] Pax. 1291.
[4] Corp. Art. Inscr. Græc, No. 545.
[5] Jahn, Ueber ein Vasenbild welches

ein Topferei vorstellt in the Bericht
d. Sachsisch. Gesellsch. 1854, p. 37.
[6] Gerhard, Neuerw. Denkm., s. 30,
No. 1605.

seven drachmæ,"—ΟΞΥ (βαφα) Ε,[1] "Five oxybapha," or
"vinegar vases." In a similar manner are written

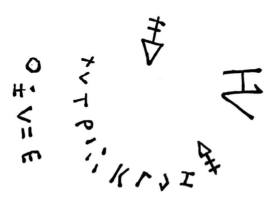

No. 126.—Incised inscriptions on vases.

memoranda of the prices of *cylices*,[2] or cups, and other
products of the kiln,[3] as Δ ΚVΑΘΕΑ, "four cyathi."[4]

Inscriptions on vases are mentioned by the ancients.
The *scyphos* of Hercules, on which was seen the fall of
Troy, had on it certain illegible characters.[5] A cup at
Capua was said to have an inscription declaring that it
belonged to Nestor. Athenæus[6] also mentions the
inscribed cup of a youth who had thrown himself into
the sea after a girl beloved by him, declaring that he had
carried with him a cup of Zeus Soter.

[1] Mus. Etr. xl., No. 1821; Cat. of
Gr. and Etr. Vas. in B. M., pl. A.
459.
[2] B. A. N. N. S., iv. p. 132, BAN. ii.
tav. i. 6, p. 23.
[3] B. A. B., 1666.
[4] C. B. L., p. 21, No. 22.
[5] Athenæus, p. 493, C.
[6] xi. 466, C.

CHAPTER VIII.

HAVING thus described the chief peculiarities of the
painted vases, and of the circumstances connected with
them, it now remains to say something respecting their
makers—the potters of antiquity. Unfortunately, however, little is known of their condition, except that they
formed a guild, or fraternity, and that they amassed vast
fortunes by exporting their products to the principal
emporia of the ancient world. The oldest establishments
appear to have been at Samos, Corinth, and Ægina, and
it was not till a later period that the Athenian pottery
attained any great eminence, or became universally
sought after. The existence of two *kerameikoi*, or pottery

districts, at Athens, and the fact that some of the principal men were connected with the potteries, show the great commercial importance of the manufacture.

By the Athenians, potters were called *Prometheans*,[1] from the Titan Prometheus, who made man out of clay, —which, according to one mythos, was the blood of the Titans, or Giants,—and who was thus the founder of the fictile art. It was not, however, much esteemed, although without doubt the pursuit of it was a lucrative one, and many of the trade realised large fortunes;[2] in proof of which may be cited the well-known anecdote of Agathocles,[3] who, at a time when the rich used plate, was in the habit of mixing earthenware with it at his table, telling his officers that he formerly made such ware, but that now, owing to his prudence and valour, he was served in gold,—an anecdote which also proves that the profession was not highly esteemed. However, the competition in the trade was so warm as to pass into a proverb, and the animosity of some of the rival potters is recorded upon certain vases.[4] To this spirit is also probably to be referred many of the tricks of trade, such as forgeries of the names of makers, and the numerous illegible inscriptions. When the potter's establishment, —called ἐργαστήριον—was large, he employed under him a number of persons, some of whom were probably free

[1] Καὶ αὐτοὶ δὲ 'Αθηναῖοι τοὺς χυτρέας καὶ ἱπνοποιοὺς καὶ πάντας ὅσοι πηλουργοὶ, Προμηθέας ἀπεκάλουν ἐπισκώπτοντες ἐς τὸν πηλὸν καὶ τὴν ἐν πυρὶ οἶμαι τῶν σκευῶν ὄπτησιν. Lucian. Prometh. in Verbis, Dindorf. 8vo., Paris, 1840, p. 6, s. 2., l. 11 and foll.
[2] Σμιχυλιων Εναυλκιδου εκ κεραμεων.

Arch. Zeit. 1853.
[3] Plutarch, Apophthegm., vol. vi., p. 673. Leipz. ed. 1777.
[4] Hesiod, Oper. et Dier., v. 25; Aristotle, Rep., v. 10; Rhet., ii. 4; Ethic., viii. 2; Plato, Lys., p. 215; Plutarch, de capiend. ex hoste util., p. 342, Leipz. ed. 1777.

but poor citizens, whilst others were slaves belonging to him. How the labour was subdivided there are no means of accurately determining, but the following hands were probably employed :—1. A potter, to make the vase on the wheel ; 2. An artist, to trace with a point in outline the subject of the vase ; 3. A painter, who executed the whole subject in outline, and who probably returned it to No. 2, when incised lines were required ; 4. A modeller, who added such parts of the vase as were moulded ; 5. A fireman, who took the vase to the furnace and brought it back ; 6. A fireman for the furnace ; 7. Packers, to pack up the vases for exportation. Hence it may readily be conceived that a large establishment employed a great number of hands, and exhibited an animated scene of industrial activity.

Some slight insight into the nature of the trade is gained from the inscriptions which the potters placed on their vases. The fullest form [1] of inscription is when both the potter and the artist placed their names on the vase ; and there is some doubt whether, when the name of a potter is found alone, he did not paint as well as make the vase. Nearly fifty names of potters have been found, but they only occur on choice specimens of art, perhaps on samples or batches, and the far greater proportion of vases have no name at all. It is so difficult to

[1] For the lists of these names see Panofka, Von den Namen der Vasen-bildner, 4to. Berlin, 1849. s. 153, 241; R. Rochette, Lettre à M. Schorn., 8vo, Paris, 1832 ; 2nd edit. 8vo. Paris, 1845 ; Clarac, Cat. d. Artist. d'Antiq., 12mo, Paris, 1849; Welcker, in the Kunstblatt, 1827, No. 81-4 ; Osann, in the Kunst-blatt, 1830, No. 83, 84 ; Welcker, in the Rheinisch. Mus. Bd. vi. 1847, s. 389-97; De Witte, sur les noms des Dessinateurs et Fabricants des Vases Peintes, Revue de Philologie, 8vo, Paris, Tom. ii. p. 387-473; Gerhard, Rap. Volc., p. 74, 75.

assign to each potter his relative position in the history of the art, that it is as well to take the names in alphabetical order.

The name of the potter *Alides* has been found upon a vase with red figures, of the strong style, found at St. Maria di Capua, having the subject of Pelops, surnamed Plexippus, with two horses.[1]

Amasis, a potter, whose name is apparently of Egyptian origin, may have had a factory at Corinth, as his works are of the early rigid school. His vases have been found only in Italy. He exercised the art of painter as well as potter, and on certain vases he states that he painted the subject.[2] He painted for the potter Cleophradas.[3] Whether he subsequently set up for himself does not appear, but he is known in connection with several vases with black figures; as, an amphora, on which is seen the dispute of Poseidon and Athene for the soil of Attica,[4] and Dionysos and his cohort; a small jug, *olpe*, with the subject of Perseus killing Medusa;[5] and an amphora, with that of Achilles and Penthesilea, and the arrival of Memnon at Troy.[6] Generally he writes on his productions ΜΕΠΟΙΕΣΕΝ, " made me," but on this last-mentioned vase appears the blundered form ΠΟΙΗΣΝ. *Anacles* is known from a cup on which is a hind.[7] *Andocides*, another maker of the same kind of vases, is known from an amphora, on which is represented the contest of

---

[1] Bull. Arch. Nap. xcv.; Panofka Vasenbildner, s. 43. This is the same name read Euergetides.

[2] Raoul Rochette, p. 31; Clarac, p. 248.

[3] Gerhard, l. c., No. 703; R. Rochette, Bull. Fer, 1831, p. 101.

[4] Gerhard Annali, 1831, 178, No. 702.

[5] Cat. Dub. No. 32; Cat. Vas. B. M., p. 172, 641*.

[6] G.A . V., ccvii.; Campanari, p. 87.

[7] Panofka, s. 32; Bull. 1835, 127; De Witte, Rev. 392.

Hercules and Gycnus, and Bacchus and satyrs,[1] and another with black figures on a white ground, having for its subject Nereids and Amazons,[2] the style of which is fine. He employed no artist. *Archecles*,[3] who also inscribes upon his vases " made me," or " made," is known from a *phiale*, a cup of a very old style, with tall foot, and small handles of figures, with the subjects of the hunt of the Calydonian boar, and the death of the Minotaur.[4] Another of his cups has a goat and satyr.[5] He employed the artist Glaucythes,[6] by whose aid he produced the celebrated vase found at Cære, one of the most remarkable for size and decoration, and which belongs to the oldest period of the fictile art. *Bryllos* is known as the maker of a *cylix* found at Vulci, painted with red figures, and having for its subject the last night of Troy ;[7] and of another, with Triptolemus, the family of Celeus, and the rape of Proserpine, also in red figures.[8] The name of the potter *Calliphon* was invented to deceive the celebrated archæologist Millin, in which it was entirely successful.[9] *Chachrylios*, was a maker of a cup with red figures, of the fine style,[10] representing Amazons and the Bacchanalian

[1] ANΔOKIΔEΣ ΕΠOIEΣE, ΕΠOEΣEN. Can. 1e Cent., 1846; Ann., 1837, 178, No. 700; Clarac, Cat., p. 37, 237-249; Mus. Etr. 1381 ; C. Dub., 79 ; C. D., 22; Campanari, p. 88; B. 1845, p. 25; Panofka, Taf. iii. 2, s. 28.

[2] His name is inscribed on the foot, which renders it suspicious. Campana Coll.

[3] C. D., No. 999 ; R. V., p. 178, n. 694.

[4] G. A. V., ccxxxv.; Panofka, s. 32, 33.

[5] Panofka, s. 31, reads this artist's name, APKITEΣ ΕΠOIEΣEN.

[6] Panofka, M. Bl., xvi. 47 ; Gerhard, A. 1831, 178, No. 694 ; Clarac, Cat. p. 251.

[7] Panofka, s. 13, B. 1843, p. 71, BPTΛOΣ ΕΠOIEΣEN.

[8] A. 1850, pl. G. p. 109.

[9] Coll. Can. 51 ; Journ. des Savans., 1830, p. 121; Raoul Rochette, Bull. Fèrus, 1831, p. 149 ; Clarac. p. 70.

[10] Coll. Can. 51 ; Cat. Can. 81; Gerhard, Ann., 1831, 179, No. 705; Campanari, p. 88 ; XAXPΤΛIOΣ ΕΠOIEΣEN ; Cat. Vas. Brit. Mus., p. 262, No. 815.*

cortège; and of another, with Theseus bearing off Antiope.[1]
A vase found at Cære, with black figures, had the name of
the potter *Charitæus*, representing the subject of Hercules
and the Nemæan lion.[2] Of *Cleophradas*, the employer of
Amasis, mention has been already made.[3] *Cholchos*,
another maker of vases with red figures, of the strong
style, appears to have worked for Euxitheos.[4] An *œnochoe*
of this maker has been found, with the subject of the
contest of Hercules and Cycnus.[5] *Chelis* manufactured
cylices with black figures, sometimes intermixed with red,
representing Bacchanalian and athletic subjects ; and one
with Apollo and Hermes contending for the lyre. He
belongs to the transition period.[6]

A jug of fine shape, having a wreath of a vine laden
with grapes depicted in black on a white ground, bears the
name of the potter *Charinos*, with which is combined that
of Xenodoros, but whether that of an artist or of a youth
is uncertain.[7] *Chærestratos* is only known from some
verses of Phrynichus. " Then, forsooth," says he, " Chærestratos, soberly pottering at home, burnt about a
hundred canthari of wine every day."[8] A person of the
name of *Cephalos*, if it be not a fictitious one, is

[1] Cat. Vas. Brit. Mus., p. 278, No.
827 ; Cat. Can., 115.

[2] ΧΑΡΙΤΑΙΟΣ ΕΠΟΙΕΣΕΝ ΕΜΕ, ΧΑΡΙ-
ΤΑΙΟΣ ΕΠΟΙΕΣΕΝ : ΕΜΕ : ΕΤ, Visconti,
Intorno gli Monumenti sepolchrali sco-
perti nel ducato di Cere, in the Dis-
sertazioni della Pontificia Accademia
Romana di Archeologia, 4to, Roma,
1836, Taf. ix.

[3] Gerhard, Annali, 1831, p. 178, No.
703; Panofka, s. 37 ; Duc de Luynes,
Choix de Vases, pl. xliv.

[4] Rochette, Lettre à M. Schorn, p.
44; Clarac. Cat. p. 273; Campanari. p.
88, ΧΟΛΧΟΣ ΜΕΠΟΙΕΣΕΝ.

[5] G. A. V., cxxii. cxxiii.; Panofka,
s. 14, Taf. i. 6.

[6] ΧΕΛΙΣ ΕΠΟΙΕΣΕΝ,Gerhard,A.,1831,
p. 179 ; No.706 ; Clarac.,p. 74 ; Cat. Dur.
180; Cat. Can. 224 ; Panofka, s. 5, 37.

[7] Brit. Mus. No. 90.

[8] Meineke, Frag. Com. Græc., ii. 386 ;
Athenæus, xi., p. 474, B. There is a
play on the word Κεραμευόων.

sarcastically alluded to by Aristophanes,[1] as making wretched dishes, but tinkering the state well and truly.

The name of *Deiniades*,[2] another potter, is recorded on a cylix, with red figures, having for its subject Hercules killing Alcyoneus. *Doris*, better known as a painter, appears as the maker of a dish, on which is a seated figure of Athene.[3] *Epigenes*, another potter, is only known from a cantharus, or two-handled cup, of peculiar shape and mediocre style with red figures, on which is painted Achilles at the ships, receiving a draught of wine from the Nereid, Cymothoe, and attended by Ucalegon, while Patroclus, attended by Nestor and Antilochos, has the same honour accorded him by Thetis. Both Achilles and Patroclus are armed, and departing from the ships.[4] *Epitimos* made vases with red figures ; as, for example, a cup of ancient style, on which is a warrior mounting his horse.[5]

Erginos, a potter, employed the painter Aristophanes, and fabricated vases with black figures.[6]

Ergotimos, another potter, is known from the Francois vase, and a *cylix* with black figures, representing the capture of Silenus in the gardens of Midas, found at Ægina,[7] of which island Ergotimos was probably a native. He was perhaps the father of the next potter, *Eucheros*, or Eucheir, in whom

[1] Eccl. v. 252.

[2] ΔΕΙΝΙΑΔΕΣ ΕΠΟΙΕΣΕΝ, Coll. Can., 1e Cent., No. 74 ; Gerhard, Ann. 1831, p. 179, No. 709 ; p. 180, No. 728 ; Campanari, p. 88.

[3] Gerhard, Fernerer Zuwachs der K. Mus., No. 1853 ; Gerhard, Trinkschalen, Taf. xiii.

[4] Ann., 1850, p. 143, pl. H. i.; B. 1846, p. 69 ΕΠΙΓΕΝΕΣ ΕΠΟΕΣΕ (ἐποίησεν) ;

Panofka, s. 40, 1.

[5] ΕΠΙΤΙΜΟΣ ΕΠΟΙΕΣΕΝ, Clarac, Cat. 240, m ; Dub. Not. descr., 56, No. 203; Campanari, p. 88.

[6] Clarac, Cat., p. 204, c, ΕΡΓΙΝΟΣ ΕΠΟΙΕΣΕ ; Gerhard, Trinkschalen, Taf. ii. iii.; Panofka, s. 8, Taf. i. 3.

[7] ΕΡΓΟΤΙΜΟΣ ΕΠΟΙΕΣΕ; G. A. V., ccxxxviii; Bull. Fér., 1831, p. 153.

some recognise the celebrated Eucheir, brought by Demaratus from Corinth to Tarquinii, who made a *cylix*, with
black figures, of the oldest style, with a representation of
the Chimæra, and on which he inscribes himself the son of
Ergotimos.[1] He is a maker of the oldest school.

Euergetides made a cup with red figures, found at
Capua,[2] representing Pelops, Plexippos, a dancer, and a
Palæstric subject.

The potter *Euphronios*, was probably the most celebrated of his day. He belonged to the epoch of the
"fine," or to the latter days of the "strong" style, cha-
racterised by red figures, or by polychrome figures on a
white ground,[3] and produced vases, mostly *cylices*, of the
finest style of art. The only vase-painter whose name
appears on his works, is the artist Onesimus,[4] who painted
for him a *cylix* with the subject of a race. Only a few of
his works remain, as a *cylix*[5] with the subject of Hercules
and the Erymanthian boar, a quadriga ; Alcæus and
a Sappho ;[6] another with the fate of Troilus,[7] a horseman,[8] Phrygians,[9] and heroes arming ;[10] one with Death
and Sleep bearing off Sarpedon,[11] and Dolon seized by
Ulysses and Diomedes ;[12] and another with a triclinium of

[1] ΕΥΧΕΡΟΣ ΕΠΟΙΕΣΕΝ ΗΟΡΓΟΤΙ-
ΜΟΥ ΗΥΙΗΥΣ, Clarac, Cat. Art. 191;
Bull. 1846, p. 78; Cat. Vas. B. M., p.
196, No. 701; De Witte, Cat. Can.,
No. 121, p. 70, M. M. I., xlii.
[2] Ann., 1849, p. 145, pl. B., ΕΥΕΡΓΕ-
ΤΙΔΕΣ ΕΠΟΙ.
[3] G. T. C., xiv.
[4] Annali, 1831, 180, No. 723; Bull.
Férusac., 1831, p. 153; Clarac. Cat., p.
109; Dubois, Cat. d. Pr. de Canino, 87,
ter; Panofka, die Vasenmaler Euthymides und Euphronios, p. 13.

[5] Vas. Cat. Brit. Mus., p. 270, No.
822; Panofka, p. 9.
[6] Cat. Dur., 61.
[7] Mus. Etr., 588; Cat. Can., 87, No.
568; Ann., 1831, 408, 824; Clarac, 272;
G. A. V., ccxxv.
[8] Cat. Dub., p. 200.
[9] Cat. Can., 81; Mus. Etr., 1091;
1831, Ann., No. 723.
[10] G. A. V., ccxxv.
[11] Panofka, p. 9.
[12] Ibid.

hetairæ.[1]   He also painted vases on which occur the name
of Panætios, an *amphora* with Hercules and the Erymanthian boar, and Acamas and Demophon with their horses,[2]
and a jar with recumbent undraped females.[3]

He has also left a *cylix* with figures in black outline, like
the later Athenian school, on which is Diomedes and a
female, or Achilles and Pontomeda;[4] and a *crater*, with Hercules and Antæus of remarkably fine and grandiose style.[5]
This potter placed on his vases the names of several
celebrated youths of the day. His vases are, perhaps, the
very finest known of the strong style.

Euxitheos, who belongs to the period of vases with red
figures, was a painter as well as a potter. He is known
from an amphora representing Achilles and Briseis,[6] and
from a *cylix* with the subject of Patroclus. For the last
he employed the vase-painter Cholchos.[7]

Execias was both a maker and painter of vases,[8] with
black figures, of the early style. He is known from
amphoræ on which are represented Hercules killing
Geryon, the chariot of Anchippus,[9] Achilles and Penthesilea,[10] Bacchus,[11] and Œnopion, and a deep *cylix* with
small figures of a winged female and stag.[12]   On cups,

---

[1] Ibid. s. 10.

[2] Ibid. s. 16.

[3] Campan. Coll.

[4] Gerhard, Trinksc. und Gefasse, taf.
xiv. 5, 6, 7 ; Panofka die vasenbildner,
taf. iv. 7. s. 11 ; Welcker, Rhein. Mus.,
vi. Bd. 1847, s. 394.

[5] Mon. v. pl. 38, 1855.

[6] ΕΥΚΣΙΘΕΟΣ ΕΠΟΙΕΣΕΝ, Cat. Dur.
386 ; G. A. V., clxxxvii. ; Panofka,
s. 17.

[7] Vases d. Pr. d. Canino, pl. 5 ;
Gerhard, Ann., 1831, p. 180, 729, No.

729; Campanari, p. 88; Brit. Mus.,
Vas. Cat., p. 246, No. 80 3; Inghirami,
Gall. Om., ii. 254.

[8] ΕΧΣΕΚΙΑΣ ΕΠΟΙΕΣΕ, Panofka, s.
s. 19, Taf. ii. 1, 2.

[9] Cat. Dur., 296 ; G. A. V., cvii.

[10] Cat. Dur., 389 ; G. A. V., ccvi. ;
Cat. Vas. Brit. Mus. p. 111, No. 554.

[11] G. A. V., ccvi. ; Panofka, s. 19,
Taf. ii. 5, 6.

[12] ΕΚΣΕΚΙΑΣ ΜΕΠΟΙΕΣΕΝ. Campana. Coll.

cylices, and amphoræ he painted the subjects of Acamas
and Demophon bringing back Æthra,[1] Achilles and Ajax
playing at dice,[2] the contest for the body of Achilles, and
Dionysos and the Tyrrhenian pirates.[3]
Echecrates is known by a single *cylix*, the subject of
which is a Gorgon's head.[4]
Glaucythes[5] has been already mentioned. His name
appears on the cup, with small figures, representing the
death of the Minotaur, and of the Calydonian boar, now
in the Museum at Munich, and on another cup in the
Berlin Museum. He must have flourished about the same
time as Tleson and Nicosthenes, and he placed on his
wares the name of Hippocritos, a youth styled " the most
beautiful." He flourished at the early period of vases with
black figures.

Other potters were *Hermæos*, the maker of a cup on
which is represented Hermes making a libation ;[6] *Hermogenes*,[7] one of the early school, who only made cups
with small figures and ornaments ; and the supposed
Hecthor.[8] *Hieron*, a remarkable name, perhaps of a
contemporary with the old Sicilian tyrant, is chiefly known
from the *cylices* he made, and which are found at Vulci,
and in the Sabine territory, with the name scratched upon
the handle. He appears to have been a partner with

[1] Ann. iii. p. 179, No. 709; Cat. Dur.,
l. c.; G. A. V. ccvi.
[2] Panofka, s. 10, taf. ii. 10-12 ; M. G.,
ii. liii., 1 a.; Etr. Vas., taf. xii.
[3] G. A. V., xlix.
[4] Ann., 1849, s. 120. EXEKPATEΣ K
. TEΛEΣEN.
[5] ΛΛΑVΚVTEΣ ΕΠΟΙΕΣEN, once ΛΛΑV-
ΚVEΣ ΕΠΟΙΕΣVEN, Gerhard, Berlins
Neuerw. Vasen., No. 1598; Bull, 1847,
p. 125.

[6] HEPMAIOΣ ΕΠΟΙΕΣEN, Clarac,
Cat., p. 240 ; Bull, 1842, p. 167.
[7] HEPMOΓENEΣ ΕΠΟΙΕΣEN, Gerhard
Ann. 1831, 178, No. 690; Cat. Dur.
1000 ; Berlins and Bildw., No. 683;
Cat. Can., 159; B. M., p. 189, 685;
Rochette, p. 46; Campanari, p. 88; Cat.
Vas. B. M., 685.
[8] HEXΘOP ΕΓΡΑΦΣEN, Mus. Etr., p.
121 ; Bull, 1830, p. 134 ; Bull. Fér,
1831, p. 155 ; Monumens, xxvii. 46.

E 2

Andocides.   The subjects of his *cylices* are Bacchanalian,[1] Peleus and Thetis,[2] the Judgment of Paris,[3] Achilles hearing the death of Patroclus,[4] and festive scenes.[5]   His orthography is not always correct,[6] and his inscriptions are scratched under the handle.

The name of *Hilinos* has been found as one of the *lecythopoioi*, or makers of *lecythi*, on a vase with red figures, of that shape, discovered at Athens.   He employed an artist named Psiax.[7]   A potter named *Lysias* has recorded his name on a plain vase.[8]

Hischylos, another potter, belonged to the period of the transition from black to red figures ; his vases have been found only at Vulci.[9]   His wares were chiefly cups. He employed one Pheidippus to paint his vases ;[10] besides Epictetus, who surpassed all the other artists of the strong style [11] of red figures,[12] and Saconides, whose name appears on a cup with the subject of Hercules and the lion.

The potter *Meidias* is known by the celebrated Hamilton vase, of the style of Ruvo, a perfect *chef d'œuvre*, of the florid style, with red figures, and gilding in the accessories ; the subject being the rape of the Leucippides, and the Argonauts.[13]

[1] Can. 1 e. Cent., No. 23 ; Mus. Etr. 565, 1183.
[2] Depolletti Coll. Clarac, Cat., p. 128; Annali, 1831, p. 179, No. 710.
[3] Campan. Coll.
[4] Cat. Dur., 758.
[5] Gerhard, Trinkschalen, taf. xi.-xii. Panofka, taf. i. 9.
[6] HIEPON EΠOIEΣEN—EΠOEΣN. Bull, 1837, p. 71 ; Bull, 1832, p. 114 ; Campanari, p. 88 ; Panofka, i. 7, 8, s. 22, 23 ; Mon., ii. xxxviii.
[7] HIΛINOΣ   EΠOIEΣEN.   Creuzer, Alt. Athen, Gefass, s. 53.

[8] ΛYΣIAΣ MEΠOIEΞEN HEMIXONEI, on a vase in the Campana collection at Rome.
[9] HIΣKVΛOΣ EΠOIEΣEN, Canino, 1 e., Cent., No. 6.
[10] Clarac, Cat., 130.
[11] Panofka, s. 30.
[12] Annal., 1831, p. 179, 725 ; Campanari, p. 88.
[13] D'Hancarville, i. p. 130 ; Millin, Gall. Myth., No. 385 ; MEIΔIAΣ EΠOIEΣEN ; Gerhard, Abh. d. K. Akad., Berlin, 4to, 1840, die Meidias vase ; Notice sur le vase de Meidias.

There is a supposed *Naucydes*,[1] who flourished during the age of the vases with black figures. *Neandros* is known from a cup with black figures, having for its subject Hercules strangling the Nemean lion.[2]

An important and extensive manufacturer was *Nicosthenes*,[3] probably one of the earliest makers of vases with black figures. He is known from a *phiale* with ornaments,[4] and *cylices* with the subjects of Dionysus, Hermes, and Hercules.[5] Æneas,[6] Theseus, and the Minotaur,[7] Acamas, and Demophon,[8] athletic subjects.[9] A Gorgonium;[10] a scene of ploughing;[11] a man running, having on one greave;[12] and a satyr and youth, painted for him by Epictetus;[13] also from a *cylix* of black and white figures, having on it Ulysses and the Sirens.[14] A *cantharus* of this potter with a dance of figures of fine style exists,[15] and an *œnochoe* or jug, with Marsyas playing on the flute.[16] He made amphoræ of peculiar shape with broad flat handles, which have for their subjects, combats, a boxing match,[17] and another is ornamented with a Bacchanalian thiasos.[18] Others have satyrs and mænads, sphinxes, Achilles and Penthesilea, the adieu of the Dioscuri, youths

---

[1] Clarac, Cat., 284-286; Cat. Can. 71; Campana Collection.

[2] NEANΔΡΟΣ ΕΠΟΙΕΣΕΝ, Clarac, p. 286; Coll. Can., 1845; Clarac., p. 287.

[3] ΝΙΚΟΣΘΕΝΕΣ ΕΠΟΙΕΣΕΝ, Panofka, s. 23; Ann., 1831, 180, No. 727.

[4] Ann., 1831, p. 178, No. 691; M. G. ii. 17; · xxvii.; Visconti, Monum. Sepolchr. di Cere., taf. ix.; Marquis of Northampton, Observations on a Greek vase discovered in Etruria, Archæol. xxxiii., pl. 16, pp. 225-262.

[5] Panofka, s. 28, 29.

[6] Mus. Etr. 567; Ann., 1831, 179, No. 711.

[7] Ann., l. c.; Mus. Etr. 1516.

[8] Cat. Can., 217.

[9] Mus. Etr., 273; Berl. ant Bildw., 1595.

[10] Coll. d. Pr. Can., 236; Panofka, s. 28.

[11] Gerhard, Coupes, et Vases du Musée de Berlin, pl. i.

[12] Cat. Dub., 59.

[13] An. 1831, 180, 727.

[14] Cat. Dur., 418.

[15] Cat. Dur. 662.

[16] Cat. Dur., 147.

[17] M. G., xxvii.

[18] Vas. Cat., B. M., 118, 563.

riding on Hippalectryons, warriors, old men, and youths, the supposed Eris, Zeus, and Heos, with friezes of animals.[1] The most remarkable vase of this potter is one entirely black, with a female figure and a dog in opaque white, having lines cut through to the black background. He also made a *crater*, differing from the usual shape, and ornamented with a frieze representing a gigantomachia.[2]

The supposed name of Panthæos appears to be more correctly read Pamaphius, or Panphæus.

Pamaphios, a potter, who flourished during the strong style of red figures, employed the artist Epictetus.[3] He was a cup maker. His name has either been confounded with, or mistaken for that of *Phanphaios*, which is itself supposed by some to be a dialectical variation of Pamphaios. It occurs on a *stamnos* with red figures, representing Hercules and the Achelous, and Marsyas and Oreithyia.[4]

The maker *Panphæos* has left his name on no fewer than seventeen *cylices*, and is by far the most common of all the makers. He belongs to the period of vases with red figures. The subjects on his productions are, a horse ;[5] Bacchanal scenes ;[6] warriors and Pegasi ;[7] Sarpedon borne off by Hypnos and Thanatos ;[8] the arming of Memnon ; Hermes, Nomios, and Mænads ;[9] a crowned

---

[1] Gerhard, Neuerw. Denk., s. 18, 159, 6; Campanari, p. 88; Gerhard, Trinsch., i. 1, 2, 3; Panofka, iii. 11, s. 24.

[2] B. M., 560; Bull., 1843, p. 59.

[3] ΠΑΜΑΦΙΟΣ ΕΠΟΙΕΣΕΝ.

[4] Trans. R. Soc. Lit., N. Ser., vol. i., 1843, p. 100; G. A. V., cxv. ; Panofka, Namen, p. 153-241, taf. v.

[5] Panofka, s. 2, der Vasenbildner Pamphaos; Gerhard, Berl. Ant. Bild. s. 27, No. 1625.

[6] Panofka, taf. ii. ; taf. iii. ; Cat. Dur. 17.

[7] Panofka, s. 4.

[8] Archæol., xxxix., p. 139.

[9] De Witte, Desc. de Vases Peints. No. 17.

youth ;[1] a scene of a *comos* ;[2] a *stamnos*, with the contest of Hercules and the Achelous ;[3] Hercules destroying Hippolyte, painted with black figures ;[4] a *cylix*, with a man crowned seated on a rock, and holding a pedum ;[5] Pelops, or Achilles, boiled in the cauldron ;[6] goats and great eyes ;[7] athletic scenes ;[8] a *hydria*, with black figures, with Dionysus and his crew ;[9] and Hercules and the other gods of Olympus ;[10] and a *cylix*, with the head of Medusa.[11] There are also *amphoræ*, with flat side handles like those of Nicosthenes, of this potter, one with the subjects of satyrs and mænads ; and another with that of Chiron and Achilles, Menelaos and Helen, found at Cervetri.[12] His style is more developed, and rather later than that of the rigid school. There is some doubt whether his name should not read Panthæus.[13]

The name which some read as Hilinus others consider to be more correctly *Philinos*.[14] *Pistoxenos* occurs as the name of a maker on a vase found at Cære.[15]

Priapos is mentioned on a cup with black figures, representing a lion running.[16]

The name of *Python* is found on two vases, so different

[1] Inghirami, Mus. Chius., tom. ii., tav. cxxxiii.
[2] Mus. Etr. du Pr. de Canino, 1116.
[3] Trans. Roy. Soc. Lit., vol. i., p. 100; G. A. V., cxv.
[4] Mus. Greg., ii. lxvi.
[5] Mus. Etr., 1513.
[6] Dubois, Notice des Vases reservés, p. 104.
[7] Braun. Bull. 1842, p. 167 ; Welcker. Rhein. Mus., 1847, s. 396.
[8] Mus. Greg. ii. lxix. 4.
[9] De Witte, Cat. Dur., No. 91 ; Brit. Mus. Cat., p. 43, No. 447*.

[10] De Witte, Cab. Beugnot, 37.
[11] Micali, Storia, 102.1 ; Braun. Bull., 1844, p. 101.
[12] Collection of M. Campana at Rome.
[13] Clarac, Cat., 164-5 ; Panofka, l. c.
[14] Creuzer, Ein alt. Athenische Gefass, ΠΙLINOΣ ΕΠΟΙΕΣΕΝ, Leipzig, 1832, s. 53, 56 ; Deutsch. Schrift. Bd. iii. n. 1, s. 6, u. ff.
[15] ΠΙΣΤΟΧΣΕΝΟΣ ΕΠΟΙΕΣΕΝ. Campanari, Intorno i vasi, p. 92.
[16] ΠΡΙΑΠΟΣ ΕΠΟΙΕΣΕΝ. Panofka, s. 31. Cat. Dur. 882.

in style and effort, that there were probably two masters
of that name. One employed the artist Epictetus[1] who
painted for him in the strong style, a hydria of red figures,
representing the death of Busiris, and an entertainment;
the other made a vase of red figures, of the shape called
lekanion, at the time of the decadence.[2]

Simon, of Elea, the supposed maker of a *hydria*,
with black figures, having for its subject the chariot of
Athene and the gigantomachia,[3] rests on very uncertain
grounds.

The name of *Smicylion*,[4] a potter, and probably a vase-
maker, occurs on an Athenian stele, and that of *Socles* on
a plate found at Chiusi.[5] *Sosias* was the maker of a cup
with red figures, representing Hermes bringing the ram
to heaven, and the healing of Patroclus.[6] The name of
Statius appears on a *cantharus* or *carchesion*, of plain
black ware of late style, inscribed, "the work of Statius,
a gift to Cleostratus."[7]

Probably one of the earliest makers was *Taleides*,
known from an amphora with a scene of weighing;[8]
a *hydria*, with Hercules and the lion;[9] a *cylix*, with a swan
in the same style of art;[10] and an *œnochoe*, with Dionysos

[1] ΠΥΘΟΝ ΕΠΟΙΕΣΕΝ. Ann. 1831,
180, n. 726; Panofka, s. 36; Micali,
Mon. Antich., xc. 1.

[2] Clarac, Cat., p. 296; Millingen,
Nouv. Ann. i., p. 495.

[3] ΣΙΜΟΝ ΗΛΕΙΤΑ ΞΕΝΟ ΗΥΥΣ ΗΠΟ-
ΝΟΥ. Cat. Can., 103.

[4] Arch. Zeit., 1850, 226. ΣΜΙΚΥΛΙΟΝ
ΕΥΑΛΚΙΔΟΥ ΕΚ ΚΕΡΑΜΕΩΝ.

[5] Bull., 1851, p. 171.

[6] Mon., i.; pl. xxiii.—xxiv.; Panofka,
p. 38, taf., iii. 6.

[7] Gerhard, Arch. Zeit., 1847, s. 190;
ΣΤΑΤΙ ΕΡΓΟΝ ΚΛ[Ε]ΟΣΤΡΑΤΩΙ ΔΩΡΟΝ;
B. A. N., iv. p. 104. An incised in-
scription of doubtful authenticity.

[8] ΤΑΛΕΙΔΕΣ ΕΠΟΙΕΣΕΝ, Millin. V.
Peints, ii. pl. 61; Gal. Myth., cxxi.
490; Panofka, s. 7; G. A. V., ii. s. 113.
The subject perhaps referring to Tantalus.

[9] Campana Collection.

[10] Gerhard, B. A. B., No. 685.

and a flute-player.[1]   The name of the youths, Clitarchus and Callias, are found on his vases,[2] and he employed the artist Takonides, or Sakonides.[3]

Theoxetos is known only from a *cylix* with black figures, representing a goatherd.[4] *Thypheitheides*, from a cup with red figures, on which are represented a deer running, and large eyes.[5]

Timagoras is known by a *hydria*, painted with black figures, representing Theseus killing the Minotaur, and Hercules contending with Nereus.   It is of the usual hard but not recherché style of Execias.[6]

Tlenpolemos, another potter, manufactured vases with black figures. Only two of his work[7] are known. He employed as his artist, Takonides.[8]   His productions have been chiefly found at Vulci. A maker, whose works are more often found is *Tleson*, son of Nearchus, probably a Corinthian potter, as a *cylix* of his fabric has been discovered in that city.[9] He was a maker of *cylices*, or cups, and many of his works are indecent.[10]   His figures, which are black, are generally finely drawn, clear in colour, and of general excellence, but of small size. The most remarkable of his subjects is Orion carrying a

[1] Bull., 1845, p. 52.

[2] The silver vase of Taleides, with the name Clitarchus is incredible. Bull. 1843, p. 13.

[3] Gerhard, Rapp. Volc. 180, 729.,

[4] ΘΕΟΞΕΤΟΣ ΜΕΠΟΙΕΞΕ, Cat. Dur., 884 ; Panofka, s. 34.

[5] ΕΠΟΙΕΣΕΝ   ΘΥΦΕΙΘΕΙΔΕΣ, Cat. Dur., 893 ; Vas. Cat. Brit. Mus., p. 309. No. 854 ; Panofka, s. 35.

[6] ΤΙΜΑΓΟΡΑΣ ΕΠΟΙΕΣΕΝ. Campana Coll.

[7] Cat. Can., 149 ; Gerhard, Ann. 1831,

p. 172; p. 178; No. 661, No. 693, p. 172; ΤΛΕΝΠΟΛΕΜΟΣ ΜΕΠΟΙΕΣΕΝ.

[8] Gerhard, Neuerworb Vasen, No. 1597; Mus. Etr., 149, [6612]; ΤΛΕΝΠΟΛΕΜΟΥ ΕΙΜΙ ΚΥΠΕΛΛΟΝ. The end of a hexameter line.

[9] Bull., 1849, p. 74; ΤΛΕΣΟΝ ΗΟ ΝΕΑΡΧΟ ΕΠΟΙΕΣΕΝ ; Panofka, s. 34.

[10] B. M. Cat., p. 189, No. 682 ; Clarac, p. 303; Dub. Cat. Can., 262; M. De Witte, Coll. d. V. Ant. de terre prov. d. fouilles faites en Étrurie, 8vo., Paris, 1843, p. 72, No. 262; Mus. Etr., 1146, bis.

fox and hare.[1] Others are a centaur,[2] an ape,[3] and two cocks.[4] The supposed name of *Tychon* on the cylix found at Hadria, is probably due to a learned blunder.[5] *Tychios* made a cylix found at Corneto,[6] also one now at Berlin,[7] and a plain cup, and Apollo playing on the lyre.[8] His name is also found on a plain *cylix*. *Xenocles*, another maker of the oldest school, is known from a *cylix* of the most archaic treatment, with the subject of the Judgment of Paris,[9] and other *cylices*, with the departure of Poseidon ;[10] the search for Poseidon, and a swan with sirens.[11] The name of *Xenophantos*, of Athens, which is not found amongst those of the makers of the cups at Vulci or in Greece, has been discovered at Kertch, or Panticapæum, one of the utmost limits where vases have been discovered, on one of coarse work with red figures.[12]

An attempt has been made to connect the choice of subjects upon vases with the names of the potters or artists, but the connection, if it exists at all, is too vague to assist the interpretation of the subjects. It is possible, that such secret allusions may have been occasionally intended ; but there has arisen no slight difficulty to decide the real names of many of the artists which occur on the vases.[13]

[1] Cat. Dur., 260.

[2] Annali, 1831, p. 178, 694.

[3] Cat. Dub., 262; Cat. Vas., B. M., p. 189, no. 682.

[4] Mus. Etr., 15, bis. ; Cat. Dub. 71.

[5] TVXON ANEOM TVXΘN ANEOIKE TO AΠΛΛ; R. Rochette, A·n., 1834, p. 194.

[6] Gerhard, Ann., 1831, 178, n. 701; Neuerworb. Vas., 1664. TVXIOΣ EΠOI-EΣEN.

[7] Gerhard, Neuerb. Vas. 1664.

[8] A. Z., 1853, 402; TVXIOΣ EΠOIEΣEN.

[9] Lenormant and DeWitte, Élite, xxiv.

p. 2, 47; Mus. Blac. xix. KΣENOKΛEΣ EΠOIEΣEN.

[10] Gerhard, Aus. Vas. i. x.

[11] Gerhard, Zuwachs., s. 26, 1662; Brit. Mus. ; Panofka, s. 40.

[12] ΞENOΦANTOΣ EΠOIHΣEN AΘHN; Bull., 1841, p. 109-113; Ouvaroff, Ant. d. Bosph. Cim. iii., pl. xlvi.

[13] See Raoul Rochette, Lettre à M Schorn., l. c.; and Questions de l'histoire de l'art, 8vo, Paris, 1846 ; Clarac. Manuel, l. c.; Panofka, Vasenbildner, &c.

ARTISTS.

From the potters, it is now necessary to turn to the consideration of the vase painters, many of whose names have been discovered on vases, although none are known from the writings of the ancients. The passage of Aristophanes,[1] about these persons, the interpretation of which is doubtful, in which " the fellow who paints *lecythi* for the dead," is spoken of in terms of contempt, does not throw much light upon the condition of the painters. Nor is much more afforded by the vases themselves. The names of some, indeed, such as Polygnotus, Nicosthenes, and Hegias, correspond with those of artists of known fame ; but it is impossible that such persons should have practised an art held in such inferior estimation,[2] and if the celebrated Zeuxis painted terra-cottas, it must be understood, that he first modelled and then drew his designs, not that he was engaged as a colourist of plastic works.

On many vases the name of the artist appears along with that of the potter, of course to enhance the value of the production, as celebrated artists were sought after, both in the home and foreign market. On others, the name of the artist alone occurs, probably because the pottery was newly founded, and the proprietor, to establish a reputation, employed the services of known artists. Some potters, such as Amasis and Euphronios, painted as well as made vases, which is natural enough, as the two arts were so nearly blended. It cannot be supposed

---

[1] Eccles., 994; Kramer Ueber die Herkunft, s. 20. The scholiast refers it to the decoration of graves.

[2] Pliny, xxxv. 40, 42 ; Kramer, l. c.

that the great artists of antiquity occupied themselves
even in furnishing designs for works of this nature ; if it
could, a sketch with the name of Polygnotus might be
recognised as a production of that celebrated master.
The names of artists follow the law which governs the
other inscriptions. There are none on the oldest vases,
and few on those of archaic style. They commence about
the most flourishing period of the strong style, and
continue till the florid style—gradually becoming rarer.
One of the oldest painters is *Æniades*, whose name is
inscribed on a *cylix* found at Vulci,[1] and now in the
Berlin Museum. Like all the vase painters, he uses the
aoristic form ΕΓΡΑΨΕΝ, " painted," the affected imperfect
not having been used by more than five painters. The
name of *Alsimos* is now read on the celebrated vase found
at *Canosa* in the Louvre, made during the decadence of the
art, but excellent in its style, on which is represented the
death of Astyanax.[2] *Amasis*, a maker of vases with black
figures of the most early and rigid style, much resembling
that of the Æginetan school, painted an *olpe* with the
subject of Perseus killing Medusa,[3] and one of rather
freer treatment.[4]

The name of *Aristophanes*, better known as that of the
comic poet than as the appellation of an artist, occurs on
a cup with black figures representing a gigantomachia.

[1] ΑΙΝΙΑΔΕΣ ΕΓΡΑ(ΦΣΕΝ), Cat. Dur.,
1002 ; Gerhard, Neuerw. Denkm., 1663.
[2] ΑΛΣΙΜΟΣ ΕΓΡΑΨΕ, Millin., Vases
Ant., i., p. 60; ii., p. 37; Visconti,
Opera. Var., iv. p. 258; Winckelman,
Mon. In., 143. This name has been
read Lasimos or Æsimos. Clarac,
Catalogue des Artistes, 16mo, Paris

1849, 30, 248 ; Panofka, s. 37.
[3] ΑΜΑΣΙΣ ΕΓΡΑΦΣΕ ΚΑΙ ΕΠΟΙΕΣΕΝ
Cat. Dub., 62 ; Campanari intron i vasi,
p. 87—89.
[4] ΑΜΑΣΙΣ ΕΓΡΑΨΕΝ ΚΑΙ ΕΠΟΙΕΣΕΝ
ΕΜΕ, Campanari, p. 88; Brit. Mus. no.
641*.

He worked for the potter Erginos.[1] The name of *Asteas*
occurs on a vase of the style of the decadence, as a painter
of a subject representing the Garden of the Hesperides.[2]
An artist, whose name some read as *Bryllus*, and others
erroneously as *Bryaxis*, painted cups with red figures of
the strong style,[3] on which are the Judgment of Paris,
Peleus and Thetis, scenes in a palace. The artist *Clitias*
painted the celebrated François vase now at Florence,
ornamented with black figures, and containing a complete
Epos of subjects[4] connected with the history of Achilles.

It is possible that *Cholchos* painted for the potter
Euxitheos the cylix with the subject of Patroclus, in
red figures of the strong style. He was, perhaps, a
Corinthian.[5] The name of the artist *Doris* is only found
upon cups with red figures in a fine grandiose style of the
best period of the art, representing Dionysos and his
crew ;[6] or the exploits of Theseus,[7] Peleus and Thetis,
the Palæstra and amatory scenes.[8]

Of the painters of the early vases with red figures, *Epictetos* is the most distinguished. His productions are more
elegant than those of Doris, and the esteem in which he

[1] ΑΡΙΣΤΟΦΑΝΕΣ ΕΓΡΑΦΕ, Gerhard, Trinkschale und Gefasse, ii. ; Clarac, Cat., p. 240 c. ; Letronne, Explic., p. 29; Bull., 1839, p. 52, 53.
[2] ΑΣΣΤΕΑΣ ΕΓΡΑΨΕ, Millingen, Anc. Uned. Mon. i., p. 67, pl. 27 ; Peint d. Vases Grec., pl. 46; Gal., Myth. cxiv., 444; Panofka, s. 37; ΕΓΡΑΦΕ Boeckh, Corp. Inscr. Grec. i., p. 42; Clarac, Cat., 58; Panofka, s. 36.
[3] ΒΡΥΛΟΣ ΕΓΡΑΦΣΕΝ. Gerhard, Annali, 1831, p. 179, No. 704* ; Campanari, p. 88 ; Clarac, p. 86; Campana Coll.
[4] ΚΛΙΤΙΑΣ ΕΓΡΑΦΣΕΝ. Braun, An.

1848, 299 ; Mon. iv., liv.-lix.
[5] [Χ]ΟΛΧΟΣ Ε[ΡΑΦ]ΣΕΝ, Mus. Etr., 1120; Vases du Pr. de Canino, Pl. 5 ; Gerhard, Ann. 1831., p. 180, n. 729 ; Campanari, p. 88 ; he uses on some vases as a potter, the Q for the X.
[6] Cat. Can., Gerhard, Ann. III., p. 179, n. 713 ; ΔΟΡΙΣ ΕΓΡΑΨΕΝ.
[7] Campana Collection.
[8] Clarac, Cat. Art., p. 99 ; Gerhard, Aus. Vas., ccxxxiv. ; Campanari, p. 67 ; Mus. Etr.,p. 106, no. 1184 ; R. Rochette, Lettre à M. Schorn., p. 3 ; Cat. Vas., Brit. Mus., p. 272, no. 824.

was held is shown by the number of potters for whom he worked. He principally painted *cylices*, with the subjects of Athene,[1] Silenus, and a wine-skin,[2] the Bacchic thiasos,[3] Theseus and the Minotaur,[4] and erotic figures.

He also painted *pinaces*, or plates, with the subjects of Marsyas,[5] an Amazon,[6] athletes,[7] Ganymedes,[8] indecencies,[9] Dionysos holding a cantharos,[10] and a warrior.[11] For the potter Hischylus he painted a cup, the subject of which is Hercules and the Centaurs ;[12] another with a Satyr ;[13] one with the subject of Busiris for the potter Python ;[14] for the potter Nicosthenes, a cup with a Satyr.[15] Other cups have women ;[16] and a youth holding vases.[17] He also worked[18] for Euxitheos. One of his cups has red figures on the outside, and black within.[19] He also painted a *pelike* with the subject of a marriage.[20] The name of the painter, *Euonymos*, has been found on a vase with red figures, and of late style, discovered at Hadria.[21] The potter

[1] Gerhard, Trinkschalen und Gefässe, xiii. ; ΕΠΙΚΤΕΤΟΣ ΕΓΡΑΣΦΕΝ ; Gerhard, Rapp. Volc. Ann. III., p. 179. From his writing εγρασφεν instead of εγραφσεν, it is probable that Epictetos was an Aeolian potter. ἐπειδὴ ἐπλανή-θησαν οἱ Αἰολεῖς κατὰ τὴν προφορὰν τὸ ζυγὸς σδυγὸς γράφοντες κὰι τὸ ξίφος σκίφος τὸ ψέλιον σπέλιον. Cramer. Anecd. Grec. iv. p. 326.

[2] Cat. Dur., 133.

[3] Vas Cat., Brit. Mus., p. 279, no. 828.

[4] Cat. Can., 53 ; Vase, Cat., Brit. Mus., p. 279, no. 828.

[5] Cat. Can., 53.

[6] Cat. Can., 117.

[7] Cat. Can. 175, 178.

[8] Cat. Can., 177.

[9] Cat. Can. 16.

[10] Bull., 1846, p. 77.

[11] Cat. Can., 189.

[12] Cat. Can., 178.

[13] Cat. Vas., B. M., p. 260, no. 814.

[14] Gerhard, Ann. 1831, 162, n. 546 ; Cat. Can., 12 Cent., no. 8 ; Vas. Cat., B. M., p. 271, no. 823 ; Micali, Storia, Tav., xc. 1 ; Panofka, Taf. iii. 4.

[15] Gerhard, Ann. 1831, p. 180, 727 ; Clarac, Cat., 103, 240 m. ; Cat. Dub., 174.

[16] Cat. Can. 124.

[17] Panofka, Cab. Pourtalès, Pl. 41.

[18] Gerhard, Ann., 1831, p. 180, 729.

[19] Gerhard, Neuerworb. Vasen., 1606 ; Coll. Feoli, p. 113, No. 58.

[20] Gerhard, Neuerw. Denk., s. 31, no. 1606.

[21] Lanzi, Giornali d. Lett. Ital. xx. p. 180 ; R. Rochette, Lettre p. 3 ; Welcker Kunstblatt, 1827, o. k. d.

Euphronios also painted vases, as appears from the cup of Troilos, and females reposing.[1] *Euthymides*, another painter, whose name is found upon amphoræ, with figures having for their subjects Hector arming,[2] and Paris,[3] was the contemporary of Euphronios, of whom he was jealous, since, upon one vase he has written, " Euphronios never did so well ;"[4] on the *hydria* with the subject of Paris is the name of the youthful Sostratus.[5]

The potter *Execias* also exercised the painter's art, and ranks, perhaps, as the best known artist of vases with black figures. The most celebrated of his efforts are the amphoræ found at Vulci, and now in the Vatican, representing Achilles and Ajax playing at dice before Troy,[6] and the departure of Castor ;[7] also one in the British Museum with the subject of Dionysos teaching Œnopion the art of making wine,[8] and the death of Penthesilea. His style, though rigid, is exceedingly elegant and finished in details, so as to become almost florid. The name of Onetorides, a youth, is mentioned on his vase.

The name of *Hermonax* is known from an *amphora*, with red figures of the hard school representing a *comos*.[9]

The name of the painter *Hegias* is found upon a *lecythus*, with black figures, discovered in the sepulchres of

[1] Cf. ΕΥΦΡΟΝΙΟΕ ΕΓΡΑΦΣΕΝ, Cat. Can., 87, n. 568 ; Gerhard, Ann. 1831, no. 403, 824 ; Panofka, Taf. iv. 3, p. 10, 11.

[2] Mus. Etr., 1836 ; Gerhard, Ann. 1831, p. 178, no. 698 ; ΕΥΘΥΜΙΔΕΣ ΗΟ ΠΟΛΙΟ ΕΓΡΑΦΣΕΝ. Panofka, s. 3 ; Welcker, A. Litt. Zeit., 1836, I. 526.

[3] Gerhard, l. c., Rochette, Bull. Férrusac, 1831, 153 ; Cat. Can., 146.

[4] ΗΟΣ ΟΥΔΕΠΟΤ ΕΥΦΡΟΝΙΟΣ, Bull., 1830, p. 140, 143 ; G. A. V., clxxviii. ; Campanari, p. 99 ; Rochette, Lettre à M. Schorn., 8 ; Bull. Fér., 1831, p. 153.

[5] Dubois, Notice d'une Coll. d. Vases du Pr. de Canino, no. 41 ; De Witte, Cat. du Pr. de Canino, 71.

[6] ΕΚΣΕΚΙΑΣ ΕΓΡΑΦΣΕ ΚΑΠΟΕΣΕΜΕ, or ΕΓΡΑΦΣΕ ΚΑΠΟΕΣΕ.

[7] M. G. II., liii. 1 a.

[8] Gerhard, Ann., 1831, p. 179, no. 709* ; Cat. Dur., 389 ; G. A., V. ccvi.

[9] ΗΕΡΜΟΝΑΚΣ ΕΓΡΑΦΣΕΝ. Campana Collection.

Ægina, and of the usual unfinished style of that island.[1]
That of the painter *Hypsis* occurs on some *hydriæ*, with
red figures, representing the arming of the Amazons,
a race of boys on horseback, and a quadriga.[2]

A painter of the name of *Onesimos*[3] decorated some
vases with black figures for the potter *Euphronios*. In
connection with the potter Hischylus, already mentioned,
Pheidippus painted a cup of red and black figures in a
style not remarkably fine, with subjects of youths and
athletes.[4] *Philtias*, another painter of the fine style of
red figures, worked for the potter Deiniades, for whom he
painted scenes of *hydriophoræ*, or water drawing.[5]

Phrynos is known from a cup with black figures, on
which is the bird of Athene, and a scene supposed to
represent her reconciliation with Poseidon.[6] *Pothinos*
painted a *cylix* of black figures, the subject of which is
Peleus and Thetis.[7]

Praxias, another artist's name, is found on a small vase
with red figures, representing Achilles delivered by Peleus
into the charge of Chiron.[8]

Polygnotos[9] is known as a painter of vases with red
figures, which are rather careless in their treatment, of

[1] Stackelberg, Die Graeber, Pl. 25—
p. 21, 22; ΕΓΙΑΣ ΕΓΡΑ.

[2] ΗΥΦΣΙΣ ΕΓΡΑΦΣΕΝ, Gerhard, Ann.
1831, 178, no. 697; Bull., 1829, p. 109;
Clarac, Cat., 133; G. A. V., ciii.; Campanari, p. 88.

[3] ΟΝΕΣΙΜΟΣ ΕΓΡΑΦΣΕ, Cat. Dub.,
87 ter.; Clarac, Cat., 161; Mus. Etr.,
1611; Gerhard, Ann. 1831, p. 180, n.
Campanari, p. 88.

[4] Gerhard, Ann. 1831, p. 180, n. 718,
722; Campanari, p. 88; ΦΕΙΔΙΠΟΣ
ΕΓΡΑΦΕ, Cat. Vas., Brit. Mus., p. 295,
no. 841.

[5] Can. 1st Cent., n. 18, 74; Gerhard,
Ann. 1831, p. 178, no. 719, 728; [ΦΙΛ]
ΤΙΑΣ ΕΓΡΑΦΣΕΝ, or rather [ΚΡ]ΙΤΙΑΣ;
Birch, Class. Mus., 1848, p. 99, 102.

[6] ΦΡΥΝΟΣ ΕΤΡΑΦΣΕΝ, Cat. Dur. no. 21.

[7] ΠΕΙΘΙΝΟΣ ΕΓΡΑΦΣΕΝ, Gerhard,
Berl. Ant. Bild., no. 1005; Panofka, s.
5; Taf. I., 2; Gerhard, Trinkschalen,
Taf. xiii—xiv. xv.

[8] Panofka, s. 30; Mus. Etr., 1500, p.
135: Raoul Rochette, p. 57; ΠΡΑΧΙΑΣ·
ΕΓΡΑΦΣΕ.

[9] ΠΟΛΥΓΝΩΤΟΣ ΕΓΡΑΨΕΝ.   Cat.
Dur. 362: Rochette, p. 66.

the commencement of the style and time of the Decadence. His name appears on a vase on which is represented the death of Cæneus,[1] and an amphora, on which is the sacrifice of a bull.[2] It is written in an indistinct, blotted manner, very different from that in which the names of the other artists are inscribed. *Priapos*, who has been recorded in the list of vase artists,[3] is probably the same as the potter.

An Athenian painter, named *Psiax*,[4] who worked for the potter Hilinus, or Philinus, has inscribed his name upon a *lecythus*, ornamented with black figures, representing a Bacchanalian subject. The artist *Python* is known from a crater with red figures, on which is depicted the apotheosis of Alcmena. His style is remarkably careful, but somewhat rigid.[5] *Taconides*, or, as some persons read his name, Saconides, painted vases, with black figures, for the potters Tlenpolemos[6] and Hischylus;[7] *Xenodoros* and *Zeuxiades* close the list.[8]

[1] Cat. Dur., 362; Rochette, p. 66.

[2] Vas. Cat., Brit. Mus. p. 220, no. 755.

[3] Campanari, p. 88.

[4] ΦΣΙΑΧΣ ΕΓΡΑΦΣΕΝ. Creuzer, Ein alt athenische Gefass, Leipz. und Darmst., 1832; Deutsch. Schrift, Bd. III., no. 1, s. 6, a. ff. Panofka, s. 16—17; Taf. iii. 9, 10.

[5] Millingen, Nouv. An., i. 495.

[6] Ann. 1831, p. 178, no. 693, p. 180, no. 729; Clarac, p. 301; Campanari, p. 88.

[7] Panofka, s. 30.

[8] Bullet. Férussac, 1831, p. 158; Clarac. p. 223.

CHAPTER IX.

Uses of Vases—Domestic use—Vases for liquids—For the Table—for the Toilet
—Toys—Decorative Vases—Prizes—Marriage Gifts—Millingen's division of
Sepulchral Vases—Grecian usage—Names and shapes of Vases—The Pithos
—Pithacne—Stamnos—Hyrche—Lagynos—Ascos—Amphoreus—Pelice—
Cados—Hydria—Calpis—Crossos—Cothon—Rhyton—Bessa—Bombylios
—Lecythus—Olpe—Alabastron—Crater—Oxybaphon—Hypocraterion—
Celebe—Psycter—Dinos—Chytra—Thermanter—Thermopotis—Tripous
—Holmos—Chytropous—Lasanon—Chous—Œnochoe—Prochoos—Epi-
chysis—Arutaina—Aryballos—Arystichos, aryter, arytis, &c.—Oenerysis—
Etnerysis—Zomerysis—Hemicotylion—Cotyliskos—Cyathos—Louterion—
Asaminthos—Puelos—Scaphe—Scapheion—Exaleiptron—Lecane—Leca-
nis—Lecaniskos—Podanipter—Cheironiptron—Holcion—Peirrhanterion
—Ardanion, or Ardalion—Excellence of the Greek cups—The Depas—Alei-
son—Cissybion—Cypellon—Cymbion—Scyphos onychionos—Ooscyphion
—Bromias—Cantharos—Carchesion—Cylix—Thericleios—Hedypotis—
Rhodiake—Antigonis—Seleucis—Phiale—Phiale Lepaste—Acatos—Trie-
res—Canoun—Pinax—Phthois—Petachnon—Labronia—Gyalas—Keras
—Vases for Food—Canoun—Pinax—Discos—Lecanis—Paropsis—Oxis—
Embaphion—Ereus—Cypselie—Cyminodokos—Tryblion—Oxybaphon.

As all the vases hitherto known have been discovered
in sepulchres, it would, at first sight, appear that their
destination was for the dead; but this seems to have
been a subsequent use of them, and many, if not all,
were employed for the purposes of life. The celebrated
Panathenaic vase, for example, discovered by Mr. Burgon,
at Athens, had been bestowed as a prize upon the
illustrious person to whose ashes it was afterwards appro-
priated. Many other instances might be cited.

D'Hancarville supposes that the large vases were dedicated to the gods in the various shrines of Greece and

Rome, as by the Metapontines in their Naos at Olympia, and by the Byzantians in the chapel of Hera. Vases of large size, painted carefully with a principal figure on one side, and having on the other figures carelessly drawn, as if intended to be placed against a wall, he considers peculiarly adapted for such uses, as the rooms of Roman villas were far too small to hold them.[1]

As the civil and domestic use of vases is the most important, it is necessary to consider it first. It is indicated by their style and shape. The painted ware was not employed for the viler purposes, nor to contain large quantities of liquids, for which it was far too expensive, but chiefly for entertainments and the triclinia of the wealthy. The exceedingly porous nature of these vases, and the difficulty of cleaning them internally, have led some writers to assert that they were ornamental. They are, however, seen in use in scenes painted on the vases themselves.[2] Thus, in the scene of the Harpies plundering the table of the blind Phineus, a painted *scyphos* with figures is seen in the hands of the aged king ; a female in a farewell scene pours a libation of wine out of an amphora with black figures, and another ornamented with painted figures is seen upon the top of a column.

These vases were used for liquids. The *hydriæ*, or water-vases, went to the well, and the various kinds of amphoræ served for carrying wine about at entertainments. Those called *craters* were used to mix wine, and the *psycter*, or cooler, to prepare it for drinking. In jugs called *œnochöœ* and *olpœ*, also of painted ware, wine was

---

[1] D'Hancarville, II. 68, 82. [2] Inghirami, Vasi Fittilii, Taf. xxxii.

drawn from the craters, which was then poured into various painted cups, as the *scyphos*, the *cylix*, the *cantharus*, and the *rhyta*, horns or beakers, which were the most common. A kind of cup, called the *cyathis*, also of painted ware, was likewise used. The cup called *phiale* was employed in religious rites. .

The vases used upon the table were the *pinax*, or plate, a vase supposed to be the *lecane*, or tureen, and certain dishes called *tryblia*, generally of ruder material and manufacture than the others. One of the most remarkable of these vases is the *cirnos*.

For the service of the toilet were the *pyxis*, the *cylichne*, the *tripodiskos*, the *alabastron*, the *lecythus*, and the *aryballos*.

Vases were also used as toys. This class is comparatively small, but its existence is proved by the discovery of several little vases in the sepulchres of children at Athens, on which are depicted children playing at various games ; whilst others are so extremely small that they could not possibly have answered any useful purpose. Among them may be cited those in the shape of animals, as apes, elephants, stags, and hogs ; imitations of crab's claws and of the *astragalus*, or knuckle-bone ; and other vessels, containing brazen balls, which produced a rattling sound when shaken.

There can be no doubt that many of the vases, especially those of later style, were used for decorative purposes, although the employment of them is not expressly mentioned in ancient authors. It is, however, partly evident, from the fact of one side only being executed with care, whilst the other has been neglected, both in the drawing and in the subject. On the later vases, too, are depicted vases of large proportions, resting upon columnar stands in interiors.

One of the noblest uses to which terra-cotta vases were applied was as prizes given to the victors in the public games. These prizes, called *Athla*, besides the honorary crowns, armour, and tripods, and other valuable objects, were occasionally fictile vases, and even coins.[1] Certain vases bearing the inscription "From Athens," or "Prizes from Athens," seem to have been given to the victors in the pentathla or courses of athletic exercises in the Panathenaia, and are mentioned by Pindar. Some of the vases, which are principally in the old style, are of two sizes,— the greater given for the athletic and the lesser for musical contests. It is also possible that some of the uninscribed vases of similar designs and shapes may have been distributed as rewards in local games. Some of the vases also on which the name of a youth, accompanied with the word Κάλος, occurs, may have been given as prizes in the training schools of athletes.

It has been supposed that certain vases were intended for presentation as marriage gifts. But the information to be obtained from classical authors on this point is by no means clear; and no satisfactory conclusion can be drawn from the circumstance that some of the subjects depicted on them appear to allude to marriages.

Millingen divides the vases used for sepulchral purposes into the following classes :—

[1] Brondsted, on Panathenaic Vases, in the Trans. R. S. Literature, 4to, London, 1834, vol. ii. p. 102.

1. Those containing milk, oil, and perfumes, which were poured upon the corpse.[1]

2. Vases placed at the door of the sepulchre, to hold the lustral water.[2]

3. Vases used at the funeral feast, of which the deceased was supposed to partake.[3]

4. Vases valued by the deceased,[4] or prizes which he had gained.[5]

To these may be added,—

5. Vases employed during the ceremonies in different operations, and subsequently broken and gathered up into the tomb.

At the earliest period of Greece, vases were not employed to hold the ashes of the dead. Those, for example, of the oldest style found at Athens, and at Vulci, do not contain ashes. In the Etruscan cemeteries, the dead were not burnt, but laid at full length, with all their personal ornaments, their furniture, their arms, and their vases. Although in the heroic ages bodies were burnt, the remains are not stated to have been deposited in earthen vessels. Those of Patroclus[6] were collected into a golden dish, carefully covered with a garment and layer of fat which was folded; and those of Achilles were placed in the golden amphora[7] given by Dionysos to Thetis.[8] In the fictitious account of the death of Orestes, introduced into the Electra of Sophocles, the expression, " his fine form circled

---

[1] Vases Grecs, p. II., n. 4; Homer, Iliad xxiii. 170.

[2] The ἀρδανίον. Pollux, viii. 7; Euripid. Alcest. v. 100 ; Aristoph. Eccl. 1025.

[3] Schol. ad Homer. Iliad xxiii. v. 29.

[4] Virgo, civis Corinthia, jam matura nuptiis, implicita morbo, decessit : post sepulturam ejus, quibus ea viva poculis delectabatur, nutrix collecta et com-

posita in calatho pertulit ad monumentum, et in summo collocavit: et uti ea permanerent diutius sub dio, tegula texit. Vitruv. iv. c. i.

[5] Schol. ad Æschyl. Choeph. 96.

[6] Il. xxiii. 241-258. Schol. ad eund. This was the φιάλη, ἀγγεῖον κοῖλον covered δίπλακι δῆμῳ and ἐανῷ λίτῳ.

[7] xxiii. 1. 91.

[8] Calaber. III. 727.

by the narrow brass " [1] of a *hydria*, shows the use of the metallic vases. The custom prevailed amongst the Romans of employing fictile vases exclusively for religious rites, amongst which that of interment was included. Hence the use of the beautiful vases imported from Greece for funeral purposes, and after the due performance of libations,[2] the vases so employed were thrown away, and left broken in the corners of sepulchres. Numerous specimens of vases thus used have been found, especially *œnochoai* and *cylices*. Other vases of considerable size, and which certainly had not been so employed, were deposited in tombs as the most acceptable offerings to the deceased, recalling to the mind of the shade the joy and glory of his life, the festivals that he had shared, the hetairæ with whom he had lived, the Lydian airs that he had heard,[3] and the games that he had seen or taken part in. Those vases were selected which were most appropriate for funeral purposes, or to contain the milk, oil, and wine, which were placed on the bier, with their necks inclined to the corpse, in order that the liquid should run over it while in the fire ; those used at the *perideipnon*, or last supper, in which the food of the deceased was placed at his side ; [4] and a vase, called the *ardanion*, which held the lustral water, placed at the door of a house where a death had taken place.[5] After the earliest or heroic ages, and during the period of the old vases with black figures, the Greeks appear to have used them for holding the ashes of the dead.

A vase of the shape of the *lebes*, probably a *crater*, found near the Piræus, which once held the ruby wine at

[1] v. 760. Schol. ad eund.
[2] Millingen, Introd. iii.
[3] Thiersch, l. c., s. 25.
[4] Millingen, Introd. iii.
[5] Thiersch, s. 22-3.

festive triclinia, and which was decorated with drinking
scenes, also held ashes. Of vases with red figures, one
representing Theseus and the Amazonomachia, discovered
by Mr. Stoddart in Sicily, and the celebrated vase discovered carefully deposited inside another at Nola, and
now in the Museo Borbonico, also held the ashes of the
dead. At Athens it was the custom to place a fictile
lecythus on the breast of those interred entire, while the
use of fictile *canopi* among the Etruscans shows that Greek
vases must have been sometimes so used by them. In the
celebrated vase representing the death of Archemoros, two
persons are seen carrying two tables laden with vases to the
tomb, while an œnochoe is placed under the funeral couch.[1]

NAMES.

We shall now proceed to give some account of the
names of ancient vases, and their supposed identification
with the specimens which have been found. It is impossible, however, to enter here into any critical dissertation, or to attempt to reconcile the contending opinions
of those critics who have written on the subject; and
the curious reader must be referred to the works of
Panofka,[2] Letronne,[3] Gerhard,[4] Ussing,[5] and Thiersch.[6]

[1] Gerhard, Il vaso di Archemoros, Inghirami iv. cclxxi.

[2] Panofka, Recherches sur les veri-
tables Noms des Vases Grecs, &c. fol.
Paris, 1829.

[3] Letronne, Observations sur les
Noms des Vases Grecs à l'occasion de
l'ouvrage de M. Theodore Panofka.
4to, Paris, 1833. Letronne, Suppl.
aux Observations, Dec. 1837, Jan. 1838.

[4] Gerhard, Rapporto Volcente; Berlins antike Bildwerke, s. 138—342,
u. f. Ultime Ricerche sulle forme dei
Vasi Grec. Ann. tom. viii. 1836, p. 147.

[5] Ussing, De Nominibus vasorum
Græcorum disputatio, 8vo, Hauniæ,
1844.

[6] Thiersch, ueber die hellenischen
bemalten Vasen, c. ii. s. 26.

Great doubts obscure the subject of the names of ancient· vases, owing to the difference of time between the authors by whom they are mentioned, the difficulty of explaining types by words, the ambiguity of describing the shape of one vase by the name of another, and the difference of dialects in which the names are found. The names of vases used by Homer and the earlier poets cannot on any just principles of criticism be applied to any but the oldest ones. Those of the second and later age must be sought for in the contemporaneous writers. The first source is the vases themselves, from which, however, only three examples can be gathered, namely, one from having the inscription ΔΙΟΝΥΣΙΟΥ Α ΛΑΚΥΘΟΣ, " the *lecythus* of Dionysius," on a vase of that shape ; and from another having ΚΗΦΙΣΟΦΟΝΓΟΣ Η ΚΥ-ΛΙΞ, " the cup of Cephisophon "[1] and ΗΜΙΚΟΤΥΛΙΟΝ incised on a two handled cup. The next source is, the names attached to vases in the paintings, among which the word ΗΥΔΡΙΑ[2] occurs written over a broken three-handled pitcher. Another source is an examination of the names inscribed by potters on the feet of certain vases, as ΚΡΑΤΕΡΕΣ, *craters* ; ΟΞΥΒΑΦΑ, *oxybapha;* ΧΥΤΡΙ(Α), *pots;* ΚΥΛΙ[ΚΕΣ], *cups;* ΛΗΚ[ΥΘΟΙ], *cruets,* &c. ; but the relation of the inscriptions to the forms is very doubtful.[3]

The various scholia written at different ages, and often embodying fragments of lost books, have occasional notices of vases. Those upon Aristophanes are the most important in this respect. Hesychius, Photius, the Etymologicum Magnum, Suidas, and others, Varro, Festus,

[1] Ussing, de Nomin., p. 24.
[2] Monumenti, iv. liv. lv.
[3] Ussing, l. c. p. 8. Cf. Chapt. on Inscriptions.

Macrobius,and Isidorus of Seville, also contain notices of the
shapes of vases. Among modern archæologists, M. Panofka
was the first to propose an identification of the shapes of
the fictile vases found in the sepulchres of Greece and Italy,
and the question has been discussed by the critics already
mentioned. In order not to embarrass the subject with
constant references and critical discussion we shall only
mention those vases which are the most important, and the
shape of which has been the most satisfactorily proved.

CLASSIFICATION.

With regard to their shapes, vases may be divided into—

1. Those in which liquids were preserved ;

2. Those in which liquids were mixed or cooked ;

3. Those by which liquids were poured out and distributed.

4. Those for storing liquids and food till wanted for use.

VASES FOR PRESERVING.

1. The chief vase of the first division is the *pithos*, or
cask ; a very large jar with wide open mouth, and lips
inclined outwards. It held figs, or wine, and was placed
in the earth in the wine-cellar, propped up with reeds
and earth. Its shape resembles that of a modern jar,
and the few examples which remain are in the plain
unglazed ware, or in the tall Etruscan vases of red ware,
with subjects in relief.[1] The *pithacne*, was a vase smaller
than the *pithos*. In such vases the Athenians are supposed
by some to have lived during the war of the Peloponnese, if

---

[1] Ussing, p. 32; Panofka, Recherches, i. 1 ; ii. 2.

indeed the word does not refer to caverns. The *pithacne* appears, from allusions in the Comic poets, to have been used for holding wine at festivals. It was of baked earth.[1] Its shape is unknown.

The *stamnos* was a vase used to hold wine and oil. It was a jar with two small ear-shaped handles, and decorated with red figures upon a black ground.[2] It is often found in the sepulchres of Northern and Southern Italy. A good reason for believing that this is the shape of the *stamnos*, is, that vases of this figure are still called *stamnoi* in Greece.[3] Those with smaller bellies are the *cheroulia*.

No. 139.—Stamnos.

The *bicos* was a vase with handles, like the *stamnos*, which held figs and wine.[4]

The name of *Apulian stamnos* has been applied to a vase with double upright handles, chiefly of the later style, with red figures, and having a vaulted cover, which is sometimes surmounted by a second vase, of the shape called the *lepaste*. They are among the latest efforts of the fictile art, and are only found in Southern Italy.

The *hyrche* was apparently a kind of amphora with a narrow neck, in which many things were imported from Athens, and which served to hold the tickets used in drawing lots.[5] It seems to have been a large kind of vase.

The *lagynos* was also a vase of considerable size, which

[1] Ussing, p. 33 ; Panof ka, Rech. iii. 2.
[2] Gerhard,BerlinsAnt.Bild.s.356;Ussing, p. 35 ; Gerhard, Ult. Rech. no. 16.
[3] Thiersch, 36.
[4] Ussing, l. c.
[5] Ussing, p. 35 ; Panofka, iii. 26.

among the Patrenses held twelve heminæ. Nicostratus mentions one three times greater than usual ; and Lynceus of Samos introduced the custom of placing one beside each guest. At a later period, it appears to have had a long narrow neck.[1] It is the bottle which, in the Fables of Æsop, the stork is represented as setting before the fox at dinner.

Many terra-cotta vases are imitations of the *ascos*, or wine-skin, which was usually made of the skin of a goat, the apertures of the legs being sewed up, and the neck, which formed the mouth, secured with a thong. In the terra-cotta imitations the mouth is open, and the four feet below, while a handle passes over the body to the

No. 140.—Ascos.

neck. Certain small vases with one handle and about a foot long, when of unglazed ware, are supposed to represent *ascoi*. The first shape is often decorated with figures of animals or men in red colour, and occasionally also the second ; while the third is decorated at the upper part with a medallion in relief, and has the body reeded. These are supposed to have been lamps, or else designed for holding oil.[2]

Perhaps of all the ancient vases the *amphoreus, amphiphoreus,* or *amphora* is the best known. It consists of an oval or pyriform body, with a cylindrical neck, and two handles, from which it derives its name, viz., from ἀμφὶ φέρω, "to carry about." Those deposited in cellars generally had their bases extremely pointed, and were

---

[1] Ussing, p 36; Panofka, v. 100; Athenæus, xi. 499.

[2] Ussing, p. 37, 38 ; Panofka, ii. 43; vi. 10 ; Letronne, Jour. d. Sav. 1833, p.

684; 1837, p. 749; Gerhard, Ult. Ricerch. Ann. 1836 ; n. 40-41; Berl. Ant. Bild., s. 366, 5, 40, 41.

fixed into the earth.[1] They were of great size, and
contained large quantities of wine, honey, oil, sand,[2]
eatables, and coin. Originally the amphora seems to
have been a liquid measure, holding eight congii. It was
always fictile, but its shape varied. The painted amphoræ
were generally provided with flat circular feet. They are
divided into several kinds : 1. The amphora,[3] called
Egyptian, the body of which is long and rather elegant,
the handles small, and the foot tapering. 2. The
panathenaic[4] amphora (ἀμφόρευς παναθεναϊκὸς), resembling
the former in shape, except that the mouth is smaller and
narrower, and the general form thinner. They much
resemble those represented on the coins of Athens.
There are some varieties of this type without the usual
representations of Pallas Athene and athletic subjects.
The most remarkable of them is that discovered by Mr.
Burgon.[5] 3. The amphora called *Tyrrhenian* differs
only in its general proportion from the two preceding
kinds, the body being thicker and the mouth wider. The
subjects on these vases are arranged as in the panathenaic
ones, in a kind of square picture at each side. The neck
is sometimes ornamented with the double helix or chain,
and the foot has the petals. Under the handles is
sometimes an antefixal ornament. Many of these vases
are decorated with figures of the usual style in black

---

[1] Ussing, p. 38; Gerhard, Berlins
Antike Bildwerke, s. 345.

[2] Cicero, in Verrem, ii. 74, 183;
Homer, IL xxiii. 170; Martial, xiii. 103;
Homer, Odyss. ii. 290, 349, 379; ix. 164.
204.

[3] Gerhard, Berlins A. B. 346.

[4] Ibid.; Panofka, Rech. i. 6; Annali,

1:31, 229; Panofka, p. 16; Mon. i. xxi.
xxii.

[5] Millingen, Anc. Un. Mon., Pl. i. ii.
iii. p. 1 and foll. According to the
Scholiast of Plato (Charmides, ed.
Bekker, 8vo, Lond. 1824, p. 17, n.
126) the contest in the Panathenaia was
one of boys, who received for their

upon a red ground. They are principally found in Etruria. Another class of these amphoræ, with black figures, has a broad, flat handle like a riband, the edges being raised. 4. The Bacchic amphora[1] is the most prevalent type at the best period of the vases with black figures. The neck of these vases is larger and taller in proportion to the body than the preceding, and the handles are not cylindrical but ribbed, having been produced from a mould. They are from five to twenty inches high.

No. 141.—Bacchic Amphora.

5. Nolan amphoræ. The character of these amphoræ differs so essentially from that of the preceding, that they have been conventionally called *Nolan* amphoræ. The body is larger than that of the Etruscan or Bacchic amphoræ ; the handles are not reeded but flat ribands ; the whole vase, except the subject painted on it, is black, and has generally but few figures at each side. It is often provided with a convex cover and a stud.[2] Another variety of this form, with twisted handles, is produced by rolling up the paste. Some slight variety[3] occurs in the feet. This kind of vase, in elegance of shape, is the finest production of the potter's art ; while the exquisite black varnish and high finish render it the admiration of all lovers of ancient art.

reward oil, an amphora, and an olive crown. They contended as in the Isthmian games.
[1] Gerhard, Berlins A. B., s. 347;
Annali, 1831, p. 231.
[2] Ibid. s. 348, 5, 6.
[3] Ibid., s. 348, 5, 6.

6. The amphora, called *Apulian* from the circumstance of its being found only in Apulia, has a thick and overlapping mouth like an inverted cone. The neck is not cylindrical, but slopes upon the shoulders, and the body is more egg-shaped.[1] Its style, varnish, and abundance of white colour, are all peculiar to the later class of vases.

7. There is also a vase of elegant shape, called the Candelabrum Amphora, with cylindrical body, spiral handles, tall neck, and narrow lip and mouth, which is always of the latest style. Some of these vases—as, for example, one in the British Museum—appear, from having a hole at the bottom, to have been used as a decoration on the top of a pilaster or column. Its complex shape seems imitated from metal work.[2] A remarkably fine vase of this shape in the Temple collection at the British Museum has its handles and feet ornamented with moulded floral ornaments. It was found at Ruvo.

8. Similar to this, but of a still later style, are the amphoræ with sieve-shaped handles. These are tall and angular, rising above the mouth, and curved upwards at the bottom. On each handle are three semicircular studs.[3] The amphora, when complete, had a cover of the same material as the vase, surmounted by a stud or button with which to raise it. An amphora in the Berlin Museum had a double cover, an inner one of alabaster, over which is placed another of terra-cotta.[4]

The *pelice* was a later kind of amphora, with a swelling base, two rather large handles, and red figures, principally of the later style, or that called Apulian. It is

---

[1] Gerhard, Berlins A. B., s. 349, no. 7.   [3] Ibid., s. 350, no. 12.
[2] Ibid., s. 350, no. 11.   [4] Ibid., s. 680.

rarely found with black figures. The name, however, is doubtful.[1]

VASES FOR DRAWING LIQUIDS.

The *Cados* (*cask*), a name given, according to Callimachus, to all pottery, was used at banquets. It appears also to have been employed as a *situla*, or bucket, and it is possible that the deep semi-oval vase of pale varnish, and generally with figures of a late style, either embossed or painted, was the cadus.[2] It is very similar to certain bronze vessels which seem also to have been *cadoi* or *cadiskoi*. In the Pax[3] of Aristophanes, Trygæus persuades a helmet-seller to clap two handles on a helmet and convert it into a cadus.[4]

The *Hydria*, or water vase, is known from the word ΗΥΔΡΙΑ inscribed over a vase of this shape, which

Polyxene has let fall in going out of Troy to draw water from the fountain. It certainly appears on the heads of females in scenes of water-drawing. The ground of this vase is generally black, and it has two subjects—one on the shoulder or neck, generally called the frieze ; the other, the picture on the body of the vase.[5] These vases are mostly of the

No. 142.—Hydria.

class with black figures — but some rare examples

---

[1] Gerhard, B. A. B., s. 349, no. 8.

[2] Cf. Ussing. l. c., 40; Aristoph. Eccl. 1002; Athenæus, iv. 102, d.

[3] 1258. Cf. Panofka, Recherches, ii. 13; Thiersch, fig. 12.

[4] Thiersch, fig. 12, makes this the antlion.

[5] Ussing, p. 43; Gerhard, Berlins Antike Bildwerke, s. 350; Panofka, i. 11; Annali, 1831, 241; Letronne, p. 10, 54.

with red figures have been found at Vulci. The two
small side handles are cylindrical; the larger ones are
riband-like or moulded, and have a small head moulded
at the point of union. The *hydria* was employed for
holding water, oil, the votes of judges, and the ashes of
the dead, and was often made of bronze. It is called by
the Italians *vaso a trè maniche.* Many fine paintings and
interesting subjects are found on vases of this shape.

The *calpis* was essentially a water vase, and only a later
modification of the *hydria ;* the body being rounder, the

No. 143.—Calpis.

neck shorter, and the handles cylindrical. It was generally used for drawing water, but unguents, and the lots
of the judges, were often placed in it.[1] This form of vase
is principally found in the sepulchres of Southern Italy,
while the older type, or *hydria,* comes chiefly from Vulci.
Callimachus alludes to vases of this shape on the top of

[1] Ussing, p. 46; Panofka, p. 8, pl. vi. 4, 5 ; Annali, 1831, 241; Thiersch, p. 37.

the Parthenon ; and Pindar mentions them at an earlier period.[1]

Of other vases of this class are the following :—the *crossos*, a two-handled vase for drawing water, the shape of which is unknown :[2] the *cothon*, also of unknown shape,

almost seems to have been a Lacedæmonian name for a military cup used for drinking water, and adapted by its recurved mouth to strain off the mud.[3] Some have conjectured it to be the tea-cup-shaped vase with horizontal

No. 144.—Scyphos, or Cothon.

handles. The *rhyton* is well known, and many examples occur. The great peculiarity of this vase was that it could not be set down without drinking the contents. It may be divided into two shapes : first, a cylindrical cup ter-

minating in the head of an animal, and with a flat banded handle, the lip slightly expanding. In the second kind the body is fluted, longer, and more horn-like, and terminates in the head or fore part of an animal, which is pierced so as to let a jet

No. 145.—Rhyton.

of liquid flow out. These vases sometimes have a small circular handle at the side, to suspend them to the wall. On the necks are subjects of little importance, and of a satiric or comic nature, in red upon a black ground ; and of the later style of art, the part forming the animal's head is often left plain or is red. Many

[1] Pindar, O. vi. 68.
[2] Ussing, p. 49.
[3] Ussing, p. 55, 56; Panofka, Rech.　iv. 72; Letronne, p. 732; Thiersch, s. 33.

are entirely of terra-cotta. It appears from a comparison of the specimens, that they terminate in horses, goats, Pegasi, panthers, hounds, gryphons, sows ; heads of rams and goats, mules, dragons, deer, the horse, the ass, the cat, and the wolf. Similar ones called gryphons or grypes, Pegasi, and elephants, are mentioned in ancient authors. When not in actual use, they were placed on a peculiar stand and disposed on buffets, as appears from the vases found at Bernay. They were introduced at a late period into the ceramic art, and are evidently an imitation of the metallic *rhyta* in use among the Egyptians and Assyrians. They are first mentioned by Demosthenes : and it appears from Polybius that there were several statues of Clino, the cup-bearer of Ptolemy Philadelphus, holding a rhyton in his hand ; and one of Arsinoë Zephyritis holding the same vase. Only one maker of them, named Didymus, is known. A remarkable one found at Vulci has an Etruscan inscription in honour of Bacchus. An attempt has been made to identify the representations on these vases with the animals in whose heads they terminate.[1]

The *bessa* was an Egyptian vase used by the Alexandrians. It is described as broad below and narrow above. Its Greek shape is not known. Certain small vases are supposed to have been of the description called *bombylios*,[2] so called from the buzzing or gurgling sound which the liquid made in dripping out of the mouth. It was mentioned

No. 146.—
Bombylios.

[1] Ussing, pp. 55, 62 ; Panofka, Rech. 32-60 ; Gerhard, Berl. Ant. Bild. 366 ; Panofka, Die Griechische Trink-horner in the Abhandlung. d. Berlins K. Akadem 4to., 1850, s. 1—38. [2] Ussing, pp. 62—63.

by Antisthenes as narrow-necked and a kind of
lecythus.[1] It is supposed to be represented by an egg-
shaped[2] body and short neck with a small handle, just
enough for a strap. Vases of this kind are principally of
the early Greek style, with brown figures on a cream-
coloured ground.

The *lecythus*, or cruet, was used for holding oil. It is
principally recognised by its tall cylindrical shape, long
narrow neck, deep cup-shaped depression,
and flat banded handle. It was often made
of metal, but still more frequently of terra-
cotta. It commences with the old period of
vases with black figures, and terminates with
the best red style and those with white
grounds. A slight difference of shape is visible;
No. 147.—Lecythus. for, while on the older vases the shoulder is
slightly convex, on the later ones it is
flattened and the neck is taller. In the oldest style
figures are often placed on the shoulder instead of other
ornaments. They principally come from Greece—
especially Athens and Sicily, and are rarely found
in the tombs of Vulci. They seldom exceed a foot in
height.[3] The earlier *lecythi* have subjects embracing
some of the myths of antiquity depicted in groups
of many figures, while but few occur in those of the
later sort. Lecythi were chiefly used for holding oil, and
were carried down to the gymnasium by means of a

[1] Cf. Ussing, pp. 63—64; 3 Gerhard, Berl. Ant. Bild., s. 368, No. 48.
[2] Panofka, v. 99; Annali, 1831,
261; Letronne, 51.
[3] Gerhard, Berl. Ant. Bild. s. 367;
Panofka, v. 93; Ussing, p. 67; Letronne, p. 616; Thiersch, s. 40, fig.
78—9; Aristoph. Eccles. 906; Batrach.
1224.

strap held in the hand to which a strigil was attached.
The whole apparatus was called ξυστρολŋκύθιον. A *lecythus*
of marble appears to have been sculptured or painted upon
the stêles of men. The peculiar sepulchral character of
the *lecythi* found at Athens has been already mentioned.
The *olpe* is supposed to be a kind of *œnochoë*
or wine jug—or rather to be intermediate
between the *œnochoë* and *lecythus*, but the
identification of it seems to be very doubtful.
It is generally mentioned as a leather bottle
or metallic vase like the *œnochoë*.[1] It was
used for holding oil and wine, and is mentioned by the oldest authors. Sappho [2] speaks

No. 148.—Olpe.

of "Hermes holding an olpis and ministering. wine to the
gods ; " and Ion of Chios [3] of " drawing wine in olpes
from mighty craters." Many of the *lecythi* of a late
period, especially those found in Magna Græcia, are
moulded to represent comic or satirical subjects, such as a
boy devoured by a sea-monster,[4] a man bitten by a great
bird,[5] pigmies and cranes,[6] a comic Hercules seated,[7] a
personage of the New Comedy,[8] a Nubian devoured by a
crocodile, and Silenus reposing and drinking out of a wine-
skin, ideas derived from the New Comedy, and consonant
with the decaying spirit of the age; no longer elevated by
the heroic epos or the tragic drama, but seeking delight
in the grotesque, the coarse, and the ridiculous.

[1] Ussing, p. 69; Schol. Theocrit. II.
156; Gerhard, Berl. Ant. Bild. s. 365,
No. 35—36.
[2] Athenæus, X. 425 d.
[3] Ibid. 495 h.
[4] Gargiulo, Racc. II. 10.
[5] Ibid. 10.

[6] Arch. Anz., 1849, p. 60.
[7] Berlins Ant. Bildw. N. 1961.
[8] Arneth, Besch. d. K. K., Münz-
und Ant. Cabin. pp. 16- -196. See Jahn,
Berichte K. Sachs. Gesellschaft, 1852,
Feb. s. 15—16.

The *alabastron* [1] was used for holding unguents, oils, cosmetics and paint, and was a kind of *lecythus*. Its name was derived from the material of which it was made, namely oriental alabaster ; and some Egyptian vases of this shape are known, bearing the name of Pharaoh Necho. The terra-cotta vase is known from its resemblance to those in alabaster, and from its

No. 149.—Alabastron.

constant appearance in the pictures, on vases and other ornaments. Its body [2] is an elongated cone, its neck short, its mouth small, and lips flat and disc-shaped ; sometimes it has a foot, and also two little projections to hold it without slipping, or to hang it up to a wall with a

No. 150.—Alabastron.

cord. These vases are very rarely found in sepulchres ; some, however, occur either with red or black figures, and often upon a cream-coloured ground, whilst others are of the Athenian white style. Their subjects chiefly relate to the domestic life of females, but some Bacchanalian and other subjects occur. No maker of them is known.

The *crater* may be considered the wine-cooler, in which the ancients mixed their wine with snow and water. It is distinguished from the *amphora* by its larger size, its wider mouth, its semi-oval body, and its two handles for occasional transport, which were small, and almost ver-

---

[1] Ussing, pp. 70—71; Herodot. III., 20; Aristoph. Ach. 1053; Callimach. Pall. 15; Ceres, 13; Plutarch, Timol. 15; Theocrit. xv. 114; Cicero, apud Non. 545; Martial, xi. 89; Pliny, N. H. 56—113.

[2] Gerhard, Berl. Ant. Bild. s. 369, No. 49—50.

tical. *Craters* are chiefly found in South Italy, and are always decorated with red figures. Of the earlier style of art are the so-called *holmos*, and the supposed *celebe*, or crater with columnar handles. The vase called *oxybaphon*, with red figures, is a very prevalent variety of this shape.[1] It is doubtful whether the amphoræ with volute or medallion handles are not craters. The *hypocraterion*, or stand on which the vase was placed, was a hollow cylindrical foot, decorated with an egg-and-tongue moulding, and a reeded body, which raised the vase almost to the height of four feet. Several kinds of craters are mentioned by ancient authors,—as the Lesbian, the Thericlean, the Laconian, and Corinthian. Some held three or four gallons.

No. 151.—Holmos.

The *crater* with columnar handles is supposed, on no very certain grounds, to be the *celebe*. The shape depicted in the accompanying cut is the oldest, having arched handles, from which springs a banded handle. Sometimes four columnar handles are substituted for these. Vases of this sort are found at the earliest period, having the subjects

No. 152.—Celebe.

disposed in friezes round the body. In the few examples known with black figures, the subject is arranged in pictures. At a later time the subjects are

[1] Gerhard, Berl. Ant. Bild. 357, 17; Ult. Rech. No. 18; Ussing, p. 84; Panofka, i. 17.

red upon a black ground.   Craters appear to have come

No. 153.—Crater.

No. 154.—Oxybaphon.

into use much later than the so-called *oxybapha*.   Although
all agree to consider the *oxybaphon* a crater, it is contested
whether the name of *kelebe* or *kelebeion* can be properly
applied to the latter description of vase.[1]

We will now pass to the Apulian craters,—the first of
which are the so-called *oxybapha*, which are bell-shaped,
and hàve two small handles at the side, recurved towards
the body.   These vases are called by the Italian antiquaries
vasi a campana.   There is some difference in the proportions, those of the earlier times being fuller in the body,
while the later ones are thin, and have an expanding lip.[2]
The correctness of the name *oxybaphon* is contested by
many critics.[3]

Some other *craters* of this tall style have been improperly
called *amphorœ* with volute handles.   These are large vases
with long egg-shaped bodies, wide open mouths, and two
tall handles curling over the lip of the vase, and terminating in the head of a swan at the lower extremity.
These, however, are rather the craters of the later Apulian

[1] Ussing, De Nom. Vas. pp. 80—
84.
[2] Gerhard, Berlins Ant. Bildw. s.

358, No. 18.
[3] Ussing, p. 81; Letronne, l. c.

potteries. They reach to a great size, and are decorated with numerous figures.[1] Similar to them are *Amphoræ*

No. 155.—Crater, with volute handles.

with Gorgon handles. This description of amphora, which is another of the later sort, only differs from the preceding in having medallions instead of volutes at the top of the handles, the ends of which also terminate in swans' necks. The medallions are stamped in moulds. These craters are found of great size, principally in South Italy, and are decorated with numerous figures[2] of the later style of art.

The *psycter*, or as it was also called, the *psygeus*,[3] or the "wine cooler," was used for cooling wine. In glazed ware,

[1] Gerhard, B. A. B. s. 349, No. 9.   [3] Ussing, pp. 76—82.

[2] Ibid. s. 350, No. 10.

this vase is of the greatest rarity. It is in the shape of a Bacchic amphora, with a double wall and an orifice projecting in front, through which snow was introduced, and a small one in the foot of the vase, by which it was withdrawn when melted. The *psycter* was one of the most celebrated vases of antiquity ; one in the British Museum has the part between the walls filled with a layer of chalk, apparently the ancient core. The subjects of these vases are always in black upon red grounds, like the amphoræ, to which they belong. Sometimes they have only a frieze round the neck. They were placed on tripods when used.

The *dinos* was made of terra-cotta, and was large enough to contain wine for a family. It appears to have been round, with a wide mouth, and to have terminated in a pointed or rounded foot, like the most ancient shape of the crater used for entertainments.[1]

Chytræ, pots, were used for drawing or warming water, boiling flesh, and various domestic purposes. They must have been of some size, for children were exposed in them; but nothing is known of their shape, except that they had two handles. It is evident that they could not have been of glazed ware, for to " paint pots " (χύτραν ποικίλλειν) was a proverb to express useless labour.[2] The *thermanter* was a vase used for warming wine or water ; but it is uncertain whether it was ever made of clay, as it is only mentioned as a brazen vessel.[3] Its shape is unknown. The *thermopotis* was a vase also used for warming wine. Its shape is

---

[1] Ussing, pp. 82—83 ; Panofka, Rech. I. 15 ; Letronne, Journ. des. Sav., 614.

[2] Ussing, pp. 87—91; Schol. ad Arist.

Vesp. 279.

[3] Ussing, l. c. Müller, Æginetica, p. 160 ; Boeckh, Corp. Inscr. 2139.

unknown, but perhaps it resembled a chafing-dish, the warming apparatus being placed beneath.

The stands of the craters, or large wine-coolers were called *hypocrateria* or *hypocrateridia*.[1] They were very different in shape, according to the age to which they belonged. At the time of the style called Ægyptian, they were tall and trumpet-shaped, and sometimes decorated with rows of figures of animals. With vases of the early style with red figures they are seldom if ever found ; with those with red figures, they are sometimes of one piece with the vase itself, and are ornamented with subjects. With the later vases of the Basilicatan style, they are of far shorter proportions, and have an egg-and-tongue moulding and reeded body ($\rho\alpha\beta\delta\omega\tau\sigma$), the foot of the *crater* fitting into a groove or rim in the upper portion. Certain shallow circular pans among the specimens of Etruscan red ware, appear to be intended for the same use, as large jar-shaped craters are found standing in them. In the black ware of the same people, certain cups, which some have called the *holkion*, are supported by female figures standing at their sides, sometimes alternating with bands. The *tripous*, or tripod, was a vase with three flat feet at the sides, and a cover, the body being hemispherical. It appears sometimes to have had fire placed under it, apparently for warming liquids. The feet and cover are ornamented with subjects. It is found only among vases of the ancient style with brown figures upon a yellow ground, and black figures upon a red ground.[2]

[1] Ussing, l. c. p. 92, 93; Gerhard, Ult. Ric. No. 26; Berlins Ant. Bildw. s. 360, 26.

[2] Ussing, l. c. Panofka, Rech. iii.

56; Gerhard, Rapp. Volci. No. 45; Stackelberg, Die Gräber, tab. 15 Brit. Mus. No. 2669.

The word *holmos*, which signifies *mortar*, and was also applied to vases, is supposed to be the name of certain large hemispherical vessels with a flat or pointed foot, which was often fixed into a trumpet-shaped stand, by which it was supported. These vases belong to the ancient hieratic style, or that called Egyptian; and both the kind with black figures, and that in the strong red style, have rows of figures round the body. The shape shows that it was a vase from which wine was drawn like the craters. The name of *deinos*, or *scaphe*, has also been considered applicable to vases of this shape.[1] They resemble the *lebes*, or caldron.

The *chytropous*, pot-foot, or trivet, was an instrument by which the pot was kept upon the fire. Possibly, some of the old Athenian vase-stands are this useful instrument.[2]

The *lasanon*, was apparently a kind of pot,[3] its shape and size are not known. It was possibly made of metal.

The *chous* appears to have been always made of clay.[4] It was a measure of liquid capacity, sometimes holding as much as the Latin congius,[5] and may be considered as the "bottle" of Athens. It was chiefly used for holding wine,[6] but its shape is unknown, some supposing that it had two, and others, that it had only one handle.[7] The *œnochoë* corresponded with the modern decanter, or claret bottle. There are several varieties of this shape, but

---

[1] Gerhard, B. A. B. 360, No. 26; Ussing, p. 96.

[2] Ussing, l. c. Pollux, x. 99; Schol. Arist. Pac. 893; Av. 436; Plut. 815; Ran. 506.

[3] Ussing, l. c. 98; Aristoph. in Pac. 891; Hor. Sat. I. 6, 109.

[4] Pollux, x. 122.

[5] Eubulus apud Athenæum, xi. 473, c.

[6] Cratinus apud Athen. xi. 494, c.; Aristoph. Pac. 537; Equit. 95; Ach. 1086; Schol. ad v. 961; Anaxandrides ap. Athen. xi. 482 d.

[7] Ussing, p. 101; Panofka, Rech. iv. 27.

their general[1] type is that of a jug, the mouth being either
round, or with a trefoil in imitation of an ivy leaf. This
first type, which appears to have been contemporaneous
with the amphoræ with banded handles, has a short neck
and banded handle rising over the lip. The subject is

No. 156.—Œnochoë.

No. 157.—Œnochoë.

generally arranged in a square picture in front ; but
sometimes the ground, especially in the cream-coloured
vases, runs all round the body. At a later period, and in
the Nolan ware, the body becomes more egg-shaped and
slender, and the handle taller, so that this series presents
some of the most beautiful examples of shape. Another
variety of figure, which is also of the best period of the
art, has a truncated base, with a mere moulding or bead,
instead of a foot. The shape of these vases is well known
from the frieze of the Parthenon and other representations
of libations and sacrifices, in which they were always
used with the *phialæ*, or pateræ, and the *thymiateria*, or
tall censers ; they were dipped into the craters,[2] and the
wine was carried round to the guests by a youth called the

[1] Gerhard, B. A. B. s. 365, No. 33—
36 ; Panofka, v. 101 ; Annali, 1831,
248 ; Letronne, p. 70.   [2] Panofka,   Rech.   vi.   6 ;   Cab.
Pourtalés, 34.

œnochoos. It was a law of the banquet never to place the *œnochoë* upon the crater, as it was considered a bad omen, and a sign that the feast was ended.[1] Œnochoæ were also employed in religious rites; whence Thucydides,[2] speaking of the anathemata which the Egesteans showed to the Athenian ambassadors in the temple of Aphrodite at Eryx, says that they displayed *phialæ*, *œnochoœ*, and *thymiateria*, all made of silver; and in Athenæus,[3] mention is made of the *naos* of the people of Metapontum, in which were 132 silver *phialæ*, 2 silver œnochoæ, and a golden œnochoë. They are often seen in the hands of figures depicted on the vases as making libations.[4]

Another jug was the *prochoos*, with an oval body, tall neck, and round mouth, but without a handle. It was used for carrying water for washing the hands, for which purpose the water was poured over them. "A maidservant bearing water for washing, poured it out of a beautiful golden prochoos," says Homer;[5] and Iris descending to Hades for the waters of the Styx, takes a prochoos to draw it.[6] It also held snow,[7] and wine. Hence we read in the Odyssey, "He laid his right hand upon the œnochoos, and the prochoos fell rattling on the ground."[8] It was also used for holding oil,[9] and libations to the dead were poured out of it.[10] M. Gerhard recognises

---

[1] Hesiod. Opp. et Dier. 744.
[2] vi. 46—3.
[3] xi. 479, f.; cf. also Boeckh, Corp. Inscr. No. 150, col. 1, v. 30; Athenæus, v. 199, b.; xi. 474, 495, 6; Pollux, x. 122.
[4] Gerhard, A. V. I. 28—30.
[5] Χέρνιβα δ᾽ ἀμφίπολος προχόῳ ἐπέχευε φέρουσα καλῇ, χρυσείῃ.—Od. i. 136.

[6] Hesiod. Theog. 785; cf. also Aristoph. Nab. 272; Pollux x. 46.
[7] Anaxandrides apud Athenæum, iv. 131, n. 26.
[8] Odyssey, xviii. 398; Xenophon, Cyr. viii. 8—10.
[9] Suidas, voce; Sophocles, Antigone, 430.
[10] Athenæus, v. 199 b.; xi. 474, 495.

the prochoos in the form depicted in the annexed cut. He also supposes the small *œnochoë*, with a bill-shaped spout and cylindrical body, to be the Apulian *prochoos*; but it is probably rather the *epichysis*. The *epichysis* was a metal vase for pouring liquids, probably so called from

No. 158.—Aryballos.

No. 159.—Aryballos.

No. 160.—Epichysis.

its spout,[1] used for holding oil and wine at entertainments.[2] The following vases were for drawing liquids. The *arataina*, shaped like a ladle, and used in baths for drawing oil, and distributing to the bathers, or for putting it into lamps. It was generally made of brass.[3] The *aryballos* was a vase always described as like a purse. M. Gerhard and Panofka attributed this name to a vase resembling a ball, with a short neck, globular body, and small handle, just sufficient for a thong to carry it with, called by the Italians *vaso a palla*. It is chiefly found among vases of the earliest style, and was carried with the strigil to the bath. In

No. 161.—Late Aryballos, or Lecythos.

the later style the form was more elongated, and a base or foot was added.[4]

[1] Ussing, p. 103.

[2] Varro de L.L. v. 1, 24; Pollux, vi. 103, x. 92.

[3] Ussing, p. 105; Aristoph. Equit. p. 1090; Pollux, x. 63; Theophrastus,

Char.; Thiersch, s. 33, 34, supposes it to be a jug.

[4] Gerhard, B. A. B., s. 367, no 44, 45; Panofka, v. 95; Annali iii., p. 263; Ussing, p. 106; Pollux, x. 63;

Small *lecythi*, or *aryballi*, of various forms, are found; for at all times the potter has manufactured these pieces as the curiosities of his art. Those found at Vulci are shaped like the bust of the archaic Bacchus, heads of satyrs and Sileni, armed heads, human-headed birds, sirens; the stag or deer, the emblem of Artemis; the hare and rabbit, sacred to Venus and Apollo; the head of an eagle, and pigeons. They are all of small dimensions, and appear to have been used for the toilet.[1]

The *arystichos* was a vase used for drawing wine out of the craters.[2] Considerable doubt prevails respecting the meaning of the passages in which its name occurs,[3] and although Panofka conjectures that he has discovered the type, his opinion on this point is by no means generally admitted.[4] It was also used for holding the judges' votes. It was called EPHEBOS, " or youth," from the boy who carried it round.[5] The *aryter*, a vase for drawing liquids, is mentioned by Herodotus.[6] The *aryseis*,[7] *aryster*,[8] *arysane*,[9] and *arystris*, were also vases used for drawing liquids. The *œnerysis* was a kind of cup used for drawing wine.[10] The *etnerysis*, a vase for serving up pulse,[11] and the *zomerysis*, a kind of vase used for ladling out sauce or soup,[12] are mentioned, but their shapes are unknown. The *cotyle*, or *cotylos*,[13] is supposed to have been

---

Athenæus xi., 781, f.; Thiersch, s. 35.

[1] Mus. Greg., p. ii., t. xciii.
[2] Ussing, p. 107; Pollux, vi. 19; Hesychius voce.
[3] Böckh Corp. Inscr. Græc., No. 2139; Athenæus, x. 424.
[4] Panofka, Rech., v. 98; Letrouve, Journ. des Savans, 1833, p. 618.
[5] Schol. Aristoph. Vesp. 855.

[6] II. 108.
[7] Sophocl. apud Athenæum, xi., 783, f.
[8] Simonides, apud Athen. x. 424 b.
[9] Timon ap. Athenæum, x., 424 b.
[10] Schol. ad Aristoph. Acharn., 1067.
[11] Schol. Aristoph. Acharn., 245.
[12] Anaxippus apud Athenæum, iv. 169 b.
[13] Ussing, p. 108 and seq.

a deep cup, used for drawing wine.   It was also a measure
of liquid capacity, equal to a *hemina*, or fourth of a sexta-
rius.   In Homer, mendicants beg for bread and a cotyle of
water ; [1] and Andromache, describing a crowd of children
approaching her father's friends, says : "Some one of
those pitying hold a cup awhile, wetting their lips, but not
moistening their palates." [2]   So the old Greek proverb :—

> There's many a slip
> 'Twixt cotyle and lip.[3]

Honey was suspended in it in the festive boughs before
the gate :—

> Eiresione bears figs and new bread,
> And honey in a cotyle.[4]

The *cotylos*, which name was more particularly applied
to the cup, was in use among the people of Sicyon and
Tarentum, the Ætolians, some of the Ionian tribes,[5] and
the Lacedæmonians, — of all cups the most beautiful
and best for drinking, as Eratosthenes calls it.[6]   It
was made of the clay of Mount Colias.   Apollodorus
describes it as a deep and lofty cup ;
and Diodorus speaks of it as resembling
a deep lavacrum, and as having one
handle.   M. Panofka and M. Gerhard
conjecture that it was a kind of deep
two-handled cup,[7] which notion, though
rejected by some critics, is rather

No 162.—Cotyliscos.

strengthened by the shape of the *hemicotylion*, as depicted

[1] Odyssey, xv. 312, xvii. 12.
[2] Iliad, xxi. 494.
[3] Athenæus, xi. 478 e.
[4] Schol. Aristoph. Equit., 729; Plutus,
1054.
[5] Athenæus, l. c.
[6] Athenæus, l. c., 482 b.
[7] Panofka, iii. 51, iv., 50, Gerhard,
ult., Ric. 28.

VOL. II.   H

in the annexed cut. A vase of this description, of clay, covered with a black glaze or varnish, and bearing the inscription HEMIKOTΥΛION, has lately been discovered at Corfu (Corcyra).

The *cotyliskos*, or diminutive *cotylos*, was a small vase, either with or without handles.[1] Some of the smaller children's vases were probably of this form.

M. Gerhard supposes the *cotyliskos* to be a vase of the shape of a lecythus, generally decorated with painting in the old or Egyptian style. It has been conjectured that certain vases, sometimes of glazed ware, are of the description called *cernos*. In the mysteries, several small vases. or *cotuliskoi*,[2] containing various scraps of food, after being bound together with wool, were tied round a larger vase, and then carried about. This type is recognised by some writers in certain groups of small cups, ranged in a single or double circle. These vases, as in an example already cited, are principally found in the sepulchres of Athens and Milo, among the unglazed painted terra-cotta vases of the earliest style. They are rudely modelled with the hand, and attached by bands of terra-cotta to a hollow cylinder in the centre. Some vases of this shape occur amongst those of the later style, and are attached to a hollow circular pipe, or crown of terra-cotta, on which they stand. In this case they sometimes have covers, and are decorated with ornaments in white. M. Ussing, on the other hand, considers these vases to be *cotylæ*. *Cyathos*, which means "the ladle," was a name applied to the small vase, by which the unmixed wine

---

[1] Gerhard, Berlins Ant. Bildw., 1, 368, No. 46.

[2] Ussing, p. 110; Gerhard, B. A. B., s. 368, No. 46.

was taken out of the craters, and put into the cups of the guests, water being added from a jug. Many *cyathi* of bronze exist in different collections.[1] An open cup, sometimes having a tall stem or foot, and with a

No. 163.—Cyathos.   No. 164.—Cyathos.

long, narrow, ear-shaped handle, well adapted for dipping the cup into the crater, but not for holding it in the hand to drink, is supposed to be this vase.

The following vases were also used for liquids : the *louterion*, for water for the bath, was generally made of marble or alabaster,[2] and it is uncertain whether it was ever manufactured of clay ; the *asaminthos*, a large vase, also used in baths ; [3] the *puelos*, or bin, which was in fact

[1] Ussing, p. 111 ; Gerhard, Berlins Ant. Bildw., s. 360, No. 24, 25 ; Panofka, No. 52, vii., 5 ; Annali, 1831, p. 251, and foll.

[2] Ussing, p. 114.

[3] Ussing, p. 115 ; Odyss. iv. 48 ; Pollux, vi. 97.

the bath tub ; [1] the *scaphe*, a vase used in the kitchen for washing culinary utensils, and also employed as a foot bath,[2] appears to have been generally made of wood or brass ;[3] the *scapheion* or *scaphion*, an hemispherical vase, for holding or drawing water, the shape of which is not identified.[4] It seems to have been also a drinking vessel,[5] for Phylarchus, in describing the mode of living of Cleomenes, the Spartan king, says that he had a silver *scaphion*, holding two *cotylæ*.[6]

The *exaleiptron* was a vase, like a *phiale* or saucer,[7] for holding ointment. The *lecane* is recognised by M. Gerhard in a deep two-handled vase, provided with a cover resembling an inverted cup. It was used for washing the feet, and for holding cups, clothes, pitch, and for other coarse work ;[8] as a basin to vomit in ;[9] and likewise in the Sicilian game of cottabus.[10] It was also employed for that kind of divination called λεκανομαντεῖα or "dish-divination." In the romantic life of Alexander the Great, written by the pseudo-Callisthenes, a long account is given how the fabled sorcerer, the Egyptian Nectanebo, employed this vessel in magic arts, and after placing in it small waxen figures of men and ships, plunged it into the sea, and so destroyed his enemies. He constantly used it for the purpose of enveigling Olympias. Julius Valerius, who wrote in Latin

[1] Ibid.; Aristoph. Equit. 1060 ; Pax. 843.
[2] Ussing, l. c. and pp. 116, 117.
[3] Pollux, x. 77 ; Æschylus in Sisypho.
[4] Ussing, p. 117.
[5] Athen. xi. 475 c.
[6] Athenæus, iv. p. 142.
[7] Ussing. p. 117 ; Clearchus. apud Athen., xiv. 648, f.; Pollux, vi. 106 ; Aristoph. Acharn., 1063 ; Athen. v.

202, c.
[8] Ussing, p. 118 ; Pollux, x. 70; Suidas, v. κέλεβε; Böckh. Corp. Inscr., No. 3071, 8 ; Aristoph. Av., 840, 1143, 1146 ; Vesp., 600.
[9] Plutarch, Moral., p. 801, B.; Aristoph., Nab. 906; Theopomp. Athen., xi., 485, c.; Pollux, x. 76; Gerhard, B. A. B., 364, 32.
[10] Schol. ad. Aristoph. Pac., 1244.

a similar apocryphal life of Alexander, calls the vessel a
bason or *pelvis*.   This magical use of the vase is also mentioned in the work called *Philosophoumena*, erroneously
attributed to Origen.

The *lecanis*, or smaller *lecane*, made of terra-cotta, was
probably of the shape figured just above.   In it the father
of the bride sent, along with her, presents to his son-in-
law, at the time of the marriage.   According to Photius,
lecanides were earthern vessels, very much resembling a
crater, which, he continues, the women now call " food-
holders."[1]

The *lecaniskos* and *lecanion* were small *lecanides*.[2]   The
podanipter was a bason for washing the feet in.[3]   Possibly
this vase may be identified with the flat, thick, circular
basons found in the Etruscan tombs.   It was generally of
bronze.   The *cheironiptron, cheironips*, and *chernibon*, were
wash-hand basons, but their shape is unknown.[4]

The vase called *holcion* was a kind of bowl, for washing
cups.   It also appears to have been used for the table and
the bath.   MM. Panofka and Gerhard suppose it to have
been a kind of small *crater*, with figures and supports ;[5]
but this is not by any means satisfactorily proved.   The
perirrhanterion, or sprinkler, was a vase which held the
lustral water in the temples, and which, in the earliest
times, was made of earthenware.   The list is closed by the

---

[1] Ussing, l. c.; Pollux, vi. 85;
Photius; Schol. ad Aristoph. Ach.,
1110; Teleclides ap. Athen., vi. 208,
c. v. 11.; Hesych., v.; Gerhard,
B. Ant. Bild., s. 364, 365, No.
32; Panofka, Rech., iii. 42.

[2] Ussing, p. 119.

[3] Ussing, p. 120; Photius, p. 118;

Pollux, x. 78; Herodot.. ii. 172.

[4] Ussing, l. c. 121; Athenæus, ix. p.
408; Homer, xxiii. 304; Andocid. in
Alcib., 29, κ. τ. λ.

[5] Gerhard, B. Ant. Bildw., s. 362, n.
27; Ussing, p. 122; Panofka, iv.,
92; Annali, 1831. p. 252.

ardanion, or *ardalion,* the lower part of which vase, after it had been broken, was placed as an emblem before a house in which a death had occurred.

VASES FOR DRINKING.

The productions of the potter never perhaps attained greater excellence as to form than in cups, many of which are of unrivalled shape. If any extant specimens of fictile ware represent the shapes mentioned by Homer, who in the true poetic spirit always speaks of cups as made of the precious metals, they must be looked for in the primitive vases of Melos and Athens. The great cup described by Homer bears, however, more resemblance to some of the specimens of the Etrurian black ware.[1] " The great cup, ornamented with golden studs, was produced, which the old man had brought from home. It had four handles, and two golden doves were placed on each ; and it had two stems. When full, any one else could hardly lift it from the table ; but old Nestor lifted it with ease." The cups mentioned by Homer are the *depas;* the *aleison,*[2] a cup with two handles ; the *cissybion*[3] so called from its being made of ivy wood, or from its being ornamented with carvings representing the foliage of ivy ; the *cupellon,*[4] or later *cymbion,*[5] which, among the Cretans and Cyprians, had either two or

[1] Iliad, xi. p. 632.
[2] Odyss., iii. 49, 50, 63, xxii., 9, 7; Ussing, l. c., p. 124.
[3] Odyss., v. 346; xiv. 78; Pollux, vi. 97 ; Theocrit., i. 59, et Schol. ; Athenæus, iv. 477.
[4] Athen., xi., 482, 483 a, 783 c. Ælian. Hist. Anin., ix. 40.

[5] Macrob. Sat., v. 21; Letronne, Journ. d. Savans, 1833, p. 605; Athenæus, 481 e, f, 482 f, 502; Schol. Arist. Pac., 1242; Nicander Ther., 526; Alexiph., 129; Hesychius voce; Demosth. in. Meidiam, 133—158, in. Euerg. et Mnesib., 58.

four handles; and the *amphicupellon*[5] formed of two *cupella*, united at their base.   The *cymbion* was a kind of cup, stated by some authors to resemble a boat.[6]   No vase of such a shape is known to exist, unless it be the rhyton in the British Museum, fashioned in the shape of the prow [1] of a vessel, with a female seated on it; or a long boat-shaped vessel with a spout, discovered at Vulci, on which is inscribed " drink, do not lay me down."[1]   This kind of vase was in common use among the Athenians.

The name for cups in general was *scyphos*; and they were called, from the places of their manufacture, Bœotian, Rhodian, Syracusan, and Heracleotan,[2] or Thericlean from their maker Thericles.   It may easily be conceived that no very distinct idea of their shape is conveyed by ancient writers.   Simonides, indeed, mentions that they had handles; and the Heracleotan *scyphos* had its handle ornamented with the Heraclean knot.   Some vases of the latest period of the art, with reeded bodies, sides ornamented with white ivy wreaths, and handles of two twigs or pieces interlaced in a knot, more resembling the *cantharos*, are probably the *Heracleotan scyphi*.   M. Gerhard supposes a kind of wide cup with two handles to be the scyphos.   These cups, which are found at Nola,[3] are of the later style, and ornamented with red figures, principally of a Bacchanalian character.   Very often, however, they are entirely plain, being merely covered with black varnish.   Another kind was, the *Panathenaic scyphos*, supposed to be a cup with two handles, of the same shape

[1] Panofka, Rech., v. 74, 75.
[2] Athenæus, p. 500 a;   Letronne, Journ. des Savans, 1833, p. 731, note 1.
[3] Gerhard, B. A. B., s. 362, No. 28; Panofka, iv. 92.

as the preceding, but having one handle placed at right angles to the cup's axis. Their usual decoration is an owl, placed between two olive branches. This vase is supposed, from the shape of its handles, to have been the *onychios*. The *ooscyphion*, or egg (shaped) cup, was without a foot,[1] and was, perhaps, the same as the vase called mastos, which had two handles, like the Panathenaic *scyphos*, and was often decorated externally with black figures upon a red ground. It often terminates like an areola, or nipple, with an oval band round it. These cups are very rare, and are ornamented with Bacchanalian subjects. They are thin and well turned, and altogether very elegant productions. They chiefly come from Vulci. The *bromias* was a long kind of *scyphos*.[2]

The *cantharos* was a kind of cup, probably so called from its resembling a beetle. It was the cup specially used by

No. 165.—Cantharos.

Bacchus,[3] and was generally made of earthenware, although sometimes of metal. It appears from the various monuments of Bacchus to have been a kind of goblet, on a tall stem, with two very long ears. In some of the older specimens of Etruscan black ware it has no stem.[4] Vases of this kind are seldom decorated with paintings, which, when they do appear, consist of red figures upon a black ground. A

[1] Ussing, p. 133; Athen. xi., 488 f, 503 e, 477 e; Panofka, v. 103.
[2] Ussing, p. 134; Panofka, iv. 65; Athenæus, xi. 784 d.
[3] Pliny, xxxiii. 53, 150.
[4] Gerhard, B. A. B., s. 359, No. 21— 23; Panofka, iv. 61; Annali, 1831, 256.

few are also found among the vases of the latest style
of the Basilicata, especially those produced from moulds.
M. Gerhard classes with them a goblet-shaped vase
without handles. In the picture of the battle of the
Centaurs and Lapithæ, painted by Hippeus, he represented
them drinking out of terra-cotta canthari.[1]

The *carchesion* was a kind of two-handled cup, the shape
of which is not very intelligible from the descriptions
of it given by the early
poets, Pherecydes, Sappho, and
others.[2] As, however, it was
the sort of cup held by
Bacchus and his "wassail rout"
in the pageant of Ptolemy
Philadelphus,[3] it was probably
a kind of cantharus. M.
Gerhard[4] and M. Panofka recognise it in a very elegant

No. 166.—Carchesion.

cup, with large ear-shaped handles, short stem, and wide
mouth, and ornamented with red figures, relating to
Bacchus. This sort of cup is chiefly found among the
later remains of Southern Italy ; but it is probable that
many of the vases called *canthari* are *carchesia*. According to M. Thiersch, they were shaped as in the annexed
cut.

Of all the cups the most celebrated was, undoubtedly,
the *cylix*, so called from its being turned on the lathe.

[1] Athenæus, 474 d, Cf.; Pollux, vi. 96.

[2] Athenæus, 474 f, 475 a.

[3] Athen., v. 198, b, c.

[4] Gerhard, B. A. B·, s. 359, No. 20 ;

Panofka, iv. 61; Annali, iii., 256, f, 6, s. 36, compared with the technical description of Callixinus of Rhodes, Athenæus, xi. 474, e.

It was a flat, shallow, and extremely wide saucer, with
two side handles, and a tall stem or foot, and was deco-

No. 167.—Early Cylix.

rated with red figures of the
finest style, both on the exterior and interior. Those of
the earliest period are distinguished by their deeper bowl
and taller stem, while the bowl

of those of a later period, with black figures, is unpro-
vided with a foot. Those ornamented with paintings of

No. 168.—Later Cylix.

the strong and fine style
have a shallow bowl, re-
curved handles, rising
rather higher than the
lip, and a stem not so

high as the earlier cylices. Their shape is one of the
most elegant of those handed down from antiquity. At
the Basilicatan period these vases resemble large flat
baskets with handles, like the crater. *Cylices* of this
style, which approach the bowl shape, are very rare,
and have subjects only inside. These vessels hold
about a pint, or even from four to seven heminæ, and
were probably passed round from guest to guest. In
banqueting scenes depicted upon them, they are often

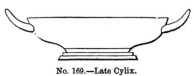

No. 169.—Late Cylix.

represented as being
twirled round upon the
finger, in the supposed
Sicilian game of cot-

tabus.[1] Athens was celebrated for its cups,[2] made of clay

---

[1] Panofka, Rech., vii. 37 ; Millingen,   Pourtalès, xxxiv. ; Thiersch, s. 31.
Vases de Coghill, Pl. viii. and 41 ; Cab.   [2] Pindar apud Athenæum, p. 480, c.

from the promontory of Mount Colias ; but the Lacedæmonian,[1] Teian,[2] Chian,[3] and Argive[4] cups were also
esteemed. These cups, when not in use, were hung up
by one of their handles on a peg, and hence Hermippus
sings of

"High on its peg the Chian cup is hung;"

a good example of which custom will be found represented on the Ficoroni *cista*.[5]

The *Thericleios* was a kind of cup invented by Thericles,
a Corinthian potter, the contemporary of Aristophanes.[6]

No. 170.—Early Cylix, with black figures. (Thericlean?)

The "Thericleans," as they were named, were, however,
soon in vogue at Athens, and are mentioned by the
writers of the middle and the new comedy. They were
all clay, and held three heminæ. Thus Eubulus exclaims
in comic bombast—

"Lately the bravest
of the Thericleans, foaming o'er, like
a cothon handled, rattling like a ballot-box,

[1] Aristophan. ap. Athen., 484, f.
[2] Alcæus ap. Athen., p. 481, a.
[3] Hermippus apud Athen, 480, c.
[4] Simonides ibid., 480-a.

[5] Brondsted, Den Ficoroniske Cista
folio Kiobenhavn, 1831.
[6] Athen., i. 470, f., 472, d., e.

> black, well circled, sharp stemmed,
> gleaming, reflecting, well cooled with snow,
> its head bristling with ivy, calling upon
> Jupiter the Saviour, I have quaffed."

It is probable that these were the *cylices* with deep bodies. They were often successfully imitated in fine wood.

Along with the "Thericleans" may be cited other cups, such as the *hedypotis*, a cup of a very cheap kind, manufactured by the Rhodians to compete with the Athenian "Thericleans,"[1] and the *Rhodiaca, Rhodiacai, Rhodiades,* or "*Rhodians,*" which were perhaps the same as the *hedypotides*. Their shape does not appear to be well known.[2] The *Antigonis*, a kind of cup, so called from King Antigonus, seems to have ended in a point, but it is uncertain whether it was ever made of earthenware.[3] The *Seleucis* was named after King Seleucus. Ussing recognises its shape in some of the paintings at Pompeii. It appears to have had four handles,[4] like a mether.

Of the same species as the *cylix*, but almost limited to religious offices, was the *phiale* (the patera or saucer), a shallow, circular vessel, so like the round Argolic buckler, that Aristotle calls it the shield of Mars,[5] and, *vice versâ*, Antiphanes [6] calls "the shield of Mars" a phiale. It rarely had handles,[7] and was chiefly used for libations, being seldom, if ever, employed at entertainments.[8] It is of rare occurrence ; the few which have been discovered

---

[1] Athenæus, xi. 464 c, 409 b.

[2] Pollux, vi. 96; Hesychius voce Athenæus, 496, f.

[3] Athenæus, 497 f; Pollux, vi. 95; Schol. Clement. Pædag., ii. 3.

[4] Athenæus, p. 488, d, f; Ussing,

p. 145, 146.

[5] Rhetor, iii. 4 and 11 ; Poetic, xxi. 12.

[6] Athen., x. 433, c ; 488, f, 591, f.

[7] Hesychius, ἀμφίθετον.

[8] Bekker, Charicles, Tab. 3, 1, 2.

belong to the later style of art, and to the class of moulded vases. Its want of handles was supplied by a boss, called the *omphalos*, in the centre of the cup, having a hollow beneath to admit of the insertion of the thumb or finger to hold it steady,[1] from which circumstance *phialæ* were also called *omphalotoi*, " bossy ; " or *mesomphaloi*, " having omphali in the middle." [2] In metallic work this umbo, or boss, appears to have been often ornamented with the head of the Gorgon. Such bosses were called " balanomphaloi," or glandular omphali, an example of which has been found.

Another variety of this shape was the *phiale lepaste*, respecting which all that can be determined is, that it was larger than the *phiale*.[3] Gerhard recognises it in the large cylix-like vessel of Basilicatan style, ornamented with studs at the sides. The *acatos* appears to have been the name of a *phiale omphalotos*, or " bossy saucer." "Some one," says Antiphanes, " has raised the acatos of Jupiter the Saviour !"[4] The *trieres*, that is the "triremis," or "first rate," was a large *phiale*.[5] The *phthois* was a broad, bossy *phiale*, or saucer,[6] but it is not certainly known whether it was made of fictile ware. The *petachnon*, or " stretcher," was a wide-spreading cup, neither resembling a *phiale* nor a *tryblion*.[7] The *labronia* was a Persian cup, probably introduced into Greece after the conquest of Asia by Alexander, and was made of gold inlaid with

[1] Athenæus, 502, a, b, 501, f.
[2] Thiersch, s. 30.
[3] Ussing, p. 152, 153 ; Athenæus, p. 485, a ; Clement. Pædag., ii. 3 ; Athen., iv. 131, c ; Pollux, vi. 95 ; Pollux, x. 75 ; Hesychius voce. Panofka Rech., iv. 36 ; Gerhard, B. A. B.

[4] Athen., xv. 692, f ; Panofka, iii. 30.
[5] Athenæus, xi. 497, b, 500, e.
[6] Athen., 490, 502, b ; Böckh. Corp. Inscr., No. 146.
[7] Ibid. ; Panofka, iv. 31, iv. 41 ; Athen., iii. 125, f.

gems.[1] *Gualas* was the Doric name of a cup.[2] With these cups may be classed the *ceras*, or "horn," so called from its imitating a natural horn.[3] It was sometimes, though rarely, made of terra-cotta. Some examples, together with a notice of it, will be found under the word *rhyton*. The body was reeded, and the horn terminated in a lion's head, with a small aperture for the liquid to flow through. The upper part was decorated with a subject in bas-relief, and at the side was a small circular handle, by which to hang it on a peg. It was sometimes supported by a collar or anclet, called *periscelis*.

VASES FOR HOLDING FOOD.

We will now proceed to the vases for holding food, of which there were several varieties in fictile ware.

The *canoun*, or "canister," also called *canastron*, *canes*, *canenion*, and *caniskion*, was sometimes made of earthenware.[4] The shape of this vase may be determined from that worn upon the heads of the canephoroi, and consesequently it must have resembled the *calathos*. The *pinax*, or "plate," of which the diminutives are *pinacion*[5] and *pinaciscos*,[6] though not mentioned among fictile ware, was probably the flat plate upon a tall stem or stand,[7] having its interior ornamented with representations of fishes, such as the tunny, or *pelamys*, the cuttle-fish or *sepia*, the maid, or *pristis*, and the *echinos* or sea-egg.

[1] Athen., 484, c.

[2] Athen. 467, c.; Letronne, J. d. S., 614, n. 3.

[3] Ussing, p. 155, 156; Panofka, v. 78.

[4] Homer. Epigr., 14, 3.

[5] Ussing, l. c., 157.

[6] Ussing, l. c., 158, 159.

[7] Panofka, iii. 59.

The *discos*, or "disk," appears to have been a flat, circular plate or *dish*, similar to the Latin *patina*.[1] The *lecanis*, *lecos*, *lecis*, *lecarion*, or *leciscion*, were dishes or tureens for holding food. They have already been described.[2] The *paropsis* was a dish, the shape of which is not known. It does not appear till a late period, and is often mentioned by the Roman authors.[3] The *oxis* was a vinegar cruet of small size, holding a *hemina*, and generally made of earthenware.[4] Aristophanes ridicules Euripides, as advising vinegar to be thrown out of vinegar cups into the eyes of the enemy.[5] *Embaphia* were vases, the shape of which is unknown. The *ereus* was a vase for holding sweets,[6] and the *cypselis*, which perhaps had a cover, was employed for the same purpose.[7] The *cuminodocos*, *cuminodoce*, or *cuminothece*, was a spice-box,[8] consisting of several small cups, called *cadisca*, united on a stand or stem. Several such vases, erroneously supposed to be *cernos*, both of late and early style, are known.[9]

Another kind of dish was the *tryblion*, a name which denoted either a dish or a cup, but is probably more correctly applied to the former.[10] The expression " to make *tryblia* badly " (τὰ τρυβλιὰ κακῶς κεραμεύειν), shows that they were fictile. All that is known about them is, that they were larger than the *oxybapha*, and that figs were eaten out of them. The *oxybaphon*, the " vinegar cruet, "

[1] Pollux, vi. 84 ; Isodorus, xx. 4.
[2] Vide suprá, Ussing, p. 160.
[3] Ibid.
[4] Ussing, p. 166, 167 ; Aristoph. Equit., 1304.; Plut., 812.
[5] Aristoph. Ranæ, 1440.
[6] Pollux, x. 92 ; Athen., ii. 67, d.
[7] Ussing, 167.
[8] Athenæus, vi. 230, d, e.
[9] Pollux, x. 92.
[10] Pollux, vi. 85, x. 86 ; Aristoph. Acharn. 278, Equit., 905 ; Phut., 1108 ; Schol. Aristoph. Aves., 371 ; Athen., iv. 169, e, f, xii. 549, f ; Ussing, p. 161, 2.

or " cup," often served the general purposes of a cup.[1] It
appears to have been small and open.[2] The name was
also applied to dice-boxes. *Oxybapha* were used in the
Sicilian game of cottabus,[3] which was played in many
different ways.

---

[1] Athenæus, xi. 494, b; Pollux, vi.
85.

[2] Athenæus, 494, c; Aristoph. Aves,
361 ; Schol. ad eund.

[3] Bekker, Charicles, i. 476–480; Athenæus, xv. 665, f; 669, h ; Pollux, vi.
109, 111.

CHAPTER X.

It now remains to enumerate the principal localities in
which the existence of potteries is mentioned by ancient
authors, as well as those in which the fictile productions
of the Greeks have been discovered. This enumeration,
however, chiefly relates to painted vases, as it would be
almost impossible to detail all the places where unglazed
terra-cotta objects have been found.

ASIA MINOR.

The most ancient potteries were probably those of Asia
Minor, the scene of the first development of Grecian

civilisation ; but our imperfect information will not permit us to follow the chronological order in describing them. Erythræ, in Ionia, was celebrated for the extreme thinness and lightness of its ware, and two amphoræ, remarkable for these qualities, the rival productions of an Erythræan potter and his pupil, were consecrated in a temple of that city.[1] Certain fragments of vases found near the circular tombs on Mount Sipylus, and in the so-called sepulchre of Tantalus, show that this ancient site had potteries which produced ware of the earliest fawn-coloured style, resembling the oldest Athenian pottery.[2] At Xanthus, in Lycia, some fragments of vases, with black and red figures, were found in the course of the excavations.[3] That potters were distributed all over Asia Minor may be surmised. An inscription at Telmissus records one who had bought a sepulchre for himself, his wife Elpis, his mother-in-law Euphrosyne, for Januarius, and his father-in-law Soterius.[4] He must have been in easy circumstances. At Halicarnassus, during the excavations made at the mausoleum, the fragments of a vase, with brown figures upon a cream-coloured coating, was found. The vases of the oldest style discovered at Smyrna are not of any great size or importance.[5] Lampsacus,[6] and Parium,[7] have also produced vases. The vases found in Ionia have the white grounds of the Athenian style ; but one had the outline of the figure traced with a graver on a pale black ground, and the principal portion retouched in black with a pencil.[8]

[1] Plin., xxxv. 12, s. 46; Brongniart, Traité, p. 578.

[2] Trans. Roy. Soc., Lit., N. S. ii. 258.

[3] Brit. Mus.; Arch. Zeit. iv. 216.

[4] Franz., Corp. Inscr. Græc., iii. n. 4212; Supp., p. 1116; Annali, 1847, p. 116.

[5] Jahn, Vasensammlung, xxvii.

[6] Walpole, Mem. p. 91.

[7] Dubois, Cat. Chois. Gonf. p. 139.

[8] De Witte, Bull., 1832, p. 169.

The determination of the characteristics of the different local styles is a point of the greatest difficulty.[1] The ware of Cnidus was renowned, even till the days of the Roman empire, but its fictile vases were probably not of the painted kind.[2] Their extreme lightness was much praised. In the days of Pliny, Tralles had a great commerce in vases.[3] Pergamus, in Mysia, was also celebrated for its potteries in the time of the same author.[4] A few vases, of very poor style and character, have been found at Tenedos,[5] a site once renowned for its potteries,[6] which lasted till the time of the Roman empire. Dion Chrysostom mentions in one of his discourses the vases which travellers purchased at this place, and which, on account of their extreme lightness, were packed with great care, but when they arrived at their destination were mere potsherds.[7] At the supposed grave of Achilles, in the Troad, *lecythi*, with polychrome figures, have been discovered, resembling in style those found in Athenian sepulchres.[8] And recent excavations made at the sites of New Ilium and Old Dardanus in the Troad, have discovered many small vases, some of the early fawn-coloured style, with figures of birds, a few with yellow grounds of the later style, and many small *lecythi*, with black figures resembling the Athenian.[9] Fragments of vases may

[1] Bull, 1840, p. 54.
[2] Eubulus in Athenæus, i. p. 28, D; Lucian, Lexiphanes, 7 and 11.
[3] Plin. N. H., xxv. c. 12, ad eund.
[4] Ibid., c. 17.
[5] Welcker, Rhein. Mus., 1843, s. 435; Annali, 1843; Chevalier, Voyage dans La Troade, title page, 8vo. Par. 1.
[6] Plutarch de vit. ær. alien Reisk., ix. 291.

[7] Orat., xlii. 5.
[8] Chevalier, Voy. dans La Troade, Reise nach Troas, 8vo, Alten., 1800, Taf. i. s. 213. Choiseul Gouffier, Voy. pitt. ii. 30.
[9] Made in 1855-56, by Mr. Brunton, of the Civil Hospital of Renkioi. These vases have been presented by Lord Panmure to the British Museum.

probably be traced throughout Asia Minor, and all the
principal cities must have had their potteries. Some have
been found at Tarsus.

ISLES.

In the Isles of Greece many vases of different styles
have been discovered. From the oldest times the island of
Samos was renowned for its fictile ware. It is to the potters
of Samos that one of the Homeric hymns is addressed—the
oldest record of the art in literature. It appears from the
life of Homer, attributed to Herodotus, that the poet had
taken refuge in one of the potteries from a storm; and that
upon the morrow the potters, who were preparing to light
their furnaces and bake their earthenware, perceiving
Homer, whose merit was known to them, called upon him
to sing some verses, promising in return to present him
with a vase or any other object they possessed. Homer
accepted their offer, and sung to them the " Lay of the
Furnace," in which the inflated language of epic verse is
applied, in a kind of satiric strain,[1] to the subject of baking
vases :—

" Oh, you who work the clay, and who offer me a
recompense, listen to my strains.

"Athene ! I invoke thee ! Appear, listen, and lend thy
skilful hand to the labour of the furnace, so that the vases
which are about to be drawn, especially those destined for
religious ceremonies, may not turn black ; that all may be
heated to the proper temperature ; and that, fetching a
good price, they may be disposed of in great numbers in

---

[1] Müller, Greek Literature. p. 132.

the markets and streets of our city. Finally, that they may be for you an abundant source of profit, and for me a new occasion to sing to you. But if you should shamelessly deceive me, I invoke against your furnace the most dreadful afflictions—fracture (*syntrips*), contraction (*smaragos*), overheat (*asbestos*), destruction (*sabacte*), and, above all, a destructive force (*omodamos*), which, beyond all others, is the destroyer of your art.

" May the fire devour your building, may all the furnace contains mix and be blended together without power of regaining it, and may the potter shudder at the sight ; may the furnace send forth a sound like the jaws of an angry horse, and may all the vases broken be only a heap of fragments." [1]

The Samian ware was distinguished for its hardness, and was used for surgical operations.[2] The earth was medicinal.[3] A lecythus, or toilet vase, of fine paste, and exquisitely modelled, with representations of the sandals attached to it, with black glaze and red accessories, procured by Mr. Finlay from this island, is now in the collection of the British Museum. Few vases have been found at Samos, notwithstanding the ancient renown of the Samian potteries, and especially of the earth, which, on account of its fineness and red colour, maintained its reputation till the days of the Roman empire.[4] In the days of the Roman empire, Samos supplied dinner services ; and

[1] Miot. Histoire d'Herodote. Paris 1822. Pl. iii. p. 263.

[2] Pliny, N. H. xxxv. 12, 46. Lucilius i. Nonn. 398. 33.

[3] Hesychius Σαμία γῆ Etymol. Magn. p. 229. 21.

[4] Plautus, Capt. 291. Stich. v. 694. Tibullus, ii. 3, 51. Cicero pro Muræna, 36. Pliny, H. N. xxv. 46. Tertullian Apolog. 25. Ausonius Epigram. 8. Isidorus Origin. xx. 4, 3.

certain vases of red ware with ivy-leaves, perhaps belonging to the Roman class, have been found there.[1]

The vases found at Melos are of different ages and
styles ; but this island was more celebrated for its plain
than its painted vases.[2] Those of the earliest period have
a paste of a greyish yellow colour, of a density and hardness resembling common stone ware.[3] Some vases from
this island, formerly belonging to Mr. Burgon, and now in
the British Museum, are of the old fawn-coloured and pale
yellow wares, and have black figures of the most ancient
style. Others exhibit a great advance in the arts, and
are as late as the period of the Roman empire. At the
neighbouring island of Argenticra *Cimolos* painted vases
have been exhumed.[4] The vases found in the sepulchres
of Santorino, the ancient *Thera*, and then an old Phœnician settlement, are all of primitive style, with fawn-
coloured grounds and brown figures.[5] Many vases from
this island are in the Bibliothèque Impériale, at Paris.
Others, in the Museum at Sèvres, were taken out of tombs
excavated in the solid limestone, the principal formation
of the island. These tombs have been covered, at a very
remote period, to the depth of 15 to 20 *mètres* by a
volcanic eruption of tufo, and are of the most remote
antiquity.[6] Some *pithoi* from this island are of huge size.[7]
Several vases which have been found in Crete, are said to
resemble those of Campania.[8] Those of the sepulchres of

[1] Bull, 1830, p. 226.
[2] Welcker, Rhein. Mus., 8vo, Franck.
1843, s. 435, 1823, p. 239.
[3] Brongniart, Traité, i. 577; Mus. Cer.,
Pl. xiii. fig 1, 2, 5, 6, 7, 10, 14.
[4] Ross, Insel. iii. 65.
[5] Brongniart, Traité, i. 577 ; Lenormant, Introd. á l' Étude, xxiii.
[6] Brongniart, Traité, i. p. 577-8 ; Mus.
Cer., xiii. 4, 13, 15, 16.
[7] Arch. Zeit. xii. 61, 62; Ross. Insel.
i. 66, 68 ; iii. 27.
[8] Brongniart, Traité, i. p. 578.

Kalymno, the ancient *Calymna*, a little isle of the Sporades, were of a fine clay, covered, like those of Athens and Vulci, with a fine lustrous glaze, but not ornamented with subjects.[1]   Cos, which was celebrated for its culinary vessels and for its amphoræ, which were considered very beautiful, and were exported to Egypt, has contributed cups of the oldest style to collections of vases.[2]   At Mytilene and Lesbos, the fragments of vases hitherto discovered have either black or red figures, resembling in their style those found in the graves of Athens.[3]   The vases of Rhodes have black figures on red grounds of the free and careless style of Greece.   In Cyprus the vases as yet discovered resemble in style and ware those of Thera.[4] At Piscopia, *Telos*, another of the small isles, a vase, with black figures on a yellow ground of bad drawing, has also been discovered.[5]   At Chiliodromia, one of the small isles of the Sporades, several vases of coarse and late style, and principally of the Roman period, have been found. They are chiefly remarkable for the peculiar manner in which they were ranged round the skeletons of the dead.[6]

Another site of the old insular potteries was the island of Ægina,[7] celebrated at an early period for the excellence it attained in the arts, and especially for its sculptures. Although Ægina chiefly imported Athenian ware, yet that it also manufactured pottery appears from an anonymous writer of comedy, calling it " the Rocky echo—the vendor

[1] Archaol. Zeit. 1848, 278.

[2] Herodot., iii. 6.

[3] Mr. Newton, H. M. Vice-Consul, has found here many fragments of painted vases.

[4] Ross. Insel. iv. 175, 194, 201, 206.

[5] Ross. Insel. iv. 44.

[6] Fiedler, Reise durch alle Theile des Königr. Griechland, Leips., 1841; Brongniart, Traité, Pl. ii. fig. 1, i. p. 581.

[7] Bull, 1829, p. 113, and fol. ; Paus, x. 17, 6.

of pots."[1] The few vases found there are remarkable for
their lightness, being made of a superficial soil, for the
most part of a siliceous base of infusorial carapaces.
They are principally *lecythi*.[2] A *cylix* with black figures
has, however, been found, with the subject of Heracles
strangling the Nemean lion, and a Bacchanalian dance,
with the names of Nicaulos, Charidemus, Empedocrates,
and an inscription,[3] probably alluding to the capture of
Midas, or the appearance of Pan to the *hemerodromos*, or
courier, Philippos. It also bears the name of the maker,
Ergotimus. Some fine *lecythi*, with white grounds and
figures, painted in the polychrome style, have been found
at Ægina. At Colouri, *Salamis*, a polychrome vase of
fine style ;[4] and at Caristo, *Carystus*, in Euboea,[5] a vase
with black figures on a white ground, accompanied by an
inscription.

GREECE.

Passing hence to the continent of Greece, the first place
to be considered is *Athens*, the pottery of which was, of
course, the most highly renowned of the ancient fabrics.[6]
The city was celebrated for its cups,[7] which, however,

[1] Meineke. Frag. Com. gr. 130. B.;
Hesych. voce.'Ηχώ. Photius and Poll.
vi. 197.

[2] Brongniart Mus. Cer. Pl. xiii. fig. 11.
Traité, p. 576.

[3] For vases found at Ægina Cf. Gerhard, Bulletino, 1829, p. 118. Wagner,
Bericht ueber die eginetischen Bildwerke, s. 80. Wolf, Bull, 1829, p. 122.
Gerhard, Bull, 1829, p. 122. Ross, Bull,
1841, p. 83. Bull, 1833, p. 27.

[4] Rochette, Peint. ant. taf. 8—11.

[5] From the Atticism of this inscription

Kramer (ueber den styl. s. 173.) is of
opinion, that the vase was made at
Athens.

[6] Rochette, Lettre a M. Schorn, 6.
Cf. Matro Parodæus. apud Athen,
iv. p. 136. f. Αττικῷ ἐν κεραμῶ πέττων
τρεῖς καὶ δεκὰ μῆνας.

[7] 'Επίσημοι κύλικες (κεράμεα ποτήρια)
αἱ τε Αργεῖαι καὶ αἱ 'Αττίκαι. Athenæus
Lib. xi. p. 480 c. Jacob ad Anth. Græc.
I. p. 2. p. 141. Eratosthenes, apud Macrob. Saturn. v. 21. Pindar. Fr. 89.
à Böckh. Athenæus xi. p. 480, C.

were rivalled by those of Argos; for its wine casks or
amphoræ,[1] its bottles, or lagænæ,[2] and its ware in general.[3]
Claiming, as it did, the honour of having invented the
potter's wheel, the manufacture was highly esteemed ; and
in very early days the Athenians exported their wares to
Ægina and the neighbouring isles. At Athens there
were two pottery quarters, or ceramici, one within, the
other, without the walls. Both seem to have had a bad
reputation from their being frequented by hetairæ.[4] The
tombs of Athens have yielded specimens of painted and
glazed ware of all kinds and periods. These have passed
into the different European collections ; and the British
Museum[5] has been particularly enriched by them, from
having obtained the collections of Lord Elgin and
Mr. Burgon. The earliest Athenian vases, with brass
figures on a fawn-coloured ground,[6] have been already
described.

Many remarkable examples of glazed ware have been
found in the tombs of Athens, and among them the sarcophagus of glazed ware found by Stackelberg in 1813, which
contained the skeleton of a child, surrounded with terra-cotta
figures, *lecythi*, and other small vases.[7] It was in a grave
beyond the Acharnian gate, and its contents subsequently

[1] Οἱ κεραμοι, Aristoph. Acarn, 910,
Corsini Fasti, Attici., Tom. ii. p. 236-7.
Diss. xii.
[2] Κεκροπὶς λάγυνε. Posidippus, Epist.
xi.
[3] Ἀττικὰ σκεύη. Pindar, p. 614.
Athenæus, xi. p. 484, f. Simonides,
Anal i. p. 72, 69, Ed. Jacobs. Athens,
had also a large trade in domestic vessels. Aristophanes, Lysistr. 557.
[4] Schol. Plat. Parmenides, Bekker,
p. 17, No. 127.

[5] For the vases discovered at Athens,
cf. Millingen, Anc. Uned. Mon., p. 1.
Stackelberg, die Graeber der Hellenen.
Panofka, Cabinet Pourtalès. Creuzer, ein
alt Athensches gefass. Leipz. and Darm.
Gerhard Ann. ix. 135. Brondstedt,
Memoir Tran. R. S. Lit. II. pt. 1. Bull.
1831, p. 95.
[6] No. 2800 and foll. Graeber der
Hellenen, s. 47. Taf. ix.
[7] Ibid., s. 42. Taf. viii.

passed with Mr. Burgon's collection into the stores of the
British Museum. The early sepulchres have also yielded
many vases of the style called Doric, with yellow grounds.[1]
Of vases with black figures the predominant form discovered is the *lecythus*, especially *lecythi* of small size, ornamented with subjects, of which the most favourite was the
return of Proserpine to earth ; but there are several with
subjects taken from the Gigantomachia, the Heracleid, the
War of Troy, and from Attic myths, as Boreas and Oreithyia, and the Theseid. Many, as might be expected, are
ornamented with scenes from the Gymnasium.[2] Of other
vases of this style, the most remarkable are that with the
subject of the Trojan women lamenting either Troilos or
Hector,[3] and a tripod vase.[4] But all these yield in
interest to the Panathenaic amphora, or Vas Burgonianum,
found ouside the Acharnian gate at Athens, in the year
1813. It is of a pale salmon-coloured clay, on which the
figures are painted in a blackish-brown colour, while the
parts not painted are of a pale black leaden glaze. The
subject represents, on one side, Pallas Athene, standing
between two columns of the Palæstra, surmounted by
cocks, the birds sacred to Hermes and the Games. She is
dressed in a talaric tunic, and armed with her ægis and
shield, the device, or *episemon*, on which is a dolphin ; in
her other hand she holds her lance. Inscribed on the
vase is a perpendicular line of Greek, reading from right to
left, TON : AΘENEΘEN : AΘΛON : EMI : "I am a prize

---

[1] One with a giant is figured in Stackelberg, Taf. 15.

[2] Cf Stackelberg, Die. Graeber., Taf.
10-16. Gerherd, Berlins Ant. Bild.

s. 230, 709 ; No. 674, 711, 716, s.
231, 717.

[3] Mon. iii. 60.

[4] Stackelberg, Ibid. Taf. 15.

from Athens." On the other side is a man driving the
biga, or *synoris*, and urging the horses with a goad, while
jingling bells are attached to their necks. There can
be no doubt bnt that this is one of the very amphoræ
described by Pindar, when he sings of the Theiæus, son
of Ulias of Argos, in the passage before cited. As a
prelude to future victories, " sacred songs twice proclaimed
him victor in the sacred festivals of the Athenians, and
the fruit of the olive tree came over in the splendid
vessels of earth burnt in fire for the manly people of Juno."
It held the holy oil from the Olive Grove of the Moiræ, or
Fates. When discovered, it was filled, as already men-
ioned, with the burnt ashes of its former owner, and also
with several small vases, which probably held the oil,
milk, and other substances poured upon the pyre. Its
age is at least as early as the sixth century B. C.[1]

The Athenian vases of this style differ considerably
from those found at Vulci, the drawing of the figures
being much more free and careless, and the incised lines
bolder and less rigid.[2] A few vases, with the white coating
and black figures, have also been discovered at Athens,
and a few, with red figures of the hard style ; the best
much resembling in their varnish and treatment the vases
of Nola ; but they are exquisitely fine and light, and certainly equal to any found in Italy. Many of the Athenian
vases are of the later period of the art, and resemble those
found in Apulia and St. Agata dei Goti ; among which

[1] Brondsted on the Panathenaic vases.
Trans. R. Soc. Lit. ii. p. 112; Böckh,
Bullet, 1832, p. 91; Müller, Comment,
S. R. Scient. Gott. t. vii. Class. Hist. p.
111 ; Bullet, Inst., 1832, 98 ; Welcker

Rheinische Museum for Philologie
Bd., i. 1833, s. 301, 346; Pindar, Nem.
x. 33, 36.
[2] Gerhard, Berl. Ant. Bild., s. 237,
No. 804.

some *pyxides*, or ladies' toilet boxes, are distinct from any yet discovered even in Southern Italy, being ornamented with polychrome figures, in red, white, and blue colours. Some of the vases found here are of the florid style of Ruvo; among which may be cited an allegorical vase, with the subject of Aphrodite and Peitho plaiting a basket, and the three graces, Paidia, "instruction;" Eunomia, "discipline;" and Cleopatra, "national glory."[1] There have also been discovered vases with opaque red and white figures, painted on a ground of black varnish. Among these is a charming little toy jug, on which is depicted a boy crawling to a low seat, on which is an apple. This specimen is unrivalled for its exquisite varnish and treatment.[2] Another vase, also ornamented with gilding, has a representation of Niké in a quadriga of winged horses, between Ploutos, "Wealth," and Chrysos, or "gold."[3] To this class must also be referred an exquisite little vase, in the shape of an astragalos, or knuckle-bone, ornamented with the subject of Pentheus and the Mænads;[4] a *cantharis*, a *thermopotis*, *rhyta*,[5] *cylices*, *pyxides*,[6] *calpides*, and *pelicæ*.[7] Some alabastra, with linear figures, in black upon a white ground, have also been found at Athens, as well as numerous *lecythi*, with polychromatic paintings on a white ground.[8] Their subjects are Orestes, Electra, and Pylades at the tomb of Agamemnon. Many Athenian vases are unadorned with figures, and many painted black, although

[1] Stackelberg xxix. It was found at the Museum.
[2] Ibid. Taf., xvii.
[3] Ibid. xvii.
[4] Ibid. Taf., xxiii.
[5] Ibid. xxiv.
[6] Ibid. xxiii. xxiv. xxvi. xxvii. xxviii.
[7] Ibid. Taf., xx. xxi. xxii.
[8] Ibid. xliv. xlv. xlvi. xlviii.

ATHENIAN LECYTHUS, ELECTRA AT THE TOMB OF AGAMEMNON.

[Vol. II., p. 124.

very elegant in shape and finish. The accounts of the rivalry in trade between Athens and Ægina and Argos,[1] and the fact of these vases being transportea to Dicæopolis,[2] and carried by Phœnician ships to Æthiopia,[3] show the extent of the Athenian trade in pottery.

In the other parts of the continent of Greece, the vases found are not very numerous. Some, however, with both black and red figures upon a black ground, as well as some with opaque white figures of the very latest style of art, have been discovered in the district of Solygia ;[4] but they are of rare occurrence. Nor has the "hollow Lacedæmon," once renowned in this branch of manufacture for dark brown cups, called *cothons*, with recurved lips, adapted for keeping back the mud of the foul water, which her valiant soldiery drank upon their marches, enriched our stores of Greek fictile productions.[5] Sicyon has only yielded a *cylix* of early Doric style. Of the potteries of *Argolis*, only a few fragments ploughed up at the foot of the supposed tomb of Agamemnon at Mycenæ, of the early fawn-coloured style, with mæander ornaments, have been discovered.[6] A vase in the Munich collection is from Tenea.[7] Near Sinano, the ancient *Megalopolis*, in Arcadia, a *lecythus*, with black figures, has been found.[8]

Some fragments have been discovered at Delphi,[9] and a considerable number of vases at Corinth, already celebrated for its earthen ware in the days of Cæsar, when

[1] Herod. v. 88. Athenæus, xi. p. 502. C.; Pollux. vi. 100.
[2] Aristophanes. Acharn. 902.
[3] Scylax. p. 54, H.
[4] See Arch. Zeit. Bull. 1830.
[5] Brongniart, Traité, p. 576. Pl. ii. fig. 1. Pl. xxxiii. 1. Plutarchus, vit.

Lycurg. Vol. i. p. 84.
[6] Dodwell Classical Tour, ii. 237.
[7] Abeken, Mittel-Italien, p. 298.
[8] Berl. Ant. Bild. 1887.
[9] Ross, Morgenblatt, 1835, 698. De Witte, Annali, xiii. p. 10.

the new Colonia Julia, as it was designated, ransacked the sepulchres for the vases, which were the admiration of the rich nobility of Rome.[1] The most remarkable ones of this site are of the old style called Doric, with black figures on cream-coloured grounds, many of which were probably made in the days of Demaratus, when Cypselus expelled the Bacchiads. The principal one is that found by Dodwell,[2] and generally called the Dodwell Vase, with a subject representing the boar hunt of Agamemnon.

The collection of Mr. Burgon also contained specimens of vases from Corinth, some with black figures upon a red ground, consisting of *pyxides, œnochoë,* and tripods with subjects of little interest ; the best specimen had a representation of a Centaur bearing off a female. Some years ago a great number of vases in very indifferent condition, having suffered much from the percolation of water through the earth, were found by boring into tombs many feet below the surface at the isthmus, or Hexamili. Most of them have passed into the possession of the Society of Arts. Lately, some *cylices,* chiefly of the early shapes, with tall stems and small figures of bulls, dancing men, ornaments, flowers, and illegible inscriptions have been found there. The discovery of a cup with the name of the maker Tleson, shows that Corinth was probably the place whence these vases were exported to Italy.[3]

Corinth, like Athens, boasted the invention of pottery,[4]

---

[1] Strabo, l. c. Zumpt, Arch. Zeit. 1846, p. 309. Osan, Zusatz. ueber Ursprung, p. 63, 85., considers the Nekrokorinthia to be bas-reliefs.

[2] Dodwell, ii. p. 197, 201.

[3] Abeken, Mittel-Italien, p. 298. Ross, Anaphe; Thiersch, Abhandl. d. Munch.

Akad. 1838. ii. 2. p. 109., contending for the so-called Egyptian style being Corinthian.

[4] Barth, Corinth, commerc. et mercat. Hist. p. 16; R. Rochette, Ann. xix. p. 237.

CANTHARUS, FROM MELOS. BACCHANTE.

and of the wheel. As the artists Eucheir and Eugrammus accompanied Demaratus from Corinth to Italy, it has been supposed that the Corinthians instructed the Etruscans in the art of making fine vases. Thericles was the most renowned of the Corinthian potters. His cups; under the name of "Thericleans," obtained a celebrity almost universal. It was here that in the time of Julius Cæsar, the colony sent here found ancient painted vases, and other remains, which excited as much interest then at Rome [1] as the discoveries at Vulci did a quarter of a century ago in Paris and London.

Vases have also been found at Patras, *Patræ*, and a small bottle, of a fine réd paste, having on it a winged and bearded head in a Phrygian mitre, is said to have been discovered there.[2] It is well known that *Megara* was anciently renowned for its vases.[3] They were chiefly of a large size and of a soft paste, as the pantomimes used to break them with their foreheads.[4] Some vases have been found on its site.[5] Laconia gave its name to a kind of *cylix*,[6] and its vases when pounded and mixed with pitch and wine, were supposed to make hens lay large eggs.[7]

From the sepulchres of Aulis, which is also mentioned by Pliny with Tenedos,[8] has been disinterred a vase with red figures, representing the Prometheus Bound of Æschylus, at the moment when the wandering Io enters on the stage.[9]

[1] Strabo, viii. 381, f.
[2] Gerhard, Annali, ix. 139.
[3] Steph. Byz. Μέγαρα.
[4] Synesius, Exc. Calv. 44. p. 77. C.
[5] Dodwell, Tour, ii. 180.
[6] Athen. xi. p. 484. F.
[7] Geoponica, xiv. 11.
[8] Plut. de vit. ær. al. 828.
[9] Millingen, Anc. Uned. Mon., Pl. ii.

Passing westward, some vases of early style with brown
figures on a yellow ground were found in the cemetery at
Castrades in Corfû, or Corcyra,[1] where stood the sepulchres
of Menecrates and Tlasias, besides numerous terra-cotta
amphoræ for holding wines of the Hadriatic,[2] which have
been already mentioned.[3]

ITALY.

The vases found in Greece are both small in size and
few in number, when compared with those discovered in
the ancient cemeteries, and on the sites of the old cities
of Italy. These are indeed so numerous, that the fictile
art of antiquity might be traced from the vases of Italy
alone. MM. Lenormant and De Witte,[4] in their work on
the subject, divide these vases into three great classes :
  I. The first division comprises those found in the south
of the peninsula, the ancient Magna Græcia, where the
cities founded upon the coast by the Greeks, infused a
certain degree of civilisation into the interior. Thus at
Locri and Tarentum,[5] the potter's art is supposed to
have been first established, and to have influenced the
semi-barbarous population of Apulia and Lucania. The
vases of these cities are distinguished for their beauty and
art, and are far superior to the specimens discovered in
the southern and eastern districts of the kingdom of
Naples, in the mountainous regions of the Basilicata, and
the Mediterranean cantons of Puglia. Of the rest of this

[1] Arch. Zeit. 1846, s. 377. For the
amphoræ, see Pseudo-Arist., Mirab.
auscult. Ed. Beckman, no. cxi.
[2] Eubulus, Atheneo, i. 28 e.
[3] Jahn. l. c. s. 34. Anth. Pal. ix.
232, 257.
[4] Élite, Introd. xxv.
[5] Gerhard, Bull. 1829, 167.

territory, the finest specimens have been found in the necropolis of Canosa, the ancient Canusium, and of Ruvo, the ancient Rubi.

II. The second class [1] embraces the vases of Campania,[2] which were discovered in three of the cities of its coast, viz., Cumæ,[3] Pæstum,[4] and Surrentum,[5] and in others in the interior. Those of the first-mentioned city are supposed from their style to have been fabricated after its subjection by the Samnites, as also were those of Nola at their finest period. The rest of the vases of Campania, as those of Capua, Avella, and St. Agata dei Goti, are far inferior to the preceding in art and fabric. As all these cities fell with the Samnite league in B. C. 272, it is probable that their potteries then ceased to exist.

III. The third, and last class,[6] are the vases discovered in Etruria, which are as abundant as that of the south of Italy. They are found in every Etruscan city of importance, from Hadria,[7] at the mouth of the Eridanus or Po, to the very gates of Rome itself.[8] These vases are, in general, of older style than those of Southern Italy. The most ancient are discovered in the sepulchres of Cære, or of Agylla, its port; in those of Tarquinii, and in the numerous sepulchres of Vulci, which have yielded an immense number of vases.

In describing these remains, the most convenient method

[1] Berl. Ant. Bildw. s. 138.
[2] Élite Introd. xxvi.
[3] Gerhard, Bull. 1829. p. 163; Schulz, Bull. 1842. 8.
[4] Gerhard, Bull, 1829, p. 163. Gerhard u. Panofka, Neapels Ant. Bildw. s. 353, no. 60, 5, 308. no. 404.
[5] Gerhard, Bull. 1829. p. 164; Schulz,

Bull. 1842, 10.
[6] Élite Introd. xxvi.
[7] Gerhard, Bull. 1832. pp. 90, 205. Bull. 1834, p. 134; R. Rochette Anal. vi. 293; Gori. Mus. Etr. tab. ii. clxxxviii.
[8] Winckelmann, Cat. Pierries Gravées, p. 215. Lanzi., Vas. Dip. 42.

will be to follow the geographical distribution of the potteries from north to south, and, accordingly, to commence
with those of Hadria, and which, at the time of Pliny,
still continued to manufacture drinking cups of the finest
quality. Painted vases have also been found in its tombs.
According to Micali,[1] the vases discovered at Hadria
differ entirely from the fabric of those found in Puglia,
the Basilicata, and at Nola. They have been exhumed
there as early as the sixteenth century;[2] and in later
excavations made at the mouth of the Po, and in some
others undertaken by the Austrian government, fragments
of Greek fictile vases were found at some depth below the
Roman remains. Of these, Micali[3] has engraved a selection, consisting of a fragment of an amphora, with the
subject of Hephaistos holding a hatchet; a vase of large
size, with part of a chariot; a female named ΚΑΛΙΟΠΑ,[4]
and a man named ΣΙΚΩΝ (Sikon); and three fragments of
cups, with the subjects of a satyr, a lyrist, and a man at a
symposium. It has been observed that, in Italy, the old
vases with black figures are rare in graves of the earliest
style, and that the greatest number of vases come from
the more recent tombs[5] of the other northern cities of Italy.
Mutina, or the modern *Modena*, in Gallia Cisalpina, was
celebrated in the days of Pliny for its drinking cups. Few
painted vases, however, have been found there, but only
some of a glazed red ware, resembling the ware of Arretium, an observation which also applies to the city of

[1] Mon. Inedit., p. 279, and foll.; Bull., 1834, p. 134.
[2] Bocchi, Dissert. dell 'Acad. di Cortona, tom. iii. p. 80, tav. viii. ix.; Mus. Etrusc. tav. 188.
[3] l. c. tav. xlv.
[4] Supposed to refer to the horses of Rhesus. See Panofka, Arch. Zeit. 1852, 481.
[5] Abeken, Mittel-Italien, s. 298.

Asti.[1] Painted vases have, however, been found in this part of Italy, some with red figures, of a style like the Campanian, having been exhumed at Pollentia,[2] which, like *Modena* and *Asti,* was celebrated in the time of Pliny[3] for its cups ; and others at Gavolda,[4] on the left bank of the Mincio, near its confluence with the Po. One, discovered near *Mantua,* had the subject of Perseus holding the Gorgon's head, and Andromeda.[5]

At *Bologna,* the ancient Bononia, in the Bolognese legation, vases, even with black figures, have been formerly discovered.[6]

ETRURIA.

Proceeding to the site of Etruria, so prolific in specimens of the fictile art, we find that many vases of the oldest style have been discovered at Valore, in the vicinity of Viterbo,[7] consisting of Archaic amphoræ with black figures, and cups with red figures ; amongst which was one made by the potter Euphronios.[8] From the sepulchres of Castel d'Asso, some ancient amphoræ and fragments of cups, with red figures, have been obtained.

Corneto, the celebrated town of Tarquinii, the birthplace of the Tarquins, and the spot to which the Corinthian Demaratus fled, taking with him the artists Eucheir and Eugrammus,[9] yielded from its sepulchres a

[1] Nat. Hist., xxxv. c. 46., ad. fin.; Bull., 1837, p. 88—97.

[2] Brongniart, Traité, i. p. 583 ; Bull., 1830, p. 21.

[3] N. H. xxxv. c. 46.

[4] Bull., 1847, p. 17.

[5] Bull., 1838, p. 62.

[6] Lanzi, ant. vas. dipint. p. 25.

[7] Also coarse vases, B. 1829, p. 201.

[8] Gerhard, Rapporto Volcente, p. 116, note 8; Bulletino, 1830, p. 233—243, 1832, p. 2, 1839, p. 199 ; Gerhard, B. A. B., s. 141, n. 5, no. 680 ; Micali, Storia, tav. xcii. xciii ; Panofka, Mus. Bart., p. 69.

[9] Livy, i. dec. 34 ; Bull., 1831, p. 5, 1832, p. 2, 3.

great quantity of the black Etruscan ware, with embossed figures.[1] Of the painted vases,[2] comparatively few have been found on this site ; but among them are a *lecythus* of the most Archaic style, resembling the vases of Corinth, or those called Doric.[3] Alabastra of this style were more frequently found here than at Vulci.[4] Archæological excavations were made on this site in 1825 by Lord Kinneir, and in 1827 by Chev. Kestner and M. Stackelberg.[5] The vases from this spot, are chiefly small amphoræ, of medium size, and good Archaic style, but for the most part either of ordinary glaze, or unglazed. One of the largest vases found in Etruria, however, came from this site ; and on fragments of cups found here are the names of the artists Amasis and Briaxides.[6]

This site has principally afforded vases of the solid black or Etruscan ware,[7] although a few painted ones have been disinterred from its sepulchres, with black figures and Athenian subjects.[8] Some came from Monte Quagliere.[9]

At *Toscanella* (Tuscania), only a few vases, and those generally with black figures, and of careless drawing, have been discovered.

At *Chiusi*, the Etruscan Camars and Latin Clusium, fragments of painted cups, with the names of the makers,

[1] Annali, 1829, p. 95, 109.

[2] Hyperb. Rom. Stud. I. 89 ; Rapp. Volc. note 3.

[3] Ibid., Bullet., 1829, p. 176,197,1830, p. 197, 138.

[4] Gerhard, Rapp. Volc. p. 121. n. 35.

[5] Bull., 1829, p. 2.

[6] Gerhard, Rapporto Volcente, p.

115, n. 3 ; Kuntsblatt, 1823, p. 205,1825, p. 199 ; Annali, 1829, p. 120; Bulletino, 1829, p. 198; Bull., 1830, p. 242,1831, p. 4.

[7] Bull, 1830, 202, 1831, 3 ; 1833, p. 80.

[8] Bull., 1829, p. 5.

[9] Bull., 1829, p. 10.

Panthæos and Hiero, and the youths Cherilos and Nicostratus, have been found.[1] Latterly however, the excavations of M. Francois have discovered the magnificent crater of the Florence Museum, representing the subjects of the Achilleis.

Many vases of all the principal styles have been disinterred at this site ; those with black figures resemble, in general tone of glaze and style, those of Vulci, and are of the usual forms. One of them has the name of the potter Anakles. Vases with red figures, both of the strong and fine styles, abound here ; the most remarkable of which are the cups, which have certain local peculiarities, and some vases of local manufacture have also been met with in the excavations.[2]

Many come from the sepulchres of the Val di Chiana.[3]

Vases of the moulded black ware have been found at *Sarteano*,[4] at Castiglione del Trinoro, in the vicinity, and at Chianciano, to the number of several thousands in all, but no painted vases.

The ware of *Orbetello* is of a pale dull clay, the glaze of a dull leaden hue, like that of the worst of the Apulian and Southern Italian vases ; the forms are rude and inelegant, and the subjects, representing satyrs and Bacchantes, and youths, are coarse and ill drawn. Vases, with subjects of the earliest Archaic style, together with the usual Etruscan black ware, have been

---

[1] Gerhard, Rapporto Volcente, s. 116, No. 5 ; Bulletino, 1830, p. 244 ; Mus. Etr. Chius. tav. xxv. 46 ; Gerhard, B. A. B., 390, 427 ; B., 1839, p. 49 ; 1840, p. 150 ; 1836, p. 35 ; 1838, p. 82, 74 ; 1831, p. 100 ; Bull., 1836, p. 25.

[2] Jahn, Vasensammlung, lxxix.-lxxxii ; Inghirami Etrusco Museo chiusino 2 ed. 4to. Fies. 1832.

[3] Bull., 1841, p. 4, 1835, p. 128.

[4] Dennis, Etruria, i. p. 464.

discovered at *Perugia*[1] or Perusia, and others at *Roselle* or Rusellæ.

The painted vases discovered in the sepulchres of *Volterra*, Volaterræ, are much inferior to those of Vulci, Tarquinii, and Chiusi. Their clay is coarse, their glaze neither lustrous nor durable.[2] Their subjects are principally large female heads, in yellow, upon a black ground, like those of the Basilicata. They betray a comparatively recent origin ; and although some fine vases are said to have been found there, none of an early style have been discovered.[3] Some contained the ashes of the dead.[4]

Similar vases have been found in *Siena*, or Sena.[5] And at *Pisa*, in the beginning of the present century, a potter's establishment was discovered. A fine hydria from this find is figured by Inghirami. At a later period vases with red figures, both of the strong and fine style, have been discovered here.[6]

The excavations in the ancient site of *Bomarzo* have produced some Archaic amphoræ, with black figures, of perfect style, and a few elegant cups. Some of the vases have red figures, and the flesh of the females is white.[7] The hydria, or water jar, has not been discovered there. The glaze is bad, and the subjects common. The place where the vases have been principally found is at Pianmiano, the supposed Mæonia of the Italian archæologists.[8]

[1] Dennis, Etr. i. p. 425; Bulletino, 1829, p. 14; Micali, Storia d'Italia, lxxiv. lxxvi. lxxviii. 2, lxxix. 1 ; xxiii. 9; Berlins Antiken Bildwerke, s. 172 and foll., No. 390, 426.

[2] Dennis, Etruria, ii. p. 203 ; Bull., 1830, p. 236.

[3] Micali, Mon. Ined., p. 216.

[4] Bull., 1829, p. 203.

[5] Lanzi, Vasi, p. 24.

[6] Jahn, Vasensammlung, lxxxiii.

[7] Gerhard, RapportoVolcente, p.116; Bull., 1830, p. 233, 1831, p. 7 ; Gerhard, 1834, p. 50 ; B. A. B., s. 141, n. 8.

[8] Bull., 1830, p. 233.

The vases found at *Orvieto* are a *cylix*, with red, and a *crater*, with black figures ;[1] one bearing the name of a youth, Hiketas, or Niketas, the other having Bacchanalian subjects.[2] Vases of the solid black Etruscan ware are also found on this site.

Veii, or *Isola Farnese*, is more celebrated for its black, or Etruscan ware, than for its vases of Greek style. Several painted vases have, however, been found at this place. Some of the Veian sepulchres consisted of a large chamber, containing sculptured couches, on which the dead were deposited ; others were mere niches cut out of the tufo, and were capable of containing one vase, and a small covered urn of terra-cotta, in which the ashes of the dead were deposited. The black vases of larger size were found placed round the body of the deceased, while those of more elegant shape were in the niches, amidst the ashes of the dead and the gold ornaments.[3] The vases were of the archaic style, with brown figures upon a yellow ground, representing two men fighting for a tripod, stags, panthers, and hind, a gryphon and crow, a lion swallowing Pegasus, a man and an androsphinx,[4] rows of animals, and a winged figure between two gryphons. Several vases were of the finished style, with black figures, consisting of craters, *celebe*, with the representation of a mænad and satyr.[5] Heos pursuing Cephalus and Deinomachus, and of amphoræ, with the Centauromachia ; the first labour of

[1] Bull., 1831, p. 23, 35, 57 ; Cf. p. 7.
[2] Bull., 1833, p. 9.
[3] A particular description of the sepulchres of Veii is given by S. Campanari, Descrizione dei Vasi rinvenuti nei sepolchri dell' antica Veii, and in the Descrizione dei Vasi rinvenuti nelle es-

cavazione fatte nell' isola Farnese, fo. Roma, 1838, 112; Bull., 1840, p. 12, Canina, Vej. fo. Rom. 1847, Etr. Marit. I. p. 123. tav. 34-38.
[4] Ibid., tav. i. p. 13-15.
[5] Ibid., pp. 18-21.

Hercules, or the conquest of the Nemæan lion ; Tyndareus and the Dioscuri ; the car of Heos ; Achilles arming in the presence of Thetis. The vases of the finished style, with red figures, consist of the shape called *stamnos*, having the subject of Jupiter, Ganymede, and Dardanus , the departure of Triptolemos ; the Dionysiac thiasos, citharædi, and athletes. Some cups, with subjects derived from the Dionysiac thiasos and gymnastic exercises ; a *scyphos panathenaicus*, with the owl and laurel branch ; and a *rhyton*, with a scene taken from a triclinium.[1]

The vases found in the very ancient tunnelled tombs of *Cervetri* or Cære [2] are of the oldest style. One from Civita Vecchia, now in the British Museum, has bands of animals, centaurs, and other figures, drawn in maroon, on a white coating, in a style of art scarcely a degree advanced beyond that of the pale fawn-coloured ware of *Athens*.[3]

The most remarkable vases of this locality are certain ones of anomalous shapes, with two or more handles— the very oldest example of the Archaic Greek ; the figures of a dark colour, on a pale red or yellow back-ground, originally traced out in a white outline, and not relieved by any incised lines ; the subject fish, and large ornaments. These vases appear contemporary with certain others, on which are painted deer and animals, in a white tempera outline, sometimes stippled.[4]

Abundance of vases of the early Phœnician or Corinthian styles, especially large craters, with stands, called by some *holmoi*, have, besides the usual friezes of animals, such subjects as the hunt of the Calydonian boar,[5] the mono-

---

[1] Ibid. Cf. for the shapes, tav. A, B.
[2] Bull, 1839, p. 20.
[3] Brit. Mus.
[4] Campana collection at Rome.
[5] Mus. Greg., ii. xc.

machia of Memnon and Achilles,[1] and the rescue of the corpse of the last-mentioned hero[2] from the Trojans. Other vases, such as an œnochoe of the Gregorian Museum, are of the same style of art, but tending towards the rigid class of black figures, and representing Ajax, Hector, and Æneas.[3] Vases of the hard style of black figures also occur, as an *olpe*, with the subject of the shade of Achilles,[4] and among those with red figures is a remarkable *stamnos*, in which is represented the contest of Hercules and the Acheloos.[5] A *cylix*, with black figures, discovered at this place, had the name of the potter Charitæus.[6] Many vases of Nicosthenes were also found there.[7] Some have incised Etruscan inscriptions.[8]

Other vases bore the names of the potters and artists— Pamphæos, Epictetus, and Euphronius. The sepulchres of Cære have produced some vases of the fine style, distinguished by a deep black and lustrous glaze, distinct in tone from those of Nola, and some few of later style.

But the discoveries made at all the other Etruscan sites combined are surpassed, both in number and interest, by those at *Vulci* (which name is universally agreed to be the ancient designation of the site of the *Ponte della Badia*), and, in its vicinity, the supposed Necropolis. It is to the elaborate report of M. Gerhard[9] that we owe an

[1] Mon., ii. 38; Annali, 1836, pp. 310, 311.

[2] Mon., i. 51; Annali, 1836, pp. 306–310.

[3] Mus. Greg., ii. 1, 3.

[4] Bull., 1830, p. 243.

[5] Roy. Soc. Lit., New Series, ii. p. 100; Annali, 1837, p. 183.

[6] Visconti, Ant. Mon. Scop., pl. 9; Canina, Cere Antica, pp. 73,78; Abeken,

Mittel-Italien, p. 299.

[7] Bull., 1830, p. 124, 1832, p. 2, 1834, p. 49, 1839, pp. 20, 21.

[8] As that with Larthia, Bull., 1836, p. 61; Bull., 1839, 21. For Cervetri Vases, see Bull., 1832, p. 3.

[9] Called the Rapporto Volcente, and published in the Annali, 1839; see also Bull., 1830, p. 4, 1832, pp. 1–3–5.

excellent classification and account of the discoveries at this
site. They appear to have commenced towards the close
of the year 1829, during which year about 3000 painted
vases were discovered by the Princess of Canino, SS. Fos-
sati, Campanari, and Candelori, at places called the *Piano* [1]
dell' Abbadia and the Campo Morto,[2] in a vast desert plain,
about five miles in circumference, between the territory of
Canino and Montalto, known by the name of *Ponte della
Badia,* from the bridge which crosses the little stream
Fiora, by which the plain is traversed. The country on
the right bank of the river, called by the inhabitants Cam-
poscala, and that on the left, distinguished by a hill called
the Cucumella, belonged to the Prince of Canino. Since
that time continuous excavations made at Vulci have
brought to light several vases of great interest, although
the numbers have materially diminished since the first
discovery. They were found in small grotto-tombs, hollowed in the tufo, and with few exceptions only a few
palms under ground. There was nothing remarkable in
them except the vases, for they were neither spacious nor
decorated, nor furnished with splendid ornaments, like the
sepulchres of Tarquinii and of Magna Græcia. Some had
seats for holding the objects deposited with the dead;
others pegs for hanging the vases up to the walls. The
wonder was to find such noble specimens of art in sepulchres so homely.[3] These vases were of all styles and
epochs of the art, from those with maroon figures upon
yellow grounds to the pale figures and opaque ones of its
last decadence. Hence they comprise specimens of the

---

[1] Bull., 1832, p. 5, 1836, p. 134, 1839, pp. 69–77; Gerhard, in the Bull., 1831, p. 161, makes them about 3000–4000.

[2] Bull., 1829, 3, 18, 39, 141.

[3] Bull., 1829, pp. 4, 5.

For a view of this, see Mon. i. xli.

style called Ægyptian, of the transition to the black
figures upon a red ground, of the hard rigid red figures,
of those of the most flourishing age of the fictile art, of
the style of the Basilicata and Southern Italy, of figures
in outline upon a white ground like those of Locri and
Athens, of opaque figures in white or red, laid upon the
black varnish of the vase, and of others of a character
unmistakeably Etruscan. Besides these, an immense number of vases painted black only, without any subject, and
others of the solid black ware, were discovered in the various sepulchres along with Etruscan bronzes and ivories,
and other objects peculiarly Etruscan.[1]

This vast discovery naturally attracted the attention of
the learned in Europe. Notwithstanding the glaring fact of
their Greek inscriptions, and the light thrown upon them by
the researches of Lanzi,[2] Winckelmann[3] and other archæologists, the Italian antiquaries, animated with an ardent
zeal for their country, claimed them as Etruscan works.[4]
It was easier to demonstrate the error of this hypothesis,
than to explain how so many Greek vases should be found

[1] Besides the already cited Rapporto
Volcente (Annali, 1830, iii.) of M. Gerhard, an account of these discoveries
will be found in the Muséum Étrusque
of the late Prince of Canino,'4to, Viterbo;
Millingen on Late Discoveries in Etruria, Tr. R. Soc. Lit. vol. ii. Supp.
1831, 409 ; Schultz., Allg. Zeit., 1831,
p. 409; R. Rochette, Ann., 1834, p. 285.
See also Archæol., xxiii. p. 130, the
Beugnot, Magnoncourt, and Durand
Catalogues, and the Reserve Étrusque,
by M. De Witte, that of the Feoli Collection, by Campanari, and all the
recent works upon antiquities. Cf.Bull.,
1829, s. 49, 1830, 1, 1831, 88, 161, 193,

1832, 74, 1834, 75, 1835, 111.
[2] Dei Vasi antichi dipinti volgarmente
chiamati Etruschi.
[3] Hist. de l'Art, iii. 3, 10.
[4] Bonaparte, L. (P. de Canino), Muséum Étrusque, 4to, Viterbo, 1829; Catalogo di Scelte antichità Etrusche, 4to,
Viterbo, 1829; Idem, Vases Etrusques,
2 livres grand folio; Annali dell' Institut. Arch., i. p. 188; Bull., 1829, p.
60; Idem, Lettres à M. Gerhard ; Bull.,
1829, pp. 113-116, 1830, pp. 142, 143 ;
Amati, sui Vasi Etruschi, Estratto
dal Giornale Arcadico Roma,1829-1830;
Bull., 1830, p. 182 ; Fea, Storia dei Vasi
fittili dipinti, 8vo, Roma, 1832.

in an inland Etruscan city. Millingen advanced the opinion that they were the productions of an Hellenic population, called by him Tyrrhenians, who were subdued by the Etruscans between B.C. 600—350. Gerhard, on the contrary, imagined them to be the work of Greek potters settled in Vulci along with the Etruscans, and enjoying equal rights[1] with them ; an opinion so far modified by Welcker[2] that he supposes these potters to have been *Metoikoi*, or foreign residents, which view was also adopted by the Duc de Luynes.[3] Hirt attributed them to the 300 Thasians who, after the failure of the Athenians before Syracuse, might have fled to Cumæ and Capua ;[4] while others imagined that they were importations, either from Sicily,[5] as Rochette supposed, from Athens,[6] or from Cumæ.[7]

This opinion was also adopted by Bunsen, but with the modification that they might principally have come from Nola in Campania, although many specimens of different styles, he imagines, were brought from Greece.[8] Kramer, on the contrary, disputes all the previous conjectures, and traces the vases, not only of Italy, but even of Greece itself, to the potteries of Athens.[9] Such was also the opinion of Thiersch ;[10] while Müller, on the other

[1] Rapp. Volc., n. 966; Bull., 1832, pp. 78-90, 1833, pp. 74-91.

[2] Rhein. Mus., 1833, s. 341 ; Berl. Ant. Bildw., s. 143.

[3] Annali, iv. 138.

[4] Annali, 1831, p. 213.

[5] R. Rochette, Journ. des Sav., 1830, pp. 122, 185 ; Lettre à M. Schorn, pp. 5, 10.

[6] Müller K. O., Comm. sec. reg. scient. Gott., vol. vii. cl.; hist., pp. 77-118 ; Böckh., Index Lect. Univ. Berol.

sem. hib. 1831-32.

[7] Müller K. O., in Bull., 1832, p. 100; Cat. Étr., avert, p. vii. n. 3.

[8] Annali, vi. p. 72. See also, Bull., 1832, p. 74.

[9] Ueber den Styl und die Herkunft der bemalten Thongefässe, 8vo, Berl., 1837, s. 146 ; see Campanari, Atti. di Pont. Acad. R. Arch., vii. p. 1.

[10] Ueber die Hellenischen bemalten Vasen, in the Abhandlungen d. I. Cl. d. Akad. d. Wiss. iv. Bd. Abth. i.

hand, considered them to be an importation from the
Chalcidians, basing his argument on the Ionic dialect of
their inscriptions, their discovery in maritime and not inland cities, the admitted exportations of Athens, and her
well-known superiority in the ceramic art.[1] Those who
inclined to the idea that the vases were a local production,
based their arguments upon grounds partly material and
partly traditional ; as, on the difference observable in the
vases found at different spots ; on the varieties of their
tone, drawing, and art, which differ in some cases most
remarkably from those of vases discovered in· Greece ; on
the difficulties of transporting, even with the appliances of
modern skill, articles of so fragile a nature ; on the universal diffusion of clay on the earth's surface ; and on the
idea, that it is much more probable that the potters were
imported than their products. Much light, they considered,
was thrown on the condition of the arts in Italy and northern
Greece at this period by the story already related of the
flight of Demaratus, the father of the elder Tarquin from
Corinth, and his introduction of the plastic art into Italy.
From this account, which rests on the authority of Pliny,[2]
it is contended that the art clearly came from Greece. It
appears, indeed, that Demaratus and his companions emi-
grated to Tarquinii, then a flourishing city of the Etruscans ; that he there married a native woman ; and that
one of his party, named Lucumo, initiated the Etruscans
in Greek civilisation.[3] Unfortunately, however, this account
of Demaratus is enveloped in much obscurity, as other

[1] Bull., 1832, p. 102. The fact which
he cites, however, of the Phœnicians
purchasing Athenian vases to export to
Cernæ on the African coast, applies to
unglazed ware.
[2] N. H., xxxv. c. 3, s. 5, & c. 12, s. 43.
[3] Cicero, De Rep., lib. ii. c. 19, s. 9.

authorities represent him as being a Corinthian merchant.[1]
The opponents of this theory contest it by alleging the
traces of an earlier independent art in Italy ; the hesita-
tion with which Pliny speaks ;[2] the Ionic character of the
ware ; the identity of its style of ornament with that of
vases found at Athens ;[3] the fact, that vases made by the
same potters have been discovered at different places, the
supposed mystery of the art,[4] and the extreme rudeness
of the Etruscan imitations.   Some writers have even gone
so far as to assert, on the authority of Pliny,[5] that Etruria
exported vases to Athens.

When we consider the great space of time occupied by
the history of Italy, it seems reasonable to believe that
vases were imported into Etruria from various localities,
and principally from Greece.   It is probable, however, that
many came from potteries established in Sicily and Magna
Græcia ; for it can hardly be conceived that an art esteemed
so trivial by the Greeks was not exercised in their colonies,
wherever founded.   The influence of these settlers upon
the Etruscan population appears to have been most marked
since Lucius Tarquinius Priscus, the last king but one of
Rome, ingratiated himself into the favour of Ancus Mar-
tius by his superior education and knowledge—and finally
obtained the sovereignty.   According to Florus[6] his elevation was due to his application to business and the elegance of his manners ; " for," he adds, " being of Corinthian origin, he combined Greek intelligence with the arts
and manners of Italy."

[1] Dionysius Halic., Ant. Rom., iii. 48,
Liv. i. 34 ; Tacit., Ann., xi. 14.
[2] Thiersch, l. c. s. 10.
[3] Thiersch, ss. 89–94.
[4] Lenormant and De Witte, Introd.
xix.
[5] N. H., xxxv. 12, 46.
[6] Lib. i. 5.

The introduction of the fine arts, as well as of writing, into Italy, is placed by Bunsen at a very remote period, when the whole of southern Etruria was in the possession of the Tyrrheno-Pelasgians. The epoch when these were expelled from Agylla, Pyrgos, and the coast, appears, according to the researches of Niebuhr, to have been later than the second century of Rome, or at least than the first half of that century. But the Attic dialect of the races here under consideration, will not the less belong to an epoch later than the invasion of the Romans, since the tombs of Tarquinii exhibit nothing but what is Etruscan.[1]

Besides these, many other vases were decidedly of Etruscan origin, and were made either at Vulci or in some of the neighbouring cities. The *tutulus*, or pointed cap, on the head of Juno, in a scene of the judgment of Paris, has been supposed to be a proof of the Etruscan origin of a vase. The same argument has been adduced from a vase on which Hermes is represented with four wings, and Ganymede with two. The properties of the figures of the vases of the paler tone, and of the style called by the Italians "national," which resemble in their short stature and thick-set limbs, the Etruscan bronze figures, has also been considered an additional proof of their origin ; and all doubt vanishes when names of persons in the language, not of Greece, but of Etruria, are found upon them.[2]

It is indeed evident that no argument as to exportation

---

[1] Annali, 1834, p. 65.

[2] Such as KAPE MAKAΘEΣA, "dear" or "lovely" Macathesa, ΠΕΛΕΙ, Peleus, AXΛE, Achilles, XIPΤN, Chiron, APΤNM, Aruns, ΛΑΣΣΑΜ, Lassas ; Annali, 1834, p. 54.

or local manufacture can be drawn from the circumstance of the different proportion in which vases with black and red figures are found at Vulci and Nola, as this may be entirely owing to the different epochs at which these cities flourished. Yet there are certain differences of style and glaze perceptible to an experienced eye, which show, at all events, a difference of importation. It is indeed possible that the early vases, or those called Doric, were introduced into Italy from the Doric states, such as Corinth,[1] and were subsequently superseded by the more active trade and more elegant productions of Athens.[2] The objection that the Etruscan Larths would have taken no interest in foreign pottery, can scarcely be serious, for the entire art of the Etruscans is filled with Greek symbolism and mythology. Greece, in fact, then stood in the same relation to Etruria as France now does to Europe in the application of the fine arts.

The vases found at Vulci consist of all styles till that of the decadence, commencing with the early Archaic Greek, with narrow figures on yellow grounds, although neither so numerous nor of so large a size as those of Cervetri. Most of the finest vases with black figures, consisting of hydriæ, amphoræ, and œnochoæ, many of large size and of finest drawing and colour, have been found at Vulci. Some vases with inscriptions, often with the names of potters or artists, of this style, have been discovered here, —a few of the vases, also, with black figures on a white ground, chiefly of small size. But as remarkable for

---

[1] Annali, 1834, p. 64.
[2] Abeken, Mittel-Italien, p. 294, places these in Olympiad 70–90.

ULYSSES AND POLYPHEMUS. (FROM A CYLIX, VULCI.)

[Vol. II., p. 144.

their beauty and number are the vases with red figures, of the strong style, found on this site, consisting of amphoræ, hydriæ, and craters of large size, cylices, and œnochoæ. These vases are distinguished by the green tone of their black colour, the vivid red of the clay and figures, the fineness, energy, and excellence of their drawing—of the later developed and fine style, comparatively few vases have been found. The numerous inscriptions with which these vases abound, the occurrence of subjects new to classical authorities, the beauty of their shapes—contemporary with the best periods of Greek art—and the excellence of their drawing, glaze, and colour, has had great influence—not only on modern manufacture, but also on the fine arts in general, and has tended more to advance the knowledge of ancient pottery than all the previous discoveries.[1]

Vases with red figures, and Etruscan ones with black and white figures on a yellow ground, have been discovered in the sepulchres at Alberoro, near *Arezzo*, in the north-west of the Etruscan territory. Arezzo itself, the ancient Arretium, so repeatedly mentioned by the Latin authors, and called by Lanzi the Etruscan Samos, has also produced a few painted vases.[2]

Other sites in the neighbourhood of ancient Rome, as Città Vecchia,[3] have yielded vases of a bad style, which were probably brought thither by the commerce of modern dealers. One, remarkable for its high antiquity, has been already mentioned. The old hut-shaped vases of the Alban lake, near Alba Longa, will be described

---

[1] Jahn, Vasensammlung, lxviii.-lxxviii.

[2] Bull., 1838, p. 74.

[3] Bull., 1832, p. 3.

under the Etruscan potteries.[1] Several lecythi have been
exhumed at *Selva Le Rocca*, near Monteroni, the ancient
Alsium,[2] and at *Monteroni* itself, dishes ornamented with
red bands, and coarse vases of the different styles.   Others
have been discovered at the *Punta di Guardiola*, near *St.
Marinella ;* and at *Poggio Somavilla*, in the territory of the
Sabines, vases of Etruscan fabric, ornamented with red
lines,[3] and other vases, with red figures, having the subject
of the gods of light, Bellerophon, and an Amazonomachia,
have been excavated, all of the later style.

CENTRAL AND SOUTHERN ITALY.

The mass of vases found in central and lower Italy,
are distinguished from those of Etruria by the greater
paleness of their clay, by the softer drawing of their
figures ; their glaze, which, in the case of the Nolan pottery, is of a jet black lustre, and in the Campanian of a
duller and more leaden hue ; by their more elaborate
shape, by the freer introduction of ornaments, and by the
abundant use of opaque colours.   Generally, the vases
from this part of Italy, whether of the Greek settlements
of Magna Græcia, or from the sepulchres of the Samnites,
the Lucanians, and the Apulians, are of the later period
of the art ; although several, even of the old or Doric
style, have been found at Nola [4] and Ruvo, and those of
the black style in the Basilicata.[5]   Their paste shows a
great proportion of carbonate of lime ;[6] and beds of clay,

---

[1] See also Abeken, Mittel-Italien, p.
824.

[2] Bull., 1839, p. 34, 1840, p. 133 ;
Abeken, Mittel-Italien, p. 267.

[3] Bull., 1838, p. 71.

[4] An., 1834, p. 78.

[5] Ibid.

[6] The analysis of Gargiulo, Cenni, p.
21, gives :—Silica 48, Alumina 16, Ox.
Iron 16, Carb. Ac. 16, Carb. Lime 8.
That of Brongniart has been cited
before.

discovered in the vicinity of Naples, and now used for making imitations of these vases, show that the ancient ones found in this locality may have been produced on the spot. It will, perhaps, afford some clue to the date of the use and fabric of many of these vases, to remember that the most flourishing period of the Doric colonies was ten Olympiads, or half a century, before the Persian war ; that Sybaris was destroyed before the expedition of Darius ; that the colonies formed by the other emigrations flourished from the LXX.-LXXXIV. Olympiad, B.C., especially those of Sicily ; that Campania was invaded by the Samnites in the LXXIV. Olympiad, B.C. 440 ; and that in the age of the second Punic war Nola is mentioned as a completely Oscan colony. After the arms of Rome had conquered Southern Italy, about the second century before Christ, the Greek settlements relapsed into utter barbarism. The subjects of the vases show an equal deterioration in moral feeling, sensual representations of nude figures, bacchanalian orgies, and licentious subjects, having superseded the draped figures, the gravity of composition, and the noble incidents of heroic myths, or epic poetry.[1]

The different condition of the states of Southern Italy accounts for the variety of the vases exhumed from the sepulchres of different sites. The Greek cities on the coast, principally founded by Achæan colonies, but some-times by Dorian adventurers, maintained, at an early period, a constant intercourse with Greece ; and their sepulchres were enriched with the vases of the oldest period and style. The inland cities were generally of more recent origin, and their sepulchres contain vases of

---

[1] Abeken, Mittel-Italien, p. 342.

the fine and florid styles.   The people north-west of
Iapygia appear to have been governed by tyrants or kings,
generally patrons of the arts.   During the war with the
Samnites, and that between Pyrrhus and the Romans,
these countries were fearfully ravaged, but enjoyed peace
from A. C. 272 till A. C. 218, the commencement of the
second Punic war, which lasted 113 years, and ended by
the Social war and the ruin of Southern Italy.

In the kingdom of Naples, and the states which compose
it, many vases of the late style have been discovered.   Many
small vases, indeed, of good style, with red figures, have been
found in excavations made on the site of Naples [1] itself,
although they have not the extremely beautiful glaze of the
Nolan vases.[2]   Others were discovered in sites in its vicinity,
as Giugliano.[3]   At *Cumæ*, the fabled residence of the Sybil,
where the sepulchres are either excavated in the tufo, or
covered with blocks of stone, have been found many vases,[4]
which belong to the later days of its ancient splendour, when
it was held by the Campanians.   The most ancient of the
Greek colonies, founded by the Chalcidians of Euboea or the
Cumæans of Æolis have produced vases of second style ;
some, however, with black figures, and most of the later style
—many of the fine style, with lustrous glaze, only inferior to
that of Nola.   These are probably about the time of its
conquest by the Campanians and Opici, A. V. C. 338, A. C.
416, after which it issued a few coins till A. V. C. 409, A. C.
345, when it fell into the Roman Protectorate.   Here were

[1] Jahn, Vasensammlung, lx., Bull.,
1829, p. 166.

[2] Bull., 1829, p. 164.

[3] Bull., 1829, p. 86.

[4] Jorio, Metodo per rinvenire i sepol-

chri, p. 11 ; Abeken, Mittel-Italien, p.
338 ; Gerhard, Rapp. Volc., n. 631, 632;
De Witte, Cat. Magn., p. 48 ; Vases de
Lucien Bonaparte, liv. i. Nos. 542, 543.

discovered in 1842, craters resembling those of St. Agata dei Goti, with pale glaze,[1] and abundance of white accessories, and decorated with the Attic subjects of Ceres and Triptolemus, and Cephalus and Aurora ;[2] also Panathenaic amphora, with black figures and inscriptions, like those of Berenice.[3] The potteries of this city were famous even in the time of the Romans, and moulded vases of their fabric have been discovered there.[4] The other sites in this province where vases have principally been discovered, are Massa,[5] Lubrense, Marano, Giugliano, Sant Arpino, Afragola, Sorrento, and Mugnano.

TERRA DI LAVORO.

In the Terra di Lavoro, *S. Maria di Capua*, the site of ancient Capua, has yielded many vases of the highest interest belonging to the strong style, some with the names of makers, as Euergides and Pistoxenos, or with those of artists, as Epictetos, have been found here. Those of fine style have occasionally been discovered here, but the style of the decadence, especially of those with red figures, having abundant ornaments, is the most prevalent. The most remarkable vase found on this spot is the calpis in the Campana collection, having a frieze of polychrome figures, with much gilding, representing the departure of Triptolemus, round the neck, and a frieze of animals round the lower part of the fluted body. One remark-

[1] Bull., 1829, p. 164.
[2] Bull., 1842, pp. 8, 9 ; Mon. I., taf. iv.; Bull., Arch. Nap., ii. p. 6.
[3] Fiorelli, Vasi rinvenuti a Cuma, fo. Nap. 1856, cf. also Mon. Ant. 4to, Nap.
1853.
[4] Martial, Epigr., xiv. 114 ; Statius, Silv., iv. 9, 43.
[5] Gerhard, Berl. Ant. Bild., s. 139 ; Bull., 1829, p. 170.

able vase had an incised Etruscan inscription. Some
recently discovered there, through the excavations undertaken by the Prince of Syracuse, are of the most
magnificent character. They are ornamented with polychrome figures, some being gilded, and representing
scenes derived either from the drama or history. One
remarkable vase had the subject of Aurora and Tithonus.[1]
A very early crater, of pale clay, with black figures,
representing a hunt, probably that of the Calydonian
boar,[2] and with very archaic inscriptions, and drawing of
peculiar style, was in the Hamilton collection. This
site has offered vases of a style,[3] distinguished for the
paleness of its clay, the bright red of its figures, and a
glaze like that of the vases of Puglia. Certain vases
with black figures, carelessly drawn, and with a bad glaze,
have also been found here, supposed to have been made
about c. Olympiad, A. C. 381.

It is uncertain whether this city was founded by the
Tyrrhenians or conquered by them from its ancient possessors. They gave it the name of Elatria, which the
Latins changed into Vulturnus, and the Samnites on their
conquest, into Campua or Capua. The arts continued to
flourish there till a late period,—its coins being all later than
the second Punic war, when it was called in Oscan Kapu.[4]

At *Teano*, the ancient Teanum, lying between Capua
and St. Germano, vases of the white style have been
discovered.[5]

---

[1] Minervini, Mon. In. 4.

[2] Cat. Brit. Mus., No. 559; D'Hancarville, pl. 1—4; Inghirami, Mon. Etr.,
v. tav. 56; Müller, Denkmäl. A. taf.
xviii. 93.

[3] Bull., 1829, 165; Bull. Arch. Nap.,
v. 52; Abeken, Mittel-Italien, p. 341.

[4] Millingen, Considerations, p. 192-
194.

[5] Bull., 1837, p. 97.

At *Atella*, the Oscan Aderl, craters with red figures, painted with a profusion of white and other colours, of the later style of art, have been discovered.[1]

The vases found at Nola consist of all the principal classes, together with a few local types. Their distinguishing characteristics are the elegance of their shapes, and the extreme beauty of their glaze, which is often of an intense black colour. Of vases of the old or Doric style, with yellow grounds and dark figures, many have been found in the ancient sepulchres. These vases are easily distinguished from similar ones discovered at Vulci, as the figures are smaller, but more carefully executed, and the colour darker. A few have human figures, representing combats of warriors. M. Gerhard, indeed, is disposed to consider these vases as imitations of the more ancient style, but it is probable that the difference is rather owing to the local fabric. Of the second period of art, viz. of vases with black figures, comparatively few have been discovered at Vulci. They are also distinguished from those of the Etruscan sites by the smallness of their size, and by the peculiar black lustrous glaze of the locality. A few are hydriæ or amphoræ, but the great proportion are œnochoæ or lecythi. Amongst them have been found a Panathenaic amphora, with the usual inscription.[2] Their drawing, also, is not so rigid in its details, approaching in this respect the vases of Greece and Sicily. The subjects of them are Greek, like those of Vulci, and show that the same Hellenic mythology prevailed there. A few vases of this style, with cream-coloured grounds, have also been discovered at Nola. The great excellence of

---

[1] Bull., 1829, pp. 165, 166.   [2] Jahn, Vasensammlung. lii.

the potteries which supplied this city is to be seen on the
vases with red figures. These vases, like the preceding,
are also of small dimensions ; and the principal shape is
the amphoræ, one type of which, almost peculiar to this
spot, tall and slim, has twisted handles. Besides this are
the *crater, calpis, cothon* or *scyphos, œnochoë, pyxis,* and
phiale. They are the most charming of the ancient vases.

Some few vases with red figures are of the strong style,
or of one intermediate between that and the fine style,—
the most remarkable of which is that with the subject of
the last night of Troy.[1]

Some of the vases of Nola are modelled in fanciful
shapes, such as that of an astragalus, or the claw of a
lobster. Besides the painting, they were often decorated
with an ornament punched in, like that on the vases of
Vulci. These decorations are antefixal ornaments,—as
stars, and bands of hatched or plain lines. A favourite
ornament of the purely black vases, which form a large
proportion of the Nolan ware, is a series of black annular
bands on the base, concentric to the axis of the vase.
Their treatment is similar to that of the same class of
vases found at Vulci, except that it is not so careful, the
extremities and outline being executed with less finish.
In many of the vases the presence of white ornaments
and letters, and the circumstance of the eye being provided with lashes and no longer represented in profile,
show that they belong to the fine style of the art. Inscriptions rarely occur on them, and those that are found
are chiefly exclamations, such as, The boy is handsome !
The girl is fair !—the names of personages very seldom

[1] Jahn, Vasensammlung. liv.   Millin., I. 25-26.

accompanying the figures. The *calpis*, or water vase, has
rarely more than three figures ; the amphoræ generally
one on each side. The *œnochöæ* have generally a single
figure, two sometimes occurring. No law can be laid
down that the subject selected alluded to the use of the
vase, though the inferior figures upon one side show that
they were intended to stand against a wall.

Among the shapes particularly local, is a kind of jug
or *œnochöe*, better adapted for metallic work than for
clay. The body assumes the shape of a head, generally,
but not always, that of a female. The face is of a warmer
tone than the body of the vase, and is sometimes covered
with a coating of lime or stucco. The hair is painted of
a light colour, and there is sometimes a necklace moulded
in the same material round the neck, which has been
gilded. The upper part of these vases, as well as the
handle and foot, are usually glazed with a black colour.
Some are in the shape of a negro's head, the mouth
being small like that of the *lecythi*, and the whole face
covered with a black glaze.[1]

The subjects found on the Nolan vases of this class are
the same as on those discovered at Vulci, consisting of Zeus,
Athene, and Apollo, Dionysos, Satyrs and Bacchanals,[2] or
Comos and Œnos,[3] Ariadne,[4] Apollo and Artemis ;[5] Nike,[6]
Linos ;[7] the story of Hermes and Herse ;[8] Phædra swing-
ing;[9] Aurora and Kephalus ;[10] Amazonomachiæ ;[11] Eros

[1] Gerhard, Berl. Ant. Bild., s. 234,
235, 236, taf. i. 38.
[2] Gerhard, Berl. Ant. Bild., s. 239, n.
806, s. 2, 40, 810 ; B. A. B., xlviii. s. 245,
845, s. 251, 867.
[3] Ibid. s. 246, 848.
[4] Ibid. s. 241, 822.
[5] Ibid. 243, s. 837.
[6] Ibid. s. 242, 833.
[7] Ibid. s. 248, 855.
[8] Ibid. s. 248, 854, s. 271, 910.
[9] Ibid. s. 249, 859.
[10] Ibid. s. 251, 866.
[11] Ibid. s. 253, 870.

and female ;[1] Penelope ;[2] the judgment of Paris ;[3] death
of Achilles.[4] The prevalence of Attic subjects on vases
found at a town apparently far removed from Athenian
influence, and certainly not an Ionian colony, together
with the difference of style, have been used as arguments in favour of their having been exported from
Athens.[5]

Many of the subjects, indeed, of these vases are difficult
to explain, and have been supposed to represent incidents of private life,—such as, females in the gynacœum,[6]
marriages, exercises of the Palæstra,[7] and the sports
of youth, or the games of Greece.[8] There are, however,
marks of the decadence of art, showing that it was passing
from the ideal to the actual—from the poetic to the
prosaic feeling. Future discoveries may clear up some
difficulties ; and to us these remains would have been
more precious had they presented scenes derived from
stirring contemporaneous events. Other vases from this site
have been burnt on the pyre. They are the *salicerni* of
Italian antiquaries, and much prized by amateurs.[9]

This city was of great antiquity, as it is mentioned by
Hecatæus, of Miletus, who wrote about A. C. 523—500,
the period of its early vases with yellow grounds, and it
was placed by him amongst the Ausonii and Opici.[10] It
however, finally placed itself under Roman protection,
A. V. C. 409, A. C. 346. Its most beautiful vases must

[1] Ibid. 254, 877.
[2] De Witte, An. 1841. p. 261.
[3] Ibid. s. 319, 1029 ; Gerhard, Berl.
Ant. Bild., taf. xxxiii.–xxxv.
[4] Ibid. s. 239, 809.
[5] Kramer, Ueber die Herkunft, s. 149.
[6] B. A. B., s. 242, 831, 243, n. 836–
840. s. 249, 856–57, s. 277, n. 989.
[7] B. A. B., s. 248, n. 852, s. 251, n.
863.
[8] B. A. B., s. 243, u. f.834, 869–71.
[9] Bull., 1829, p. 19.
[10] Steph. Byz. voce Nola.

have been made before its final subjection.   Its predilection for Greek art and institutions is well known.[1]

The existence of Greek potteries at Nola has been conjectured from the vases there found ; and the Greek inscriptions on its coins tend to show that a dominant Greek population was established there.   Nola was a colony of the Chalcidian Greeks, who were invited thither by the Tyrrhenians, and it is possible they may have brought with them the art of making vases.   The clay of which their vases were made is said to have been found in the district.[2]

Vases of Nolan fabric are distributed far and wide throughout the peninsula as far as Pæstum and Locris. The age of the beautiful vases of Nola is certainly that of the apogee of the Greek colonies in Italy.   Their age is placed about Olympiad XC., and they have been attributed to the potteries of Ionian cities.[3]

Generally speaking, the Nolan vases have attracted less attention than those of Vulci and Cervetri, from their smaller size and their less interesting subjects.[4]

Other sites in this province, being those of cities once renowned in Campania, have also produced several vases of late style, as *Acerra*,[5] *Sessa*, and *Calvi*, or Cales, the tombs of which have yielded some of the finest and largest specimens of modelled terra cotta of the latest style of art.   The vases of *Avella*, or Abella, were distin-

---

[1] Dionys. Halicarn, Excerpt. Reiske, p. 2315.

[2] Annali, 1832, p. 76.

[3] Abeken, Mittel-Italien, pp. 340–341.

[4] A volume of engravings of Nolan vases, prepared by Angelini, was in the possession of the late Dr. Braun at Rome, who was to have edited them with an accompanying text.   They were engraved in the style of Tischbein, and had been printed at Naples.

[5] Bull., 1829, p. 162; Gargiulo, Cenni, p. 15.

guished by their bad glaze, the pale colour of their figures, the fineness of their clay, and occasional good drawing.[1]

Still more renowned from its vases, being among some of the first discovered, is the site of *St. Agata dei Goti*, the ancient Plistia, which at one time gave its name to all the vases of later style and fabric. Their shapes were principally *craters*, their drawing skilful, but careless, especially in the extremities resembling those of Nola, but with the introduction of more red and white tints; their clay is fine, their glaze black and lustrous.[2] It is supposed that they were made after the occupation of this city by the Samnites.[3] Vases with black figures are rarely found here.

PRINCIPATO CITERIORE.

The vases discovered in the Principato Citeriore come from Salerno, from Cava, and *Nocera dei Pagani*,[4] or Nuceria Alfaterna. Those from the celebrated *Pesto* or Pæstum, the ancient Poseidonia, resemble in style those of the Basilicata, having red figures on a black ground, but of a better style of art, the varnish dull, the figures pale, with accessories of various colours.[5] One of the finest vases of this locality is that of the painter Asteas, in the Louvre, representing the story of Cadmus and the dragon, the principal figures now have their names inscribed. Some other vases of this spot, of inferior style, represent the toilet of Venus, jugglers,[6] and similar

---

[1] Bull., 1829, p. 163; Gerhard, Berl. Ant. Bild., l. c.
[2] Bull., 1829, p. 165.
[3] Abeken, Mittel-Italien, p. 341.
[4] Bull., 1829, p. 165.
[5] Ibid. p. 163.
[6] Quaranta, Mystagogue, p. 214.

subjects. They are said to be discovered outside the sepulchres.[1]

The vases found at *Eboli* do not appear to have had any particular or distinct style, although some had engraved inscriptions in the Doric dialect, under their handles. Their subjects were uninteresting.[2] Vases had also been discovered at *Battipaglia*, in the vicinity.[3] No details have been given of those from the sepulchres of *St. Lucia*. Those from the plains of *Surrento*, the ancient Surrentum, resembled in style the fabric of St. Agata dei Goti, and had the ordinary subjects of vases of this class, such as Sirens, Bacchanalians,[4] and triclinia. There were potteries here in the time of Pliny, celebrated for producing excellent cups.[5]

PRINCIPATO ULTERIORE.

Avellino and *Monte Sarchio*, in the Principato Ulteriore, have also produced vases, probably of later style ; so have *Isernia*, in the Contada di Molise, *Sansevera*, and *Lucera* in the Capitanata.[6]

BASILICATA.

The vases of the *Basilicata* comprise a large portion of those of the later style of art, and exhibit the local peculiarities of a native fabric, through the barbaric and other costumes represented on them. The Alpine countries of Lucania have produced vases differing in style from those of the maritime districts of Magna Græcia. Some, indeed,

---

[1] Bull., 1829, 119.
[2] Bull., 1829, pp. 151, 164; 1836, p. 136; one was a Siren.
[3] Bull., 1829, 163.
[4] Mus. Pourt., .pl. xxiii. xxv. p. 73,

and foll. ; Bull., 1829, p. 164; 1842, pp. 11–13.
[5] N. H., xxxv., s. 46.
[6] Gargiulo, Cenni, p. 16.

have supposed that a colony of foreign potters, located here, introduced amongst the Lucanians the art of painting vases. Their tint is pale, the glaze of leaden hue, their ornaments are distinguished by an abundance of white accessories, and their style of art has already been described in the account of the decadence. The high price which vases of great beauty or interest obtained in the European market during the 17th century, caused researches to be carried on in this province with enterprise, and on a settled plan. Here the earth is still trenched on sites which appear favourable, and when the original soil has been disturbed, the excavators continue their labours till they have arrived at a part where the earth shows decided proofs of being still intact, and by this means are assured that nothing remains below. Many of the vases in this locality are found broken into fragments, either owing to the roofs and tops of the sepulchres having been destroyed or burst by the roots of trees. All the vases found in this province, are of the latest style, with pale red figures on a dull, leaden, black ground, and subjects chiefly relating to the Dionysiac orgies.

Many vases of the finest red style have been excavated from the sepulchres of *Anzi*, the ancient Anxia, a spot teeming with the remains of ancient art. It is the principal place where the vases of Lucania are found. Their style much resembles that of Ceglie, and is better than that of the generality of vases of the Basilicata. A fine *calpis*, found at this spot, and now in the Berlin Museum, represents the subject of Zeus and Io.[1] Some of the vases

---

[1] Gerhard, Berl. Ant. Bild., s. 260, n. 902; Hirt, Die Brautschau, Berlin, 1825; Avellino, Opuscoli diversi, vol. ii. tav. 7, pp. 169, 174.

were of the style of Nola, others of that of Apulia, and were supposed to be made by foreign potters established there.[1] At *Armento*, vases have been found[2] with black figures of the finest style, an example of which will be seen in a crater now in the British Museum, and others of an intermediate style, between the latest Nolan and early Apulian. Other vases of large size, fine style, and heroic subjects, have been found at Missanello, where a vase of ancient style, and many of later style, generally with good, but occasionally of careless drawing, have been found in the vicinity.[3] The other sites of the Basilicata, in which vases have been exhumed, are *Potenza*, or Potentia, *Calvello*, and *Pomarico* (distinguished for its well-painted dishes, with supposed representation of nuptial ceremonies), *Venosa* or Venusia, and *Pisticci*.[4]

Some vases from *Grumento*, the ancient Grumentum, founded by a Greek colony from Thurium, and which evidently was flourishing at the time of the second Punic war,[5] exhibited the same style as the vases of Puglia. One had for its subject an Amazonomachia. A magnificent vase, with the subject of Perseus, but of mediocre drawing, was found at Missanello, in the vicinity of Grumento, and is now in the museum of the Cav. St. Angelo.[6] Other sites in the same province, as *Rocca Nova* and *St. Arcangelo*, *St. Brancato*, *Ardarea*, and *Nice*, *Timpani* and *Sodano*[7] had also produced vases of similar style. At *Marsiconuova* was found a vase with an Amazonomachia,

[1] Bull., 1829, pp. 162, 169.
[2] Gerhard, B. A. B., ss. 139, 234.
[3] Bull., 1829, p. 170.
[4] Gargiulo, Cenni, p. 15; Bull., 1829, p. 165.

[5] Livy, xxiii., c. 37; xxvii., c. 4.
[6] Bull., 1830, p. 24.
[7] Lombardi, Memorie de l'Institut., p. 195, and foll.

others of both styles occurred at Castelluccio,[1] so also at *Vaglio Oppido*, or Velia, and *Ruoti* [2] *Calvello, Acerenza*, or Aceruntia.[3]

BARI.

The vases of Puglia [4] on the coast of the Hadriatic are described as so much resembling each other in character and style, as to lead to the inference that they must have been fabricated about the same period, and almost in one pottery. Their epoch is probably that of later days of the potteries, and of the Senatûs consultum A. U. C. 564, suppressing the licentiousness of the Bacchic orgies. They are distinguished from those of Northern or Southern Italy, by the paler colour of their clay, the duller tone of their glaze, the size and *recherché* character of their shape, the mystic nature of their subjects, the abundance of heroic figures, and their general resemblance to the vases of the Basilicata. They differ essentially in the Alpine countries from those of the cities of the Gulf of Tarentum.[5] The most remarkable of which are a rhyton, with the name of its maker Didymus, that of the maker Asteas, in the Louvre, and the vase in the British Museum, with the subject of Mars and Vulcan contending over Juno, entrapped on the golden throne.[6]

Many of the vases of Puglia are the most beautiful of the later style of art. They have been found throughout the tract of level country extending

---

[1] Panofka, Hyperbor. Rom. Stud., i., p. 168.
[2] Mem., p. 218, 221, 227.
[3] Mem., p. 208.

[4] Bull., 1829, pp. 166, 172, 173.
[5] Ibid. p. 162.
[6] Jahn, Vasensammlung, xxxix.

from Bitonto to Ruvo, and at Polignano or Neapolis-
Peucetiæ, Putignano, Alta Mura,[1] and Carbonara,[2] Terra
di Bari, Canosa, Ceglie, and Ruvo, the vases of which,
from their superior excellence, merit a separate description.
These belong to the district called the Terra di Bari.

The vases of *Bari*, the ancient Barium, are like those of
Rubastini, Canosa, and St. Agata dei Goti, and have red
figures upon a black ground. Among them was one in
the shape of the head of a female, resembling those of
Nola, and several were deep bell-shaped *craters*, called
oxybapha, having on them mystic and Dionysiac subjects.[3] They have been found in tombs on the sea shore.[4]

The vases of *Canosa* (or Canusium, a city supposed to
have been founded by Diomed, and an Ætolian colony,
which at one time had attained considerable grandeur
and power, probably in the interval before the second
Punic war, and was one of the largest cities of Greek
origin in Italy),[5] consist of large *craters*, decorated with
subjects derived from the mysteries, the drama, and other
sources which inspired the later artists, and are known
from the work of Millin. They rank as some of the
very finest of the florid style of the decadence of the art,
and bear considerable resemblance to the vases of Ruvo
and Ceglie.[6] Lately a magnificent vase, with the
subject of Darius and Hellas, taken from the Persæ of
Æschylus, has been discovered at Canosa.[7] One of the

[1] Bull., 1829, p. 172; Arch. Zeit., 1851, s. 81.
[2] Bull., 1829, p. 173.
[3] Abeken, Mittel-Italien, p. 349; B. A. B., s. 139, Nos. 729, 742, 753; Bull., 1837, p. 33.
[4] Bull., 1829, p. 172.
[5] Strabo, vi. 284.
[6] Millin, Tombeaux de Canosa, fo. Paris, 1816; Bull., 1829, p. 174; Gerhard, Ant. Bild., ss. 139 and 192, no. 604.
[7] Gerhard, Monatsbericht. d. K. Akad. Wissen. zu Berlin, 1857.

tombs opened here, which contained vases, had a Latin inscription, dated A. C. 67, but the kind of vases found in it have not been recorded. Some unimportant vases of the style of black figures of the last decadence, have also been disinterred at Canosa.[1]

Close to *Bari*, at a little distance from the sea, lies *Conversano*. Its vases appear in style to resemble those of other parts of Puglia and those of Nola.[2] Putignano, in the same territory, has also produced vases.[3]

The vases found at *Ruvo*, the ancient Ryps or Rubastini, are of the same style and composition as those of the rest of Southern Italy, and of some found at Athens.[4] This city, of which so little is known from the ancient authorities, has produced many of the finest vases found in Southern Italy. Several styles have been found on this site, showing that it was colonised probably by the Achæans at an early epoch. Only a single vase with animals on a yellow ground, of the style called Dorian, Corinthian, or Phœnician, has been exhumed. The most remarkable with black figures are two Panathenaic vases with the usual inscriptions, and a vase with Priam ransoming the corpse of Hector, of the strong red style ; and of the fine style like that of Nola, only a few vases have been found. A polychrome vase, with the figure of a satyr, and the name of Alcibiades, as a καλὸς, has been discovered at Ruvo ; and another, in the possession of Sir Woodbine Parish, represents Aurora. The great proportion of vases, however, of this ancient city are of the florid style, of large size, with volute and ornamented handles, with numerous

---

[1] Jahn, Vasensammlung, xlv.

[2] See the *œnochoe* with the head of a Satyr and Bacchante, Gerhard, Berl.

Ant. Bild., p. 234 ; Bull., 1829, p. 172.

[3] Bull., 1829, p. 172.

[4] Bull., 1829, p. 174 ; Bull. 1837, p. 97.

figures, and arabesque ornaments, sometimes enhanced by gilding. Of these large vases, the most important for its subject, the elaboration of its details, is that with the death of the Cretan giant, Talos, at the hands of the Argonauts. It would be too long to specify here all the subjects of the vases of Ruvo. Besides amphoræ, craters, hydriæ, and rhyta of fantastical shape are by no means of uncommon occurrence in the sepulchres.[1] They are often of considerable size, and most of the finest vases of late style have come from this spot. The celebrated vase of the potter Meidias, in the British Museum, with the subject of the rape of the Leucippides, is supposed to have come from thence, on account of its resemblance to many other beautiful vases known to have been discovered on the spot. Their details are executed with great elegance, the hair and also the drapery being indicated by fine wiry lines,[2] while the figures are of more slender proportions than those of the vases of the Basilicata. In fact, they resemble the known works of the young Athenian School, which commenced about the age of Alexander, in the middle of the 4th century B.C., and of which, in another branch of art, such brilliant examples may be traced on the coins of Pyrrhus and those of Tarentum.   Vases of the latest style have also been found here.[3]

The sepulchres of the comparatively unknown site of *Ceglie*, the ancient Cælia, in Apulia, have much enriched the collections at Berlin.[4] In style these vases have the

---

[1] For the Ruvo vases, see Jahn, Vasensammlung, xl.-xlv.

[2] For the account of the finest Ruvo vases in the Naples Museum, B., 1837,

pp. 97, 98; 1840, p. 187.

[3] Bull., 1834, pp. 164, 228; 1836, p. 114; 1838, p. 162.

[4] Bull., 1829, p. 173.

general Apulian type, and their art is of the same late
period. They are remarkable for their size. The principal
shapes are cups and amphoræ, with volute handles and
gorgon masks. Some have subjects of great interest from
their representing scenes taken from the drama. Among
the subjects are the usual Eros and Aphrodite[1] of this style,
Phrixus crossing the Hellespont on the ram,[2] Orestes at
Delphi, the sacrifice of the ram of Tantalus,[3] Actæon
seized by his dogs, the burial of Chrysippus,[4] Bellerophon,
Meleager, and the Calydonian boar, Hercules, and Geryon;[5]
the judgment of Paris,[6] the arming of Penthesilea,[7] Europa,
the Centaur, and Amazonomachiæ,[8] Omphale,[9] and others
of a similar kind. The finest of these vases represents
the subject of the marriage of Hercules and Hebe.[10] These
vases show the prevalence of Greek ideas and civilisation,
and were probably fabricated on the spot by Hellenic
potters.

In the province of Calabria Ulteriore the vases discovered at *Locri* are perhaps some of the most beautiful
of the South. The Locri, a branch either of the Opun-
tii or Epizephyrii, established themselves at C. Zephyrium,
OL. XXVI., A. C. 673, and appear to have been accompanied
in their emigration by Corinthians and Lacedæmonians,
finally becoming a Dorian colony. Their coins are not
earlier than OL. C., A. C. 374. All these states appear to

[1] Gerhard, B. A. B., s. 139, s. 279, n. 995; Bull., 1834, p. 55.
[2] Ibid. s. 279, n. 996.
[3] Ibid. 1003; Raoul Rochette, Mon. Ined., pl. xxxv. pp. 192-196.
[4] Gerhard, B. A. B., 1010, ss. 295, 296.
[5] Ibid. no. 1222, s. 309.
[6] Ibid. s. 296, no. 1011.
[7] Ibid. 1019, s. 307.
[8] Ibid. 1023, s. 313.
[9] Gerhard, B. A. B., 1024, s. 315.
[10] For these vases, see Jahn, Vasen., s. xxxviii.; Gerhard, Apulische Vasen-bilder, fo. Berlin, 1845.

have suffered from the ravages of the Lucanians, who,
OL. XCVI., B. C. 396, advancing rapidly, seized part of the
country and the maritime cities. These were succeeded
by the Brettii, who, forty years later, revolted in OL. CVI.,
A. C. 356, and who issued gold coins of great beauty,
probably struck in the maritime cities, showing the high
state of the arts of the period. The vases are not found
in covered sepulchres, like those previously described, but
in the cultivated ground, as if scattered by a barbarian and
plundering population. So thoroughly have the vases on
this site been destroyed, that it is almost impossible to discover all the fragments of any single one. Those in the
Berlin Museum, which formerly belonged to Baron Koller,
were found broken within a sepulchre, and a vase holding
the ashes of the dead was discovered deposited in another
of coarser ware, which served as a kind of case for it,[1]
much in the same manner as glass vases are found holding
the ashes of the ancient Romans or Britons in this
country. They are of different styles of art, commencing with those of black figures. In the fainter
colour of their paste, and the duller tone of their black
glaze, they differ from those of Vulci, and few of the
earlier kind are known. Among them may be cited a
hydria or *calpis* with an erotic subject,[2] and a *lecythus*
with a Bacchanalian one.[3] The most remarkable of these
with red figures are the *hydria* or *calpis*, on which is
represented the last night of Troy, Neoptolemus slaying
Priam on the altar of the Herceian Zeus, the death of
Astyanax, and the rape of Cassandra; a *lecythus* with an

[1] Gargiulo, Cenni, p. 13; Bull., 1834,
p. 166.

[2] Gerhard, Berl. Ant. Bild., s. 231, 721.
[3] Ibid. 232, 725.

erotic scene ;[1] an *œnochoe*, with a Bacchanalian one ;[2] a
Nolan amphora, with figures of Marsyas and Olympus ;[3]
a vase with the Dioscuri and their names ;[4] a two-handled
vase with Triptolemus,[5] and an amphora with Zeus and
Nike.[6] Of the later style of art, and resembling the local
style of Lucania is an amphora, with the subject of Venus,
Adonis, and Eros.[7] In the Durand collection were also
some *lecythi* of the late Athenian style, with polychrome
figures on a white ground, and of a coarser kind of drawing
than those of Athens. One vase of this site has a remarkable inscription.[8]

In the department of Otranto, *Brindisi*, the ancient
Brundusium, founded before Tarentum and the arrival
of the Spartan Parthenii, a formidable rival to Tarentum, and one of the great ports of Italy, colonised by
the Romans A. V. C. 508, A. C. 246, has produced several
vases. Besides the numerous black glazed plates impressed
with small ornaments stamped from a die, a great *crater*
in the Naples Museum, painted with the subject of Eros
mounted on a panther,[9] came from thence. Vases have
also been found in the vicinity of *Oria*,[10] or Hyria, between
Brindisi and Taranto, a town of great antiquity, founded
by the Cretans sent in pursuit of Dædalus, and which
successfully resisted the people of Tarentum and Rhegium. At *Torre di Mare* (the ancient Metapontium,
supposed to be the Alybas of Homer, but colonised by
Achæans from Sybaris, the great head-quarters of the

[1] Gerhard, B. A. B., s. 232, 726.
[2] Ibid. 728.
[3] Gerhard, l. c. s. 244, 841.
[4] Jahn, Vasensammlung, s. xxxv.
[5] Gerhard, B. A. B., s. 259, 896;
Panofka, Mus. Bart., p. 133.
[6] Gerhard, B. A. B., s. 259, 898.
[7] Ibid. 332, 1057.
[8] ΚΑΛΕΔΟΚΕΣ, Bull., 1829, p. 167.
[9] Bull., Arch. 1829, p. 172.
[10] Bull., 1834, p. 55.

Pythagoreans, and subsequently, during the Peloponnesian war, in alliance with Athens; finally subjugated by the Romans after the retreat of Pyrrhus, but subsequently revolting to Hannibal), the circumstance of Roman sepulchres having been constructed over the Greek ones appears to have been unfavourable to excavations in search of vases. Some of late style have also been discovered at *Castellaneta*,[1] at the site of the ancient Salentum in its neighbourhood, and at *Fasano*,[2] or Gnathia, at *Ceglie, Genosa*, and *Ostuni*, all of late style.

At *Taranto*, or Tarentum, where it might have been expected from its ancient renown for luxury that many vases would have occurred, few have been turned up amidst its ancient ruins. Those, however, which are met with maintain the old pre-eminence of the city for its works of art, especially as manifested in its coins. Their clay is of a fine glaze like the vases of Pomarico, and often resembles the finest red figured vases of Nola.[3] Vases with black figures are rarely found; a fine crater with an Amazonomachia was discovered here;[4] and on the fragment of a *crater* in the British Museum is the Pallas Athene of the Parthenon, in red upon a black ground. It is of the best style of this School, probably not much older than Alexander, B. C. 330, if not over half a century later, or of the age of Pyrrhus, B. C. 280; although the medallic art of that time is more like the style of drawing found on the vases of Ruvo. Generally, the subjects of the vases discovered here are unimportant.

[1] Bull., 1836, p. 167.

[2] A vase with a siren between two owls, was there discovered. See Bull.,

1849, p. 174.

[3] Bull., 1829, p. 171.

[4] Duc. de Luynes, choix. pl. 43.

Some objects, supposèd to be moulds, have also been discovered on this site,[1] and the vases here, as at Locri, are
found broken into fragments.   Vases with black figures
are comparatively rare on this site, those with red figures
of a free style, having been principally found.   This
agrees with its history, the most flourishing period of the
city having been from B. C. 400, under the government of
Archytas till its final fall to the Romans, during which
time the principal sculptors and painters of Greece embellished the public monuments of Tarentum.   Its treasures
of ancient art at the period of its fall were equal to those
of Syracuse ; and there can be no doubt, from the beauty
of its coins, that it not only imported the choicest ceramic products of Greece, but also employed in its city
vase painters and potters of eminence.   Other specimens
come from Molto, La Castellaneta, and La Terza, in the
vicinity ; from the latter they are principally dishes.
Vases of Campanian style have also been found at *Lecce*,
the ancient Lupiæ,[2] at *Rugge*, or Rudiæ, and at Rocca
Nova and Valesio.[3]

At the island of *Ischia*, Ænaria, was found a *crater*
with the subject of the infant Dionysus consigned to the
Nymphs.[4]

SICILY AND MALTA.

Sicily, so celebrated for its magnificent works of art,
has not produced a very great number of fictile vases,
and the greater part of those discovered are by no means
pre-eminently distinguished from those of Italy ; some

---

[1] Bull., 1842, p. 120.   [3] Mommsen, Unterital. Dial., 58–60.
[2] Reidesel, Reise, 230.   [4] Schulz, in Bull., 1842, p. 10.

resembling in style the early vases, with black figures of
Greece Proper; while others are undistinguishable from
those of Southern Italy. The vases with red figures
especially resemble those found in the Apulian tombs.
Many of the vases from the Peninsula are however carried over to Palermo and sold as Sicilian, so that it is by
no means certain which are really Sicilian vases. This
island was anciently renowned for its potteries, and Agathocles, the celebrated tyrant of this island, was the son
of a potter, and was reported to have dined off earthenware
in his youth. The various sites in which vases have been
found at Syracuse, Palermo, Elima, Himera, and Alicata,
will be found subsequently mentioned. In Sicily the cities
of the southern coast have produced the greatest number
of vases, Agrigentum, the modern Girgenti, abounding in
the treasures of ceramic art. Fine vases have also been
discovered at Gela and Camarina. On the east coast,
south of Syracuse, the cemeteries of the Leontini and
Acræ have produced more vases than the necropolis
of Syracuse, which was probably the first destroyed.
Palermo, Messina, and Catania,[1] on the north and east
coast, have produced but a small number of vases. On the
whole, Sicily has produced far fewer ancient vases than
Italy.[2]

The principal sites where vases have been discovered
are *Centorbi*, the ancient Centuripæ, where a vase was
found, with encaustic painting, the colours having
been prepared with wax, and laid upon a rose-coloured
ground. This vase is ornamented with gilding, and is of

[1] Serra di Falco, Bull., 1834.   si trovano in Sicilia, 8vo, Pal., 1829,
[2] Avolio, Delle fatture di argilla che   p. 6.

a late style and period.[1]   At *Lentini*, Leontini, vases,
chiefly of the later style of art, have been discovered,
many polychrome, and one or two with red figures of
the strong style.[2]   The vases found at *Syracuse* have
both red and black figures, and are of both styles,
but unimportant.[3]   At *Palazzolo*, the ancient Acræ,
vases of the ancient Doric or Phœnician style, of the
Archaic style, and some with red figures, have been discovered; one of the most interesting is that in the British
Museum, representing Dionysos in a car in the shape of a
ship.[4]   Fine vases have been found at *Kamarina*; at
Terranova, the ancient Gela, one of the earliest settlements of the island, vases had been found a century ago,
both with black and red figures,[5] and in style like those of
Nola.[6]   In 1792, a pottery with furnaces and vases appears to have been discovered in the vicinity.[7]   Quite
recently vases with black and with red figures, of the
finest style, have been discovered here.

In *Selinunte*, or Selinus, famous for its two ancient
Doric temples, its archaic sculptures, and for the beauty of
its coins, both of the ancient and finest style, lecythi of
archaic style have come to light.[8]   *Himera* has produced
only one vase [9] with red figures, and the single specimen
found at Solus has been doubted.[10]

[1] This mode of painting vases is
alluded to by Athenæus, v. 200 b. The
vase is not unique, similarly painted
fragments having been discovered in
the Biscari Museum in Catania, at
Kertch, and in the Durand Collection :
Rochette, Peint. Ant. In., p. 430, taf. xii.;
Bull., 1833, p. 490.

[2] Jahn, Vasensammlung, s. xxxi.

[3] Gerhard, Aus. Vas. 68, i.; Bull.,

1832, p. 177.

[4] Judica, Antichita di Acre, fo. Messina, 1819.

[5] Dorville, Sicula, p. 123 b.

[6] Böttiger, Vasen, i. p. 39.

[7] Uhden, Arch. Intell. Bl. 1836, p. 33.

[8] Gerhard, in Arch. Int. Bl., 1834, p. 55.

[9] B. Romano, Antichita Termitane
Pal. 1838, p. 139, taf. i. H.

[10] Jahn, Vasensammlung, s. xxxiv.

Several vases are described in various accounts of these remains as coming from Sicily. Several of these with black figures exhibit a style of drawing so rude and peculiar as to entitle them to be considered decidedly of local fabric, as they are readily to be distinguished from those of Vulci, Nola, and Campania. Those with red figures have also certain characteristics, such as defects of shape and careless style of drawing, which connect them with the vases of Greece Proper. One of the most interesting specimens of this class discovered of late years, is a fragment, with the subject of Telegonos, Circe, and Ulysses.[1] Most of the vases come from Girgenti, and few from Palermo.[2] The vases of *Girgenti*, or Agrigentum, with black figures, resemble those of Vulci in the rigidity and mechanical finish of their details ; among them may be cited, a Panathenaic amphora, with Hercules and Cerberus, Hermes and Bacchanals ;[3] a *lecythus*, having on it the destruction of the Lernæan Hydra ;[4] another, with a warrior leaping from his horse ;[5] the *amphoræ* of the maker Taleides, with Theseus and the Minotaur, and a scene of weighing ;[6] another with Achilles and Hector, and Aurora bearing off Memnon.[7] A curious vase of the maker Nicosthenes [8] has also been found there. From these and similar subjects, such as Hercules and Tritons,[9]

[1] Bull., 1843, 82; Arch. Zeit., 1843, 143.

[2] One, with birth and marriage of Dionysos, Bull., 1834, p. 201, 1843, p. 54 ; Arch. Zeit., 1843, 137.

[3] Politi, Anfora Panatenaica, 8vo, Girgenti, 1840.

[4] Politi, Il mostro di Lerna lekitos Agrigentino, 8vo, Palermo, 1840.

[5] Politi, Esposizione di sette vase Gr.

Sic. Agr., 8vo, Palermo, 1832.

[6] Millin, Peint. d. Vases Ant., pl. i. lxvi. ; Explic., ii. p. 88, n. 7.

[7] Millingen, Anc. Un. Mon., i. pl. 3, 4.

[8] Panofka, Mus. Blac., pl. 111 ; Gerhard, Lettres, p. 40.

[9] Politi, Lettera al S. Mellingen su di una figulina rappresentante Ercole e Nereo, 8vo, Palermo, 1834.

Achilles dragging Hector,[1] and Bacchanals,[2] it will be seen that they are of the usual class found on the best and rigid school of vases with red figures. Numerous examples of this style have been found in Sicily, such as *lecythi* with females,[3] Hera and her peacock,[4] Nike,[5] the Dioscuri, scenes from the Amazonomachia,[6] warriors,[7] Dionysus,[8] and birds.[9] Among the finest vases of this style are the *amphoræ* of Munich, representing Tityus seizing Leto, and Mr. Stoddart's *crater* with an Amazonomachia.[10] But that representing the meeting of Alcæus and Sappho, now in the Museum of Munich, is the most renowned of all.[11]

Most of the vases of Girgenti however are of the shape of the *craters* of *oxybapha* and resemble those of the tombs of Lucania. They have such subjects as the Hyperborean Apollo,[12] Dionysiac representations,[13] the return of Hephaistos to Heaven,[14] the Centauromachia,[15] scenes of leave-taking,[16] triclinia,[17] and Achilles and Amazon.[18]

---

[1] Politi, Cenni su di un vaso fittile Greco-Agr. rapp. Achille vincitore di Ettore, 8vo, Messina, 1828.

[2] Politi, Esposizione di sette vasi, l. c.; Bull. d. Inst., 1834. p. 59.

[3] Politi, Illustr. sul dipinto in terracotta, 8vo, Girg., 1829.

[4] Politi, Esposizione di sette vase Gr. Sic. Agr., 8vo, Palermo, 1832.

[5] Ibid.

[6] Ibid.

[7] Politi, Un lekitos, 8vo, Palermo, 1840.

[8] Politi, Due parole, 8vo, Pal. 1833.

[9] Politi, Esposizione di sette vase, l. c.

[10] Politi, Illustrazione sul dipinto in terra-cotta, 8vo, Girgenti, 1829.

[11] Millingen, Anc. Un. Mon., xxxiv.; La borde, Vase de Lamberg, pl. lii.

[12] Politi, Illustrazione d'un vaso Græco Siculo rappresentante Nemesi trovato nell antica Agrigento, 8vo, Palermo, 1826, p. 22, tav. iii.

[13] Politi, Cinque Vasi di Premio, extracted from La Concordia Giornale Siciliano, Num. 14–20. Laglio Anno Secundo; Minervini; Bull. Arch. Nap., i. 14; Gerhard, A. Z., s. 61.

[14] Politi, Illustrazione sul dipinto in terra cotta, 8vo, Girgenti, 1829, tav. 4.

[15] Politi, Cinque Vasi di Premio., tav. vi.; osserv. 8vo, Ven. 1828; Minervini, Bull. Nap., i. p. 14; Gerhard, A. Z., 1843, s. 60.

[16] Politi, Descr. di due Vasi Græco-Sicoli Agrigentino, 8vo, Girgenti, 1831.

[17] Politi, Illustraz., tav. 3.

[18] Politi, Due parole su tre Vasi fittili, 8vo, Palermo, 1833. The name of the Amazon is ΣΛΔΕΣΙΣ.

Many interesting vases of the shape called *celebe* also come from Girgenti, and are of the more perfect style of art, representing Zeus bearing off Ægina,[1] the Eleusinian deities,[2] Dionysos confided to the nursing of Ariadne,[3] the departure of Triptolemus, Aurora and Thetis pleading for their sons,[4] Peleus and Thetis,[5] and some general scenes.[6] Cups with white ground, and with subjects in linear outline, have also been discovered there, and one in the Museum at Munich has the subject of Bacchanals, Hercules killing Cycnus, or the Amazons.[7] The Atticisim of the inscriptions[8] has been alleged as a reason for supposing the vases of this island to have been imported, but the Ionic colonies, such as Acragas, and the prevalence of Ionic and Attic Greek as a polite language, may account for the appearance of this dialect. Vases of fine style have also been discovered at Catania and some with black figures at Alicata.[9] Vases with red figures, of good style, have been found at *Aderno*, Adranon, at the foot of Etna.[10]

In the public Museum at *Malta* are also some vases of Phœnician and later Greek style, with Bacchanalian subjects. One represents the capture of Midas.[11] Another

---

[1] Politi, Cinque Vasi di Premio, tav. iv.

[2] Politi, Illustr. di un Vaso fittile rappr. Apollo il citaredo e le pace en Girgenti, 8vo, Palermo, 1826.

[3] Mon., iii. pl. 17; Ann., 1835, p. 82.

[4] Politi, Cinque Vasi di Premio, Concord., ii. 14; Bull. Arch. Nap., ii. p. 16; Gerhard, Arch. Zeit., 1843, p. 14.

[5] Politi, Illustr. ad un Vaso rappr. Cassandra e Ajace, d'Oileo, 8vo, Palermo,

1828; Minervini, Bull. Arch. Nap., i. p. 14; Gerhard, A. Z., 1843, 61, Poseidon und Amymone.

[6] Politi, ibid., also Descr. di due Vasi Greco-Sicoli, 8vo, Girg., 1831.

[7] Politi, Desc. di due Vasi. l. c.

[8] Kramer, Ueber die Herkunft, s. 119.

[9] Jahn, Vasensamml. s. xxxii.

[10] Bull., 1843, p. 129.

[11] De Witte, Bull., 1842, p. 43.

has Eros, with his name.[1] These vases are said to resemble those found in Sicily and Campania.

AFRICA.

Passing from Sicily to the coast of Africa, the site of *Bengazi*—the old *Euhesperis* of the Cyrenaica, which subsequently obtained the name of *Berenice* from the queen of Ptolemy Philadelphus—abounds in sepulchres, in which have been found a very large number of vases of the later style of art, like those of Lucania and Apulia. Of these the most remarkable are the Panathenaic vases, which have black figures on a red ground, and the usual inscription of "[I am] one of the prizes from Athens," accompanied with the names of the following archons :—Hegesias and Nicocrates, who were archons at Athens in the 4th year of CXI. Olympiad, A. C. 334 ; Cephisodorus, who was archon in the 2nd year of CXIV. Olympiad, A. C. 323 ; Archippus, who was archon of the 4th year of the same Olympiad, A. C. 321 ; and Theophrastus, whose name occurs as that of archon of the 1st year of CX. Olympiad, A. C. 340, or of CXVI. Olympiad, A. C. 313.[2] They are remarkable for showing the late period at which black figures

[1] Reidesel, Reise, p. 74 ; Jahn, Vasensammlung, s. xxix.

[2] Cf. ΑΓΑΣΙΑΣ ΑΡΧΟΝ ΤΟΝ ΑΘΕΝΕΘΕΝ ΑΘΛΟΝ, R. Rochette, Ann., vi. 287, n. 2 ; Böckh, Corp. Inscr. Græc., ii. p. 70, No. 2035 ; P. Lucas, ii. 84. Some of these vases from the Cyrenaica are in the Museum of Leyde ; Lenormant and De Witte, Élite des Monumens, Introd. p. xix. Many of these vases are like those found at Nola, while others resemble the pottery of Melos, especially the coarser fabrics ; while the appearance of the head of Jupiter Ammon on a vase indicates a local fabric ; Lenormant and De Witte, Élite, Introd. xxiv. and n. 2. Jahn, Vasensammlung, s. xxviii. xxix.

were used.[1] These vases, from the Atticism of their
inscriptions, are conjectured to have been imported
from Athens. Two other vases of a supposed historical
import have also been found there—one representing a
Persian king attacked by a lion, the other Aristippus
between Arete, his daughter, and Aphrodite.[2] These last
have inscriptions in the Doric dialect.

The principal excavations on this site are those recently
made by M. Vattier de Bourville and Mr. Werry.
Besides the prize vases, many small vases and a few large
of later style, some few polychrome, with subjects of little
interest, and resembling the later vases found at Ruvo,
Apulia, and the Basilicata, have been exhumed here, and
at the adjoining spots of *Ptolemata*, or Ptolemais, and
Tukera. A selection of Mr. Werry's vases are in the
British Museum.

Of the vases in the Louvre, Mr. Newton, Vice-Consul at
Mytilene observes : " The collection of the vases from the
Cyrenaica is very interesting. The two vases with black
figures, with the names of Athenian archons, are in a
style of complete decadence. The figures have the small
heads and general proportions of the school of Lysippus ;
the drawing is very coarse, and, compared with the
drawing of other vases, may be called cursive. On each
of the two columns, between which Pallas stands, is Nike,
holding an aplustron. Their form is the late Basilicatan
kind of amphora. A number of very interesting vases
and terra-cottas have been brought from the Cyrenaica.

[1] Lenormant, Revue Archéologique,
1848 p. 230; Paul Lucas, t. ii. p. 84,
ed. Amst., 1714 ; Böckh, Corp. Inscr.
Græc., t. ii. p. 70, No. 2035.
[2] Lenormant, Nouvelles Annales,
1847, 391.

The vases seem to be of Athenian manufacture. Among
them are many polychrome, like the pyxis of Mr. Burgon's
collection. They have ornaments in relief, gilt. On one
most curious vase is a mixture of painting and bas relief.
Cupid is seen, seated on a rock, fishing. The rock is raised
in slight relief, the wings of the Cupid are painted red, the
accessories are gilt. Before him are two figures hauling
in a net ; the whole in a very slight relief, on a black
ground. The composition is elegant and graceful, like
the mural paintings of Pompeii. There is also a vase
with a curious caricature of Hercules, after his Libyan
victory, standing in a chariot driven by Victory, to which
four Centaurs are harnessed. The faces are of the
Nubian type ; those of the Centaurs very grotesque, and
full of comic expression. These are now in the Museum
of the Louvre."

Vases have also been found at Tripolis, on the same
coast. They are also of late style, few with black figures,
the greater portion with red figures, and unimportant
subjects, principally ornaments. A few of like style have
also been discovered at *Leptis*.[1]

To the other vases found on the African coast and in
Egypt, allusion has been already made—such as those
of Coptos, famous for being made of an aromatic
earth.[2] Naucratis was celebrated for its *phialæ* having
four handles, and a glaze so fine that they passed for
silver. They were not made upon the wheel, but modelled
with the hand.[3] In the catacombs of Alexandria, vases
with a pale paste, and painted in the last style of

---

[1] Jahn, Vasensammlung, s. xxix.
[2] Brongniart, Traité, i. p. 582.
[3] Brongniart, ibid ; Athenæus, x. c. 61.

Greek art, have been discovered, some of which are now
in the Louvre,[1] and others in the British Museum.   Their
paste occasionally is of a violet colour.[2]

CRIMEA.

The northernmost point at which vases have been found
is *Kertch*, the ancient *Panticapæum*, one of the other colonies
of the Milesians, in the Cimmerian Bosphorus, celebrated at
a later period for its commerce, and in A. C. 120, finally
subdued by Mithradates.   About 400 vases, scarcely a
fourth of which have subjects of the least importance, have
been found in this locality.   Few have black figures, and
their drawing is in the careless and free style of the Greek
potteries.   The rest are principally small vases, with red
figures, of the later style of art, and some of these are
polychromatic, and ornamented with gilding.   The most
remarkable of these vases is that of the Athenian potter,
Xenophantus, having for its subject a combat of gryphons
and the Arimaspi, a story of local interest.   These vases
appear to be about the time of the Bosphoran king Leucon,
who flourished A. C. 393-353.   Fragments of a vase of the
artist Epictetus have also been discovered in this vicinity.[3]
Most of these are now in the Hermitage of St. Petersburg.
They are probably Athenian, most of them ill-preserved.
M. Brongniart describes one from this site, at present in

[1] Brongniart, l. c. 582.
[2] Mus. de Sèvres, i. 18.
[3] For the vases found here see Annali,
1832, p. 6; Dubois de Montpéreux,
Voyage autour du Caucase. Pad.
1843, Pl. 7-15; Ashit, Bosph. Reich.
4to Od. 1848-49, iii. t. 3. 26; Bull. 1841,

p. 105; Köhne in the Bulletin de la
Soc. Arch. & Num. de St. Petersburg, ii. 7. ; Jahn, Vasensammlung,
s. xxviii.   A coin of Leucon was found
with a vase. Annali. xii. 13.; Ouvaroff,
Antiquités du Bosphore Cimmerien,
vol. iii., p. xlvi.-lxviii.

the Bibliothèque Imperiale at Paris, as having a beautiful
black glaze, and a bas-relief in the midst of it.[1] The vases
have red figures, and are of the style of the decadence
of the art, the workmanship being coarse, and the subjects
uninteresting ; such as, the Dionysiac thiasos,[2] gymnastic
scenes,[3] and those of private life.[4] Their shapes were the
hydria, calpis, pelice, and *lecane.*[5]

ENAMELLED WARE.

In the sepulchres of Greece, the Islands, and Italy,
a class of ware has been found, quite distinct from the
preceding, and resembling the enamelled stone ware of
the Egyptians and Babylonians already described. Many
Egyptian perfume vases have been found in the sepulchres
of Etruria ; and as their hieroglyphs [6] are identical with
those found in Egypt, it is probable that they were
imported into Etruria from that country. There are,
however, some other vases of this class of ancient fayence,
or porcelain, which are not so decidedly Egyptian—such
as certain jars, ornamented with zigzag white ornaments
and maroon petals, on a pale, dull green ground, and

[1] Brongniart, Traité, i. 578. Engravings of these vases will be found in
Dubois de Montpéreux, Voyage autour
du Caucase, etc., Paris, 1843, 6 vols.
atlas folio, and Anton Ashik, Bos-
phorische Alterthumer, Odessa, 1848 ;
Cf. Annali, 1840, p. 6.
[2] Gerhard, l. c. s. 195; Dubois de
Montpéreux and Ashik, l. c.
[3] Ibid. These principally are draped
and enveloped figures.
[4] ΞΕΝΟΦΑΝΤΟΣ ΕΠΟΙΗΣΕΝ ΑΘΗΝ.

Bull., 1837, p. 47, 1841, pp. 108, 109;
Dubois de Montpéreux, Voyage autour
du Caucase, V. Classe at Kertch;
these vases exhibit proofs of a local
fabric; Lenormant and De Witte,
Introd., xxiii.
[5] Bull., 1841, p. 108. Dubois de
Montpéreux, Atlas, pl. vii.; Gerhard,
Denkmaler Forschungen und Berichte,
1850, s. 193.
[6] Micali, Mon. Inedit., tav. vii.

which may be imitations by Greek potters of this foreign ware.[1]

The specimen here represented was found by Campanari in a tomb at Vulci.
Some very beautiful specimens have been discovered in the tombs of southern Italy. A beautiful small *calathus*-shaped vase, procured by the late Mr. Chambers Hall at Naples, and by him presented to the British Museum, is of a pale green, inlaid with blue and white ornaments ; and a *prochoos*,

No. 171.—Jar of enamelled Ware. Vulci.

or bottle, in his possession, is most delicately decorated with ornaments of the same kind.

Several *lecythi*, or little toilet vases, of this ware, have been discovered in the tombs of Melos and Cære, and at Vulci. Their shapes show that they had not an origin purely oriental, having been delivered from moulds, and then glazed. They are in the shape of a female kneeling, and holding a jar, the heads of satyrs and nymphs, alectryons and hedgehogs. In the Egyptian grotto of the Polledrara at Vulci were found scarabæi and beads, also of this ware. At Athens one was found in the shape of a double head of Hercules and Omphale,[2] and at Melos another in the form of a hedgehog.[3]

---

[1] Mus. Etrus. Vatic. ii. iv.
[2] Panofka, Rech., p. 25, pl. iii. 55.

[3] Bull., 1831, pp. 184–90.

IMITATIONS.

The discovery of painted vases, and the general admiration which they excited among the lovers of the fine arts, gave rise to several imitations. The first of these were made by Mr. Wedgewood. His paste is, however, heavier, and his drawings far inferior to the antique in freedom and spirit. At Naples, chiefly through the researches and directions of Gargiulo, vases have of late years been produced, which in their paste and glaze resemble the antique, although the drawings are vastly inferior, and the imitation is at once detected by a practised eye. They are far inferior in all essential respects to the ancient vases. Even soon after the acquisition of the Hamilton collection by the public, the taste created for these novelties caused various imitations to be produced. Some of the simplest kind were made of wood, covered with painted paper, the subjects being traced from the vases themselves, and this was the most obvious mode of making them. Of late Mr. Battam has made very excellent facsimiles of these vases, but they are produced in a manner very different from that of the ancient potters, the black colour for the grounds or figures not being laid on with a glaze, but merely with a cold pigment which has not been fired, and their lustre being produced by a polish. Such a process by no means gives them the extreme beauty of the better specimens of the ancient potteries, and in technical details they do not equal the imitations made at Naples, some of the best of which have occasionally deceived both archæologists and collectors. Even in the

times of antiquity many counterfeits existed, for the
potters evidently often endeavoured to assume the names
of their rivals, without infringing the laws of their respective states, by inscribing them on their vases in an illegible
manner. These, however, can scarcely be classed in the
category of ancient forgeries, like the Etruscan painted
vases, imitated from the Greek. These are chiefly found
on Etruscan sites ; but some few from Athens itself show
that they were manufactured at home. They may possibly
have been a particular style of fabric, introduced as a
novelty to attract the popular taste, and subsequently
abandoned.

One of the most remarkable fabricated engravings of
these vases was that issued by Brondsted and Stackelberg, in a fit of archæological jealousy. A modern
archæologist is seen running after a draped female figure,
called ΦΗΜΗ, or " Fame," who flies from him exclaiming,
ΕΚΑΣ ΠΑΙ ΚΑΛΕ, " Be off, my fine fellow ! " This vase,
which never existed except upon paper, deceived the
credulous Inghirami, who too late endeavoured to cancel
it from his work. Other vases, evidently false, have also
been published.[1]

PRICES.

In the ancient times of Rome, these vases bore a high
value, and sold for enormous sums to connoisseurs, which
has also been the case in modern times. Cleopatra spent
daily on the fragrant or .flowery ware of Rhossus, a
Syrian town, six minæ.[2] Of the actual prices paid for

[1] Inghirami, Vasi Fittili, i. tav. xiii.;
a false vase also is published in Passeri, ccc., and another in D'Hancarville,

ii. 84 ; D'Hancarville, ii. 71.
[2] Athen. vi. 229, e.

painted vases, no positive mention occurs in classical
authorities, yet it is most probable that vases of the
best class, the products of eminent painters, obtained
considerable prices. Among the Greeks, works of merit
were at all times handsomely remunerated, and it is
probable that vases of excellence shared the general
favour shown to the fine arts. For works of inferior
merit only small sums were paid, as will be seen by
referring to the chapter on inscriptions, which were
incised on their feet, and which mentioned their contemporary value. In modern times little is known about the
prices paid for these works of art till quite a recent
period, when their fragile remains have realised considerable sums. In this country the collections of Mr.
Townley, Sir W. Hamilton, Lord Elgin, and Mr. Payne
Knight, all contained painted vases ; yet, as they included
other objects, it is difficult to determine the value placed
on the vases. A sum of 500*l.* was paid in consideration
of the Athenian vases in Lord Elgin's collection, which
is by no means large when the extraordinary nature of
these vases is considered, as they are the finest in the
world of the old primitive vases of Athens. 8400*l.* were
paid for the vases of the Hamilton collection, one of the
most remarkable of the time, and consisting of many
beautiful specimens from southern Italy. The great
discoveries of the Prince of Canino, in 1827, and the
subsequent sale of numerous vases, gave them, however,
a definite market value, to which the sale of the collection
of Baron Durand, which consisted almost entirely of
vases, affords some clue. His collection sold in 1836 for
313,160 francs, or about 12,524*l.* The most valuable

specimen in the collection was the vase representing
the death of Crœsus, which was purchased for the Louvre
at the price of 6600 francs, or 264*l*. The vase with the
subject of Arcesilaus brought 1050 francs. Another
magnificent vase, now in the Louvre, having the subject
of the youthful Hercules strangling the serpents, was
only secured for France after reaching the price of
6000 francs, or 240*l* ; another, with the subject of
Hercules, Dejanira, and Hyllus, was purchased for the
sum of 3550 francs, or 142*l*. A *crater*, with the subject
of Acamas and Demophon bringing back Æthra, was
obtained by M. Magnoncourt for 4250 francs, or 170*l*. A
Bacchic amphora, of the maker Execias, of the archaic
style, was bought by the British Museum for 3600 francs,
or 142*l*., in round numbers. Enough has, however, been
said to show the high price attained by the most remarkable of these works of art. The inferior vases of
course realised much smaller sums, varying from a few
francs to a few pounds ; but high prices continued to be
obtained, and the sale by the Prince of Canino in 1837,
of some of his finest vases, contributed to enrich the
museums of Europe, although, as many of the vases were
bought in, it does not afford a good criterion as to price.
An *œnochöe*, with Apollo and the Muses, and a *hydria*,
with the same subject, were bought in for 2000 francs,
or 80*l*. each. A *cylix*, with a love scene, and another with
Priam redeeming Hector's corpse, brought 6600 francs,
or 264*l*. An amphora with the subject of Dionysus, and
a cup with that of Hercules, sold for 8000 francs, or
320*l*., each. Another brought 7000 francs, or 280*l*. A
vase with the subject of Theseus seizing Helen, another

with the arming of Paris, and a third with Peleus and Thetis, sold for 6000 francs, or 240*l.* Nor can the value of the finest specimens of the art be considered to have deteriorated since. The late Mr. Steuart was offered 7500 francs for a large *crater*, found in southern Italy, ornamented with the subject of Cadmus and the dragon ; 3000 francs, or 120*l.*, were paid by the British Museum for a fine *crater* ornamented with the exploits of Achilles ; 2500 francs, or 100*l.*, for an amphora of Apulian style, with the subject of Pelops and Œnomaus at the altar of the Olympian Zeus. For another vase, with the subject of Musæus, 3000 francs, or 120*l.* were paid, and 2500 francs, or 100*l.*, for the Athenian prize vase, the celebrated Vas Burgonianum, exhumed by Mr. Burgon. At Mr. Beckford's sale, the late Duke of Hamilton gave 200*l.* for a small vase, with the subject of the Indian Bacchus.

The passion for possessing fine vases has outstripped these prices at Naples ; 2400 ducats, or 500*l.*, was given for the vase with gilded figures discovered at Cumæ. Still more incredible, half a century back, 8000 ducats, or 1500*l.*, was paid to Vivenzio for the vase in the Museo Borbonico representing the last night of Troy ; 6000 ducats, or 1000*l.*, for the one with a Dionysiac feast ; and 4000 ducats, or 800*l.*, for the vase with the grand battle of the Amazons, published by Schulz. But such sums will not be hereafter realized, not that taste is less, but that fine vases are more common. No sepulchre has been spared when detected, and no vase neglected when discovered ; and vases have been exhumed with more activity than the most of precious relics.

The vases of Athens, with white grounds and polychrome

figures, have also been always much sought after, and have realised large prices, the best preserved examples fetching as much as 70*l.* or 100*l.* Generally those vases which are finest in point of art have realised the highest

No. 172.—Lecythus.   Triumph of Indian Bacchus.

prices, but in some instances they have been surpassed in this respect by others of high literary or historical value. As a general rule, vases with inscriptions have always been most valuable, the value of these objects being much enhanced when inscribed with the names of potters or artists, or with remarkable expressions. The inferior kinds have fetched prices much more moderate, the *cylices* averaging from 5*l.* to 10*l.*, the *amphoræ* from 10*l.* to 20*l.*, the *hydriæ* about the same, the *craters* from 5*l.* to 20*l.*, according to their general excellence, the *œnochöe* about 5*l.*, and the miscellaneous shapes from a few shillings to a few pounds. Of the inferior vases, the charming glaze and shapes of those discovered at Nola have obtained the best prices from amateurs. Those of Greece Proper have also fetched rather a higher price than those of Italy, on account of the interest attached to the place of their discovery. Many charming vases of unglazed terra-cotta have rivalled in their prices even the best of the painted vases.[1] Although there are scarcely limits to the desire of possessing noble works of art, it will be seen that vases have never excited the minds of men so much as the nobler creations of sculpture or of painting; nor have they reached the fabulous value of Sèvres porcelain or Dutch tulips. Even at the present day their price in the scale of public taste has been disputed, if not excelled, by the porcelain of the supposed barbarian Chinese, and Chelsea may pride itself that its china in value, if not in merit, has surpassed the choicest productions of the furnaces of Italy and Athens.

[1] Some account of the prices paid for vases will be found in the "Description des Antiquités et Objets d'Art qui composent le cabinet de feu M. le Chev. E. Durand," by M. J. De Witte, 8vo, Paris, 1836; in the "Supplement à la Description des Antiquités du cabinet de feu M. le Chev. E. Durand;" and in the "Description d'une collection des vases peints et bronzes antiques provenant' des fouilles de l'Etrurie," 8vo, Paris, 1837; also by M. De Witte.

PART III.

——◆——

ETRUSCAN POTTERY.

CHAPTER I.

Etruscan Terra-Cottas—Statues—Busts—Bas-reliefs—Sarcophagi—Vases—Brown Ware—Black Ware—Red Ware—Yellow Ware—Painted Vases—Imitations of Greek Vases—Subjects and Mode of Execution—Age—Vases of Orbetello and Volaterra—Vases with Etruscan Inscriptions—Latin Inscriptions on Enamelled Ware—Other sites.

FROM Grecian pottery we naturally pass to the Etruscan, as that people derived their arts from their Hellenic masters. Few remains, however, of their productions have reached the present day with the exception of vases, of which an immense number has been found, and which convey a very distinct notion of the Etruscan art. It is not, however, possible to trace the Etruscan arts in clay in so distinct a manner as the Greek or Roman, owing to the want of a literature among the Etruscans. Bricks and tiles they seem to have seldom employed, most of the public buildings and sepulchres having been composed of tufo. Gori has, indeed, published several tiles, some plain and others with flanges,

from the Museum Buccellianum,[1] having inscriptions in the
Etruscan language, either engraved or painted upon them,
commemorating the name and titles of the deceased, like
the inscriptions upon the sarcophagi. According to
Buonarotti, tiles were employed for closing the recesses in
the chambers within which were placed the little sarcophagi
which held the ashes of the dead.[2] These were principally
found in the sepulchres of Chiusi or Camars. One specimen had, besides the usual inscription, the figure of the
dead incised upon it.[3] At a later period, such tiles were
also used in graves, to cover the body laid at full length.
Some, which bear bilingual inscriptions, in the Etruscan and
Latin languages, show them to be not much older than the
latter days of the Roman republic, or the commencement
of the empire. According to Strabo, the walls of *Arretium*, or Arezzo, were made of these tiles, but no traces of
these ancient walls remain.[4] Some portions of the architectural decorations of tombs were made of terra-cotta;[5]
and sometimes certain altars, or other embellishment of
sepulchres, decorated with bas-reliefs, were moulded of
the same material. At Cervetri have been found the
antefixal ornaments at the end of the large imbrices or
joint tiles, with representations of the Gorgon's head,
modelled in the style of the earliest vases with yellow
grounds, and painted with colours in *engobe*. From the
same locality are said to have come the revetment of
the walls of a tomb made of slabs, about four feet high
and one inch thick, having painted on them a series of

[1] Gori, Mus. Etrus. tom. III. p. 134
and foll. t. xxviii. xxx.
[2] Dempst. ii. supp. xxvi. p. 36.
[3] Gori, p. 135.

[4] Strabo, V. p. 226; Dennis, II. p.
421.
[5] Dennis, II. 479.

mythical representations, treated in an archaic style, having some resemblance to the figures on the vases with yellow grounds.   The figures on these slabs are principally painted in red and black on a cream-coloured ground, but it is difficult to say whether all the colours have been burnt in.

STATUES.

Notwithstanding the reputation of the Etruscans for their works in clay, few statues of importance have descended to us.   Although some of the Greek authors,[1] and of the modern Italian writers,[2] claim the priority of the art of making figures in terra-cotta for Italy, there can be no doubt that the Etruscans, in their modelling, imitated the Greeks.   It must be conceded that the art of modelling in clay preceded that of working in metals, in which last the Etruscans particularly excelled,[3] especially in the mechanical treatment.   The arrival of the Corinthian Demaratus, and of the artists in his train, in Italy, is the earliest record, that can be referred to, of the art of modelling clay ; working in bronze having been imported from Greece.

The most remarkable for its size and execution is a group of a male and female figure, reposing on a couch, in the Campana collection, of the same style of art as the early bronzes, and wall paintings of the sepulchres of Italy,—the figures life-size, of rather slender proportions, with smiling features, and flat and formal drapery.   This group is made of a clay, mixed with volcanic sand,

---

[1] Tatian. Orat. adv. Græc. c. i.   p. 10.
[2] Campana, Ant. op. in Plastica, c. iv.   [3] Pliny, xxxv. c. 16-44.

resembling the red ware, and is decorated with colour.
It is said to come from Cervetri, where similar figures in
relief, of pale red terra-cotta, have also been discovered,
all probably older than the foundation of Rome.

It is chiefly from the Roman writers that our knowledge of Etruscan statues in terra-cotta is derived, as the
Romans, unable themselves to execute such works, were
obliged to employ Etruscan artists for the decoration of
their temples, as will be subsequently seen in the description of Roman statues. Volcanius or Turianus of Fregellæ,
at Veii, was employed by Tarquinius Priscus to make the
statue of Jupiter in the Capitol, which was of colossal
proportions.[1] The quadriga placed on the acroterium of
the same temple, and a figure of Hercules in the Forum
Boarium, were modelled in the same material.[2] Numa
also consecrated a double statue of Janus, or a statue of
the two-headed Janus, of terra-cotta.[3]

According to Pliny, the art of statuary was so old in
Italy that its origin was unknown.[4] There was an export
trade thence even to Greece the greater part of which,
in all probability, consisted of works in metal.[5] The art
of working in terra-cotta, according to the same author,
was principally cultivated in Italy, and by the Etruscans.
They may indeed have worked from foreign models, and
perhaps from the statues of the Egyptians, with which they
first became acquainted when Psammetichus I. (A. C. 654)

[1] Pliny, N. H. xxxv. xii. 45; Cf.
Sillig. Dict. of Artists, 8vo, London,
1836, p. 137.
[2] Plutarch, Vit. Poplic. i. 409; Pliny,
N. H. xxxv. c. 45; Cf. also Martial,
xiv. Ep. 178.

[3] Pliny, loc. cit. xxxiv. vii. 16.
[4] Ibid. xxxiv. c. vii. 16 ; xxxv. 44, I.
c. 54 ; Dionysius, III. c. 46; Strabo, V.
c. 2.
[5] Ibid. loc. cit.

threw open Egypt to the commerce of the world, in the second century of the era of Rome. It was subsequently that the Romans employed Etruscan artists, and Tarquinius Priscus placed in the Capitol a terra-cotta statue of Jupiter, made by Volcanius of Veii or Turianus of Fregenni.[1]

Besides these, there were numerous fictile statues in the temples of Rome called *signa Tuscanica*, distinguished by their barbarous rigidity, and resembling in many respects the works of the Æginetan school. The Etruscans probably continued to supply Rome with statues till southern Italy submitted to her arms. The popular legends invested these fictile statues with a halo of superstition. The horses in the quadriga on the apex of the temple of Jupiter Capitolinus were reported to have swollen instead of contracting in the furnace—a circumstance which was supposed to prognosticate the future greatness of Rome.[2]

BUSTS.

No vestiges of any of these statues remain, and remarkably few small figures have been found in excavations made in Etruria, but some singular busts and models of viscera have been discovered on the sites of the ancient Gabii and at Vulci. The busts represent the face in profile and the neck ; the back is flat, to allow of the busts being attached to the wall, and has in the centre a hole for a peg to fix it. Models of hands, feet, of the breast

---

[1] Pliny, N. H. xxxv. c. 45 ; Campana (loc. cit. p. 13), prefers the reading "Fregenis" to "Fregillis," the Volscian town. See Sillig's notes to Pliny, loc.

[2] Festus, v. Ratumena.

and viscera, have also been found, some having plug-holes [1] for fixing them to statues, either made of other materials,

No. 173.—Etruscan Female Bust.   Vulci.

or in separate pieces, like the acrolithic statues of Greece. Some of these may have been *charisteria*, or thank-offerings, like those at Athens.

BAS-RELIEFS.

No bas-reliefs like those employed by the Romans to decorate the walls of edifices have been discovered in recent excavations, although it is probable that some of the temples were decorated with terra-cotta friezes. In the tombs, however, a considerable number of sarcophagi have been discovered, the greater part of small proportions, ornamented with subjects in bas-relief. The bas-relief models found at the ancient Gabii have been already mentioned ; in connection with which we may advert to some

D'Agincourt, Recueil, Pl. xviii. 4-7 ; xxii. 1-5.

bas-reliefs found in the Sabine territory, and engraved in the work of D'Agincourt.

SARCOPHAGI.

Although the more important sarcophagi of the Etruscans were made of alabaster, tufo, and peperino, a considerable number, principally of small size, were of terra-cotta. Some few were large enough to receive a body laid at full length. The reliefs in the smaller ones seem to have been moulded. The colour of their paste is either pale red or pale yellow, and some which were discovered in the tombs of Tarquinii and Volterra contained traces of pyroxene. Two large sarcophagi, removed from a tomb at Vulci, are now in the British Museum. The lower part, which held the body, is shaped like a rectangular bin or trough, about three feet high and as many wide. On the covers are recumbent Etruscan females, modelled at full length. One has both its cover and chest divided into two portions, probably because it was found that masses of too large a size failed in the baking. The edges at the point of division are turned up, like flange tiles. These have on their fronts either dolphins or branches of trees, incised with a tool in outline. Some of the same dimensions are engraved in the works of Inghirami and Micali, and are imitations of the larger sarcophagi of stone. Many of the smaller sort, which held the ashes of the dead, are of the same shape, the body being a small rectangular chest, while the cover presents a figure of the deceased in a reclining posture. They generally have in front a composition in bas-relief, freely modelled in the later style of

Etruscan art, the subject being of funereal import ; such as
the last farewell to the dead, combats of heroes, especially
one, in which an unarmed hero is fighting with a plough-
share ;[1] the parting of Admetus and Alcestis in the presence of Death and Charon,[2] and demons appearing at a
repast.[3] Some few have a painted roof. All these were
painted in water-colours, upon a white ground, in bright
and vivid tones, producing a gaudy effect. The inscriptions were also traced in paint, and not incised.

A good and elaborate example of taste in the colouring
of terra-cotta occurs on a small sarcophagus, presented by
the Marquis of Northampton to the British Museum, and
obtained by him at Florence. Here the flesh is red, the
eyes blue, the hair red, the wreath green, and the drapery
of the figure is white, with purple limbus, and crimson
border. The pillars are red, with purple and blue stripes.
The beards and hair are bluish purple, the arms blue, the
inside of the shield yellow, with a blue ground ; the
chlamydes yellow, purple, and crimson ; one blue, lined with
purple ; the mitræ red and blue. Even the pilasters are
coloured white, with red flutes ; the festoon of the capital
is green, and the abacus red, the dentals yellow, with a
red boss. The inscription is in brown letters, on a white
ground.

Some specimens of terra-cotta sarcophagi have been
engraved by Dempster[4] and Gori.[5] According to Lanzi
and Inghirami[6] they are seldom found at Volterra, while

[1] Brongniart, Mus. Cer. I. 3 ; Inghirami, Mon. Etrusc. tab. xxxviii.
p. 25.
[2] Inghirami, i. p. 324.
[3] Bull. 1844, p. 87.

[4] De Etruria regali, i. tab. liii.-lv.
[5] Mus. Etr. III. Præf. xxii., tom. I.
p. 92; Cf. Tab. clvii. clviii. cxci.
[6] Mon. Etrusc. i. tav. iii. p. 15.

they are frequently discovered in the sepulchres of Chiusi and of Monte Pulciano.[1] They are the prototypes of the Roman urns, which were ranged in niches round the columbaria or sepulchral chambers.

VASES.

We will now proceed to the consideration of vases, of which several, differing in paste and composition, have been discovered in the different tombs of Etruria. The principal varieties are, 1, Brown-ware ; 2, Black-ware ; 3, Red-ware ; 4, Yellow-ware.

BROWN WARE.

The brown-wares are apparently the oldest. Their colour is a grayish brown, probably from their having been imperfectly baked ; sometimes, however, they are red in the centre. Some vases of this class, the fabric of which is exceedingly coarse, and which are ornamented with rude decorations, consisting of punctured or incised lines, spirals, raised zigzags, bosses, and projecting ornaments applied after they were made, resemble in their character the Teutonic vases found on the banks of the Rhine, and certain Celtic ones that occur in France and Britain, from which they are often scarcely to be distinguished.[2] They consist of jugs, œnochoæ, small vases with two handles, and wide cups like the

[1] See also Mus. Etr. lxxiii. xcvi. ; Gori, I. tab. lxvii. I. p. 155; tab. clvii. clviii. clx.

[2] Brongniart, Traité, i. p. 417; Dorow, Poteries Étrusques proprement dites, 4to. 1829.

cyathos. In the rudeness of their shapes, and peculiar treatment, they seem to be imitations of vases carved out of wood, such as we know the cissibion to have been. The most remarkable and interesting of them are those found under the volcanic tufo, near the Alban lakes, which are in the shape of a tugurium or cottage, and must have contained the ashes of the early inhabitants of Latium. Considerable difference of opinion has however prevailed respecting the age of these vases.[1] By some they are supposed to be relics of the primitive inhabitants of ancient Rome ; by others, of those of Alba Longa. One in the British Museum, presented by Mr. W. R. Hamilton,

No. 174.—Tugurium vase from Albano.

is filled with the ashes of the dead, which were introduced by a little door. This door was secured by a cord passing through two rings at its sides, and tied round the vase. The cover or roof is vaulted and apparently intended to represent the beams of a house or cottage. The exterior has been ornamented with a mæander in white paint, traces of which still remain. They were placed inside a large two handled vase which protected

---

[1] Urns in shape of cottages, of brown Etruscan ware (Bull. 1846, p. 94), supposed to be of the Swiss guards in the service of the Romans, were found near Albano. They were excavated in 1817, by Guiseppe Carnevali of Albano, and illustrated by Sig. Alessandro Visconti, *Sopra alcuni vasi sepolcrali rinvenuti nelle vicinanze delle antica Alba-Longa.* Roma, 1817.

them from the superincumbent mass. Although the fact of their having been found under beds of lava, originally led to an exaggerated opinion of the antiquity of these vases, there can be no doubt that they are of the earliest period of Etruscan art. The curious contents of one of them, published by Visconti, confirm their very primitive use. They have no glaze upon their surface, but a polish produced by friction. At Cære have also been found some of the earliest specimens of painted vases, evidently manufactured upon the spot by the native settlers, and exhibiting traces of Greek rather than of Etruscan art. The

No. 175.—Group of vases, one in shape of a hut. From Albano.

paste of which these vases are made is pale reddish brown, speckled black, with volcanic sand, and gleaming with particles of mica. Upon the ground of these vases the subjects have been painted in white upon a coarse black back-ground, or in the natural colour of the clay. Dental, helix, herring-bone, and calix patterns abound, some covering the whole vase, but on some of the vases of this class are introduced birds, lions, gryphons, and even fish.

Some of the figures of animals are small and drawn in outline like those of the fawn-coloured vases found at Melos, Thera, and Athens, but many of the others are large coarse figures, resembling in style and treatment those of the earliest Greek vases of the style called Phœnician or Egyptian. None of these early vases have incised lines scratched on the figures to aid the effect of the painting, which was an opaque colour, laid on as fresco, and not burnt in as encaustic on the vases. The drawing was sketched out in white outline, sometimes consisting of a line of dots, by the artist, and the background subsequently filled in.

The shapes of these vases also differ considerably from those of the later Hellenic vases, but resemble those of the fawn-coloured vases.

Similar to these are two other ones, published by Micali, which were found at the ancient Cære or Cervetri. One in the shape of a Panathenaic amphora has more mica or tufo in its paste ;—but the other, a hydria or three-handled water jar, more resembles the paste of the vases just described, and has a polish on its surface. All these have had subjects painted upon them in opaque colours, like those used on the sarcophagi, and in the mural paintings of the tombs, in blue, white, and vermilion ; one with the Athenian legend of the destruction of the Minotaur.[1]

From the remote antiquity of their shape, the absence of human figures, the tempera character of their drawing, they are evidently to be referred to the oldest period of Cære or Agylla, probably to that historically designated as the age of the Pelasgi and Aborigines, which succeeded

---

[1] Monumenti Inediti, Pl. iv. v.

the occupation of the Siculi, during which period Agylla had maintained an intercourse with Greece Proper.[1] The subsequent conquest of the Etruscans probably introduced a different style of art,[2] that of the black and red Etruscan stamped and modelled ware —while the Greeks supplied the city, through the Port of Pyrgi, at a later period, with vases of all the principal styles of their art.[3]

Some objects resembling curling pins or *bilboquets* of this ware have also been found at Vulci.

No. 176.—Cone.   Vulci.

BLACK WARE.

The next class are made of a paste entirely black, though rather darker on the edges than in the centre,[4]—and when imperfectly baked, the black has sometimes a lustrous jet-like polish. Some think that this ware is made of a black bituminous earth found in the Etruscan territory ; according to others it is of a clay naturally yellow, but darkened by casting the smoke of the furnace upon it. Although some have conjectured that it is sundried, yet an attentive examination shows that it has been baked in kilns, but at a low temperature.[5] There are, however, several varieties of this ware, dependent upon the place of manufacture. Sometimes it is thick and heavy, at others thin and light. It is found only in the sepulchres of Etruria, and belongs to the subdivision of lustrous vases

[1] Lepsius, Ueber die Tyrrhener, p. 39; Dennis, ii. p. 58.

[2] Brongniart, Traité, l. c.

[3] Canina, Cere Antica, p. 16. Cf. the dedication of treasures to Apollo at Delphi, Strabo, v. 220, and its consulting the oracle, Herodot. i. 167.

[4] Brongniart, Traité, i. p. 413–419.

[5] Micali, Mon. In. p. 156.

with a tender paste. In many specimens the lustrous appearance is a mere polish, probably produced on the lathe. This ware was an improvement on the brown Etruscan sort already described, and exhibits the highest degree of art attained by the Italian potteries. An analysis of its paste gives a mean of 63·34 Silica, 14·42 Alumina, 7·9 Ox. Iron and Manganese, 3·25 Carb. Lime, 2·12 Magnesia, 7·34 Water, 1 83 Carbon. They are for the most part made with the hand, rarely if ever turned on the wheel. The ornaments are often incised with a pointed tool, and in such cases consist of flowers, resembling the lotus, festoons, rude imitations of waves, or spirals resembling the springs or armillæ known at a later period, and very similar to the ornaments on the early vases of Athens. Sometimes they appear to have been punched in with a circular stamp, and run round the vase ; while in other instances figures of horses and other animals are stamped in the interior.[1] Many of these vases have bas-reliefs, either modelled on the vase, or pressed out from its mould, which are disposed as a frieze (ξωίδιον) running round its body. These friezes have been produced by passing a hollow cylinder round the vase, while the clay was moist, and before it was sent to the furnace, a process identical with that employed by the Assyrians and Babylonians, in order to prevent the cylinders which they used for written documents being enlarged after they had been inscribed.[2] The treatment of the subject on the friezes is peculiar. The conventional arrangement of the hair, the rigidity of the limbs, the smile playing on the features,[3] the

[1] Dennis, ii. 352.
[2] Storia d'Italia, tom. ii. p. 278, et seq.
[3] Campanari, Intorno i vasi fittili di-

pinti, in the Dissertazione dalla Pontificia Accademia Romana di Archeologia, tom. vii. 1836, p. 5-7.

rudeness and archaism of the forms, not unmixed, however, with a certain plumpness and softness of outline,
reminds us of the early schools of Asia Minor and Ægina,
as well as of the bas-relief of Samothrace, and the coins
of Magna Græcia ; all which belong to the style of art
called by some Egyptian. In some instances the rudeness
of the forms seems to be the effect of the material rather
than of the artist's conceptions ; and in this respect their
bas-reliefs may be compared with the rude *asses* of the
Etruscans, the circulation of which did not extend below
the fourth century B.C. Other specimens exhibit all the
characteristic of Oriental art in the
arrangement and treatment of the
recurved wings, the monstrous animal combinations, such as the
scrupulous exactitude of detail, and
the ornamental repetition of the
subject. The monotony of the
moulded figures is often relieved by
incised marks by which the minor
details of the dress are indicated.
Those who conceive that they exhibit traces of imitation should
remember that imitative art is the
product of a universal decadence—
the evidence that a nation has exhausted its intellectual capacity :

No. 177.—Vase with moulded
figures and cover. *Vulci.*

and that Etruria fell in her meridian, when the arts of her
neighbours bloomed in unrivalled beauty.

The only traces of imitation which they display are
those of other Etruscan works in metal. The bronze

vases and shields found at Cervetri, Cære, are ornamented
in the same manner with circular friezes chased on the
metal.

The idea of imitation from works in metal is still more
strongly suggested by the detached figures in complete
relief which decorate the covers of these vases—the
rows of animals'
heads—such as
cows, rams, and
lions, which pass
round their lips
—and the pro-
jecting   knots
which   radiate
from   their
sides.[1] One most
remarkable vase
of this class is
modelled like a
man standing in
a biga, and the
mouths, which
are at the top
of the horses'
heads, are pro-
vided with bow-

No. 178 —Oenochöe of Black Ware.

shaped stoppers.[2]

From the shapes of this class of vases we may draw
some conclusions derived from Egyptian, Chaldæan, or
Phœnician sources, respecting the uses to which they were

[1] Mus. Etr. Vat. G. II. xcvi.-xcvii.   [2] Mus. Etr. Vat. xcviii.

applied. They evidently formed part of the furniture of the Etruscans.[1] We find among them the *cantharos*, or two-handled cup ; the *cyathus* or *cissybion*, another kind of drinking vessel somewhat resembling the modern tea-cup, the *cothon*, or deep cup with two handles ; and a small *cylix*. A peculiar kind of goblet, to which the not very satisfactory name of *holcion* has been given—as to judge from the description given by Herodotus of that made by Glaucus, it is rather a kind of *crater*—is by no

No. 179.—Tray or table of vases of black ware. *Chiusi.*

means uncommon.[2] The *phiale*, or saucer, and *pinax*, or trencher, frequently occur ; and the vessel called *holmos*, probably a crater for holding wine at a banquet, is also found. The *oenochöe*, or wine pitcher, either with the vine-leaf shaped or the circular mouth, is of frequent occurrence ; but the *lecythus*, or oil cruse, is uncommon, and the *alabastron* altogether unknown. The two-handed vase with a cover, called *lecane* is found, which seems to have served the purpose of a box or basket among the ancients. There are also vases of unusual shape, and even of grotesque

[1] Dennis, ii. 352.   [2] Ibid. Cf. Brongniart, Traité, Pl. xx.

appearance ; among them a kind of cubital, the use of which is utterly unknown. Objects supposed to be braziers, or trays,[1] are also to be found among them ; but these are probably stands to hold other vases. They often contain spoons as well as other curious little vases of unknown use. The celebrated *rhyton* or drinking cup which could not be set down, is also found among this ware.[2] The most extraordinary application of it, however, was to sepulchral purposes. Here the potter has exhausted all the resources of his art. He has endeavoured to invest the clay with metallic power, and to work it up into shape that conveys an idea of metallic strength. One of the simplest forms of these vases is the *canopos* or jar resembling those in which the Egyptians placed the entrails of their mummies.

The Etruscan canopi are rude representations of the human figure, the heads which are coifed in the Egyptian manner forming the covers.[3] The eyes are sometimes inlaid. They have large earrings which are moveable. They have holes supposed to be intended to allow the effluvia of the ashes to escape. When they had received the last remains of mortality, they were placed in the tombs on chairs of oak or terra-cotta. In this respect they resemble the tufo sepulchral figures of early style found at Chiusi, which separate into two pieces, and have in their lower part a hollow bowl scooped out to receive the ashes of

[1] See Dennis, ii. 325 ; Inghirami, Mus. Chius. tav. 40, p. 39; Mon. Etrusc. vi. tav. 6, 5 ; Micali, Antic. Pop. tav. xxvi.–xxiii. ; Brongniart, Traité, Pl. xx. fig. 12.

[2] For vases see Micali, l. c. xiv.-xxvii.

[3] Dennis, II. 356, n. 8 ; Micali, Mon. In. p. 151.

the dead. This method of placing the mortal remains of a person within a representation of himself, is peculiarly Egyptian, and recalls to mind the orientalism of certain Etruscan remains. The circumstance of burning the dead cannot be considered as a fatal objection to the antiquity of these vases ; and although the canopi are probably not anterior to the 4th century B.C., they are not to be regarded as modern.[1]

A vase found at Cervetri is a remarkable instance of this style. It is a modification of the *holcion*, and is supposed to have been used as a thymiaterion. The bowl or upper part is ornamented with a star and lune, it is attached to the side, or upper part of the stem by objects resembling studs rather than columns, and the stem is divided into two bowls or inverted cups.[2]

Unfortunately the subjects in the small friezes are imperfectly defined, especially the attributes ; yet enough is seen to enable us to draw some general conclusions.[3] They seem to be later than the early vases of Athens, with their elongated animal forms, or than the early Doric ware with its extraordinary human and animal figures, as seen on the vase of Civita Vecchia, representing the battle of the Lapithæ and Centaurs. Yet the mythology which they present seems obscure and shadowy, and in a state of transition from its Asiatic prototypes. It is not Etruscan, for none of the local divinities appear ; it is rather oriental Greek, with all its primitive monstrous combinations of human and animal

---

[1] Abeken, Mittel-italien 273 thinks them modern ; Dennis, l. c. p. 359.

[2] Dennis, ii. p. 58.

[3] Brongniart, Traité, Pl. xx. fig. 1, 3, 4, 5, 6, 7, 9, 10, xx. 11a. 12.

forms, before it had been refined by the national genius and taste, and endowed with ideal beauty. It is ante-Homeric, since the legends are either entirely different from those of the Epic cycle, or else such as are alluded to, or borrowed, as antecedent traditions, in the Iliad and

No. 180.—Oenochöe of Black Ware. Perseus and the Gorgons.

Odyssey. The Corinthian legend of Bellerophon repre-sented on them, has like the Milo terra-cotta an unwinged Pegasus, the hero and his son Peisander. The grand exploit of the Perseid has two Gorgons, one with the head of the horse Pegasus issuing from the neck, and the swan or Graia. On others are divinities grouped like those on the Harpy monuments at Xanthus. The vases of this style have no inscriptions referring either to the subjects, the artist or the potter. This is a remarkable fact, and confirms their high antiquity; for in the middle period the use of inscriptions was common. When inscriptions do occur they are not essential, being subsequent to the fabric and scratched in with a point after it has been made. These subsequent inscriptions which seem to be the potter's memoranda, are placed at the bottom of the vases, having black and red figures, and are generally in the *Etruscan* language.

Many vases of Etruscan black ware have these inscriptions, and that on a cinerary urn is *mi tesan keia tarchumenai*.[1] One jug is known that has an inscription, and several inscribed slabs have been found. In the tombs of Cervetri,[2] two of these vases, which had probably been employed as an ink-stand, had a Greek alphabet and syllabarium scratched on them, but this, like the other inscriptions, is incidental rather than necessary. All these vases precede the period when names, whether of the figures or of the artists, were introduced. As the arrangement of the alphabet just alluded to differs from that established by the Alexandrian grammarians it may be useful to give it here, viz. : B, C, Z, H, Th, M, N, P, K, S, Kh, Ph, T.

At Bomarzo[3] another vase had an Etruscan alphabet

---

[1] Micali, Mon. In. tav. lv. 7.
[2] Dennis, ii. p. 54.
[3] Lepsius, Annali, 1836, p. 186, 203,

Ueber die Tyrrhener-Pelasger, p. 39, 42.

thus arranged : A, C, E, F, Z, H, Th, I, L, M, N, P, S, T, U, Th, Ch, Ph.

From the form of the letters, especially from the 日 or aspirate, and the R, it is evident that the inscription is contemporary with that on the helmet of Hiero I. in the British Museum ; while the introduction of the double letters proves it to be of the age of Simonides. Of these the Archaic H, written 日, is excessively remarkable, and points out the original form as analogous to the aspirate which is thus shaped on the early coins of Thebes. On another vase of this class was found what has been called a Pelasgic inscription, supposed to be two hexameters.[1]

The vases of this class are discovered only in a limited range of country. They scarcely appear to the south of the Tibur, and the most northern sepulchres in which they are found are those of Siena. In the old tombs of Cervetri[2] or Cære Vetus, on the site of Veii, Orte,[3] and Viterbo,[4] at Vulci,[5] at Palo, the ancient Alsium,[6] at Chiusi or Clusium, Sarteano, Castiglioncel del Trinoro, Chianciano,[7] and Cesona,[8] six miles to the west of Chiusi ; also at Magliano,[9] Orbetello,[10] Orvieto,[11] especially at Volaterra,[12] and Cortona,[13] numbers of these vases are found.

The vases of the different localities are, however, distinct in style : those from Chiusi, Volaterra, Magliano, and its neighbourhood, have figures in bas-relief, while those

[1] Dennis, Cities. 1, 225, v.
[2] Dennis, Cem. and Cit. p. 58.
[3] Ibid. 164.
[4] Ibid. 197.
[5] Ibid. 410.
[6] Ibid. ii. p. 72–73.
[7] Dennis, ii. p. 101, 409 ; Micali, Ant. Pop. Ital. tav. xxii. xxvi. ; Mon.

In. xxviii.-xxxi. ; Mus. Chius. xii.-xix. xxi.-xlv- lxxxii. ; Dennis, ii. 348.
[8] Ibid. p. 402, 425.
[9] Ibid. ii. 296.
[10] Ibid. ii. 265.
[11] Ibid. ii. 528.
[12] Ibid. ii. 203.
[13] Ibid. ii. 442.

from Palo and Veii, have the figures incised or engraved.
In many instances, they are entirely plain. The solution
of the question as to their relative antiquity has been
much retarded by the uncritical and careless manner in
which the tombs have been opened. At Palo the incised
vases were found in excavated tunnel tombs, like the
Egyptian *speoi*, and in these were what have been called
Egyptian remains, as painted ostrich eggs, and beads of
an odorous paste. At Magliano such remains were found
in sepulchres with the scarabæi. The vases with subjects
in bas-relief, appear to be found in tombs with the alabaster
sarcophagi, most of which cannot be placed earlier than
the third century, B. C. In none were found coins which
would have been of much service in fixing the age
of the vases of this class. Most
of them appear to be prior to the
circulation of the *as grave* of
Italy.

There is some reason to believe
that this black ware was that
supposed to have been made by
the corporation of potters in the
days of Numa, B.C. 700 ;[1] for
Juvenal mentions it as being in
use at that period : "who dared
then," he says, "to ridicule the
simpuvium and the black saucer of Numa ? " (*nigrumque
catinum*)[2], while Persius[3] styles it the *Tuscum fictile* or
Tuscan pottery ; and it appears from Martial that

No. 181.—Painted ostrich egg. Vulci.

[1] Pliny, N. H. xxxv. xii. 46.
[2] Juvenal, vi. 343.
[3] Ibid. ii. 60, Schol. Vet. "Vilem fictilemque a Thuscis olim factum."

Porsenna,[1] B.C. 507, had a dinner set of the same ware.. Horace also speaks of the *Tyrrhena sigilla,* or Tyrrhene pottery.[2]

RED WARE.

The next class of vases to be considered is that of the red ware, of which there are two or three different kinds. The first consists of certain large jars resembling the cask (*pithos* or *keramos*) in which wine and other things were stored, and which, long before the time of Diogenes, afforded a retreat to Eurystheus when he fled at the sight of the Erymanthian boar. Such a vase also formed the prison of Ares, when bound by the twin Aloids— Otus and Ephialtes. The bodies of these vases are reeded, and there is usually a bold modelling running round the neck, for which a frieze, with figures of animals, is sometimes substituted, resembling those on some of the black ware. Sometimes the friezes have hunting scenes of animals chased by persons in chariots ; at other times they represent entertainments. These vases often have handles, thus forming a kind of large amphoræ or diotæ. They generally stand in flat circular dishes of a similar ware, but of finer paste, the broad and flat lips of which have friezes of similar subjects impressed in bas-relief with a cylinder. These vases are very old, probably B.C. 700, and are chiefly found in the old Etruscan cemeteries, in the tunnelled tombs of Cervetri[3] or Cære Vetus, or at Tarquinii, and on the site of Veii. Their paste is of a dullish red

---

[1] " Lautus erat Thuscis Porsenna fic- tilibus."—
   Martial, Epig. xiv. 98.

[2] Epist. II. 2, v. 180.
[3] Mus. Etr. Vat. ii. xcix. c.

colour, and of a gritty material, apparently mixed with the tufo of the soil. Sometimes they are of a pale salmon hue, mingled with black specks or ashes, probably of a volcanic nature. The bodies of these vases are too large to have been turned upon the wheel, and they must consequently have been modelled.

As they are found in tombs which contain no painted vases, they evidently belong to the earliest period of the Etruscan conquest. They are about three feet four inches. with expanding mouth, and body tapering to a cylindrical foot. A festoon or zigzag line in relief usually runs round the neck of these vases, the body of which is reeded, and a ring or band in bas-relief round the foot. On the shoulder of these vases is a frieze or zoidion either impressed from a cylinder and then run in a continuous repetition round the neck, or else stamped from a mould about $2\frac{1}{2}$ inches square, depressed like metopes. Their upper surface is flat like work in ivory, and they seem moulded from bronze or other metallic work. That these were separately stamped is evident from some having been double struck, and others having been only half struck, owing to their interfering with the part already impressed. These latter ornaments or metopes contain generally only one figure, while the friezes have a subject successively repeated. The connection of these vases of Cære with the early metallic works of Egypt and Assyria will appear from the animals and monsters represented, which show an acquaintance with Asiatic art, either derived from the early commerce of the Etruscans, or introduced to them by other means from Asia. Such patterns probably passed over to Greece and

Italy from the Western coasts of Asia Minor and from the Phœnician sea ports in Syria. The most remarkable of these representations indeed are to be found on the silver cups and other gold objects discovered in the tombs of Cære, which show a style of art immediately derived from Egypt, and such as existed in Egypt during the reign of the Psammetichi, when the ports of the Nile were thrown unrestrictedly open to Greek commerce, and Egyptian art and even language appears in the annals of Corinth about the 7th and 8th century before Christ. At this period the Etruscans had probably developed a brisk trade in the Mediterranean, and ivory, ostrich eggs, amber, Egyptian porcelain, and tin found in the articles of adornment of the oldest sepulchres, show the extent and activity of the national adventure. The vases of Greek Proper indeed had not yet been imported, but the great casks or dolia, of which mention is now made, were manufactured on the spot, probably under the direction of colonies of Greek and other potters. This admixture of Hellenic art is visible in the subjects, which are Sphinxes, centaurs, horsemen, wild birds perched on the back of the horse, Pegasi, Gorgons, and Chimæras, winged lions uniting in a common head, man hunting a stag, lions, birds, and similar subjects. These so nearly resemble the vases of pale clay with friezes of animal figures, that they must have immediately preceded them.

Of a deeper red, but of rather finer paste, and covered with a coating of red paint, are certain dishes found in the sepulchres of Vulçi and other places, and almost resembling the Aretine ware. Many jugs or œnochoæ, phialæ or saucers, ascoi or bottles, and a few cups, are also found of a red paste, more or less deep in colour and fine in quality.

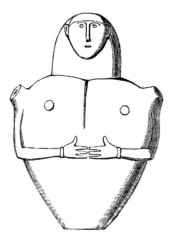

No. 182.—Etruscan Canopus of Terra-cotta.

The most remarkable vases of this sort are those which held the ashes of the dead, rudely modelled in shape of the human form, the cover representing the head, and having in front small rude arms and hands. These were placed in the tombs in curule chairs, as if the dead still sat there in state.

YELLOW WARE.

Of pale yellow ware of fine quality, but imperfectly baked, are certain *lecythi* and perfume vases, found in the more ancient sepulchres. These very much resemble the painted vases called Doric, but are not decorated with figures. They are modelled in the shape of animals, of Venus holding her dove, &c. ; and some were perhaps made by the Etruscans. Various unglazed vases of a light-coloured paste come from the Etruscan sepulchres, and such may be occasionally contemporary with the earlier vases, but the general mass of this pale ware appears referable to a later period.

PAINTED VASES.

Although the Etruscans executed such magnificent works in bronze, exercised with great skill the art of engraving gems, and produced such refined specimens of filagree work in gold, they never attained high excellence in the potter's art. The vases already described belong to plastic rather than graphic art, and are decided imitations of works in metal. Their mode of painting certain vases in opaque colours, in the manner of frescoes, which were not subjected a second time to the furnace, has been already described. These were probably their first attempts at ornamenting vases with subjects, and such vases are as old as the sixth century B.C.

These vases are quite distinct from the glazed vases of the Greeks, which, however, the Etruscan potters imitated, although not at their first introduction into the country. They subsequently produced imitations of the black and red monochrome vases, as appears from a few specimens which have reached the present time, and which are in the different Museums of Europe. In order to make these imitations they used different methods. The vases with black figures upon a red ground were produced, either by making a vase of pale paste and painting upon it a subject in a black glaze of leaden hue, or else by painting an opaque red ground in an ochrous earth over the black varnish of a vase entirely coloured black, of which an example may be seen in the *hydria* now in the British Museum, representing the subject of a giant attacked by two gods. In this case the inner engraved lines are usually omitted. This mode was, however, not exclusively Etruscan, for a vase found at Athens by Mr. Burgon has its subject painted in a similar manner, in red upon a black ground. Another vase in the Bibliothèque Impériale, at Paris, with the subject of Chiron, has been painted upon the same principle, and this process has been adduced as a proof that the art of making painted glazed vases was a mystery to the Etruscans. But there are several vases of pale clay, painted with a dull leaden glaze, and of treatment so bad, and drawing showing such remarkable analogies with other works of Etruscan design, that their origin is undoubtedly local, and they are called by Italian antiquaries "national."

The subjects of these vases generally show traces of Etruscan influence, and often resemble the friezes of the solid black ware, abounding in winged figures and monstrous combinations, not capable of explanation by Hellenic myths, or else have scenes derived from private life. Many of these vases are evidently much later than the vases with black figures, which they attempt to imitate, and must have been fabricated at a late epoch. To produce imitations of vases with red figures, the Etruscan potter adopted the processes already described. In the vases with black figures he stopped out, with an opaque red ground, all but the required figures ; but to produce a vase with red figures, the required figures were painted in an opaque red, apparently a pulverised clay, on the dull leaden back ground of the vase. The figures were relieved by passing a tool, not so sharp as to cut through the black glaze, through the required details of the opaque red figure down to the black glaze, thus producing the

inner black outlines usually painted on the red figures of
the Greek vases of the more finished style. But they also
manufactured a ware of paler paste, with figures of a
pallid tint, and glaze of a leaden hue, drawn in imitation
of the finer Greek vases. Their drawing is bad, and the
subjects generally unimportant. Sometimes Etruscan
deities, such as Charon with his mace, are represented on
them, which decides their Etruscan origin. The general
mass of the vases of this style and period resemble those
of the later Greek potteries found in the sepulchres of
Puglia, and of the Basilicata. Although their shape is
less elegant, their clay less fine, and their inscriptions
generally more local than those of the Greek vases, yet
their subjects are generally derived from the Greek
mythology, treated in a manner consonant to the Etruscan
taste, and to the local religion, while their drawing is of
the coarsest kind. On a vase of this class (formerly
belonging to Dr. Braun, at Rome, having for its subject
the farewell of Admetus and Alcestis,[1] with Etruscan
inscriptions accompanying the figures, and an Etruscan
speech issuing from the mouth of one of them), there is
depicted, behind Admetus, one of the horrid demons of the
Etruscan hell, probably intended for *Hades* or *Thanatos*,
girdled in a short tunic, and holding in each hand a snake.
Behind the faithful wife is Charon, with his mace. On a
second vase of the same style and fabric, found at Vulci,
Neoptolemos is represented killing a Trojan prisoner, probably Polites, also in the presence of the Etruscan Charon ;
while, on the reverse, Penthesilea, or her shade, is seen,

[1] Engraved in Dennis, "The Cities and Cemeteries of Etruria," vol. ii.
Frontispiece.

accompanied by other figures, to which are attached an undecyphered Etruscan inscription.[1] A third vase of the same class has on it Ajax, designated by his Etruscan name, committing suicide by throwing himself upon his sword, after the fatal judgment respecting the armour of Achilles ; while, on the reverse, is the unfortunate Actæon, also designated by his name, killed by his own dogs.[2] On another of these vases, the Etruscan name, *Elenai*, of " Helen," inscribed upon an oval object held by a female, and addressing a man, is supposed to represent Leda showing Tyndareus one of the eggs from which spring the Dioscuri, Helen, and Clytemnestra.[3] The age of these vases is universally referred to the very latest time of the existence of the potteries, and those with the opaque red figures are supposed to have been made between the fall of Veii, A. V. C. 359, B. C. 395, and the civil wars of Marius and Sylla, B. C. 90.[4]

Connected with these vases are certain others of pallid clay, figures of a light tone, white accessaries, dull glaze, and coarse shapes, discovered in the sepulchres of Orbetello and Volaterra, on which are painted figures, armed with the long oval buckler, and the square Roman scutum.[5] These vases are almost the last examples of the glazed kind produced in Italy, and were succeeded by a class of excessive interest, of which, however, only a few examples have been found. Their subjects are painted in opaque white colour upon a black ground, in drawing of the

[1] Raoul Rochette, Sur deux vases peints du style et de travaille Étrusque, Annali, 1834, 274 ; Campanari, Dissertaz. l. c.

[2] R. Rochette, l. c.

[3] Micali, Mon. In. xxxviii.

[4] Annali, 1834, p. 81-83 ; Gerhard, Rap. Volc. p. 31, n. 177.

[5] Inghirami, Vas. Fit. ccclviii.

coarsest kind, far inferior to the best examples of this class
of vases found in southern Italy, and consist of figures of
Cupids or Erotes, accompanied with old Latin inscriptions,
such as Volcani pocolom, Heri pocolom, Belolai Acetai
pocolom, the cup of Vulcan, of Hera, of Bellona or Acetia,
in Latin as old as the age of Ennius and Plautus : why
these inscriptions were placed upon them is uncertain.
Perhaps, as all of them have the names of deities, they
may have been placed before the images of the gods, or at
their lectisternium.　　The archaic form of the word *Poco-*
lom, resembling that of *Romano-m* of the coins of the
Romans struck in Campania, shows that they were
made about the time of the Social War, B.C. 200, at the
earliest, and probably much later.　　They were found
at Orte.[1]

INSCRIPTIONS.

The inscriptions which accompany the Etruscan vases
are of two kinds, like those on the Greek, namely, such
as are painted on the glaze of the vase itself, descriptive
of the figures and other circumstances connected with the
subject, and such as are incised.　　The former are painted
in an opaque colour, white or red, and are in the Etruscan
language, resembling those which accompany similar
figures on the engraved scarabœi, or bronze mirrors.
Such are the names of the deities ꓤAꓒV, Charu[n], or
Charon ; of the Centaur ꓦIꓒV, Chiru[n], for Chiron ; and
of the heroes AIFAZ, Aivas or Ajax ; ATꓒESTE, Atreste,
or Adrastus ; AKTAIVN, Actaiun, or Actæon ; and of the

---

[1] Secchi. Bull. 1837, p. 130, 1843, p. 127; 1843, p. 72.

THE FAREWELL OF ADMETUS AND ALCESTIS

from an Etruscan vase in the possession of Dr Emil Braun

females EⱯINAI, Elinai (of) Helen; AⱯC STI, Alcestis; and ΓENTASIⱭⱭ, or Penthesilea. Some other of these painted inscriptions are not equally intelligible, having such words as ΒINΘIⱭⱭTⱯPMⱯCAS, Hinthia(l) Turmucas, "the crowds of shades" which accompany Penthesilea, and EⱭ A : EⱭSCE : NAC : AⱯⱭVMɧ : ⱭLEⱭODCE, *eche : ersche : nac aqrum : wlerthche*, the speech of Charon at the parting of Alcestis and Admetus. Some few of the inscriptions, painted on the vases after the baking, seem to refer to the vase itself, ⱭⱯAAⱭIⱭAIɧ,[1] *mi laris aaqs* AIɧⱯⱭIⱭΘAⱭAIɧ,[2] *mi arathsil guna*, which are painted in white and red. On a deep crater is found ⱭⱯⱭƎ7ⱭⱭAⱭ:ⱭƎIƎⱭƎⱭ *veneies Larthoelus*, and on another crater :ⱭⱯΦA:ⱭƎⱭƎⱭƎⱭ, *veneies Aphns*.[3] As the Etruscan word *mi* is supposed to stand for "I am," it is probable that the inscriptions refer to the vases themselves, or to their proprietors.

A still larger class of inscriptions are the incised, or engraved. They are found on Etruscan vases of all classes, but more frequently on the solid black ware than on the painted vases, on which last, however, some examples occur. Thus, a *rhyton*, formerly in the collection of the Prince of Canino, and now in the British Museum, has under one of its handles, ⱭƎIⱯAⱭⱭ :ⱭⱯⱯⱭⱯⱭ.IOⱭⱭⱭƎ, *Efpupoi ūlūlun plaqies* apparently an address to Ululuns, or the Etruscan Dionysos.[4] Generally, however, the name alludes to the proprietor, as on the vase found at Tarquinii, republished by Inghirami, reading, ⱭƎ+ⱭƎⱯ ⱭƎI+ⱭƎⱭ ⱭAAⱯⱭAɧ Iɧ *mi*

---

[1] Mus. Etr. Vat. II. xcix. 2.
[2] Ibid. 3.
[3] Ibid. 3.
[4] M. De Witte, Descr. d'une Coll. de Vases peints," 8vo, Paris, 1837, no. 198. Perhaps "plaqies" is for "places," " thou pleasest."

Marqaas Senties Questes, "I am [the dish of] Marcus Sentius Cestius."[1] In the numerous examples given in the work of Micali,[2] other inscriptions are unmistakeably the names of the ancient proprietors, as, ΖΑИΙϤ√ΛΖ, Spurinas ; Ι√VИƎΗ, Senuli, or Menuli ; ΖΑИΖΑⰆ, Lasnas. Some other inscriptions appear to refer to ladies, and are prefixed by the word, Ǝ√ΑϏ, imitated from the Greek, as ΑΖƎΘΑϾΙVᴹƎ√ΑϏ, *Kale Mukathesa,* "the lovely Mukathesa ;" but it is difficult to feel sure about the meaning of many of these inscriptions, as they frequently consist of truncated words, whilst others do not recur elsewhere. A small vase found at Bomarzo, and another at Cervetri, were incised with the Etruscan alphabet. The presence of incised inscriptions[3] in the Etruscan language under the feet of vases has been alleged as a proof that these vases were made in Italy; but this, of course, turns on the circumstance, whether the inscriptions have been incised after the clay was baked.[4] Even at Nola a few vases have been found inscribed with Oscan inscriptions,[5] supposed to be the names of their former possessors, and some terra-cotta tablets inscribed with Oscan characters were found in the valley of Gavelli, at a place called La Motte, six miles from Hadria.[6] A few vases of the later style of art, when pottery had fallen into discredit, have the Latin inscriptions already-mentioned painted in white letters on them, and intended to describe their use, as KERI : POCOLOM,

[1] Inghirami, Mon. Etr. Tav. vi. s. vi. T. O. 3 7.
[2] Antichi Monumenti, fo. Flor. 1832. Tav. ci.
[3] Arch. Zeit. 1844, s. 335.
[4] Bull. 1844, p. 13; Berl. Ant. Bild. no. 1667.
[5] Berlins Ant. Bild. no. 1613, 1629.
[6] Muratori, dix. 2.

the cup of Kerus, or Janus; VOLCANI : POCOLOM,
the cup of Vulcan ; BELOLAI : POCOLOM, the cup of
Bellona ; LAVIIRNAI : POCOLOM, the cup of Laverna ;
SALVTES : POCOLOM, the cup of Salus ; AECETIAI :
POCOLOM, the cup of Aecetias.

ENAMELLED WARE.

The enamelled perfume bottles, and other objects of this
ware, sometimes found in the tombs of Etruria set as
jewels, in frameworks of gold, and considered by Italian
archeologists to be certainly discovered in these sepulchres, are products of the Egyptian potteries.   The
Etruscans, masters of the seas, imported enamelled ware
from Egypt, glass from Phœnicia, shells from the Red
Sea, and tin from the coast of Spain or Britain.   This
ware is generally with a tarnished hue, and often
of a pale grass green colour, resembling that which
was made in Egypt at the time of the 26th dynasty
or the 7th century, B. C.   It has been previously
described.

OTHER ITALIAN SITES.

Many terra-cotta statues, bas-reliefs, have been found
in other cities, the art of modelling and working terra-
cotta having been in activity all over the Italian Peninsula.
Notices of the vases, and other objects in glazed ware will
be found in the chapter on the distribution of the potteries.   It would require a long research to describe all

the Italian sites where terra-cotta remains have been found, and in style of art and method of execution they resemble Greek or Roman terra-cotta, according to the site where they have been discovered. Those from the cities of Southern Italy, Magna Græcia, and Lucania, such as Calvi or Cales, Canosa, Pæstum, Tarentum, are in all respects similar to contemporary productions of Greece Proper. Some bas-reliefs found at Capua,[1] not of very early work, about B. C. 200, are supposed from their style and representation to be Samnite, while a considerable collection of terra-cotta statues from Ardea, in the Campana collection at Rome, exhibit the style of Latium in the days of the Republic, and consist of figures of considerable merit, of rather a severe style of art. They are important, as this city had a great celebrity for its ancient fresco or tempera paintings.

---

[1] Riccio, Not. d. scav. d. suol. d. ant. Capua, 4to, Napoli. 1855.

PART IV.

ROMAN POTTERY.

CHAPTER I.

Bricks—Lydia—Tetradora—Pentadora—Size—Paste—Use—Houses—Tombs—Graves—Tiles—Tegulæ—Imbrices—Antefixal ornamentation—Tile-makers—Flue tiles—Wall tiles—Ornamentations—Drain tiles—Tesseræ or tessellæ—Inscriptions on tiles—Stamps—Farms—Manufactories—Legionary tiles—Devices—Columns—Corbels—Spouts—Friezes.

BRICKS.

In treating of the Roman pottery it is not necessary to repeat the description of the technical parts, as they were the same as among the Greeks. We shall, therefore, commence with bricks, which were called "*Lateres,*" "because," says Isidorus, "they were broad, and made by placing round them four boards."[1] Their use was most extensive, and they were employed as tiles for roofing houses, as bricks for structures, as slabs for pavements, and covering graves.

The simplest kind were made of clay merely dried in

---

[1] Origin, xv. 8.

the sun, called *lateres crudi*, or raw bricks, and were used for building walls. The clay of which they were made was called *argilla* or *limus*; and they were cemented together by clay or mud, called *lutum*.[1]

According to the Roman writers, bricks were divided into three classes. "Three kinds of bricks," says Vitruvius, "are made ; one, which the Greeks call *Lydion* which our people use, one foot and a half long, and a foot broad. The Greeks build their edifices with the two other kinds. One of these is called the *pentadoron*. For the Greeks call a palm δῶρον ; whence the presentation of gifts is called *doron*, for that is always borne in the palm of the hands. Hence, that which is five palms long every way is called *pentadoron*, πενταδῶρον, and that which is four, *tetradoron*. Now public edifices are built with the *pentadoron*, private with the *tetradoron*."[2] Pliny states nearly in the same words, "Their sorts [of bricks] are three, the *Lydion*, which we use, one foot and a half long, and one foot broad ; the second, the *tetradoron ;* the third, the *pentadoron*. For the ancient Greeks called a palm a *doron*, and hence *dora* are gifts, which are given with the hand. Therefore, they are named from their measures of four and five palms. Their breadth is the same. The smaller are used in Greece for private buildings, the larger for the public edifices."[3] There is, indeed, some discrepancy in the dimensions of bricks, as Palladius makes them measure two feet long and a foot wide, while the others give their dimensions as a foot and a half long

---

[1] Pliny, N. H. xxxv. 13, 49. Varro, de Rè Rusticâ, i. 14 ; Columella, de Re Rusticâ, ix. i.

[2] Vitruvius, ii. 3.

[3] Pliny, N. H. xxxv. 14, s. 49.

by a foot wide and four inches thick, but their dimensions may have been altered in the interval between these writers. Two dimensions are recorded by the brick-makers in the numerous inscriptions, *bipedales*, or two-foot bricks, and *secipedales* or *sesquipedales*, one and a half, which occur amongst the names of the makers of the opus doliare. The *Lydian*,[1] were probably so called from their resembling those used in the palace of Crœsus, at Sardis, the dimensions of which were rectangular like the *didoron*, of which they appear to be but another name. In their proportions they resemble our tiles rather than bricks, being very flat and thin in proportion to their size. They are generally square or rectangular, with the exception of the cylindrical hand bricks. The smallest size, the *tetradora*, generally measure between seven and eight inches square. *Pentadora* are often found measuring fifteen inches, by seven and a half inches broad. Some of the larger, which are twenty inches square, are the *bipedales*. Their thickness varies from one and a quarter inches to two inches. They are not made with mechanical accuracy, the edges being rounded and the sides not always parallel. In military works they were often used alternately with flint and stone, and for turning arches of doorways. For this purpose the two sizes were sometimes combined, in order to bond the work, or, the *bipedales tegulæ*, or " two-foot tiles," as Vitruvius calls them, and the *sesquipedales*, or " tiles of one and a half. feet." The dimensions of the bricks found in Sicily varied from two palms six inches to one palm nine inches in length. Those of Trèves were one foot

---

[1] De Re Rusticâ, vi. 36, 12.

three inches broad, one and a quarter inches thick; others from Civita Vecchia, in the Museum of Sèvres, measured 0·65° long by 0·5° thick.

The general size of the Roman bricks was 15 × 14 inches by two inches thick. The hypocausts had the pillars of their floors formed of bricks, from seven or eight inches to ten inches square, *bessales*, and sometimes of two semicircular bricks joined at their diameter, and so forming a circle.[1] Occasionally the upper bricks diminished in size, in order to give greater solidity to the construction. The upper floor bricks, or tiles, were from eighteen inches to twenty inches square, and formed the floor of the laconicum. All these were laid with mortar.[2]

The great building at Trèves, called the palace of Constantine, is built of *pentadora* burnt bricks, 15 inches square and $1\frac{1}{4}$ inches thick.[3]

Baked bricks, called *cocti* or *coctiles*, were in general use. Clay, which was either whitish or decidedly red, was preferred; and, as is evident from inspection, was well ground and mixed with straw. It was then kneaded and stamped out from a frame or mould of four boards. The bricks then went through the usual process of drying in the brick-field, indeed some of them bear the marks of the feet of animals and birds, which passed over them while the clay was yielding and unbaked, and on

[1] See Caumont, Cours. D'Antiq. ii. Pl. xx. figs. 1-5, p. 161-5.

[2] Caumont, Cours. Pl. xx. p. 170-1; cf. Buckman and Newmarch, Illustrations of the remains of Roman Art in Cirencester, the site of the ancient Corinium, p 64—66. The bricks of the pilæ were 8 inches square; the floors were made of flange tiles.

[3] Wyttenbach, Guide to the Roman Antiquities of Trèves, p. 42.

a brick at York are the nails of the shoes of a boy ; on those in the Museum of Shrewsbury, the imprint of the feet of a goat. The bricks were then baked—an operation expressed by the phrase lateres ducere [1]—in kilns apparently covered as the fornax. They were then ready for use, but were kept for two years before they were employed. Much care was taken in their preparation, and it was generally considered that the spring was the most favourable time for making them, probably because they dried more slowly and were less liable to crack during the operation, in autumn the rain interfered with the making, and in winter the frost.

The paste of the Roman brick is remarkably hard, and generally of a fine red colour, although sometimes of a pale yellow intermingled with fragments of red brick ground up with it to bind it together. Both kinds are found even in the same locality.

In the museum of Sèvres are fragments of bricks of a red paste, from different parts of France and Italy, as the Thermæ at Civita Vecchia, the pavement of the Coliseum, the theatre at Lillebonne, and the Thermæ of Julian [2] and Trajan. Among those from Civita Vecchia, were some similar to the so-called hand bricks, which are rude conical lumps of red paste, roughly fashioned with the hand, and supposed to be used for raining marshy roads, one having been found in the bog of Mareuil near Abbeville,[3] cut in facettes, and with striated marks. Some from Italy were baked almost to a stone ware, and others from Byzantium were of a similar red

[1] Pliny, N. H. vii. 57. [3] Ibid. 17.
[2] Brongniart, Musée, p. 16-18.

paste.[1]   The bricks formed one of the great staples of the
manufacture in baked earth among the Romans, who appear
to have derived it from their Etruscan ancestors.   Baths,[2]
whether public or private, military towers, and walls were
constructed with bricks, as they were better able to resist
the battering ram than stone ; as well as tanks for holding
water, amphitheatres, palaces, temples, and other public
edifices.[3]   The tombs of Cumæ of the Roman period are
made of brick.   Gigantic brick walls erected near Cumæ,[4]
and great arches of brick still remain in the amphitheatre
at Puzzuoli.[5]   The magnificent aqueducts, the prototypes
of the modern viaduct, broad enough for a horseman to
travel along them, were constructed of the same material.[6]

The villæ, insulæ, and houses of Rome were of brick
during the time of the republic, and Dio mentions how
an inundation of the Tibur destroyed the bricks of the
houses in the time of Pompey.   Augustus boasted that
he had found Rome of brick and left it stone,[7] and
Vitruvius mentions that brick was no longer adopted for
Roman houses in consequence of the laws which prohibited the thickness of the walls exceeding $2\frac{1}{2}$ feet, thus
preventing their being made two or three bricks thick,
which was required for the joists.   From the time of
Trajan however the use of bricks revived,   and public
edifices were made wholly of them.   They were laid in a
manner called the *opus reticulatum*, or ' network.'   A
common mode of construction, especially in the military

[1] Brongniart, Musée, p. 18.

[2] Martial, Epigram vii. lxxvii.

[3] Avolio, p. 10.

[4] Avolio, p. 34 ; Guida Ragionata per
le antichità et per le curiosita naturali

di Pozzuoli, di Gaetano d'Ancora, p. 120.

[5] Avolio, p. 35 ; G. d'Ancora, p. 61.

[6] Avolio, p. 35.

[7] Sueton. Aug. c. 29.

works, was to lay them in double courses horizontally with
stone above and below, which bonded the stone-work and
lessened its monotony by the red veins which they presented to the eye of the spectator. Sometimes they are
disposed in chevrons or vandykes.

A hand-brick found in Guernsey is in the collection of
the Museum.[1] It is $3\frac{3}{4}$ in. long, $2\frac{1}{4}$ in. diameter above,
and $1\frac{1}{2}$ below ; of a coarser and more gritty composition
than the regular tiles.

TILES.

The word *tile* (tegula) was evidently derived from
tegere, "to cover ;" called "*tegula,*" says Isidorus,[2]
"because it covers the house." The curved tile was
called imbrex, because it received the showers, *imbres* ;[3]
and those which resemble the
French festieres are called by
Pliny [4] "laterculi frontati." The
tile is distinguished from the brick
by its greater thinness in proportion to its superficies, and by its
being employed generally for
roofing houses. Tiles are much
more commonly found than bricks
The margin of the tiles is called
hamata.[5]

No. 183.—Flange Tile. London.

The most distinctive mark of tiles is the flanges. The

---

[1] Archæological Journal, vol. vii. p.
70.

[2] Origin. v. 8, " Tegulæ, quod ædes
tegat."

[3] Ibid. " Imbrex, quod accipiat.
imbres."

[4] N. H. xxxv. 12.

[5] Vitruv. vii. 4.

paste of which they are composed is compact and dense, very similar to the brick, but generally not so fine. Their clay when baked is either of a pale salmon or light straw colour. In some specimens, portions of bricks appear to have been ground up and mixed with the paste in order to bind it. Small stones, and fragments of vegetable remains, are also occasionally seen amidst the paste.

Tiles, like bricks, appear to have been made by means of a mould, but two boards were probably sufficient for the purpose. A hole was then driven through them by a peg when they were intended for roofing, especially for the *opus pavonaceum*, or "peacock's work," in which they are arranged like scales, being hung by one corner. The flange tiles were probably made in the same way, and the flanges subsequently turned up by the hand of the workman. They were then dried in the sun, evidently by being laid flat upon the ground, and subsequently baked in a kiln. How they were transported, or what they cost, or were taxed, unfortunately are among the particulars which have not reached us.

M. Brongniart, in his catalogue of the Museum of Sèvres, has described many of these tiles either of yellow or of red paste, and turned up at the edges, and showed that they were used for roofing, from the remains of Roman villas and baths in France. Some were for hypocausts,[1] others for pavements,[2] and others for roofs of houses.[3] Similar tiles are found all over England and

---

[1] As the one from Heilenburg, Mus. Pl. II. 13, p. 17.

[2] From the Tower of Dagobert at

Laon, p. 17; also at Pontchartrain; ibid.

[3] From Mt. Ganelon, ibid. 18; at

Germany, wherever traces of Roman occupation occur, and were made on the spot.

Tiles having their edges turned up, were principally employed for roofing, but some were occasionally placed in the walls when others were not at hand.[1] Those found in France are said to be distinguished by the sand and stones found in their paste.[2] In the ruins of villas they are found scattered about the floor, the roofs having fallen in. The flanges are generally about $2\frac{1}{4}$ inches higher than the lower surface of the tile. They are bevelled on their inner side in order to diminish the diameter of the imbrex, but have no hole by which to nail them to the rafters. In order that the lower edge of one tile might rest on the upper edge of that which came next to it, the two sides were made to converge downwards, as seen in the cut. These joints were of course covered by the semi-cylindrical tiles called *imbrices*, and the roof was thus rendered compact.[3] The rain flowed down each row of broad tiles into a gutter; the end tiles being lapped up at their outer edge, and provided with a spout, in shape of a lion's head in bas-relief, for the purpose of carrying off the water. The *imbrices* were plain semi-cylindrical tiles, except the last, which had an upright, generally semi-oval, and ornamented with antefixal or other ornaments. The end tiles were always flanged on their exteriors, and had a mæander or antefixal ornament painted upon them.[4]

Blizon, ibid. 18; mixed with white quartzose sand at Noyelles-sur-Mer, ibid.

[1] Caumont, Cours. ii. p. 182.

[2] Ibid. 184.

[3] Xenophon, Memorabilia, III. s. 1, c. 7.

[4] Dict. Antiq. Tegula, p. 939.

The tilés from private houses, as will be seen by the one found at Ostia, were upon the same plan as those used for the temples. The use of tiles for the roofs of private edifices as well as temples is proved by the ordinary expression of descending from the tiles, being applied to those who came down from the roof.[1]

The tiles with two of their parallel edges turned up called flanged tiles, were principally used for roofing ; but they were also employed for the floors of the laconica and the hot baths, in which case they were inverted, the flanges being placed on the pilæ, and the stucco floor was laid on them.[2] Several of these tiles, of red and yellow paste, from the Roman Thermæ near Saintes are in the Museum of Sèvres, as well as others from the ancient potteries at Milhac de Nontron ; also some tiles of red paste mixed with calcareous remains found at Palmyra.[3] In England in the military castra these flange tiles are also found of a red or yellow colour, the latter apparently having fragments of red tiles mixed in the paste.   They are worked in the brick bonding of the walls.

Of two tiles found at Boxmoor, and now in the British Museum, the one plain, the other a flange or roof tile, the dimensions are nearly similar. The plain tile measures 1 foot 4 inches long, by $10\frac{1}{2}$ inches wide, and $1\frac{1}{2}$ inches thick.   The flange tile 1 foot $3\frac{1}{2}$ inches long, by 1 foot wide, and the highest part of a flange $2\frac{1}{4}$ inches high. These are probably the tiles of one foot and a half in

---

[1] Terent. Eun. iii. 5, 60 ; Gellius, x. 15 ; St. Luke, v. 18.

[2] Cf. Buckman and Newmarch, p. 64.

[3] Brongniart and Riocreux, Mus. de Sèvres, I. 18.

length, the *sesquipedales* of the inscriptions. In the same collection are two tiles, sub-multiples of the above, measuring 8½ inches square, by 1½ inches long. They are not quite square, as usual. In the same collection are several other fragments of flange tiles, which have apparently been of the same dimensions. The flanges, however, are always bevelled on the inner side.

One of the most interesting facts connected with tiles is their use in the graves of the ancient Romans. The large *bipedales* tiles were set up in a prismatic form, one forming the floor, and the two others the pointed covering (*en décharge*), which protected the body from the superincumbent earth. In some of the graves of Greece, apparently of the same age, semicircular or vaulted tiles were used. On these bricks were impressed in large letters the names of the legions which garrisoned the various cities. Thus the tiles of the Roman graves at York [1] are inscribed with the name of the sixth and ninth legions which were there quartered, while at Caerleon, the old Isca Silurum, the bricks bear the name of the second or Augustan legion.[2] The stations of the twenty-second legion may also be traced by the bricks placed over the graves of its soldiers in this manner.[3] They were placed at the foot of the sepulchre in order to indicate, like tomb-stones, who was buried beneath. The inscriptions in most cases are written across the breadth of the tiles in Greek or Latin.[4] The inscriptions given by Gori

---

[1] Wellbeloved, Eburacum, p. 33, 34, 118.

[2] Lee, Delineation of Roman antiquities found at Caerleon, Pl. xiii. ; Gent. Mag. Nov. 1845, p. 490.

[3] Wiener De Legion. Rom. 1838, p. 106-137.

[4] See Gori, Mus. Etr. iii. Tab. xxvii.-xxx.

are of very different age, some apparently as late as the introduction of Christianity.

At Royston, in a supposed *ustrinum*, roof tiles either covered the mouths of the sepulchral urns, or they were placed around them as a *septum*.[1]

The name of the *imbrices*, as already stated, from their use in keeping off the showers, *imbres*, from the joints of the roof tiles ; and the roof of a bath, found at Ostia, will illustrate the manner in which they were placed over them. They were semi-cylindrical, about 3 feet long, and 3 inches in diameter, and $1\frac{1}{4}$ inches thick, made of the same material as the flange tiles, and apparently with the hand, but are not stamped like them with potters' names. The imbrex close to the edge of the roof had a perpendicular semi-elliptical piece, called the antefix. The tiles were connected at their edges, being laid for that purpose across the rafters, *postes*, of the roof, *tectum*.[2] The semi-oval upright plate, or *antefixa* of the *imbrices*, was not large enough to admit of much ornament. The usual one is the floral antefixal ornament, sometimes, indeed, replaced by acanthus leaves, accompanied with the mæander. Busts, from their elongated shape, were peculiarly appropriate to these plates, and those of Juno,[3] Venus, heads of the Gorgon, and Neptune between two dolphins, and tragic masks, have been found.[4] In this case the bust is stamped in a mould, and applied to the antefixal ornament. Two found at Ostia had groups instead of

[1] Archæol. xxvi. p. 370.
[2] Bayardi, Catalogo degli Antichi Monumenti di Ercolano, p. 284-285; Smetius, Antiq. Neomag. p. 88.

[3] Campana, Pl. xi. on specimens found on the Palatine Hill.
[4] Campana, Tav. vii. at Ostia.

busts,—such as Neptune sailing over the sea in his car drawn by hippocampi, and the statue of Cybele in the ship drawn by the Vestal Claudia.[1] These came from the ridge of a house, the tiles of which were inscribed with the names of Consuls in the reign of Hadrian.

Sometimes the antefixa of the *imbrex* was strengthened by a band behind, examples of which occur in the roof tiles at Pompeii. The edge tiles of the roof were flanged so as to form a gutter, and either externally decorated with subjects moulded in bas-relief,—such as antefixal and floral, and floral architectural ornaments, —or else painted in encaustic with mæanders, and other patterns. A space was cut out to admit of the insertion of the antefixal ornament of the imbrex. The ancient tiles were made by special makers, distinct from the brick-makers, and called *tegularii*,[2] tilers, or *figuli ab imbricibus.*

FLUE TILES.

For warming the rooms of the baths and other chambers a peculiar kind of tiles were used. The manner in which they were placed along the walls of the room will be seen from a plate of M. Caumont. They are hollow parallelopipeda, with a hole at one side for the ejection of the air which traversed them. Sometimes the whole side of the wall was composed of flue tiles covered with cement. Their sides are always scored with wavy or diagonal lines, apparently to make the cement adhere

---

[1] Campana, Tav. vi. at Ostia.
[2] Muratori in Mongez; Brongniart, Traité, I. 367.

better to them. Sometimes these marks assume a more regular and ornamental appearance, such as the shapes of lozenges or chequers, and the fleurettes, as on those of the Roman villa at Hartlip,[1] and the lower tiles have scores of squares.[2] They are generally of the same paste as the roof tiles, and are found scattered amongst the desolate Roman houses. The flue tiles were sixteen and a half inches long, six and a half inches wide, five inches deep.[3] A similar mode of constructing walls is found in the building called the house of Agathocles at Acradina,[4] some of the walls of which were made of hollow cylinders. The tepidaria of baths were lined with rectangular hollow tiles, with holes for the introduction of warm air to heat the walls of the chambers. These tiles were plastered over with stucco.[5] Cisterns for holding water were made of brick, fine examples of which are found at Taormina or Taurominium[6] and Selinunte or Selinus.[7]

No. 184.—Flue-tiles, ornamented.

---

[1] R. Smith, Collectanea, vol. II. p. I. p. 21, Pl. viii. fig. 1, 2.

[2] Ibid.

[3] Specimens of these tiles will be seen engraved in Caumont, Cours d'Antiquities, t. ii. p. 172, Pl. xxii. fig. 3 and 5; and Buckman and Newmarch, Illustrations of the remains of Roman art in the Ancient Corinium, 4to, 1850, p. 64, 65.

[4] Torre Rezzonico, Viaggio di Sicilia e Malta, tom. v. p. 227; Avolio, p. 9.

[5] One at Cassibili, near Syracuse; Avolio, p. 21; cf. Avolio, p. 2, 4.

[6] Biscari Viaggio, p. 7.

[7] Avolio, 8.

WALL TILES.

Of the nature of tiles were large thin squares of terra-cotta, which were often two Roman feet square, and hence called *bipedalis*, used for casing or reveting the walls of rooms. They are found in the different Roman villas, and are ornamented on one side with various incised ornaments by the potter, apparently with a tool upon the wet clay. The decorations of some, found in Essex,[1] represent mæanders, the Greek border, rosettes, and other ornaments. They were often covered with the stucco with which the rooms were plastered.

DRAIN TILES.

Terra-cotta pipes, *tubuli*, joined with mortar, were especially used for draining lands,[2] and for drains of amphitheatres.[3] They were eight inches in diameter.

As among ourselves, fragments of brick and tile were used to the very last, being employed for the second of the five strata, called the *ruderatio*, of the road, while the third, called the *nucleus*, was formed of bricks and of large stones.[4] The Roman mortar was made of sand, chalk, and pounded brick.[5]

---

[1] Archæologia, xiv. 64, 72; Brongniart, Traité, I. p. 367.
[2] Some have been found at Terra Nuova, Alesa, and Alicata in Sicily,
Fazzelli, Decad. I. lib. ix.
[3] Avolio, p. 21.
[4] Avolio, p. 37.
[5] Pitiscus.

TESSERÆ.

The tessons used for Mosaic pavements were made of marbles, glass, and of a red brick. These pieces were called by the Greeks *psephoi* ψηφοὶ, or *psephides* ψηφὶδες, pebbles ; and by the Romans *tessellæ, tesseræ, laminæ*. They vary in size from an inch to almost a quarter of an inch square, and were made either by fracture and cutting of the ordinary Roman tile into small squares, or else were stamped in a small mould. They supplied the red colour for the *opus musivum*, or mosaic work, especially for pavements, and aided in the composition of the various subjects. At the time of the Byzantine empire such mosaics were introduced into ceilings. The early mention of mosaic pavements in the book of Esther, and the anecdote of Aristarchus, show that they were in use before the time of Augustus, although no extant mosaic is earlier than that age, and most of them are of the period of the Antonines.

The larger tiles of the tesselated pavements were called *tesseræ* or *tesseræ magnæ*, the smaller *spicata testacea*. The word *tessellæ* was particularly applied to the pavements. It evidently comes from the Greek word *tessera*, "four" (sided), of which *tessella* is the diminutive ;[1] and thus signifies a diminutive cube or die. The term *testacea spicata* was applied to pavements, the *tesseræ* of which were not flat cubes, but packed with their ends pointed upwards.[2]

---

[1] "Tesseram a verbo Græco τεσσαρα dictam esse putat." Turnebus, Adv. xix. 26.

[2] Vitruvius, Arch. vii. 1 ; Pliny, N. H. xxxvi. 25, 63.

INSCRIPTIONS ON TILES.

A considerable number of the Roman tiles are inscribed with the names of the consuls of the current year in which they were made, presenting a long and interesting series, commencing with the consulship of L. Licinius Sura and C. Sosius Senecio, A.D. 107, and terminating with that of Alexander Severus, A.D. 222. Many of these consul-ships, however, do not appear to have been recorded in the regular *fasti consulares*, or official lists, and they were probably the "suffects" whose names were not recorded after their temporary elevation. Since many of the potters indifferently inscribed, or omitted, the names of the consuls upon their ware, it is probable that the tiles so dated were destined for the public buildings, and were so marked to prevent their being stolen with impunity. They are fewer in number than those which have merely the names of the potteries, or of the farms from which the clay was procured, but are yet sufficiently numerous to be an invaluable aid to the chronological inquirer in tracing the succession of consuls for upwards of sixty years. Inscriptions of this class belong to the *opus doliare* only, and are found on the tiles of Italy alone, and it is pro-bable that their appearance is owing to some law passed by the senate, about the reign of Trajan, to regulate the potteries. It has been, indeed, stated that the law obliged the brick and tile-makers [1] to affix their distinctive mark or emblem upon their bricks. The emblem in the circular stamps is in the centre, surrounded with the inscription,

---

[1] Cassiodor. I. s. xxv. ; II. s. xxviii.

as on medals, and resembling the countermarks or little
adjuncts on the currency of the republic, and the seals or
stamps of the eponymi of Rhodes.   On the Roman tiles
these marks are generally circular, with a circular portion
cut out at one part, but they are occasionally oblong or
rectangular.   The use of such a mark was to guarantee
the quality of the clay of which the tiles were composed,[1]
and which, in some instances, is found so remarkably fine,
so compact, and so well baked, that when struck it rings
with a metallic sound.   It is of these bricks and tiles that
the greater part of the edifices of ancient Rome were
made, and Theodoric,[2] when he repaired the walls, made a
present of 25,000 tiles for that purpose.   The boast of
Augustus, that he had found Rome built of brick, and left
it constructed of stone, could only apply to some of the
principal monuments and quarters of the city.   The
visitor of the Vatican will remember a great number of
these tile marks inserted in a wall of that magnificent
museum.   Such tiles have been removed from the principal edifices of ancient Rome ; the Coliseum, Circus
Maximus, the so-called Thermæ of Titus, the Thermæ of
Caracalla, the Basilica of Constantine, the Prætorian Camp,
the Cemetery of Priscilla, the Mons Cœlius, Mons Viminalis,
Mons Vaticanus, and the Pons Sublicius.   Such marks
have also been found on tiles removed from the ancient
edifices, and now placed on the roofs of many of the
churches of modern Rome.   Large collections of them
are, and were, in the museums of the Vatican, and in the
Villa Albani.   Cortona, Bologna, Tibur, Pagnani, and

---

[1] Seroux d'Agincourt, Recueil, p. 82,   [2] Cassiodorus, Variar. i. 25, ii. 23.
Pl. xxxii.

Ostia have also revealed numerous tiles of this class,—important remains of the golden days of the imperial city, when the best of the emperors embellished it with new edifices, or restored those of their predecessors which exhibited symptoms of decay. To the topographer they are of the greatest value ; and had the Romans stamped on them the names of the buildings for which they were destined, the sites of the great edifices of the city might have been indisputably fixed. Besides the value of these tiles in settling the succession of the consuls and the sites of the monuments, they also throw great light upon the economy of the Roman farms, and the possessions of the great landed proprietors. Perhaps from Nero, and certainly from Domitian, till the age of Commodus, after which these marks almost disappear amidst the general wreck of the fine arts which then ensued, an uninterrupted series of names of proprietors, potters, and estates, tells much of the internal condition of Italy, and one of the sources of revenue to the Roman nobility.[1]

STAMPS.

Before, however, entering further upon this subject, it is as well to show the nature of these inscriptions ; and the accompanying example, taken from a tile removed from one of the edifices at Rome, will illustrate their nature in the fullest manner. The whole is in bas-relief, and was probably made with a stamp or die of bronze,[2] wood,

---

[1] Fabretti, Inscr. Antiq. fo. 1699, 502, 503; Boldetti, Osservazioni sopra cimeterij, p. 557; Gori, Inscr. Ant. III. p. 152, 153; Caylus, III. Pl. lxviii. p. 253, 254.

[2] Gori, Inscr. III. 118.

stone, or terra-cotta, a bronze stamp of this kind hav-

No. 185.—Stamp on a Tile. British Museum.

ing been discovered.[1] In the centre of the circular stamp or medallion is seen a figure of Victory —the mark or sign that the potter used. Commencing with the inscription on the outer band, the following words may be read :—OPVS DOL[iare] DE FIGVL[inis] PVB-
LINIANIS. EX PREDIS AEMILIAES SEVERAES. " Pot work from the Publinian potteries, from the estate of Æmilia Severa." The most complete stamps have the date of the emperor or of the consulship, the name of the estate which supplied the clay, that of the pottery which baked it, and of the potter who prepared it ; sometimes even of the slave who moulded the tile, and the very dimensions of the tile itself. The earliest stamps look like the first attempts at a methodical manner of impression, and the later ones betray a comparative neglect. Not only are the names of the Emperors and Cæsars given at the beginning and end of the series, without indications of the consulships, farms, or proprietors, but singular expressions are also introduced. Thus the tiles of

[1] Gori, Inscr. iii. 118.

Theodoric show that his gift excited national or official enthusiasm, for he is styled upon them the good and glorious king, with the addition of " Happy is Rome ! " At all times, indeed, as is shown in the stamp already figured, the inscriptions were in contraction, and even the consuls were mentioned only by the initial letters of their name. Still, by comparing the numerous series, it is possible to place them in their order. Many tiles, indeed, have no date, although it is evident that they were made in the imperial times, but the general impression, on examining the series of stamps, is that the potteries of tiles or bricks were in active operation during the reigns of Trajan and Hadrian, especially in that of the last mentioned emperor, and continued so till the close of the reign of Marcus Aurelius. After the twentieth year of Antoninus, till the eighth year of Alexander Severus, the inscriptions are few and irregular. Most of the public edifices had been built or amply repaired. The political convulsions left no time for architecture ; the law respecting the stamps had probably been abrogated, and estates had changed hands.

FARMS.

The estates from which the tiles came, or to which some probably belonged, are called " possessions," *possessiones ;* private property, *privata;* shares, *rationes ;* blocks, *insulæ;* or more generally estates, *prædia.* There is indeed, some ambiguity about the expression *ex prediis,* but it apparently means that the brick or tile was " from the estate," the uncertainty being in what sense this is to be taken.

Prædium, indeed, means a property, either in the town or country ; but the word *fundus*, which means a country farm, is also found impressed upon some bricks. It will however be seen, from some apparently exceptional instances, that the names of the edifices to which the tiles belonged are combined with those of the potteries and potters, so that the expression *ex prædiis* possibly means that the tiles or bricks belonged to the houses or other property in the city of Rome of the person named. The designation of the place, for example, for which the tiles were made occurs on those stamped with the name of the Prætorian Camp, and of the Chapel of the Augusti, and can hardly refer to potteries established in that quarter. A critical examination of the series would enable the enquirer to arrange the entire sequence of the properties to which the tiles refer, and, on comparing the evidence, it is probable that the *prædia* are the estates which produced the clay. The proprietors of these estates were the Emperors and Cæsars, persons of consular dignity or equestrian rank, and sometimes imperial freedmen. The names of the estates are rarely mentioned, although the Salarian, the Ulpian, and a few others are recorded. Many of the tiles record merely the imperial estates, without designating the name of the reigning emperor ; and at a later period, as on the tiles of the Basilica of Constantine,[1] the stamps record the estates of our Augusti and our Cæsars. Of the family of the Antonines there are several names. The Empress Plotina was evidently a large landed proprietor. Annius Verus, and his wife Domitia Lucilla, the parents of M. Aurelius, have left their

---

[1] Annali, 1848, p. 158.

names upon many tiles ; so have that emperor himself,
Aelius Cæsar, the adopted heir-apparent of Hadrian ;
Arria Fadilla, the aunt of M. Aurelius ; Julia Procula,
Cusinia Gratilla, Faustina, and others. It would be
tedious to repeat all the names of inferior proprietors
unknown to fame, such as Q. Servilius Pudens and T.
Tatinius Satrinus. Some belonged to imperial freedmen,
for such names as Umidius Quadratus and Quintus
Agathyrsus are evidently of this description. The most
remarkable fact connected with the history of the proprietors is the prevalence of female names ; and the
quantity of tiles which came from their estates is
enormous. The occasional renunciation by the emperors
of their private fortune in favour of their female relations ;
the extensive proscriptions by which, owing to a defect of
male heirs, estates devolved upon females, as well as the
gradual extinction of great families, consequent on the
corruption of public morals, may be traced on a tile as
readily as in the page of a historian. As to freedmen,
their rise and progress is not in the scope of the present
chapter, but they were alike the ministers of the palace,
the agents of the nobility, and the wealthy proprietors of
Italy.

POTTERIES.

The potteries of the tile makers were of two kinds ; the
figlinæ, or " potteries," and the *officinæ*, " or manufactories." The *figlinæ* are the most numerous, and form a
class by themselves ; the term *officina*, or workshop, being
commonly stamped on lamps and smaller vases. The potteries are mentioned in a subordinate manner to the

prædia, or farms, and, in many instances, the names of both occur on the same tiles. The *prædia*, too, are often omitted, and only the *figlinæ* recorded. Attached to the term *figlinæ* is often an adjective, expressive of some quality or name. These epithets are sometimes geographical, as the Corinthian, Macedonian, Rhodian, or Tempesine, and the greater or lesser Ocean potteries. Sometimes their names were derived from the reigning Emperor, as the Neronian and Domitian potteries, but the greater number were called by a Gentile or family name, as the Bucconian, Camillian, Furian, Terentian, and Voconian potteries. There are, however, many potteries only distinguished by the names of their proprietors, who were generally freedmen or slaves. One of the names which most frequently recurs in the series is that of L. Brutidius Augustalis, a freedman ; while other tiles are stamped " from the potteries of Primigenius, the slave of our Lord " the Emperor. There were many potteries of imperial slaves ; but there are also numerous tiles from the potteries of the Emperors and other wealthy proprietors, although undoubtedly under the administration of of freedmen or slaves.

MANUFACTORIES AND MAKERS.

The *officinæ*, which are also recorded upon tiles, served to distinguish the quality of the different *figlinæ*. Thus tiles are stamped with the title of the officinæ of L. Aurelius Martialis, of Domitius Decembris, and of M. Publicius Januarius, freedmen, named after the months in which they were born. The establishment of the last of these freedmen was called the *doliariæ officinæ*, a term which will be more fully explained in the sequel. Another officina is called "Domitian," either after its proprietor, or out of flattery to the Emperor. Sometimes a second manufactory of the same proprietor is mentioned. Other tiles are stamped with the fanciful names given them by the potters, as Claudians, Domitians, Brutians, &c. A few tiles are stamped both with the name of the potter and that of the proprietor of the estate, as the tiles of C. Cosconius, from the potteries of the celebrated Asinius Pollio, and the *tegulæ doliares*, or pot-work tiles of Julia Procula ; the *Bipedales*, or two-foot tiles of one Crispinianus, and the "*Secipedales*," or "one foot and half" tiles of Julia Procula. This expression is distinguished from the previous one by having after it the name of the wealthy proprietor, and not of the poor slave who made the tile. While, indeed, the potteries of private proprietors were under the direction of liberti and libertini, those of the Imperial estates were chiefly managed by slaves, from whose labours the Roman nobles derived so large a portion of their revenue. The work itself was called *opus figlinum*, "earthenware," or *opus doliare*, "pot-work ;" and, in the contracted form of either, "*opus*" or "*doliare*." Such work is always found accompanied with the names of freedmen or slaves. The imperial slaves have two names, those of private individuals only one ; but the liberti had three names. Such names as Arabus, Arestius, Modestus, Tertius, Zosimus, are clearly servile. In some cases, the form fecit is substituted for *opus ;* but in all instances the makers were of inferior condition, A regent of France might amuse himself with making glass,

and a German Emperor with compounding sealing-wax,
without the loss of the respect of their subjects; but a
Roman historian cites, as an instance of the degraded
taste of Commodus, that in his youth he had amused
himself with making cups of earthenware.[1]

"Let him who made it, and who belongs to Cneius
Domitius Amandus, prosper," is stamped on one remarkable tile. Sometimes the work is stated to come from
particular potteries, without mentioning the potter. Some
of the potters, indeed, impressed mottoes on their tiles, as
utamur felices, "may we use happily," "Fortune who
brings back is to be worshipped," and "the Constantinian
age." But such an inscription as *Poppina talis*, "what a
tavern," is hardly credible, and probably a joke.

LEGIONARY TILES.

Only few of the tiles have inscriptions indicating the
places for which they were destined. This is particularly
the case with those employed for military purposes. These
inscriptions probably had a double use. First, they showed
that they were made by the soldiers, thus indicating that
in the legions, as in modern armies, there were many
soldiers acquainted with handicraft trades; secondly, they
prevented the tiles being stolen or removed, and were thus
stamped with the Roman broad arrow of the public property. At Rome, indeed, there was no necessity for the
legionaries themselves making tiles and bricks; and,

---

[1] Æl. Lampridius, Vit. Commodi, Init.

accordingly, one Sextus Attius Silvanus appears to have supplied the camp. The clay he obtained from the estate of Umidius Oppius. The actual maker was a freedman, who bore the name of L. Silvinus Helpidianus. The sacellum, or shrine, of the Augusti, which held the standards and eagles of the Prætorians, appears to have been roofed, or partly constructed of tiles from the potteries of Paniscus, Hermetianus, and Urbicus. A few tiles from the Via Salaria, had only on them " Castrum," or camp. Some fragments of tiles or bricks, evidently the *semilateres*, or half-bricks, of Vitruvius, dug up on the site of the Post-office in London, were impressed with the letters P P. BR. LON., denoting the residence of the Roman proprietor in Britain.[1] Still more interesting are the inscriptions stamped on the tiles relating to the legions and other military divisions stationed throughout the provinces of the vast empire. These are chiefly found in their graves, camps, and quarters. They contain the number and titles of the legions, and mark the limits of the Roman conquests. The route of the XXII. legion has been traced through Germany ; and in our own country an examination and comparison of these tiles show the distribution of the military force, and the change of the quarters of the different legions which held Britain in subjection. These are seldom circular like those of the imbrices and flange tiles, but are in shape [2] of a foot, or oblong, with the letters in relief, sharply impressed, probably with a metallic die. The principal legions of which

[1] Mr. Roach Smith, Collectanea, i. p. 143.　　[2] Arneth. Hypocaustum, 4to, Wien, 1856, taf. iii.

tiles have been found are the 1st assistant; the 2nd august;
the 6th victorious, pious, and fortunate, and 9th Spanish [1]
legion, stationed at York ; the 8th august, Armenian and
fortunate; the 10th, called the double, pious, and fortunate;
the 20th, Valerian and victorious, discovered at Chester ;
and the 22nd and 30th legions, the tiles of which have been
traced throughout Germany.[2] Subordinate to the legions are
the cohorts, the tiles of which have been also found, as, for
instance, those discovered at Niederbieber of the 4th
avenging ; [3] and of the 4th of the Breuci, exhumed at Slack,
in Yorkshire.   Besides which are the tiles of the "three
standards" of the British fleet or marines, found at Dover
and at Lymne, the ancient Portus Lemanus.[4]   Sometimes
a maker's name is added to that of the legion.[5]   Some tiles
appear to have been numbered in the order in which they
were to be built into the public works.   Thus, a tile discovered at Nola was inscribed " the water is received in
the chapel, tile 90."   Many tiles have only initial letters
of words inscribed upon them, and when so contracted,
it is always difficult, and often impossible, to guess what
the inscriptions were intended to express.

DEVICES.

All that remains to be considered is the devices which
accompany these stamps.   The device occupies the centre

---

[1] Wellbeloved, Eburacum, 8vo, York,
1842, p. 104.

[2] See List in the Appendix.

[3] R. Smith, ii. 140.

[4] R. Smith, Ant. Richborough, 4to,
Lond. 1850, p. 258.

[5] R. Smith, ii. 132.

as in a medal, and the inscriptions on the oval stamps are
disposed on the outer circle running round it.   A common
ornament, or device, is a plain circle or ball, touching the
inner edge of a larger circle at one point, thus giving the
rest of the stamp a lunated shape.   Sometimes the device
is left out altogether.   The devices are not numerous, nor
is it always possible to discover the principle upon which
they were adopted.   They were, of course, the potter's
seal, and he selected his devices, or coat-of-arms, as it may
be termed, as he chose.   Some can, however, be traced
to their origin.   One potter, named Aper or Boar, adopts
that animal for his device ; another, called Hermes. or
Mercury, has a caduceus.   Other devices represent a
favourite deity, or some idea connected with the estate.
Rome, of course, is found.   The Caninian potteries had a
star, in allusion to the dog-star.   Divinities, animals, stars,
crescents, palm branches, pine cones, crowns, &c., are among
those found.   It was the practice of the ancient world to use
these emblems in various manners.   The Rhodian and
Cnidian potters placed them upon their amphoræ, the maker
of strigils on the handles of that instrument ; the mint-
masters of Greece and of Rome in the consular times, introduced them upon the area of the coins issued during their
tenure of office, and the potter followed the general rule.
So interwoven was art in the mind of the ancients, and so
dominant was the love of animal form, that the work of
the potter was deemed incomplete unless he impressed his
device upon it.   This resumé of the information afforded
by the marks on tiles, is drawn up from an examination
of a very great number of inscriptions.

COLUMNS.

The use of terra-cotta in architecture was most extensive for capitals and columns, bases of columns, sills and
frames of windows, the crowning portions of cornices,
gutter spouts, &c.[1]

CORBELS.

The corbels which supported the cornices were also
made of this material, either moulded or else stamped out
of mould. Indications of the use of terra-cotta corbels
occur in a *lararium* at the entrance of the house of the Faun,
and in the fragments discovered amidst the ruins of the
buildings at Pompeii. Some of the wall paintings in
which interiors are represented, also show cornices
supported apparently by figures of terra-cotta, which
have been painted entirely in accordance with the mural
decorations.

Between the columns were suspended masks and heads
of terra-cotta, called *clypea*, painted and decorated and
suspended by long cords, in the same manner as lamps
are in religious edifices at the present day. On some of
the Greek vases similar objects, *oscilla*, are seen suspended

---

[1] Seroux D'Agincourt, Recueil, p. 78.
Some of the columns and windows of
this material were found outside the
gate of St. John Lateran, and in the
valley of the Fountain of Egeria; Cf.
also D'Agincourt, Histoire de l'Arts
Architect. Pl. xii. xx.

from the boughs of trees, along with tablets or paintings, *pinakes*.

SPOUTS.

The gutter spouts under the ridge tiles were a very decorative and interesting part of terra-cotta architecture.[1] The most ordinary form of these spouts was a lion's head, which is constantly seen in fountains, and which is found on the walls of the bath at Ostia and at Pompeii, moulded in salient relief. Sometimes the whole fore-part of a lion is substituted, with a trough placed below the feet for the water to flow out.

The head and the fore-parts of dogs,[2] and comic and tragic masks, whose open, shell-shaped mouths (*conchæ*) were particularly adapted for this purpose, were sometimes used, and also female heads.[3] These objects are generally of the same piece as the gutter tile, and were stamped out of moulds. Yet, after all, spouts of this description must have been a very imperfect contrivance, and disagreeable beyond measure to pedestrians in the streets.

FRIEZES.

Terra-cotta ornaments were used largely both in the interior and exterior decoration of houses, a custom which

---

[1] See the one, Duc de Luynes, Metaponte, pl. vii.

[2] Cf. d'Agincourt, Pl. xxix.; Histoire de l'Art. xx.; Marquez, Dell' ordine Dorico riczerche, 8vo, Romæ, 1803; and Boni, Lettera, 8vo, 1805; Guattani, Mon. Ined. 4to; 1805, p. 108.

[3] Three masks of terra-cotta found at Musarna, Bull. 1850, p. 44.

probably arose from the imperfect knowledge possessed by the ancients of the uses of gypsum, especially in ornamental work ; hence they substituted terra-cotta for such purposes. Bas-reliefs of terra-cotta, *antefixa*,[1] formed the decorations either of the impluvium[2] of the house, or else went round the exterior. They were formed of flat slabs, about eighteen inches in length, and nine inches wide, and were decorated with a variety of subjects. The style of art is bold and vigorous, and the slabs were evidently cast in a mould, although in some instances they were apparently retouched before they were transferred to the kiln. Circular holes are left in them for the plugs by which they were attached to the woodwork or to the masonry. They were painted after they were fixed. No great variety of subjects occurs ; but the treatment, which is essentially Roman, exhibits illustrations chiefly borrowed from mythology, such as the birth of Zeus, who is cradled by the Corybantes; the Gigantomachia; the birth of Dionysos—his thiasos—especially his being supported by the satyr Comos; Pan; the Tritons and Nereids; Neptune, Apollo Musagetes ; the dances of the Spartan Virgins at the statue of Minerva ; Minerva and Tiphys fabricating the Argo, the Centauromachia ; Theseus destroying the huge Eurytus ; Perseus, aided by Minerva, killing Medusa ; Æneas consulting the oracle of Apollo ; Machaon curing Antilochos ; Victory ; sacrifices ; Barbarian prisoners, and architectural ornaments. Some few slabs have been found which, in the false taste of the

---

[1] "Antefixa, quæ ex opere figulino tectis adfiguntur sub stillicidio." — Festus, voce.

[2] Festus, voc. Impluvium. Varro, de LL. 4.

period, represent the land of the Pigmies, hippopotami browsing on the banks of the Nile, and gigantic cranes perched on the cottages of the diminutive race, who are navigating the river in boats. As many of these slabs went to the formation of a large composition, they were numbered, in order to assist their arrangement.[1] The subjects on these slabs are disposed in bas-reliefs on the flat surface, and their treatment is of two kinds. In the first sort the figures are grouped with large flat surfaces between them, in accordance with the later style of Greek art; in the second, they are introduced as accessories to floral and scroll ornaments, forming centres from which these ornaments radiate. The slabs are ornamental, with bands or corniches, in the shape of artificial flowers, or with the usual egg and tongue moulding above, while plain moulding and artificial ornaments occur below. The bas-relief is exceedingly high in the narrow bands and friezes destined for some of the architectural mouldings, but in other instances it is flat and scarcely raised a quarter of an inch above the surface. The treatment, although free, and in many cases noble, is essentially architectural. These slabs are by no means choice specimens of ancient art, like those which decorated public buildings, but were intended merely as ornaments for private dwellings, or for sepulchres.

All these ornaments, even when used externally, were coloured generally with pure colours, such as red, blue, and black; while, in some instances, as in the decoration of the antifixæ, green and yellow were used. In Greek

---

[1] Campana, Antiche opere in plastica, fo. Roma, 1842.

edifices, it is probable that the painting was in wax, as mentioned by the pseudo-Dicæarchus ; and some, indeed, of the Pompeian buildings appear to have been coloured in encaustic. These ornaments were probably not much. later than the time of Severus. In some instances the name of the potter occurs upon them, as those of Annia Arescusa, and Antonius Epaphras. Some late examples of this style are in the Museum at Sèvres, and exhibit Vulcan standing between Apollo and Abundance, Minerva and Mercury, and Minerva, Vulcan and Mercury, or else subjects such as Perseus and the Graiæ.[1] Two of these reliefs bear the names of their makers, Fecinus and Verecundus, who were either freedmen or slaves.

The bas-reliefs in the collection of the British Museum were found in a dry well, near the Porta Latina at Rome.[2] In 1761, a subterraneous place, divided into many chambers, was discovered at Scrofano, about sixteen miles from Rome. The dome of the largest chamber was enriched with paintings in fresco, representing animals. The whole of the frieze below the dome was enriched with bas-reliefs in terra-cotta, which were fastened to the wall with leaden nails. Many tombs on the Appian Road, as well as the temple dedicated to Romulus, near the Circus of Maxentius, were ornamented in a similar manner with terra-cottas ; and there are several ancient chambers still visible in the neighbourhood of Rome, in which, though the bas-reliefs have been long since removed, the places which they occupied are per-

---

[1] Brongniart and Riocreux, Mus. de Sèvres, p. 16. One of these was 0·33 o 0·45 b. One has "Fecinus fecit" — the other, "Verecundus f [ecit]."

[2] Taylor Combe, Descr. of Ancient Terra Cottas, 4to, London, 1810, p. vi. vii.

fectly distinguishable. Similar slabs were discovered, forming a frieze round the four sides of a chamber of the house of the Cæcilii, at Tusculum.[1]

Some found between the Porta Salaria and Pinciana were used for roofs, and stood considerably raised above the height of the roof, with a narrow gutter and a ridge, over which was placed an imbrex.[2]

---

[1] Campana, p. 31.   [2] D'Agincourt, Recueil, pl. vii.

CHAPTER II.

STATUES.

MOST of the ancient statues of the Romans are of terra-cotta,[1] a fact which is constantly alluded to by their writers.[2] In the early days of the republic the fine arts were at the lowest ebb, all objects coming under this denomination being either imported from Greece, or procured from their more refined neighbours the Etruscans who cultivated the glyptic and plastic arts with complete success. Hence the Romans purchased such statues as they required; and these which appear to have been terra-cotta and called *signa Tuscanica*,[3] adorned all the principal temples of their

---

[1] Pliny, N. H. xxv. 12, 46.

[2] Pliny, N. H. xxxv. 12, 46; Muratori Thesaur. tom. ii. p. 237.

[3]   " Jupiter angusta vix stabat in æde,
Inque Jovis dextra fictile fulmen erat."
            —Ovid, Fasti, 1, 201-202.
    " Fictilibus crevere diis hæc aurea
        templa."
    —Propertius, Eleg. lib. iv. 1, 5.

" Fictilis et nullo violatus Jupiter
    auro."
            —Juvenal, Satyr. xi. 1, 16.
" Cogita illos [deos] cum propitii essent
    fictiles fuisse.
        —Seneca, Epistol. xxxi. a fin.
" Tunc per fictiles deos religio jura-
    batur."
        —Consolat ad Helv. c. 10, 2.

gods. The most celebrated works of republican Rome were made by the artists of Veii, and those of the Volscian Fregellæ or the Etruscan Fregenæ. The celebrated quadriga made by Volcanius of Fregellæ, which surmounted the pediment of the temple of Jupiter Capitolinus, which was treated with superstitious awe and considered one of the safe-guards of the Imperial city, shows the low state of the arts among the Romans.[1] Numa, however, ever attentive to the Roman arts and institutions, is said to have founded a corporation of potters.[2]

In A.C. 491, Gorgasus and Demophilus ornamented with bas-reliefs and terra-cotta figures the temple of Ceres at Rome. They were natives of Himera in Sicily, and their labours were probably rather of Greek, than Etruscan style, which was previous to them. In the reign of Augustus the temple was burnt, and so great was the esteem in which the works of these old masters were held, that they were taken out of the walls and framed in wood. They were of the Æginetan style of art.[3] It has been conjectured that the want of white marble in Italy, none being discovered till the Imperial times, caused the extensive use of terra-cotta.[4] The gradual conquest of Campania and of Greece Proper, which supervened after the fall of Etruria, unfolded to the eyes of the Romans a new school of art, and after the siege of Corinth the old terra-cottas fell into contempt and neglect. From this time the temples of the gods and the houses of the nobility became enriched and beautified with the spoils of Grecian

[1] Pliny, N. H. x. xxv. c. xii. 45.

[2] Servius ad Virgil, Æneid, vii. 188.

[3] Tacit. Annal. ii. 49 ; Dio Cassius, 50, 10.

[4] Hirt, Gesch. d. Bild. Kunst. s. 117, 123.

art, in stone, marble, bronze, and terra-cotta. The artists
of Greece hastened to pay their court to their new masters,
and received great encouragement, in spite of the protests
of the old conservative party of the aristocracy led by
Cato. On the occasion of the attempt to abolish the
Oppian law, which was in fact a sumptuary one for women,
Cato, who was then consul, inveighed against the increasing
luxury of the state, and especially against the statues
which conquest had brought in its train. "Hateful,
believe me," says he, "are the statues brought from Syracuse into this city. Already do I hear too many who
praise and admire the ornaments of Corinth and Athens,
and deride the terra-cotta figures, *antefixa*,[1] of the Roman
gods. For my part, I prefer these propitious gods, and hope
they will continue to be so if we allow them to remain in
their places." [2]

Towards the close of the republic, great works continued to be executed in terra-cotta, and were much
esteemed. The modellers, Possis and Arcesilaus, are cited
by Varro,[3] and the former made for Julius Cæsar a statue
of Venus, which was highly prized, although the artist
had not completed it. Virgil's father was a potter in the
neighbourhood of Mantua ; and some of the remains of
terra-cotta, extant in the Museums of Europe, can be safely
referred to the first century of our era.[4]

---

[1] "In æde Concordiæ, Victoria, quæ in culmine erat icta decussaque ad Victorias quæ in antefixis erant."—Livy, lib. xxvi. ; Vitruvius, iii. c. 2.

[2] Livy, xxxiv. c. 4.
[3] Pliny, xxxv. c. 12, 45.
[4] Seroux D'Agincourt, Recueil, p. 7.

SIZE.

Few statues of any size in this material have escaped the injuries of time. In the regal days of Rome, Numa prohibited all statues above three feet high, a regulation probably agreeable to the practice of the neighbouring nations, and by no means favourable to the arts. At least there are no large Etruscan figures. Of the few large figures known, one is the Torso in the British Museum, the arms, legs, head, and extremities of which were mortised to it in another material in separate pieces. That such was the practice appears from the fable of Phædrus about Prometheus, who after he had made the human race out of clay, in separate pieces, having been invited to supper by Bacchus, on his return home applied the wrong limbs to the bodies.[1]

Four figures in this material found at Pompei are larger than life. They represent an Æsculapius and Hygieia, and a male and female comedian. There is also a bust of Pallas, rather larger than life, with a buckler at the right side. Figures however of this size are of great rarity,[2] one of the latest of these terra-cotta figures, mentioned in ancient authors, is that of Calpurnia, wife of Titus, one of the thirty tyrants, " whose statue," says Trebellius Pollio,[3] " made of clay, but gilded, we still see in the temple of Venus."

In the Vatican is a figure of Mercury of this material,

---

[1] Phædrus, lib. iv. Fab. xiv.
[2] Winckelmann, Stor. ii. p. 273.
[3] Vita Titi, " Cujus statuam in templo Veneris adhuc videmus Argolicam sed

auratam." Triller, (Ob Crit. I. 4 c. 6, p. 328) reads " Argillaceam." Winckelmann, Hist. de l'Art. iii. p. 256.

about the size of life. Some figures, about three feet high, representing Muses, and some terminal busts of Bacchus, almost the size of life, used to decorate gardens, were found in the same well as the friezes near the Porta Latina. These were of the same coarse red material as the friezes. They are in the British Museum.[1]

MODELS.

It appears that the artist was obliged to make first a model in clay of the statues in bronze or marble, which he intended to execute. This process was however not very ancient, as Pliny states that it was first used by Lysistratus, the brother of Lysippus. Pasiteles, an artist of the time of Augustus, is stated by Pliny never to have made a statue except in this manner ; but the custom was by no means general. These sketches, called *proplasmata*, were often much sought after, as they exhibited the full freedom of the artist's conception and style, and those of Arcesilaus, an artist of the period, fetched a high price.[2]

SIGILLARIA.

The majority of figures were of small size, called *sigilla*, or *sigillaria*, and were used for votive purposes, or as toys, presents, and for the *lararia*. They represent all kinds of figures of gods, actors, aurigæ, moriones or buffoons, dwarfs, portraits of Imperial personages, and philosophers, like those of Greece, but of coarser execution, and are found throughout the Roman Empire. Few specimens, indeed,

[1] Ancient terra-cottas in the British Mus. Pl. 1, et seq.   [2] Clarac, i. p. 25.

have been discovered in Britain, and those found are of a coarse red clay.[1] Some were found in the rubbish pits of Richborough.[2] More than 200 at a time have been discovered in France.[3] A very common type is a nude figure of a female seated in a chair, sucked by two children, supposed to represent the Deæ Matronæ, or Matres. A manufactory of them was discovered some years ago at Heiligenberg, near Mutzig, on the Brusche. Many of these figures, in the British Museum, found in the neighbourhood of Lyons, are of a very white paste, and represent Mercury, Venus Anadyomene, and other figures.

A great number of figures were probably prepared for the festival of the Sigillaria. This is particularly described by Macrobius, and like all the Roman fêtes was supposed to have had a mythic origin. Hercules, after the death of Geryon, and the capture of his cattle, was stated by tradition to have thrown from the Pons Sublicius, into the Tiber, the images of the companions whom he had lost in his wanderings, in order that they should be carried by the sea to their native shores. The hypothesis of Macrobius is equally fanciful, for he thinks that candles were used by the Pelasgi, because the word φῶς, or φώς signified both *man* and *light*, and that *oscilla*, or masks of terra-cotta,[4] were substituted instead of human heads around the altar. "They keep," says Ausonius, "the festivals so called from the figures."[5] Macrobius thus touches on the Saturnalia. "The Saturnalia were [originally] celebrated

---

[1] Cf. that of Lidney Park, Lysons, Reliq. Britann. Rom. ii. xxix. 6.

[2] Wright, The Celt, Roman, and Saxon, 12mo. London, p. 224.

[3] Caumont, Cours. xxxviii. p. 222.

[4] Macrobius, Saturn. i. c. 11.

[5] "Festa sigillorum nomine dicta colunt."—Idyll, xxv. 32.

for only one day, on the fourteenth of the Kalends, but were afterwards prolonged to three. The celebration of the *Sigillaria*, which was added, extended the public pastime and the joy of the fête till the seventh day. It was called the Sigillaria because sigilla, or little images,[1] and other trifling gifts were sent about." Martial[2] alludes to many of these being of terra-cotta, which were either bought for joke, or by parents for their children in honour of Saturn. They probably alluded to the stone or image which Rhea gave the god to devour instead of his children. The Saturnalia commenced on the 14th or 16th of the Kalends of January, and were continued for three days. On the 12th of the Kalends of January, the feast of the Sigillaria commenced.[3] All classes of society indulged in this festival. Hadrian, says his biographer, sent the Saturnalian and Sigillarian gifts even to those who did not expect them, or had no right to do so.[4] Commodus, when a child, gave them to his tutors as a mark of great condescension. The whole feast reminds us of Twelfth Night.

Although it is not possible to trace a succession of these small figures in the Imperial times, yet the age of the greater part of them is of the middle period of the Empire. Some representing the Deæ Matres just cited, are of the latest time of Paganism, when taste and knowledge had declined.

Some were actual portraits of deceased persons.[5] One

---

[1] Saturn. lib. i. c. 10.
[2] Lib. xiv. clxiv. clxvi.
[3] Rosinus, Antiq. Rom. p. 295.
[4] Spartianus, in vita, Lugd. Bat.

1632, p. 23.
[5] Seroux D'Agincourt, Recueil, Pl. xvi. fig. 1. One of these heads was in Mr. Hertz's collection.

of the most interesting of this nature is the small head discovered in the sepulchral chambers of the Cornelian family near the urn of Scipio Barbatus. It is at present in the collection of Mr. Mayer, and is an excellent specimen of the art of the time.

A few notices of terra-cotta figures [1] are found in the Latin authors. Martial speaks of a deformed indecent figure of a man, perhaps Clesippus, which was so horrid that he thought Prometheus must have made it when intoxicated during the Saturnalia,[2] and of a mask of a red-haired Batavian, the conceit of the potter.[3] The makers of Sigillaria do not appear to have deemed them of such importance as to place their names upon them.

FABRIC.

The Roman artists followed the same process as the Greeks. The figures were made upon a stick (crux et stipes[4]), with moist clay, and afterwards baked. "You will imitate," says Horace,[5] "in wet clay whatever you choose." From these figures moulds were taken in a more porous clay, which produced a succession of other figures.[6] The torso was often a separate piece.

D'Agincourt finds some difficulty in accounting for the mode in which the terra-cotta figures were hollowed. "Si ces statues ont été moulés," he observes, "elles sont été

[1] For sigillaria, D'Agincourt, Pl. x. 1; xiii. 1, 2, 3 xiv. 1, 3 ; xv. 14 ; xvi. 3.

[2] Epig., xiv. 176.

[3] Ibid., 182.

[4] Tertullian, Apologet. 12. "Quod si-mulacrum non prius argilla deformat cruci et stipiti nuper structa."

[5] Horace, lib. ii. Ep. 1, 8, "Argilla quid vis imitaberis uda."

[6] Festus, in Rutumena, 6.

déchargées adroitement et à mesure de leur formation, de l'epasseur intérieure de la terre. Quelques ouvertures plus ou moins grandes pratiquées au dos et même dans le bas des figures donnent la preuve de cette opération ; elles laissent apercevoir la traces des doigts ou de de l'ébauchoir de l'artiste qui a pris le soin de les évider." [1] This is however evidently not quite correct, as the figures were made by pressing the crust into the mould with the fingers.

POTTERS.

Although the names of makers are constantly found upon all kinds of lamps, vases, tiles, friezes, and mouldings, especially those of terra-cotta, the sigillaria are not found marked by them. Passeri [2] indeed has engraved a figure of Minerva, on which is stamped or impressed the name VLPIANI, " of Ulpianus," probably the name of its maker— but as this figure has two wings or handles behind, it probably belonged to a lamp—and might even have been put on by its possessor. An account of the potters will be found attached to the respective classes of ware.

Although among the Greeks, the potter as a manufacturer and often an artist, held a respectable position, the social condition of the Roman potter was low. He was generally a slave, sometimes a barbarian, while the masters of factories or shops were only liberti, or freedmen. Sometimes the potter appears to have worked on the estate of a wealthy proprietor, who received through his name the profits accruing from the establishment. The fullest account of the potters will be found in the

---

[1] D'Agincourt, Pl. xviii. fig. p. 43.   [2] III. tab. 84.

description of tile and lamp makers, who formed a numerous class.

MISCELLANEOUS USES.

It is impossible to enumerate all the purposes to which the Romans applied terra-cotta ; but some are so remarkable as to deserve a special notice. Such are the cages employed to fatten dormice,[1] called *saginaria, gliraria,*[2] in order to prepare them for the palates of Roman epicures ; and the cones of heated terra-cotta placed before hives, in order to burn the butterflies, and other insects which attacked the bees, called *milliaria testacea.* There are specimens of both these instruments in the Museum of Naples.[3] Bees, too, seem to have been hived in terra-cotta amphoræ,[4] a use of the material peculiar to antiquity. Toys, as among the Greeks, were also made of this material, and called *crepundia* and *sigillaria*, from their being stamped in moulds.

Small altars, which have been found, are supposed to have been dedicated in the *lararia* to the lares, for the holding of lamps or the burning of incense.[5]

Of terra-cotta were also made the little money-boxes which the successful charioteers or athletes carried about, to receive the donations of the spectators of the circus. One of these, found on the Aventine hill, of a conical shape, like an ancient furnace, is engraved by D'Agincourt.[6] On

---

[1] Verde, Guide pour le Musée Royal Bourbon, Naples, 1833, p. 114, n., 516–518.

[3] Varro, lib. iii. c. xiv.

[3] Verde, l. c. no. 4860, p. 140.

[4] Porphyry, Ant. Nymph. p. 261.

[5] D'Agincourt, Recueil, xxi. 1, 3 ; xxii. 9, p. 53.

[6] Recueil, Pl. xx. p. 50–52.

one side is the victor, in the dress of the auriga of the third century ; on the other, the words Ael(ia) Max(ima). A second had a head of Hercules ; and a third, engraved by Caylus,[1] is of an oval form, like a snuff-box, and has upon it a head of Hercules. It was found upon Mount Cælius, with another, on which was Ceres. A fourth was discovered in the baths of Titus, in 1812, filled with coins of the time of Trajan.[2] The three figures on the front of this were explained as the tutelary gods of the capitol. It had on the outside a branch and horse.[3]

A few tickets, or tesseræ, used for admission to the games of the amphitheatre and the circus, were also occasionally made of red ware, intermediate between terra-cotta and stone ware. On them were either impressed or incised the number of the cuneus and the steps, such as, V IIII. :—namely, the 4th division of the 5th row, or cuneus, or else a representation of the animals exhibited. On the reverse of one with such a representation is the letter A.

COINERS' MOULDS.

Terra-cotta moulds for making false coins have been discovered, of a paste composed of fine clay, containing the fossil infusoria of the genus navicula. Other moulds are of a dark red clay, and as hard as brick.[4] The clay was first worked up to form a tablet, flat on both sides, and about one-eighth of an inch thick. A piece of coin

---

[1] Tom. iv. Pl. liii. 3, 4, p. 157.

[2] Fea, Dissertation sur la Pretendue Statue de Pompée, p. 12.

[3] A. de Romanis, Terme di Tito, fo. Romæ, 1822, p. 25, 50-51.

[4] On the subject of these moulds, see Caylus, i. 286, cv. ; M. Hiver, Rev. Num. 1837, p. 171 ; Poey d'Avant (de Melle,) Rev. Num. 1837, p. 165; Rev. J. B. Reade, Num. Chron. vol. i. p. 161.

was pressed into this pillet on each side, so as to leave an impression on the clay. The clay was cut round this, and a triangular notch was made at one side of the clay. The pillets or moulds intended for the ends were impressed on one side only. The moulds were then piled in rouleaux or stacks, one above another, with the obverse and reverse of the coins adjusted so as to give out proper casts, and the notches inside, to allow the metal to flow through. The greatest number of piles or rouleaux placed together was eight, but there were often not more than three. The whole was then luted externally, to prevent the liquid metal from escaping ; and a kind of small basin or funnel was made at the top of the mould to facilitate the pouring in and circulation of the liquid mass, which was poured into a channel of a star-shape, formed by the union of the triangular notches. How the coins were extracted is not known : in all probability the external terra-cotta luting was removed, and the jet of the mould pared ; after which the coins were washed with tin or silver. Such is the apparatus for coining found in Roman stations in France and England. In the former country such an apparatus was found in an ancient building, close to the public baths at Fourvières, near Lyons ; and in another in the park of the castle of Damery, near Epernay, built on the ruins of Bibé, the first station on the military road between Rheims and Beauvais. In the latter place were found two thousand pieces of base silver coin, three-fourths of the Emperor Posthumus, and the rest coins of the Emperor Philip and his successors ; also several of the Constantines, and of all the principal imperial mints. An apparatus and thirty-nine moulds were found here, comprising the types

of Caracalla, the elder Philip, and Posthumus.   The dates
of these moulds range from the time of Severus, who first
adulterated the silver currency, till Diocletian, who restored
it.   They were thus made when the empire was distracted
with civil dissensions, rapid revolutions, and hostile camps;
and it is very difficult to decide whether they were the
work of forgers of the public money, or intended for the
issues of usurpers, who, being removed a considerable
distance from the capital, were unable to fill their military
chests except with cast coins.   At the Lingwell Gate, in
Yorkshire, where several of these moulds were found, they
were made of the clay and sand belonging to the spot.
A mould from Egypt, in the British Museum, of a deep
brick-red colour, is quite dissimilar from the moulds of
the Lingwell gate, and is probably made of Egyptian
clay.[1]

TOYS.

In the sepulchres of the Romans, several dolls of terra-
cotta, with movable arms and legs, are found, like those of
bone and ivory which occur more frequently,[2] especially in
the cemeteries of a late period, and of Christian children.[3]
Horace mentions them as made of wood, so also Apuleius,[4]
and M. Antoninus uses the Greek term of νευρόσπαστα,[5] neu-
rospasts.

Other toys were also made of this material, such as

---

[1] Other of these false dies for coins
are given in D'Agincourt, Recueil, xxxiv.
p. 90; Ficoroni, Piombi Antichi, tom. i.
pl. cv. no. 2.

[2] Seroux D'Agincourt, Recueil, p.
91; Caylus, Recueil, tom. iv. pl. lxxx.

no. 1, p. 259.
[3] Boldetti, osservazioni sopra i cime-
terii, 1720, p. 496.
[4] De Mundo, 8vo, Franc. 1621, p. 70;
cf. Aristotle, de Mundo, l. c.
[5] In Vitâ, lib. vi. c. 2.

the astragalus, or knuckle bone,[1] fruits, carts, animals, and other objects.

LAMPS.

Lamps, *lucernæ*, are often of terra-cotta. They are made of a fine clay, and are one of the most interesting products of the art. Several are covered with a thin coating of slip, or silicious glaze, and consequently belong to M. Brongniart's sub-order of lustrous pottery composed of a tender paste. The later lamps are of the red Roman ware. As the greater number, however, are of terra-cotta, the general description of their manufacture, subjects, and epigraphs, will be given here, and the other kinds referred to in their respective places.[2]

The Greek name for a lamp was *lychnos* (λύχνος), and for the stand in which the lamp was placed, *lychnuchus*, or " lamp holder." The lamp *lucerna*, says Varro, was afterwards invented, so called from *lux*, light, or beaming, the Greeks call it λύχνος.[3] The. parts of the lamp are the nozzle, or the nose, *nasus*, the handle *ansa*, and the upper part *discus*, in which was a hole for pouring in the oil, anciently plugged with a stopper. The word *myxa*,

---

[1] Agincourt, Recueil, xxiii. ii.

[2] Oct. Ferrarius, de veterum lucernis sepulchralibus; Grævius, Ant. Rom. xii. 998. Veterum lucernæ sepulchrales delineatæ a P. S. Bellorio, cum observationibus G. P. Bellori ex Italico, Romæ, 1691-1729 ; Gronovius, Thes. t. xii. 1702; Böttiger, Amalthæa, Bd. iii. s. 168, a Silenus lamp; kl. Schrift v. III. s. 307, new-year's lamp ; Walz.— in Pauly, Real Encyclopedie der classi-

schen Alterthumwissen. 4 Bd. 1846, s. 1162; F. Licetus, De lucernis antiquorum, libri vi. fo. Udin. 1652; P. Santi Bartoli, Le antiche lucerne sepolcrali figurate et designate ed intagliate nelle loro forme, fo. Roma, 1691 ; Lucernæ fictiles Musei Passerii, folio, Pisauri, 1739—43-51. ; Le Lucerne d'Ercolano. fo. Nap. 1792; Seroux D'Agincourt, Recueil, p. 63 et seq.

[3] L. L. v. 34.

the French *mèche*, which was applied to the wick, gave the
name *polymyxos* to lamps with many nozzles. Lamps are
sometimes circular, with a spout and handle, sometimes
elliptical or shoe-shaped. The Greeks applied to terra-
cotta lamps the term *trochelatus*,[1] or made on the lathe,
although, as already stated, they were obviously made in a
mould. Those used in dining-rooms, *tricliniares*, generally hung by chains from the ceiling,[2] candelabra being
only used to hold lamps in temples. Those found in
sepulchres, *sepulchrales*, were placed in a shoe-shaped
stand, fastened with a spike into the wall. The chamber
lamps, *cubiculares*, burnt all night.[3] The invention of
lamps is attributed to the Egyptians, who thought
that they were first fabricated by Vulcan, that Minerva
supplied the oil, and that Prometheus lit them.[4]
Lamps are first mentioned by Pherecrates, the Athenian
poet, who flourished in the reign of Alexander the Great.
We find no further mention of them till the age of
Augustus, and none of the terra-cotta lamps are earlier
than that period. The principal parts of these lamps
are the cup or hollow portion, *crater*, the upper part,
discus, and the handle, *ansa*, behind. The discus has
a hole, *infundibulum*. Round the crater is the limbus,
which is a decorated border of floral or other ornaments.[5]

The *infundibulum*, or hole, by which the oil was poured
into the lamp had a movable cover, or stopper, which is

---

[1] Aristophanes, Eccl. 1.

[2] Virgil, Æn. I. 730.

[3] Martial, xiv. 39, x. 38. For the
mode of using lamps, see Böttiger, Die
Silenus lampen, Amalthæa, III. p. 168,

&c.; Becker, Charicles, II. p. 215;
Gallus, II. p. 209.

[4] Passeri, Lucernæ, folio, Pisauri,
1739, p. 4.

[5] Pollux, Onomasticon, x. 27.

rarely found. This, which was an inch or an inch and a quarter in diameter, was stamped in a separate mould, and is generally ornamented with the subject of a head in full face. A fictile lantern was found in the pyramid of Cestius.

The wick, *myxa*, was made either of tow, *stuppa*, or rush, *scirpus*, of amaranth, *amaranthus*, or papyrus. The pin or needle with which the wick was trimmed was sometimes placed in a hole at the side.

SHAPE.

The earliest lamps have an open circular body, with a curved projecting rim to prevent the oil from spilling, and occur both in terra-cotta and also in the black glazed ware found in the sepulchres of Nola. Many have a projecting hollow pipe in the centre, in order to fix them to a stick on the top of a candelabrum. These lamps have no handles. They may have been placed in the sacella or lararia, and were turned on the potter's wheel.

The shoe-shape is the most usual, with a round body, a projecting spout or nozzle having a hole for the wick, and a small annular handle, which is more or less raised. Some of the larger lamps, and especially the Greek ones, have a flat triangular handle, which is sometimes elaborately ornamented in bas-relief with figures, the helix ornaments, dolphins, and other subjects. Another kind of handle was in the shape of the crescent moon, and was very common in bronze. In a few instances it was in the form of the neck of a vessel. The bust of the god Serapis was a much more unusual form.　A singular variety of lamp,

well adapted for a table, was fitted into a kind of small altar, the sides of which were ornamented with reliefs.　Several however, from their unusual shape, may be considered as fancy ware, the upper part, or the whole lamp, being moulded into the resemblance of some object.　Such are the lamps in the British Museum in the shape of a female head surmounted by a flower, or of the head of a negro or Nubian with open jaws, through which the wick was inserted.　Some elegant little

No. 186.—Lamp.　Crescent-shaped handle.

lamps were in the shape of a foot, or a pair of feet, shod in

No. 187.—Lamp, with bust of Serapis.

the caliga, and studded with nails.　A bull's head was a

favourite device. Some lamps in the shape of a pigeon are of very late fabric. A lamp for two wicks, in the collection just referred to, is in the shape of the wine skin of old Silenus, whose head is seen above, and through whose gaping jaws it was fed. Another is also of a comic nature, having a satyr's head in front. It was for many wicks.[1]

No. 188.—Group of lamps—altar-shaped—with many spouts, and ordinary one for one wick.

Some are in the shape of tall jugs, the upper part being the lamp. In this case the front and sides are ornamented with figures in bas-relief, such as Apollo,[2] or the triform Hecate—one figure on each side.[3]

AGE.

Most of these lamps appear to have been made between the age of Augustus and that of Constantine. The style, of course best at the earlier period of the empire, degenerates under the later emperors, such as Philip and Maximus, and becomes at last Byzantine and bad.

[1] Seroux D'Agincourt, Recueil, Pl. xxxvii. xxxviii.
[2] Passeri, i. tav. lxix.
[3] Passeri, i. tav. xcvii. iii. lxxvii.

T 2

Most lamps had only one wick, but the light they afforded must have been feeble, and consequently some have two wicks, the nozzles for which project beyond the body of the lamp. In the same manner were fabricated lamps of three, five, and seven wicks. If more were required the nozzles did not project far beyond the body of the lamp, which was then moulded in a shape adapted for the purpose, and especially the favourite one of a galley. Sometimes a conglomeration of small lamps was manufactured in a row, or in a serrated shape, which enabled the purchaser to obtain what light he required ; still the amount of illumination must have been feeble. As many as twenty wicks are found in some lamps.

The greater number average from three to four inches long, and one inch high ; the walls are about one-eighth of an inch thick, and the circular handles not more than one inch in diameter. Some of the larger lamps, however, are about nine inches or a foot long, with handles eight or nine inches high.

The paste of some is white, chalky, and easily scratched ; of others, hard and clayey ; of a few, of a bluish-black colour. Red, is however, the prevalent tone, either owing to the earth called *rubrica*, or ruddle, by Pliny, or to the use of bullock's blood, which washes out.[1] The lamps found at Rome on the Via Nomentana, celebrated for its potteries, are of a white colour.[2] The Neapolitan lamps are of a dingy brown, or yellow. Those made of earth from the Vatican hill are red.[3] The lamps from Cumæ are also made of red clay,[4] and those

---

[1] Livy, lib. iii. dec. 1.
[2] Passeri, p. xiii. xiv.
[3] The fragiles patellæ of the Vatican are mentioned by Juvenal, Sat. vi. 343.

[4] Passeri, xiv.; Martial, xiv. Ep. 112, speaks of the red clay of this locality.

found at Arretium and Perusia are of the same colour.[1]
The lamps of Pisani are both red and white clay, from the
fundus accianus. The Etruscan are of black clay, the
Egyptian of red, brown, or black clay, fully baked. Many
of the lamps from the vicinity of Naples are of an ashen
or yellow clay. Those from Greece are remarkably pale
and pure.

PROCESS.

Lamps were manufactured by means of moulds, which
were modelled from a pattern lamp, in a harder and finer
clay than the squeeze or pattern. The latter was divided
into two parts, adjusted
by mortices and tenons,
the lower part forming
the body of the lamp, the
upper the decorated su-
perficies. The clay was
pressed in with the fin-
gers by a potter called

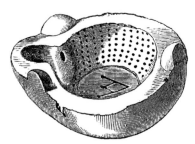

No. 189.—Mould of a lamp (lower part).

the *figulus sigillator*,[2] or stamper. The two portions were
joined while the clay was moist, and pared with a tool, and
a small hole was pierced for introducing the oil. They
were then dried and sent to the kiln, and baked carefully
at a not very high temperature. Some moulds were
prepared with considerable taste and good workmanship,
and as the same type was used by different potters, it
appears that they were sold ready made, and that the
potter merely added his name.

[1] Passeri, xiv.
[2] Passeri, p. x. " Dis manibus Aga-

tobolus, Lucii filius Pyrrhus figulus
sigillator."

RELIEFS.

The simplest kind of lamps, and which may be considered of the earliest and best style, have their subjects
in the centre, which is concave, like a votive clypeus, which
it appears intended to represent. The subject is only
surrounded with a plain bead or moulding. Such lamps
are probably of the best period of Empire, and may be
traced down to the time of Philip.[1] They generally have
simple semi-oval nozzles and moulded handles, and are
distinguished by their simple circular bodies. In some
cases the moulding is divided, leaving a channel to the
neck.[2] These lamps have never more than one hole for
the oil. Such specimens as have not handles, generally
have the part for the wick elongated, and ornamented
either with mouldings resembling the Amazonian pelta
(which are sometimes seen combined with architectural
flowers on those with handles), or else the nozzle seems
intended for an ivy leaf, flower, or pelta. On some of the
later lamps, the borders are much more elaborate ; egg
and tongue mouldings, wreaths of laurel, bunches of grapes,
and oak leaves, are distributed round the subject ; or the
acanthus leaf, and antefixal ornament, and a trefoil
flower or leaf, an egg and tongue border, wreaths appear.
The number of figures is generally small, it being contrary to the principle of ancient art to crowd a work with
minute figures and accessories. Many lamps have no subject, the majority only one figure ; and two, three, and more
figures are rare in the ratio of the increasing number.

---

[1] Cf. the one in Passeri, iii. xxix.   [2] Ibid. iii. xxvii.

Some of the largest lamps, indeed, have several figures, but such are very rare. Nor are lamps impressed with distinct and well preserved subjects common ; only a few of this description can be selected out of the hundreds that are found. Many are of grotesque and humorous workmanship. Such lamps, when of small size, generally fetch from a few shillings to a pound ; but there is no limit to the price that amateurs will pay for extraordinary specimens. Considering their smallness, they are amongst the most interesting remains of Roman terra-cottas ; and it is only to be regretted that the Romans possessed so little historical taste, as they might by this means have transmitted to us more interesting information than is conveyed by the representation of barren myths, the exploits of gladiators, or the lives of courtesans.

SUBJECTS.

The subjects of these lamps are calculated to convey the same relative idea of Roman civilisation, as the plates now made to be sold among the working classes are of that of our own day. The lamp-maker sought to gratify the taste of his customers by ornamenting his ware with familiar subjects. The purchasers of terra-cotta lamps were generally persons of inferior condition : he would therefore copy from memory well-known statues of the principal gods, or represent incidents in the lives of heroes whose fame was popular. In Rome the stage exerted little influence, and the lamp-maker rarely took a subject from the drama ; but the games of the circus, the incidents of gladiatorial life, the contest, the pardon, or

the death, as well as the tricks of the *circulatores* or
mountebanks, recalled scenes familiar to every eye.
Under the empire the Romans had become vain and
frivolous, and their masters sought to obliterate from
their minds the cruel scenes of imperial bloodshed and
public rapine by spectacles and diversions. There are
also some subjects taken from fables, which always make
so much impression on uneducated minds ; but a great
number have nothing except ornaments.

DEITIES.

A few only of the great gods are found represented.
A lamp published by Passeri, has Cœlus, surrounded by
Sol, Luna, and the stars.[1] Jupiter often occurs, seated on
a throne ; probably a potter's copy of the statue of the
Capitoline Jove ;[2] at other times he is seen in the
company of Juno and Minerva,[3] or allied with Cybele, Sol,
and Luna.[4] A very common subject is the bust of this
deity, sometimes with his sceptre placed on the eagle,
which is flying upwards.[5] His consort Juno seems to have
had but few admirers.[6]

Of the incidents in the life of Minerva, the lamp
represent her birth, Jupiter being attended by Vulcan
and Lucina.[7] Her head[8] or bust is[9] of common
occurrence. She is also seen standing[10] as Pacifera,[11]
having at her side a vase and cista ;[12] advancing as
Promachos,[13] having at her side an owl ;[14] or sacrificing at

[1] P. I. vii. In this and the following
pages B. M. stands for the Collection of
the British Museum; B. for Bartoli; and
L. for Licetus.
[2] B. M.   [3] B. M.   [4] Pass. I, xv.

[5] B. M.   [6] P. I. xii.   [7] P. I. lii. lx.
[8] P. I. liii.   [9] P. I. liv.   [10] P. I.
[11] P. I. lix.   [12] P. I. lxii. lxiii.; B. ii. 18.
[13] P. I. lxiv.   [14] P. I. lxv.

an altar.[1] Sometimes only her helmet,[2] or her ægis is represented,[3] having on it the head of the terrible beauty Medusa. The lame Vulcan is scarcely ever seen,[4] and his servant, the grim Cyclops, only once.[5]

Apollo often appears as the Pythian, or the Lycian,[6] seated [7] and playing on the lyre ; or as the Hyperborean [8] with the gold-guarding gryphon at his side. Other lamps have Diana hunting,[9] or without her dogs,[10] or driving in her character of the Moon, or Luna.[11] Another form of Diana, as the three-fold Hecate, whose statue was placed in most of the Roman triviæ is often found.[12] Mercury occurs in various attitudes, with the caduceus and purse, as the god of commerce,[13] with a goat, dog, and cock,[14] or allied with Fortune and Hercules.[15] The bust of this god, with a purse and caduceus as the god of merchandise, or with the ram [16] is constantly repeated.[17] On one lamp, the exchange of the lyre, which he invented, for the caduceus of Apollo is represented.[18] Mercury was always a popular Roman god.

Mars, although pre-eminently the deity of Rome, the Gradivus Pater, is rarely distinguishable from ordinary heroes. He is represented disarmed by Cupid,[19] meditating war,[20] and bearing a trophy.[21] One lamp, on which are the busts of Mars, Venus, and Sol, probably refers to the amours of the god.[22] Venus, a favourite goddess of the Roman people, and consequently of the lamp-makers, is

[1] B. M.   [2] P. I. lxvi.   [11] P. I. xci. xcii.   [12] P. I. xcvii.
[3] P. I. lxvi.   [13] P. I. ciii. cv.
[4] P. II. xxxv.   [5] P. II. xxxv.   [14] Passeri, I. cii.; B. ii. 18.
[6] P. I. lxxi.   [7] P. I. lxxii.-v.   [15] B. M.   [16] P. III. xcvii.
[8] P. I. lxxv.   [17] B. M.; P. I. c.   [18] P. I. civ.
[9] P. I. xcvi.; B. M.   [19] B. M.   [20] B. M.; P. II. xxx.
[10] B. M.; P. i. lxxxvii.   [21] P. II. xxiv.-xxvi.   [22] P. I. lxxxix.

seen as Cytherea, or rising from the sea,[1] with a star and crown,[2] at the bath,[3] as the Coia of Praxiteles,[4] as Victrix,

No. 190.—Lamp.—Mercury, Fortune, and Hercules.

or the vanquisher, and arming, attended by Cupids,[5] like the Venus of Capua.

The representations of marine deities are limited to those of Neptune,[6] Triton, Proteus wearing the mariner's cap,[7] and Scylla,[8] and the head of Thetis ornamented with a crab. Many lamps have Cupids, who appear invested with the attributes and performing the functions

of the gods. Sometimes the merry little deity holds the club and quiver of Hercules,[9] reclines upon a couch,[10] sails over the sea in a galley,[11] fishes from a rock, plays on pipes,[12] holds a crater and inverted torch,[13] gambols with companions,[14] holds a bird,[15] sounds the lyre like Apollo,[16] sacrifices,[17] seizes the arms of Mars,[18] fills a crater or winebowl out of an amphora, like a Satyr,[19] holds grapes,[20] shoots a serpent, a parody of Apollo and Python,[21] or blows

[1] P. II. xiv. [2] P. II. xiii. [13] B. M. [14] B. M.
[3] B. M. [4] P. II. xv. [5] B. M. [15] P. III.xci.
[6] P. i. xlii. [7] B. M.; B. 5. [16] P. I. lxxvii.
[8] P. i. xlvii. [9] B. M. [10] B. M. [17] P. I. ci. [18] P. I. lxvii.
[11] B. M. [12] B. M. [19] B. M. [20] B. M. [21] B. M.

Pan's pipe.[1]   Sometimes his amour with Psyche is represented, from the tale of the Golden Ass by Lucian and Lucius Apuleius ; [2] sometimes only his bust is seen,[3] or he appears as a terminal statue.[4]

Bacchus was always a popular god at Rome, and the edicts against his worship show how deeply it had taken root in the minds of the people of Italy.   On lamps he is seen holding his cantharus for a panther to lick,[5] or with the cantharus on his head,[6] drinking,[7] as a boy with grapes,[8] or in his ship.[9]   Several lamps have Ampelus,[10] a Satyr, with torches[11] or with pipes,[12] Comus or Marsyas, Satyrs pouring wine from the *ascos* or wine-skin,[13] or pounding in a mortar,[14] the old Pappo-Silenus,[15] Satyrs pursuing Nymphs,[16] Bacchantes tearing a kid over a lighted altar,[17] or a Bacchante at an altar,[18] and Pan.

The host of minor deities and demi-gods also often exercised the ingenuity of the modeller of lamps. Among these is found Sol in a quadriga,[19] standing with Luna,[20] Sol or the Colossus of Rhodes, full face,[21] and his bust surrounded by the stars and planets ; [22] Nox or Ariadne also occurs.[23]   Luna also appears in an infinite variety of shapes. So many of the lamps were made on the occasion of the secular games that they seem to allude to them.   Among Roman gods are seen Janus,[24] Silvanus with the falx and basket,[25] his bust,[26] Vesta, and some others.[27]   Pluto,[28] Salus, and Æsculapius rarely occur.[29]

---

[1] B. M.   [2] P. III. t. xx. ; B. i. 7.   [14] B. M.   [15] B. M.   [16] B. M.   [17] B. M.
[3] B. M., P. II. i.   [18] B. M.; B. ii. 22   [19] P. I. lxxxv.; B. ii. 9.
[4] P. III. viii.   [5] B. M.   [20] P. I. lxxxviii.   [21] P. I. lxxxiv.
[6] B. M.   [7] P. II. xxxix.   [22] P. I. xii.   [23] P. I. vii. xv.
[8] B. M.   [9] B. M.   [24] P. I. iv.   [25] P. I. x.
[10] P. II. xxxvi.   [11] P. II. xxxviii.   [26] P. I. ix.   [27] B. M.
[12] B. M.   [13] B. M.   [28] B. ii. 6. 8.   [29] B. ii. 45.

Hercules is seen killing the serpent Ladon, which guarded the tree of the Hesperides,[1] holding the gathered apples,[2] seizing the stag of Mount Cerynitis,[3] sacrificing,[4] reposing,[5] holding the cup as Hercules Bibax,[6] in the company of Minerva,[7] or as Musagetes playing on the lyre.[8] The Dioscuri, so propitious to the Romans at the lake Regillus, sometimes appear as busts in full face, as the "lucid stars, the brothers of Helen;"[9] Castor is seen accompanied by his horse,[10] or with his horse's head and spear.[11] Of the inferior deities there is Rome seated alone,[12] or crowned by Victory;[13] Fortune having before her a star and rudder,[14] or standing with other gods; the Dii lares,[15] the Genius of the army,[16] Hymen,[17] the four Seasons,[18] and Vesta.[19]

Victory is beheld holding a shield,[20] on which is often an inscription, invoking a happy new year,[21] having in area the head of Janus and other emblems;[22] sacrificing at an altar; accompanied by the Lares;[23] holding a shield;[24] sacrificing a bull, or elevating a trophy high in the air.[25]

FOREIGN DEITIES, EMBLEMS, ETC.

The prevalence of exotic religions at Rome is shown by the representations of Diana of Ephesus,[26] Cybele, with her lions, and the youth Atys,[27] Mithras;[28] Serapis supported by

[1] B. M.; P. III. 93. [2] B. M.
[3] P. II. iv. [4] P. II. iii.
[5] P. III. xciv. [6] B. M.
[7] P. II. vii. [8] P. II. vi.
[9] B. M.; P. I. lxxxvii.
[10] B. M.; P. II. xxviii.
[11] P. II. xxvi.
[12] P. III. i. [13] P. III. ii.
[14] B. M. [15] B. M.
[16] P. II. xxvi. [17] P. I. xxxviii.
[18] P. I. xi. [19] P. I. xiii.
[20] B. M. [21] B. M.
[22] B. M. [23] B. M.
[24] P. I. t. vi. [25] B. M.
[26] P. I. xcviii. [27] B. M.
[28] P. I. xc.

two sphinxes[1] or alone,[2] or on a throne with Isis ;[3] Isis,[4] with her son Harpocrates,[5] in the company of Anubis ;[6] Harpocrates alone,[7] and other Egyptian gods.[8] Some lamps have an Egyptian hunt,[9] a crocodile, and the god Canopus.[10]

Many lamps have merely the emblems of deities, as the sword, club, and lion's skin of Hercules ;[11] the lion's head, cantharus, and vine leaves of Bacchus ;[12] or a cantharus with wreaths of vine leaves and panthers, of which Passeri possessed 500 repetitions, made by the lamp maker L. Cæcilius Sætinus ; [13] the dolphin and lyre of Apollo, allied with the hippocamp and rudder for Neptune ; [14] the gryphon and patera of Apollo ;[15] or the raven, laurel, and caduceus,[16] allied with the thunderbolt of Jupiter, the staff of Æsculapius, the helmet and shield of Mars ;[17] the joined hands and caduceus of the goddess Peace ; [18] a goat, and armour on a column.[19]

Few subjects were taken from the old stories of the cyclic poets and the Iliad, which were familiar only to the learned public ; yet some appear which Virgil, Ovid, and the other poets of the Augustan age had rendered familiar. Among these are Ganymede playing with the bird of Jove ;[20] the amour of Jupiter, under the form of a swan, with Leda ; [21] the judgment of Paris ; [22] the combat of Achilles and Hector ;[23] the death of Hector, of Penthesilea,[24] and of other Amazons ; [25] Diomed and Ulysses with the Palladium ; the flight of Æneas ; [26]

[1] P. III. lxx.
[2] P. III. lxiii. lxviii. [3] P. III. lxx.–i.
[4] P. III. lxix. [5] B. M.
[6] B. M. I. xxxii. [7] P. I. i.
[8] P. I. lxxviii. III. lxxx. lxxxi.
[9] B. M. [10] P. III. lxxiv.
[11] P. II. ix. [12] P. III. civ.

[13] P. III. ciii. [14] P. I. l.
[15] P. I. lxx. [16] B. M.
[17] P. I. iii. [18] B. M.
[19] P. I. lxviii. [20] B. M.
[21] B. M. [22] B. M.
[23] B. M.; B. i. 10 ; iii. 9. [24] B. M.
[25] B. M. [26] B. M.

Ulysses passing the Sirens ;[1] Polyphemus devouring the companions of Ulysses ;[2] the same hero escaping under the Ram ;[3] receiving the wind-bags of Æolus ; the cranes and pigmies ;[4] Œdipus and the Sphinx ; Prometheus ;[5] Perseus and Andromeda ;[6] Meleager ;[7] Actæon ;[8] the fall of Bellerophon ;[9] and Orestes haunted by the Furies.[10]

FABLES.

A few of the fables of popular writers are also represented. One lamp, found near Naples, and now in the British Museum, has the well known tale of the fox and the crow, treated in a peculiar style. The fox has slipped on a chlamys, and stands erect on his hind legs, holding up a pair of pipes to the crow, which is perched on the top of the tree. Another in the same collection represents a fable taken from an unknown source, perhaps the veritable Æsop, in which a stork holds in its beak a balance, and weighs in one scale an elephant, while a mouse is seen in the other. A third lamp has on it the cock that has found the grain of barley, which he preferred to all the precious stones on earth. There are also numerous caricatured subjects,[11] consisting of grotesque heads and figures, with diabolical countenances, the meaning of which is very obscure ; but they are supposed by many to be dwarfs.

[1] B. M.   [2] Avolio, 116.   [7] B. i. 31.   [8] B. i. 28.   [9] B. ii. 24.
[3] Lamp in S. W. Parish's collection.   [10] P. II. xciv.–ciii.
[4] B. M.   [5] B. i. 1, 2, 3.   [6] B. i. 9.   [11] P. III. xx. xxi. 6.

HISTORICAL SUBJECTS.

There are but few historical subjects, and those which occur are taken from sources more piquant than true. One lamp represents the celebrated interview of Alexander the Great and Diogenes, who addresses the hero out of his jar ;[1] Romulus found by Faustulus [2] is seen, the twins Romulus and Remus suckled by the she-wolf,[3] and Remus alone.[4] The immolation, perhaps, of Curtius,[5] and a few other events in Roman history are found. Neither are subjects derived from real life numerous, although some may be cited; as an Emperor sacrificing, soldiers,[6] a battering ram,[7] and soldiers fighting ; [8] galleys sailing over the ocean ; [9] fishermen either at the Tiber or at Ostia ; [10] Tityrus [11] tending his herds ; a shepherd with a caged animal; [12] the rustic chapel of the gods of the countrymen ; [13] persons pounding in mortars; [14] preparing the vintage,[15] or bringing the wine in casks.[16] The scenes of love are far too numerous to describe ; neither are they treated in the chaste style of modern art, but repeat the orgies of the debauched Tiberius at Capreæ.

GAMES OF CIRCUS.

Many lamps have bas-reliefs representing the popular subjects of the games of the circus, and the gladiatorial exhibitions of the amphitheatre. The finest of these in the British Museum has a race of quadrigæ ;[17] the spina,

[1] B. M.; P. III. lviii.
[2] P. III. iv.　[3] P. III. iii.
[4] P. III. v.　[5] B. M.
[6] P. II. xxii. xxiii; III. xxxv.-xxxviii.
[7] P. II. xxviii.　[8] B. M.
[9] B. M.　[10] B. M.
[11] B. M.　[12] Avolio, 120.
[13] B. M.　[14] B. M.　[15] B. M.
[16] B. M.
[17] B. M.; B. i. 24-25-27.

the metæ, the obelisks, the carceres, from which the
chariots have started, and the seats with the spectators
are represented. Others also occur with chariots,[1] sometimes bigæ.[2] Gladiators[3] are very often seen—either
Samnites or mirmillones,—with a palm,[4] crowned by Victory.[5]

No. 191.—Lamp—Games of the Circus—in the British Museum.

A lamp from Naples, now in the British Museum, has
the names of two gladiators, FVRIVS and COLVMBVS,[6]
in bas-relief at their sides. A common subject is the
victor holding up his sword, while the vanquished, fallen
upon one knee, expects his fate. Another lamp in the
same collection has a *retiarius*, holding his trident and

[1] B. M. ; P. III. xxvi. xxvii. xxviii.   [4] B. M.   [5] B. M.
[2] B. M.   [6] Cf. B. i. 22. Sabinus and Popillius.
[3] B. M. ; P. III. v. ix. ; B. 20-21-22.

mucro, with his name CALVISIVS, and that of his fallen
opponent MAXIMVS. Combats with beasts are seen,[1] also
boxers,[2] flute and cymbal players.[3] Busts of comedians,[4]
and comic and tragic masks [5] often occur, and several of
those deformed and obscene dwarfs called *Moriones*, holding pipes,[6] boxing with others,[7] wearing the petasus,[8] or
the hat of the slave.[9]

ANIMALS.

Animals form a numerous class of representations, such
are the gryphon,[10] pegasus,[11] lions, often devouring a stag[12]
or a bull,[13] panther,[14] boar[15] bitten by a dog,[16] bears,[17]
horses,[18] deer couchant,[19] dogs, sometimes fighting,[20] a
stag chased by dogs,[21] sheep[22], goats,[23] hares or rabbits
devouring grapes,[24] sphinxes,[25] a crocodile attacking a
lion,[26] an eagle,[27] a peacock,[28] the crow of Apollo,[29]
snails,[30] parrots,[31] dolphins, the same entwining an anchor,
a pelamys or tunny,[32] a hippocamp,[33] scorpion,[34] serpents
and lizards,[35] toads, scorpions,[36] shells,[37] locusts devouring
grapes,[38] capricorns,[39] and marine monsters.

[1] P. III. x. xiii.; B. i. 23.
[2] P. III. xxii. xxiii.
[3] P. III. cvi.   [4] P. III. xxxv.
[5] B. M.; D. 100.   [6] P. III. xxi.
[7] B. M.   [8] B. M.   [9] B. M.
[10] P. I. lxxix   [11] P. I. lxxx.
[12] B. M.   [13] B. M.
[14] B. M.   [15] B. M.
[16] B. M.; P. I. lxxxvi.
[17] B. M.   [18] B. M.
[19] B. M.   [20] B. M.
[21] B. M.   [22] B. M.
[23] B. M.   [24] B. M.
[25] B. M.   [26] B. M.
[27] B. M.   [28] P. III. xv. xvii.
[29] B. M.; P. I. xlix.
[30] P. III. lviii. lix.
[31] P. III. lxi.–lxxxiii.
[32] B. M.   [33] B. M.
[34] B. M.   [35] P. III. li.
[36] P. III. cv.   [37] B. M.
[38] P. I. xlviii.   [39] P. I. v.

MISCELLANEOUS SUBJECTS.

There are many subjects which it is difficult to class, such as the *as* and its divisions,[1] which must have been numismatic curiosities at the time the lamp was made ; the arms of the salii,[2] of foreigners, vases,[3] or a cupboard filled with

No. 192.—Lamp. Monogram
of Christ.

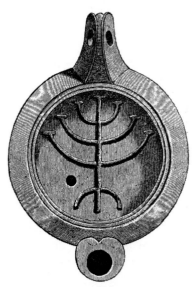

No. 193.—Lamp with the Golden
Candlestick.

vases,[4] a lectisternium to the infernal gods,[5] a lighted altar and genii,[6] serpents,[7] the dolphins of Neptune,[8] a sepulchral cippus,[9] a Bucraniun,[10] two palms,[11] a wreath,[12] of laurel, myrtle,[13] of oak leaves, the civic crown,[14] a curule seat with

[1] B. M.   [2] B. M.   [9] P. iii. liv.   [10] B. M.
[3] B. M.   [4] P. iii. li.   [11] B. M.   [12] P. iii. xliii.
[5] P. III. li.   [6] P. III. lii.   [13] B. M. iii. xli.   [14] P. iii. xliii.
[7] B. M.   [8] P. iii. xlv.

lictors,[1] tombs with genii [2] crowning sepulchral urns,[3] urns,[4] lustral vases,[5] crowns and palm branches.[6]

One of the most remarkable subjects of the later lamps is the golden candlestick,[7] as it appears upon the arch of Titus at Rome ; either a copy of that object at the time, or else in allusion to the Church, as figured in the Reve- lations. Many lamps indeed occur with Christian sym- bols—such as crosses, the monogram of Christ,[8] the good shepherd,[9] the great dragon, Jonas swallowed by the whale, and other emblems ; but these are generally of the bright red ware, of the class called the false Samian, under which they will be found described.

INSCRIPTIONS.

A considerable number of lamps have inscriptions, dis- posed in different manners. Those which have reference to the subject, being impressed in relief along with it, while those which relate to the lamp itself, or its maker, are always on the bottom, and consequently out of sight. These are either in relief, or else incised with a tool in cursive letters ; on the lamps of Arretium and Cumæ they are in relief in small tablets, on the upper surface. They were impressed with bronze stamps.

The inscriptions found upon lamps are—1. marks ; 2. names of makers ; 3. names of places where they were fabricated ; 4. name of pottery ; 5. name of proprietors ;

---

[1] P. III. xxxix.
[2] P. III. xliv., xlv., xlvii; I. 13, 14.
[3] P. iii. xlvi.
[4] P. III. xlviii.
[5] P. III. xlix., l.
[6] P. iii. xlii. xlviii.
[7] B. iii. 32.
[8] B. iii. 22.
[9] B. iii. 28, 29.

6. date of manufacture ; 7. dedication to deities ; 8. acclamations used at the public games ; 9. facts.[1]

Of the first class are the little marks used by the potter, either instead of his name, or in conjunction with it. There is no very great variety of symbols, and those found are of the simplest kind, such as circles, half moons, the print of a human foot, wheels, palm branches, the colt's foot, or vine leaf.

Although the inscriptions relating to the fabric of lamps are by no means so numerous or complete as those upon tiles, yet they are instructive with regard to the potteries. A considerable portion only indicate that they were made by slaves, since they bear single names, such as Agatho, Attius, Arion, Aquilinus, Cinnamus, Bassa, Bagradus, Draco, Diogenes, Heraclides, Fabrinus, Fortis, Faber, Faustus, Inulisuco, Memmius, Monos, Maximus, Muntripus, Nereus, Oppius, Primus, Priscus, Pastor, Publius, Probus, Rhodia, Stephanus, Successivus, Tertullus, and Vibianus. These names generally occur in the genitive, the word "manufacture," or "factory," being understood. One rare specimen has "Diogenes fecit." Many makers appear to have been freedmen, and the most remarkable of these was Tindarus, the freedman of Plotina Augusta, the wife of Trajan.[2] It has been already seen from the inscriptions upon tiles, that Tindarus was also a tile-maker, many of the tegulæ doliares having been prepared in his potteries. Some examples of the use of the word *officinæ* occur, as the officinæ of Caius Clodius Successivus, the officinæ of Publius and Titus already mentioned, that of P. Asisus, that

---

[1] Seroux D'Agincourt, Recueil, p. 67.　　　[2] P. i. xxxi.

of Patricius and Chrestio, and Ionis, but the expression is
uncommon.   That of *Manu*, or hand, is still rarer ; only
one potter, L. Muranus, is known to have employed it.

   Another remarkable inscription under a lamp, engraved
by Passeri, runs, *"from the manufactory of Publius
and Titus, at the Porta Trigemina."* [1]   A considerable
number of the names have a simple prænomen, such
as Aurelius Xanthus, Ælius Maximus, Caius Cæsar,
Clodius Heliodorus, Caius Memmius, Caius Faber, Caius
Fabricius, Claudius Lupercalis, Egnatius Aprilis, Lucius
Primus, Turcius Sabinus.   None of these names is of
historical importance, although it is just possible that the
last may be the Tyro-Sabinus mentioned by Pliny, who
wrote de Hortensibus.   They were probably freedmen
who manufactured lamps.   Of still higher rank than these
freedmen were the persons who possessed three names,
and who occasionally record their descent.   These must
be regarded as Roman citizens.   Such were probably
Publius Satrius Camillus, Caius Oppius Restitutus, Caius
Lucius Maurus, Caius Clodius Successivus, Caius Julius
Nicephorus, Caius Pomponius Dicax, Caius Julius Philippus, Caius Iccius Vaticanus, Lucius Fabricius Æveius,
Lucius Fabricius Masculus, Lucius Cæcilius Sævus.   Whether they were proprietors of the establishment, or of the
farm from which the clay was procured, is by no means
certain, but none of them are mentioned elsewhere ; which
renders it probable that they were persons of inferior
condition, such as masters of the potteries, who were probably rich freedmen.   A few words occur in a contracted
form which refer to the fabric, such as the Accianian of

------

[1] P. iii. vii.

Publius Satrius Campestris, son of Caius," on lamps found at Pesaurmu; "the Caninian," "the thirds (tertia) of Commodus," and those already mentioned, called "Flavians" and "Domitians;" also "the Heraclians," "the fourths of Oppius," and "the thirds of Publius Fabricius." It is of course uncertain what such expressions mean, as they may refer either to the officinæ or establishments, or to the names of the lamps themselves. If some may be interpreted "the Vatican lamps of Caius Iccius," this would appear to mean the celebrated clay of that hill, and the word *figlina*, or "pottery," is to be supplied. In the appendix will be found a list of the marks borne by other lamps. Some have the names of certain shops, such as C. Oppius Rest., Caius Rest., Clodii res., Publii Fabricii tertia, Oppedi quarta.

A third class may contain the name of the place where the lamps were made, as, *Caii Iccii Vatican(æ)*, for "Vatican (lamps) of C. Iccius," on lamps found at Rome. The fourth class has the name of the lamps or fabric, as the Caninian, Flavian, Domitian, Heraclian, Thirds, Fourths. This expression may refer to the names of the *figlinæ*, or potteries, similar expressions occurring on the tiles.

The fifth kind is supposed to contain the name of the Patroni in whose houses the lamp-makers lived. On these the names of Antoninus, Commodus, Philippus, Diocletian, and Maximus occur, and one, more distinct than the rest, has *Tindarus, Plotinæ Augustæ libertus*, "Tindarus,[1] the freedman of Plotina Augusta." One only contains the date of the consulship of the Emperor Philip, during the celebration of the Secular games. These

---

[1] Passeri, xi.

inscriptions observe the usual laws of contraction. The most
contracted form in which the names of emperors appears,
is AA. NN. (*Augustorum nostrorum,* of our two Augusti);
a phrase which cannot date earlier than the joint reign of
M. Aurelius and L. Verus. It is indeed possible that
the name of Titus, which occurs on one lamp, may be as
old as that of the emperor of that name, for upon several
lamps is found inscribed, "the Flavians of our god and lord;"
an expression particularly referable to Vespasian or Titus,
both of whom bore that surname ; while other lamps are
inscribed " the Domitians of our god and lord," showing
that they allude to the Emperor Domitian. Much light
is, however, thrown upon this point by the tiles, some of
which, as we have seen, were called "the larger Neronians"
after the Emperor Nero. The name of Trajan is found
upon a lamp, showing either that it came from the imperial
potteries or from others named after that emperor ; while
a large number of lamps are inscribed " of Antoninus," or
" of Antoninus Augustus," which probably refers to one
of the two Antonines, or else to Caracalla, or Elagabalus.
To this middle period of the Roman empire most lamps
may be referred, as some occur with the name of Severus,
others with that of Maximus, and several [1] with that of
M. Julius Philippus, some of which have the addition of
his third consulship—thus showing that they were made
during the remarkable epoch of the celebration of the
Secular games, A.D. 247. It is of course impossible to feel
certain that such names as Probus refer to the emperor of
that name, and no Roman lamps bear the name of a later
sovereign, although one Greek one has that of Diocletian.

[1] P. i. xxix.

The inscriptions upon some lamps are votive exclamations resembling those of the Decennalia and Secularia, such as, ANNVM NOVVM FAVSTVM FELICEM, " a new and propitiously happy year ! " [1] ANNVM IN QVO FAVSTVM FELIX TIBI SIT, "a year in which may all be fortunate and propitious to you;" or ANNVM NOVVM FAVSTVM FELICEM MIHIC, " may the new year be happy and propitious to me." These inscriptions seem to show that the lamps were given away or sold on new-year's-day, or on the celebration of the Secular games. On one is inscribed HAVE,[2] 'hail!'; SVTINE, 'oh Sutinus.' These inscriptions sometimes occur upon victors' shields, on which are often found inscriptions relative to victories, and other subjects. One remarkable lamp has DEQ QVI EST MAXIMVS,[3] " to the god who is greatest." Another, IOVI SERENO SACRUM, " sacred to Serene Jove." [4] Nor are certain expressions adapted for funeral purposes less interesting, such as SIT TIBI TERRA

No. 194.—Foot of Lamp, with name of the Secular Games.

LEVIS, " earth lie light on thee ;" or ANIMA DVLCIS, " O sweet soul ! " [5] A great number are stamped " SAECVL, or SAECVLARIA," in reference to the games of the period.

USES.

An immense number of lamps must have been used during the illuminations which seem to have taken place

---

[1] Passeri, i. 6 ; Fabr. vii. 5.   [4] P. i. xxxiii.   [5] Passeri, iii. 46.
[2] Avolio, p. 112.   [3] Passeri, I.

on occasion of triumphs. During the celebration of the Secular games the city was illuminated for three nights, and it is probable that some of the subjects found in lamps have reference to this festive use of them.[1] They were used for illuminations as early as that for the suppression of the Catiline conspiracy.[2] Lamps were also used in the Isiac worship. "Moreover," says Apuleius, "in the festival of Isis there was a great number of either sex, with lamps, torches, wax candles, and another kind of torches, imitating the light of the celestial stars. The first of them held forth a lamp, gleaming with a clear light, not much like those which illuminate our evening entertainments, but a golden boat or cup, sending forth a very long flame out of the midst of it."[3] They were also lighted in the lararia and sacilla and in the thermæ,[4] which Alexander Severus opened at nights.

They appear, indeed, to have been in general use for illuminating public buildings. For domestic use they were employed in the dining room, the study, and the kitchen.

Several lamps have been found in sepulchres, but these are chiefly of the Christian period, or connected with the worship of the Manes, and were not placed there, as some authors of the preceding century imagined, with the idea of their burning eternally.[5] In an inscription on a sepulchral cippus in the Museum, the heirs of a deceased person are enjoined on all the kalends, ides, and nones of

---

[1] Passeri, p. xx.; Sueton. Vit. Jul. Cæsar c. 37; Dio. Neron.; Xiphilin, i. xxxiii.; Sueton. Dom. c. 4; Lamprid. Vit. Alex Sev. c. iv.; Tertull. in Apologet.; Capitolinus, vita Gordian. ad fin.; Martial, x. ep. 6; Symmachus, l. ii.   [2] Plutarch. Cic. c. 22.

[3] Lamprid. vit. c. 24.   [4] As. Aur. xi.

[5] Fort. Licetus, de lucernis antiquorum reconditis, 1622.

each month[1] to place a lighted lamp in his sepulchre ; and the same is enjoined upon alternate months as a condition on which her slaves received their liberty, in the testament of Mævia.[2]   That this was common under the empire appears from the story of the Matron of Ephesus,[3] and from the following remarkable inscription : " May a golden shower cover the ashes of whoever places a lighted lamp in this tumulus." [4]

Among other superstitions connected with lamps was that of choosing the name of a child.   Several lamps were named, and then lighted, and the name of the child was taken from that of the lamp last extinguished.[5]   At the end of the eighteenth century a great number of lamps were discovered in a furnace, where they had been baked, together with the moulds and other utensils for making them.[6]   Great numbers are found at Rome, Naples, and on the sites of the principal cities of ancient Italy, Germany, France, and Britain.   Some numbers also occur in the rubbish heaps of the different cities of Greece and Africa.   According to Avolio seventeen lamps, placed one upon another, were found close to the mouth of a reverberating furnace, near Anzi.[7]   These lamps were placed in stands, also of pale red coarse terra-cotta.[8]

---

[1] Brit. Mus. Marbles, pt. v. viii.
[2] Digest. i. lx. 44.
[3] Petronius, Sat. c. 3, " positum in tumulo lumen renovabat."
[4] Gruter, mcxlviii.
[5] Joh. Chrysost. Homelia xii.
[6] Avolio, p. 117.   [7] P. 123.
[8] Lysons, iii. Pl. xvii. 6.

CHAPTER III.

VASES.

THE decorations of lamps are analogous with bas reliefs used for architectural purposes, and hence they may be considered as connected with the fine arts, since they required not merely the technical manipulation of a potter, but also the skill and taste of an artist to produce them. They are the last link in the chain of the glyptic art. Of the unglazed Roman pottery it now only remains to consider the vases, a class of objects which demanded for their manufacture no higher skill than that of the potter. The technical part of Roman pottery is probably better known than that of the Greek ; kilns, furnaces, moulds, tools, clays, and other objects connected with it being distributed all over Europe, and consequently having attracted the attention of various scientific inquirers. In point of shape and elegance the Roman vases are far inferior to the Greek—nor does the paste seem to have been prepared with the same regard to fineness and compactness. Nevertheless, many shapes and pastes often possess very superior qualities for useful purposes. The art was evidently held in lower estimation among the Romans, and committed to the hands of slaves and freedmen. The Roman potteries produced useful but by no means fine or beautiful vases, and they were only adapted to the necessities of life.

PASTE.

The paste of the Roman vases is by no means so fine as that of the Greek, except the glazed red ware, which is of so bright a colour as to resemble coral.[1] Since red clay does not retain this colour in the furnace, either a peculiar clay must have been used, like some varieties found in this country, or it must have been heated to a certain temperature and combined with peculiar earths to produce the colour. The pipe-clay used was called the figlina or potter's chalk. Other kinds of paste are of a pale or deep yellow, with small pebbles intermingled, and fragments of red bricks worked in. It was generally fine. Some ancient terra cottas have little pebbles mixed in their composition, either from the use of ill-prepared clay, or in order to prevent the contraction of the clay. Other pastes are black, of a deep thick gray, cream-coloured, nearly white, light red, pale red, brown, and even of a

---

[1] γῆ κεραμίκη, Geopon. ii. 49.

yellow colour. The clay was probably ground, trodden out with the feet, and worked up with the hand.[1] The Romans evidently availed themselves of the earth of the different localities in which they found themselves ;[2] with the exception of the Samian ware, the paste and colour of which is uniform. The vases from different countries are easily distinguished from one another. There is also a variety of paste of a pale red colour intermixed with flakes of mica, of the nature of that of the vases commonly called chrysendeta.[3] There is a great difference of opinion among the commentators about this paste. The ancients employed several processes, and paid the greatest attention in preparing their different clays for use. An analysis of the fragments found in the excavations at Rome, Pompeii, and Herculaneum, shows that the clays were mixed in certain proportions with volcanic earth and sand, especially pozzolano. Even the time of making was carefully observed. "Bricks are best made in the spring,[4] for those made at the solstice," says Pliny, " are full of chinks ;" an observation repeated by Vitruvius, who says, " Bricks are to be made in spring and autumn, in order that they may dry equally;"[5] and they were often prepared two years before.

PROCESS.

In the manufacture of vases the Romans used the

[1] Varro, Re Rustica, iii. 9 ; Mr. Yates in Smith's Dict. Antiq. p. 418.

[2] Clarac, part. Tech. I. 31.

[3] Clarac, Mus. d. Sculpt. P. Tech. p. 30. The Chrysendeta are mentioned as used by the wealthy ; but some suppose them to have been of metal.

Mart. xi. 29.

[4] "Finguntur optime vere nam solstitio rimosi fiunt."—Pliny, N. H. xxxv., xiv. 49.

[5] "Ducendi autem sunt per vernum tempus et autumnale ut uno tenore siccescant."—Vitruvius. ii. 3.

same process as the Greeks. They were made by
the table or wheel, called *orbis*, or *rota figularis*. The
mass of clay was placed on this, and worked up with
the hand to the requisite form. Most vases were
made by this process, except the *dolia*, or casks, which
were made by the same means as the *pithoi*. The
handles were either modelled with tools or else pressed
out of moulds ; and zones, concentric circles, hatched and
punctured lines, and imitations of thorns were produced
by pressing pointed pieces of stick or bone against the
sides of the vases while revolving. Sometimes ornaments
were modelled upon the moist clay before the vase was
sent to the furnace. Moulds were very extensively used
by the Romans, and the entire vase was often made by
pressing the clay with the fingers into one of the requisite
size. Besides these ornaments, the potter impressed upon
certain vessels an inscription from a metal mould, containing the name of the establishment which manufactured
them. These inscriptions are found upon amphoræ, and
the so called mortaria ; but seldom on the smaller vases of
unglazed ware. It appears that under the Lower Empire
the potters were compelled by law to place their names on
their ware.[1] The Romans were acquainted with several
ways of perfectly drying their wares before they submitted
them to the action of the fire. As the greatest attention
was paid to the proper manner of preparing tiles, bricks,
and architectural members, it is probable that the clay of
vases was also an object of great attention.[2]

---

[1] Cassiodorus, Variar. lib. i. form. xxv. lib. ii. form. xxiii.

[2] Vitruvius ii. c. 3 ; Campana, p. 22.

FURNACES.

The furnaces were arched with bricks moulded for the purpose. The side of the kiln was constructed with curved bricks set edgeways in a thick slip of the same material, made into mortar, to the height of two feet. A singular furnace was discovered, over which had been placed two circular earthen fire vessels, one close to the furnace, of about eight gallons contents. The fire passed under both of these, the smoke escaping by a neatly plastered flue, from seven to eight inches wide. These vessels were suspended by the rims fitting into a circular rabbit or groove formed for the purpose. They contained some perfect vessels and many fragments, and are supposed to have been used for glazed ware, and probably had covers.[1]

A uniform heat in firing the kiln is supposed to have been produced by first packing up the articles which were required to be fired to the height of the side walls, the circumference of the bulk was then diminished, and finished in the shape of a dome. As this arrangement progressed, it is supposed that an attendant followed the packer, and thinly covered a layer of pots with coarse hay or grass. He then took some thin clay, the size of his hand, and laid it flat on the grass upon the vessels ; he then placed more grass on the edge of the clay just laid on, and then more clay, and so on until he had completed the circle. The packer then raised another tier of pots, the plasterer followed, hanging the grass over the top edge of the last layer of plaster until he

[1] Brongniart, Traité, i. p. 426-7.

had reached the top, in which a small aperture was left, and the clay scraped round the edge ; another coating would be laid on as before described. Gravel or loam was thrown up against the side wall, where the clay wrappers were commenced, to secure the bricks and the clay coating. The kiln was fired with wood.[1] In some kilns, indeed, has been discovered a layer of ashes four or five inches deep. Other kilns at Sibson, near Wandsford,[2] Northamptonshire, exhibited peculiar differences in the mode of arranging the furnace. Instead of the usual dome of clay and straw, bricks were modelled and kneaded with chaff and grain, and made of a wedge shape, interlapping at the edges, with a sufficient curve to traverse the circumference of the kiln ; the floor had perforated arc-shaped bricks. These kilns appear to have been used for making a great quantity of terra-cotta, Samian and stone ware. The blue ware is supposed to have been produced by smothering the fire (or rather smoke) of the furnace upon it when in the kiln, and the colour is so volatile that it flies when forced a second time in an open kiln. Mr. Artis has traced these potteries in England for twenty miles on the gravel banks of the Nen, in Northamptonshire, and tells us that the kilns generally resemble one another, consisting of a cylindrical shaft three feet deep, four feet diameter, walled to the height of two feet. The length of the furnace, which communicated with the kiln, was one-third its diameter. In the centre of the circle formed by the furnace and the kiln was an oval pedestal, the same height as the side, with the end point-

[1] Mr. R. Smith, in the Journal of the British Archæological Association, vol. i. p. 5.

[2] Same Journal, li. 165.

ing to the kiln's mouth. Upon this pedestal, and upon the side wall, the floors of the kilns, formed of perforated arch-shaped bricks, rested." The furnace itself was arched, made of moulded bricks to form the arch, and the side constructed of curved bricks set edgeways.

Mr. R. Smith mentions a kiln at Colchester, and a portion of one of the sun-dried bricks, of which the furnace was composed, was discovered at Colchester in 1819, with about thirty vases. The vases stood on circular vents above the hollow chambers, through which the heat was conveyed to them. Some of the vases, all of which were of the same coarse material, and nearly of the same form and size, were less baked than the rest, and broke unless handled with great care. [1]

One of the furnaces, which appears to have been used for baking the gray Roman ware, was discovered at Caster. The furnace was quite different from those for the black and only calculated for a slight degree of baking. It was a regular oval, and measured 6 feet 4 inches in breadth. The furnace holes were filled in the lower part with burnt earth of a red colour, and in the upper part with peat. The exterior was formed of strong blue clay 6 inches thick, and the interior was lined with peat. The kiln was intersected by lines of the same, and divisions of blue clay. Some of the vases were inverted and filled with a core of white sand. [2]

The supposed *pistilla*, or pestles for mortars were also made of baked clay,[3] they were really supports used in the kilns to steady vases while baking.[4]

---

[1] R. Smith, Collect. ii. p. 38.
[2] Vol. xxii. p. 413, Pl. xxxvi.
[3] Arch. xxiv. p. 199, Pl. xliv. 4.
[4] Arch. Journ. vii. 176.

DIMENSIONS OF VASES.

At all periods specimens of immense vases were fabricated. The great Roman amphoræ were sometimes as high as two metres, and required two oxen to draw them. The enormous dish prepared to cook the gigantic turbot presented to Domitian must have been above seven feet long ; [1] and another dish, called the Ægis of Minerva,[2] composed of tongues, brains, and roes, must have been of the same size. Ciampini mentions an ancient Roman vase so large that a man required a ladder of twelve steps to reach the mouth.

PRICES.

Martial describes the tiresome man as going about the town, and winding up the day by purchasing two cups for an *as*, or penny, but it is not certain whether these were earthenware or glass.[3] They were probably worth a sesterce or large brass Roman coin, for one of the amusements of the fast young Lucius Verus, the colleague of the staid Marcus Aurelius Antoninus, was to break *calices*, or cups, with these pieces of money—probably for

[1] " Incidit Hadriaci spatium admira-
        bile rhombi, ...
Implevitque sinus . . . .
Sed deerat pisci patinæ mensura. . . . .
. . . . Montanus ait, testa alta paretur,
Quæ tenui muro spatiosum colligat
        orbem.
Debetur magnus patinæ subitusque
        Prometheus.

Argillam, atque rotam citius properate ;
        sed ex hoc
Tempore jam, Cæsar, figuli tua castra
        sequantur."

—Juvenal, Sat. iv. 39-41, 72, 131-135.

[2] Pliny, N. H. xxxv. c. xii. 46 ;
Sueton. vit. Vitell. 13.

[3] " Asse duos calices emit, et ipse
tulit."—Martial, ix. 60.

two reasons, they were sufficiently heavy to effect their purpose, and at the same time paid for the damage they occasioned.[1] Juvenal speaks of Plebeian cups purchased for a few asses.[2] Pliny states that some terra-cotta vases sold for more than the celebrated myrrhine vases ;[3] and for gigantic proportions of this ware may be cited the immense plate made by Vitellius, to bake which a furnace was prepared in the open country. It cost him a million sesterces, or about 8000*l.*

USES AND SHAPES.

One of the great uses of earthenware was for the transport of wine, figs, honey, and other commodities— being used in the same manner as casks are at the present day. The *lagena,* or large bottle, was used to hold wine or figs, and articles were imported from the African coast in the *testa.* In this manner a preparation from the blood of the tunny was sent from the Phrygian Antipolis to Rome.[4] Another vessel for transporting and pre- serving viands was the *cadus.* Martial speaks of *cadi vaticani,*[5] which are supposed to refer to the wine ; how- ever, when he speaks of the yellow honey taken out of the red pot,[6] he also mentions the red cadus pouring out foreign wine.[7] Vases were also used for religious rites, the operations of metallurgy, chemistry, and medicine ; but above all for domestic purposes—for the cellar, the kitchen, and the table.

[1] Jaciebat et nummos in popinas maximos, quibus calices frangeret.—Jul. Capit. vit. Veri, 12mo, Lugd. Bat. 1671, p. 102.
[2] Sat. xi. 145.
[3] N. H. xxxv. c. 12, 46.
[4] Martial, iv. 88.
[5] Epigram i. xix. 2.
[6] Epigram i. 10, " Flavaque de rubra premere mella cado."
[7] Ep. iv. 66.

The feet of tables were also made of this unglazed ware,[1] and one of the jests of Elagabalus[2] was to place before his parasitical guests, at a lower table, a course, the viands of which were made of earthenware, and make them eat an imaginary dinner.

The gigantic earthenware casks, resembling the Greek pithoi, were used for holding enormous quantities of wine, corn, and oil—in fact whole stacks of cellars have been found at Antium and Tunis, at Gergovia near Clermont, and at Apt in the department of Vaucluse.[3] They bore marks of the withes by which they were held, or of being made from moulds. In various caves and other places in France they are mixed up with fossils,[4] the supposed remains of a primitive race.

It appears from the ancient jurists that it was unlawful to remove the gigantic dolia in which the Romans kept their stores of wines in the cellar, for fear of endangering the safety of the house.[5] From the dolia, the wine, as among the Greeks, was put into another vase, probably an amphora, and decanted off.[6] As the amphora had a pointed base to fix it more securely into the earth of the cellar, it was when brought up placed in a tripod stand,[7] which among the poor was of wood but among the rich was made of brass or silver. The dolia were sunk in the ground, and one of these prodigies which was supposed to predict the future fortune

---

[1] Fulcitur fagina testâ mensa mihi."
—Martial, ii. xliii.

[2] Lamprid. vita Heliogab. 12mo Lugd. 1632, p. 317.

[3] Brongniart, Traité, i. 407, 408, 409.

[4] Ibid. 409.

[5] Paullus Manutius, Comm. in Cic. Epist. famil. lib. vii, Epist. xxii.

[6] Cicero, de Clar. Orat.; Seneca, Epist. xxxvi.; Pliny, xiv. c. 13.

[7] Doni, l. c. p. lxxxviii.-lxxxix.

of the Emperor Antoninus Pius was the discovery above ground of the dolia in Etruria, which had been sunk in the earth.[1] Juvenal represents them as deep casks,[2] and as being cemented with pitch, gypsum or mud.[3] They held twenty amphoræ, or forty-one urns.

The makers of the casks called dolia, and of the larger amphoræ, were called doliarii ;[4] a term, however, applicable to all kinds of coarse ware, since the roof tiles were also called *opus doliare*, while the workmen were called *fabriles*.[5] Makers of smaller vases were styled *vascularii*,[6] *fictiliarii*,[7] or *urnamentarii*.[8]

Large dolia, with leaden hoops have been found at Palzano, seven miles from Modena, and at Spilamberto one was also discovered broken in fragments, with an inscription containing the name of T. Gavelius and the numbers XXX and XX, probably its contents ; while another of thirty-six amphoræ capacity had an inscription and contained a coin of Augustus.[9]

" Bind your casks with lead," says Cato,[10] in his treatise upon agriculture, and Pliny speaks of scraping the hoops or making new ones.[11]

A few rare inscriptions, recording the names of the owners or makers of the dolia have been preserved as " L. Calpurnius Eros," on the mouth of a cask found in the

[1] " Etruria dolia, quæ defossa fuerant, supra terram reperta sunt."—Capitolinus, Vita Anton. Pii. s. 1.
[2] Sat. vi. 430, " Alta dolia."
[3] Sat. ix. 58.
[4] Doni, Inscript. p. 289, tab. xi. no. iv.; see the bas-relief with the dolia and amphora.
[5] Ibid. p. lxxxvi.
[6] Gruter, Thes. p. dcxliii. 4, 5, 6, 7.
[7] Ibid. p. dcxliii. 1.
[8] Spohn. Miscell. s. vi. p. 238.
[9] Bull. 1846, p. 35.
[10] " Dolia plumbo vincite," R. R. 39.
[11] " Dolia quassa sarcire ipsorumque lamnas scabendo purgare."—Pliny, N. H. xviii. 64.

villa Peretta.[1] "T. Cocceius Fortunatus," on that of another
discovered in the ruins of Bæbiana.[2]   Another large
vase had "Stabulum P. Actii,"[3] *the Stable of P. Actius;*
which is, however, certainly not a potter's mark, but probably incised by the slave of the stable where it was
used.   Two of these dolia will also be seen in the
gardens of the Villa Albani.   They are
about four feet diameter, and as many
feet high and about three inches thick, of
a coarse gritty earthenware, and of a pale
red colour.

The Roman amphoræ were coarser than
those made in Greece ; the body more
globular and less elegant.   The clay is
reddish, and sometimes covered externally
with a siliceous coating like the Egyptian
vases.   Amphoræ were pitched internally
to retain the wine,[4] and the mouth was
closed with clay or else with a bung.

No. 195.—Terra-cotta
Amphora.

When of moderate size, they were made
on the wheel, the larger like the Greek,
were moulded.   The name of the maker was in a square
label stamped out of an incuse mould on the handle.
This name is in the genitive, as Maturi "of Maturus," or
" of Maturius ; " the word "officina" or " factory " being
understood.[5]

Several amphoræ have been found at Rome, and 120
were discovered in a subterranean cellar near the baths of

[1] L. CALPVRNIVS EROS. F. Fabretti, 502.

[2] T. COCCEI FORTVNATI.   Ibid.
503.

[3] STABVLVM P. ACTII. Doni, 98.

[4] Horat. Carm. i. 20, 3 ; Pliny, N. H.
xiv. 20, 27 ; Palladius, iii. 24.

[5] Seroux D'Agincourt, pl. xix. xxxvi.

Titus. Doni[1] has engraved a remarkable one, five Roman palms high, holding eight congii, discovered in the gardens of the Villa Farnese, amidst the supposed ruins of the Golden Palace of Nero. On its neck was traced in large letters ex cel(la) L(ucii) Purelli Gemelli M(amertinum). " Mamertine wine from the cellar of L. Purellus Gemellus." Cæsenniæ, "from the estate of Cæsennia." The neck of another found on the Aventine hill, now in the Kircherian Museum, has inscribed upon it, *Fabriles Marcellæ n(ostræ) ad felicitatem*—" the workmen of our Marcella to wish her joy." [2] It is supposed to have been a present during the Saturnalia. On others found in a house at Pompeii were painted, in red and black ochre, such words as MES. AM. XVIII., "the amphora measures eighteen[3];" BARCAE, 'of Barce,' near Cyrene ; FORM. ' Formian' ; KOR. OPT, ' best Corinthian'; RUBR. VET. 'old red,' which seem to be the names of the wine deposited in the cellar. Other amphoræ were marked LIQVAMEN OPTIMVM, ' the best dripping,' or ' grease,' showing for what purpose the vessel had been used. On one of them was inscribed TVSCOLANON OFFICINA SCAV[RI] " Tusculanum " or " Tusculan," OFFICINA SCAURI, " from the manufactory of Scaurus." Other letters refer to the contents of the amphoræ, its age or number in the cellar.

Several which were found in an excavation close to the Porta del Popolo, and consequently near the Flaminian Gate, in a subterranean chamber, supposed by some to be a cellar, contained various materials and objects, such

---

[1] Inscrip. p. lxxxii.
[2] Doni ; ibid. p. lxxxvi.
[3] Mr. Falkener, Museum of Classical

Antiquities, vol. II. pp. 70, 79 ; Bull Arch. Nap. ii. 85.

as ivory and bone pins, portions of animals, lamps,
and fragments. On some of these amphoræ were letters ; and on a piece of terra cotta, probably a tile, was
stamped,[1] "from the establishment of Domitia Lucilla,"
a name already mentioned among the tile makers.

The letters on these amphoræ are described by
Plautus and Juvenal.[2]

The use of amphoræ was very various and extensive
among the Romans. They were employed at entertainments, sacrifices, dinners, in cellars and granaries, and
for holding the sand of the bath and gymnasium with
which the body was rubbed,[3] as well as for many purposes to which the moderns have applied wood and
iron.

Amphoræ and other vases, inscribed with the names of
the consuls under whom they were deposited, were called
(literatæ) " lettered,"[4] or " fictile letters,"[5] and so were the
urns which bore the names of the temples to which they
belonged.[6] Two fine glass scyphi, which Nero broke in his
terror when he heard of the revolt of Galba, had on them
some verses of Homer,[7] and on the glass amphoræ of
Trimalchio was inscribed "the finest Falernian wine one

[1] EXOFICFATDOMIT LVC. Seroux
D'Agincourt, pl. xix., fig. v.
[2]   " Itaque in totis ædibus,
Tenebræ, latebræ : bibitur, estur, quasi
    in popina, haud secus,
Ibi tu videas literatas fictileis epistolas,
Pice signatas : nomine insunt cubitum
    longis literis,
Ita vinariorum habemus nostræ
    delectum domi."—Pœnulus, act.
    iv. s. 11, v. 14.
" Cras bibet Albanis aliquid de monti-
bus, aut de

Setinis, cujus patriam, titulumque
    senectus
Delevit multa veteris fuligine testæ."
—Juvenal, v. 33.
[3] Doni, l. c. p. lxxxvii.-xci.
[4] Brodæus, Miscell. i. c. 3 ; Turneb.
Advers. i. 1 ; Brisson. de For. viii.
715 ; Illustr. di un vaso Italo-Grec. d.
R. Mus. Borb. 4to, Napoli, 1822.
[5] Plautus, Pæn. act iv. s. 2, 15.
[6] Plautus, Rudens, act iv. s. 5, 17.
[7] Sueton. Nero, 47.

hundred years old." [1] A cup of gold had the other names of Cicero, with a *vetch*, instead of Cicero.[2]

They are of various sizes, from about two to four, or even six feet in height. Their paste varies much in colour, from a pale red to a cream colour, like the bricks and tiles. It is compact and heavy, somewhat resembling that of the mortaria.

Like the mortars, they were made either by slaves or freedmen ; but the names of the makers of the amphoræ are distinct from those of the makers of mortars. They have been found throughout the ancient limits of the Roman empire.

One of the most curious stamps upon these vases is a square one, having a caduceus and twelve compartments, with symbols and the following inscription : M(arci) PETRON(ii) VETERAN(i) LEO SER(vus) FECIT. "Leo the slave of M. Petronius Veteranus made it." [3]

Sarcophagi, even at a late period were made of the same paste as the amphoræ—such having been found in the Roman potteries at Saguntum.[4] The *obrendaria*, or urns in which the ashes of the dead were deposited, were also of this coarse ware, and globular shaped, and were used as cases for more precious vases. It will be remembered that Cato and Cicero are both stated by Varro to have wished to be buried in terra cotta vases.

Roman amphoræ have been found at London, Kingsholme, Gloucester, and Woburn.[5] One of the large

---

[1] "Falernum Opimianum annorum centum."—Petronius, Sat. 34.

[2] Plutarch, Apophthegm. p. 205.

[3] D'Agincourt Recueil, xxii. 7.

[4] Brongniart & Riocreux, Musée de Sèvres, i. 18.

[5] Arch. xxv. Pl. lxix. p. 606.

amphoræ, containing ashes of the dead and other objects was found at the Bartlow Hills.[1] Another remarkable vase of this ware found at Littington near Royston, was apparently a kind of colander, of a cup shape, and having inside a hollow domed portion, perforated with holes, which formed the letters IN-DVLCIVS.[2]

Vessels of terra cotta were extensively used by the Roman people, in the earlier days of the republic, for all purposes of domestic life,[3] and the writers under the Empire often contrast their use with that of the costly vessels of the precious metals then employed. This ware appears to have been called "Samian," either because it was imported from that island, or because it was made in imitation of the ware procured thence. "For the necessary purposes," says Plautus, "in religious ceremonies Samian vases are used;"[4] and Cicero repeats that the simpuvia and capedines of the priests were of the same ware.[5] It appears indeed to have been discontinued even for religious rites under the Empire. "Gold," says the Satirist, "has driven away the vases of Numa and the brass (vessels) of Saturn—the urns of the Vestals and Etruscan earthenware."[6] "Who formerly presumed to laugh at the bowl and black dish of Numa, and fragile plates from Vatican Hill."[7] And again, "There-

---

[1] Arch. xxv. Pl. xxxiii. p. 304.
[2] Arch. xxvi. Pl. xlv. p. 376.
[3] Tibull, I. i.
[4] Capt. II. ii. 4.
[5] De Nat. de Or. III. 17.
[6] Persius, Sat. ii. 60.
[7]   " Aut quis

Simpuvium ridere Numæ, nigrumque catinum,
Et Vaticano fragiles de monte patellas,
Ausus erat."—Juvenal, i. vi. 341-3. Cf. Juvenal, i. 4, xi. 19; Seneca, Epist. 97; Tertullian, Apol. c. 25.

fore then they placed all their porridge in a Tuscan bowl."[1]

The vases used in sacrifices were principally of earthenware, and comprised the *simpulum* [2] or the *simpuvium*,[3] a vessel for pouring out wine, or according to some the bowl in the shape of a ladle, in which the priests washed. The *capis capedo* or *capeduncula*,[4] the *discus* and the *catinus* [5] or patera, the *aquimenarium* to wash the vessels, or *amula* which held the lustral water. To these must be added the *urna* or *urnula*, which appears the equivalent term of the Greek hydria, or water pitcher, and a small earthen vessel called *lepesta* in use in the temples of the Sabines.[6]

For eating and drinking, fictile vases were only used by poor people. Juvenal speaking of his time says—" no aconite is quaffed out of fictile vases." [7] But this must be accepted with some reservation, as it is evident that fine red glazed ware was used by the upper classes. Thus the celebrated consul Curius is said to have preferred his earthenware service to the gold of the Samnites.[8] "It is a reproach to dine off earthenware," [9] says the Satirist in the days of Domitian. This is proved by the example of Catus Ælius whom the Ætolian ambassador in his consulship found dining off vessels of earthenware,[10] B.C. 169 ; and in the entertain-

[1] "Ponebant igitur Tusco farrata catino Omnia tunc."—Sat. xi. 109, 110.
[2] Varro, iv. 26 ; Schol. Juvenal, vi. 341-3.
[3] Isidorus, xx. 4 ; Pliny, N. H. xxxv. 12.
[4] Capedines et fictiles urnas Pliny, N. H. xxxv. 12 ; Cicero. Paradox. 1.
[5] Pliny, N. H. xxxiii. 69.
[6] Varro, L. L.
[7] "Sed nulla aconita bibuntur Fictilibus." —Juvenal, Sat. x. 25, 26 ; cf. xi. 20.
[8] Florus, i. 18.
[9] "Fictilibus cœnasse pudet."—Juv. iii. 168.
[10] Pliny, N. H. xxxiii. c. 11, 51.

ment given before the Cella of the temple of Jupiter,
Q. Tubero placed fictile vases before the guests.[1] At the
entertainment, however, given by Massinissa, the second
course was in the Roman manner, served up on silver,
B.C. 148, which the Greeks had not substituted for earthenware till after the age of Alexander.[2]

In the early times of the Republic even persons of
wealth used only pottery at their meals, as well as for
other domestic purposes ; but the increase of wealth
caused vessels of bronze to be made for many uses
for which pottery had been formerly deemed sufficient.
Under the empire glass was used even by the poor
for drinking-cups, while the rich disdained meaner
materials than gems, precious metals, moulded or engraved glass. Earthenware was left for the service of
the gods, and the tables of the poor. Numerous small
vessels, especially bottles and jars of various shapes, which
are found either in graves or houses, seem to show that
earthenware was employed for the purposes of life.

It is however difficult, if not impossible, to decide
whether the various small flat plates, dishes, and bowls
which are found, were the *paropsis*, which is known to have
been made of red ware, the *patina*, the *patera*, the *catinus*,
the *gabbata*, or *lanx*, mentioned as made of red terra
cotta. The *trullæ* or bowls, were probably made of red
ware. The *patella* or plate was made of black ware.
Martial speaks of "a green cabbage in a black plate."[3]
Some clue might perhaps be obtained to their size from

[1] Seneca, Epist. 95, 72.

[2] Athenæus, vi. 229, a. It does not
appear quite certain whether Athenæus
refers to his own time or that of the
republic when he cites this fact.

[3] " Nigra cauliculus virens patella."
                        —v. 78, l. 7.

the descriptions of ancient authors. The *catinus* was large enough to hold the tail of a tunny,[1] the *lanx* could hold a crab.[2] Another dish was called *scutula*. Speaking of the course of a luxurious entertainment, Martial says, "Thus he fills the gabatæ, and the paropsides, the light scutulæ, and the hollow lances.'[3] The *patina* was flat, and held soup,[4] and was the generic name for a dish, the most remarkable example of which was that made by Vitellius, and which has been already mentioned. This was called the "marsh of dishes," by Mutianus;[5] The wretched emperor, when dragged to death, was insulted by the epithet of *patinarius*, or dish maker.[6] Small vases called *acetabula*, or vinegar cups, which were certainly made of terra cotta, probably appeared on the table.[7]

The great vessels for holding the wine in the cellar, the dolia, and amphoræ, have been already fully described. Besides the amphoræ the *cadus* held wine in the cellar. The cadus held more than two quadrantes or six cyathi,[8] and it was hung up in the chimney in order to give the wine a mature flavour, especially that of Marseilles.[9] The diota held wine.[10] The wine was transferred from the cadus into a fictile vase called the *hirnea*, but its shape is unknown.[11] Another large vase for holding wine was the *sinus*, which also held water.

Many bottles are found in the coarser kinds of ware, and

[1]   " Rubrumque amplexa catinum Cauda natat thynni."—Pers. v. 182.

[2] Juv. v. 80 ; Martial, ii. 43.

[3] "Sic complet gabatas, paropsidasque, Et leves scutulas, cavasque lances."— Martial, xi. 31, 19.

[4] Phædrus. I. 26.

[5] Paludem patinarum, Pliny, N. H., xxxvi. 12.

[6] Suetonius, Vita Vitellii, c. 17.

[7] Acetabula fictilia. Tertullian, Apolog. c. xxv.

[8] Quadrantem duplica de seniore cado. —Martial, ix. 94.

[9] Martial, x. 36.

[10] Hor. Car. i. 9,

[11] Varro, L. L.

were probably used even at table for pouring the wine
into the cups of the guests. The *lagenæ*, narrow necked
bottles, with one or two handles,[1] when destined for the
next day's entertainment were sealed by the master of the
feast with his ring that they should not be changed. No
crater of the Roman times can be identified in terra cotta.
The *œnophorum*,[2] a large wine pitcher, and the *urceus*, a
vase with one handle,[3] sometimes made of red ware, and
the *urceoli*, or little pitchers, are of frequent occurrence.
Another vase for holding wine, probably the same as
the œnophorum, was the *acratophorum*. The *ampulla*,
a kind of jug, was used for bringing wine to table after
having been duly labelled.[4] The wine was mixed into a
crater, and thence transferred into cups.[5] These vases
are probably represented by various terra cotta bottles.

There are a great number of little cups found in
different localities, and in all kinds of ware, but chiefly
in the glazed varieties. These were perhaps known under
the generic name of *pocula*[6] " cups," *calices* " goblets,"
cotylæ "gills,"[7] and *scaphia* or " boats."[8] The shapes known
under the names of *cantharus*,[9] *carchesion*,[10] *scyphus*, and
rhyton were rarely if ever made of earthenware ; indeed,
the pride of the wealthy Romans at this period was to
show magnificent cups of metal embossed by Mentor, Mys,
and other celebrated masters of antiquity, and hence
earthenware cups were only used by persons in moderate

[1] Symposius; Aenigm.
[2] Juv. Sat. vi. 425; Pers. v. 140; Hor. Sat. i. 6, 109.
[3] Martial, xiv. 106.
[4] Pliny, Epist. iv. 30 ; Suetonius,Vit. Domit. 21 ; Martial, vi. 35-3, xiv. 110. Ovid, Fasti. v. 522, of red terra cotta.
[6] Martial, xiv. 108, refers to Saguntine cups.
[7] Martial, viii. 71.
[8] Plaut. Stich. v. 4, 11.
[9] Virgil, Ecl. vi. 17.
[10] Macrobius, vi. 41.

circumstances. There were, however, certain cups peculiarly Roman, their names not like those just mentioned,
derived from the Greek. Such were the *ciboria*, in shape
of the leaves of the *colocasia*, or Egyptian bean,[1] the
cymbia, or milk cups,[2] the *nasiterna*, which had three
handles. Besides these, the *guttus*, a small bottle used for
conveying oil to the bath, and which is probably the little
long-necked bottle, called by antiquarians the lachryma-
tory, was often made of terra-cotta. The *matella*[3] or *matellio*
was also made of earthenware, as well as a large vase
that used to be placed in the highways.[4] The *bascauda*,
imported to Rome from Britain, were probably baskets.

Several obscure names of vases are mentioned by the
etymologists and others, as the *pollubrum*, a wash-hand
bason, the *escaria*, or vegetable dishes, the *obba*, which
was probably a kind of ampulla, being in the shape of
the helmets of the Dioscuri,[5] the *craticula*, a small goblet,
the *myobarbum*,[6] in shape of a mouse, the *galeola* and
others. The *pelvis*, or pan, is probably the so-called
mortarium ; the *sinus*, which was also used as a wash-hand
bason, may be a vase of similar shape, but there is as
much difficulty in recognising the true names of the
Roman as of the Greek vases. The *olla*, or jar, was of
sepulchral use, and the *urna* was also adapted to hold the
ashes of the dead.

---

[1] Porphyrion in Horat. Ep. II. 7.
[2] Pliny, N. H. xxxvii. 8.
[3] Martial, xii. 32; xiv. 119.

[4] Persius, v. 148.
[5] Ausonius, Ep. iii.
[6] Pliny, N. H. xxviii. 1.

PLACES OF THE FABRIC.

It is not to be supposed that all vessels were made at one place, for different towns excelled in the production of their respective wares, which were imported in large quantities into Rome. Anciently this city was supplied with earthenware by the Etruscans and probably by the Greeks, as Plautus mentions *Samian* ware almost as synonymous with earthenware. Still it cannot be doubted that extensive manufactories of vases existed at Rome, although they are only occasionally mentioned. Martial speaks of the fragile plates of the Vatican Hill, and Horace of the potter's wheel,[1] as though he had seen it revolving. He also speaks of cups made at Allifæ in Samnium. Yet Rome itself does not appear to have excelled in any of the finer vases, as Pliny, when he mentions pottery, does not praise its productions,[2] although Numa had instituted a guild of potters.[3] He mentions eight principal places of the manufacture ; Arretium or Arezzo, famous for its dinner services, which he compares to the wares of Samos ; Asta ; Pollentia, upon the banks of the Tanarus ; and Surrentum, upon the eastern coast of the Bay of Naples, renowned for drinking cups ; Modena and Rhegium which produced the most durable ones, and Cuma, already mentioned by Martial. The foreign manufactories were Saguntum, in Spain, so often praised by the same poet ; Pergamus, in Asia ; the island of Samos, Erythræ, in Ionia, where two amphoræ of remarkable thinness existed ; Tralles, Cos, and Hadria.

[1] Sat. ii. 8, 39.
[2] N. H., xxxv. xii. 46.
[3] Ibid. xxxv. 12, 46.

At a later period the glazed red ware is found distributed all over the European limits of the old Roman world, and was evidently manufactured at one place and exported.

The services used at a Roman entertainment presented the same spectacle as those of persons possessing wealth and taste at the present day, to which the potteries of Staffordshire, of Sèvres, Dresden, and China, contribute their respective portions. The most exquisite enjoyment was derived from the contemplation of a variety of the products of the human mind and hand, which please by their association and improve by their presence.

ARCHITECTURAL USE.

The vaulted top of an oven at Pompeii is formed of jars, *ollæ*, fitted one into another. These ollæ are about a foot high and six inches wide, of the usual ware. The span of the arch is five feet six inches. The object of it was to produce extreme lightness and dryness. A similar construction occurs at Syracuse ; part of St. Stefano alla Rotonda at Rome, and the dome of the church of St. Vitale, at Ravenna, built by Justinian, is constructed of amphoræ and tubes on the same plan.[2]

In the chapter Vitruvius has written on the ' *Echea*,' or sounding vases, which were distributed in the Greek theatre, he mentions that they were often for economy made of earthenware.[3] The Greeks seem indeed to have

---

[1] N. H. xxv. c. 12, s. 46, 47.

[2] Seroux D'Agincourt, Storia dell' Arte. Tav. xxiii. tom. v., p. 56. See

tav. xxii. tom. v, p. 52-6.

[3] Vitruvius, v. c. vii. vol. i. p. 284, a Marinio ; Pliny, N. H. xi. 112.

employed both pithoi or casks and lagenæ to make rooms,[1] and they were sometimes nsed as in the case of vaults, domes, or other elevated erections, for the sake of diminishing the weight rather than for augmenting the sound.[2]   Such, at all events, is supposed to be the case of the vases found at the top of the wall of the circus of Maxentius, at Rome.   There is a row of amphoræ arranged with their necks downwards, and their long axis inclined obliquely to the top of the wall.   All these are now broken, but they show an ingenious method for rendering lighter the upper part of the arches which held the wall of the seats.   Vases are also found used in the construction of the Tor Pignatarra, the Mausoleum of the Empress Helena.[3]

[1] Seneca, Quæst. Nat. vi. 19; Aristotle, Probl. xi. 8.

[2] Blanconius, Descr. dei Circhi, p. 98; Scamotius, Arch. Un. viii. 15; Venutius Rom. Ant. Pl. ii. i.; Winckelmann, Stor. d. Art. iii. p. 29.

[3] Nibby, Analisi della carta di Roma, 8vo.   Roma, 1837, III. p. 343.

CHAPTER IV.

Division of Roman pottery : Black—Gray—Red—Brown—Yellow ware—Shapes —Red ware—Paste —Shapes—False Samian—Paste and shapes—Lamps of Christian period—Ollæ—Gray ware—Mortaria — Paste —Pelves—Trullæ — Names of makers—Black ware—Paste—Colour—Mode of ornamentation —Shapes—Brown ware—Paste—Shapes—Ornamentation.

CLASSES.

GREAT confusion prevails in the classification of Roman pottery, and each author adopts a system of his own, owing to the subject not having been yet studied with the necessary minuteness. Many local circumstances, such as the clay, firing and manipulation, produced differences in the ware. As the scope of this work is not so much to follow the technical march of science as to give the literary and archæological results of an examination of ancient pottery, it will perhaps only be necessary to take colour for a guide, as it is a distinction easily followed. The glazed wares, irrespective of their colour, will be reserved for a subsequent chapter.

Brongniart[1] groups the Roman pottery in the following manner :—

---

[1] Traité, p. 381.

1 Division.—Pale yellow paste, almost white.
2   „   Dull reddish paste, passing to a reddish
                   brown.
3   „   Gray, or ash-coloured paste.
4   „   Black paste.

The 1st division comprises the jars and amphoræ ; the
2nd division, the Roman pottery of the 1st century ; the
3rd division, Roman ware later than the 1st century ; the
4th division, Gallo-Roman ware, and that of the local
potteries.

The system of Brongniart follows the age of the potteries
more closely than that of Professor Buckman, although
it must be remembered that the different descriptions of
ware are found together, and were consequently employed
simultaneously.   Thus, the amphoræ and ollæ which filled
the cellar, the bottles in which the wine and other liquids
were carried about, the lagenæ and cadi were of the first
and second divisions.   The so-called mortaria, some bottles,
and other small vases were of the third division.   The
jars which covered the ashes of the dead were of the
brown paste of the second division ; and the cups and other
bottles out of which persons drank were of red or black
ware.

Professor Buckman,[1] who has more recently examined
the technical qualities of the unglazed ware found in
Britain, divides them as follows : —

1 Division.—Black.
2   „   Gray.
3   „   Red.
4   „   Brown.
5   „   False Samian.

[1] Buckman and Newmarch, Corinium, p. 77.

The only objection to this division is that it does not present the vases according to their relative ages, as that of Brongniart professes to do.

YELLOW WARE.

Distinguished by its coarse paste, of a grayish white or yellow colour, verging more or less to red. It is to this division that all the larger pieces of wares belong, such as the remains of amphoræ [1] and *dolia*, or tubs, casks which form the Monte Testaceo at Rome. These vases were made by different processes. Some were turned upon the wheel; others, such as the casks, *cadi*, were modelled with the hand, and turned from within.[2] The globes, in which the urns and glass vessels holding the ashes of the dead, were deposited, were of this class. They appear to have been amphoræ with their handles broken off. Mortaria were also made of this ware, and it was extensively used for long narrow necked bottles with one or two handles, probably lagenæ : and trullæ, or deep bowls.

A finer paste of this colour, often of a rosy tint, or white and micaceous, was used for making the smaller vases, which are all turned upon the wheel, and are thin and light.[3] They are ornamented with zones, lines, hatchings, and leaves, slightly indicated by a dull ochre, laid on and baked at the same time as the paste.[4] These vases are often covered with a white coating of a flat

---

[1] Musée Ceramique, Pl. iv. fig. 2. 3, 5.
[2] For various fragments of this ware found with other specimens of red ware, see Archæologia, viii. Pl. 6.

[3] Brongniart, Traité, i. 435; Mus. Cer. viii. 5, 10, 14.
[4] Arch. xiv. Pl. 14, p. 74.

colour, harder and more equally laid on than in the Athenian vases.

Some of this ware has its paste mixed with grains of quartz.[1]   A subdivision of it is a very white kind, which has been occasionally found in England, consisting of little jars ; small bottles, pateræ, or dishes, painted inside with a dull red ornament ; vessels of the same shape, painted ; a vessel, apparently a dish, ornamented with red lines crossing and hooked ; and others with brown lines.   The paste of these is very white, and by no means adapted for common uses.   They must have formed a fine kind of ware for ornamental purposes, such as those of the table.

RED WARE.

The largest division of Roman pottery is the red ware, as it comprises nearly all the vessels used for domestic purposes.   It varies in colour from a pale salmon to a deep coral—and in quality from a coarse gritty and cancellated structure to a fine compact homogeneous paste.   The greater part of this pottery is red, and without any glaze, and of it are made a great number of plates, dishes, bottles, amphoræ, dolia, and jars.   It is often distinguished by an engobe or white coating of pipe-clay, with which the potter has covered the vase, in order to give it a neater appearance ; but in many specimens this is completely wanting.   Sometimes the paste of this red ware is mixed with grains of quartz.[2]

The following are the principal shapes of this ware ;

---

[1] Caumont, iii. p. 214.   [2] Caumont, Cours. i. 214.

the olla or jar for holding the ashes of the dead ; the amphora ; the urceolus or small jar ; vases in the shape of a small barrel, one of which was found near Basingstoke, and presented to the British Museum by Lord Eversley; a little bowl, patella, patina, or lanx. Innumerable small bottles with a long neck, of a very fine red paste, formerly called lachrymatories, but now supposed to be unguent vases, are found in the Roman graves all over Europe.

Many illustrations of this ware may be taken from the vases in the collections of the British Museum,[1] consisting of amphoræ, and large open mouthed jars, with two handles, probably *diotæ* ; conical vases, with a small mouth, adapted for holding liquids, perhaps the *cadus*,[2] which held fruit or honey ; and *lagenæ*, or bottles, and bottles with a female head, probably the *guttus*, painted with white ornaments upon a red ground ; a *colus*, or colander, of red ware, from Cissbury, curiously moulded at the sides, pierced for straining. Some of these have a polish or very thin glaze, and belong to the division of glazed wares. A jar with six holes at the bottom, was found at Minchinhampton, Gloucestershire.

Of this pale red ware were also made the jars or *ollæ* which held the ashes of the dead, mostly of slaves which were deposited in the Columbaria. Some singular lamps of this ware are in the shape of the helmet of a gladiator.[3]

Specimens of this pale unglazed ware were found at Étaples, near Boulogne, with hatched and wreathed patterns in a very bad style, and apparently of a late age.[4]

---

[1] Journal, Brit. Arch. Assoc. i. 238.

[2] Martial, v. 18, 3, " Et acuta senibus testa cum damascenis."

[3] Journ. Brit. Arch. Assoc. v. 136.

[4] Roach Smith, Collectanea, Vol. i. Pl. iii. 3.

In the Sèvres Museum are the remains of a vase or cup found at Souaire, near Bourges, made of a reddish brown paste mixed with a great number of little particles of mica. The exterior is covered with a perfectly black coating, with micaceous particles shining through it. The polish is owing to the friction the potter has given it while turning it. The interior is flat. Some other specimens in the Sèvres Museum, and fragments of cups and bottles, exhibit the same peculiarities.[1] This is, however, rather a glazed or lustrous ware.

Another division of ware with a red paste is that called false Samian, made of fine red clay, by no means so brilliant as the Samian, and covered with a thin coating of a red colour, produced by dipping the clay into a slip made of sulphate of iron. The subjects, as in the case of the Samian ware,[2] have been impressed from a mould ; but they are generally of ruder execution, and more indistinct than upon the true Samian. The vases with reliefs are, however, often hollowed on the inner side. This ware is of a rarer occurrence than the true Samian. Specimens of it in the shape of dishes, lances, patinæ or patellæ, cups, pocula, cyathi or calices, are found in England, France, Germany, the Peloponnese, and the Archipelago.

Of the very fine brick-red paste the principal shapes are the class called *mortaria*, the inside having small black pebbles inserted into it, to grind or pound the food ; another is probably the *urceolus*, or cup of some kind ; a third, a *guttus*, or oil vase ; others are lagenæ, or bottles.

[1] Brongniart, Traité, i. p. 434.   [2] Buckman and Newmarch, p. 93, 94.

Of this fine red unglazed ware, were made a great number of lamps in the latter days of the Roman Empire. They are long and shoe-shaped, having subjects stamped on a flat bas-relief. These consist of the monogram of Christ—the great dragon—a fish—alluding to the monogram IXΘΥC,[1] in which was contained "Jesus Christ, son of God, the Saviour ; " necklaces of crosses, and other objects and symbols. Such lamps were particularly common in Egypt, with inscriptions as already cited, evidently made for ecclesiastics.

The ollæ which held the ashes of slaves in the columbaria, are also of unglazed terra-cotta. They are tall jar-shaped vessels, with a moulded rim, and a flat saucer-shaped cover. They are humble imitations of the glass or alabaster vessels, in which were deposited the mortal remains of their wealthier masters. In the Roman sepulchres of Britain and Gaul, the ashes of the Reguli or chieftains, were also deposited in ollæ, or jars, which were placed inside a large dolium, or broken amphora, to protect them from the weight of superincumbent earth.[2] Near the urns were often deposited several small vessels and different instruments. The urns were often placed in coffins or coverings of different kinds : one of the most remarkable, which was found near Lincoln,[3] was a sphere with an orifice sufficiently large to allow the urn to be introduced. Great numbers of these urns are found on the sites of the ancient Roman provincial cemeteries, as in the Dover Road. Twenty thousand were

---

[1] Avolio, p. 126, lamp from Puzzuoli.
[2] Wright, Celt, Roman, and Saxon, p. 223.
[3] Archæologia, xii., p. 108, Pl. xiv. 7 & 8.

found near Bordeaux.[1]　　An amphora of pale red ware, containing a jar, with a lid of pale gray pottery,[2] was found near Colchester.　After the introduction of Christianity in the third century this practice was abandoned ; when the body ceased to burnt, similar vases, but of smaller size, containing charcoal were placed near the dead.

GRAY WARE.

This ware was made of fine clay, and may be divided into two classes.　The first of these was made of a kind of sandy loam, such as that of the softer bricks made from clays on the border of the chalk formation.　Its colour is rather light and its texture brittle.[3]　By many it is called stone-coloured ware.　This ware was chiefly employed for amphoræ, mortaria, and dishes used in cooking, which were exposed to the heat of the fire.　The small pebbles, which some suppose to have been placed inside the vessels for the purpose of preventing unequal contraction in baking, others regard as intended to grate the corn, flour, or meat.　The *mortaria* resemble in shape modern milk-pans, being flat and circular with overlapping edges, and a grooved spout in front, though these may be the *pelvis* or *trulla*.　Most of them appear to have been used for boiling, as appears from holes burnt through them, or from their having become much thinner. This may also be the result of the grinding to which the materials placed in them were subjected.　They are of a hard ware, rather coarse, but compact in texture, and

[1] Brongniart, i. p. 437.

[2] Journal Brit. Arch. Assoc. i. 239.

[3] Mus. Pract. Geol. Cat. p. 88, 89.

heavy. On the upper portion inside are the remains of the small stones, which some think were introduced into the paste in order to render it harder to grind upon.[1] Sometimes ground tile was used, apparently to prevent the vessels from shrinking when they were baked. They are often impressed with iron scoria. Their colour is a pale red, bright yellow, or creamy white, resembling stone ware. Some of them have upon their lips a square stamp with a potter's name, like those upon amphoræ. These names are generally of persons of servile condition, such as Albinus, Aprilis, Catulus, Brixsa, Sollus, Ripanus, and Paulus ; but some are apparently the work of freedmen, such as those inscribed Quintus Valerius, Sextus Valerius, Quintus Valerius Veranius, Quintus Valerius Esunertus. The most remarkable are those which read upon one edge *Ripanus Tiber f(ecit) Lugudu(ni) factus,*—" Ripanus Tiberinus,—made at Lyons." The names of the potters are accompanied with the words F or FECIT, he made ; OF. or Officina, the factory ; M. or Manus, the hand ; as in the red Samian ware. These *mortaria* are from 7 to 23 inches across, and 4 inches high.[2] They are found in France,[3] England, Switzerland, and Germany. Several urns were found at Aosta, and amongst them a mortarium inscribed C. Atisius Sabinus.[4]

A group, in the Collection of the British Museum, exhibits some of the principal shapes of this ware. One is a dish, patera, or patella ; others, small bottles,

---

[1] Cf. Buckman and Newmarch, p. 79.

[2] Artis, Journal Brit. Arch. Assoc. ii.

p. 166, 167.

[3] Caumont, Cours. Pl. xxviii. 4.

[4] Muratori, i. p. 134, fig. 3.

gutti, for oil or vinegar ; an *urceus,* found in Moor-
gate Street, in the City ; an amphora, the sides of
which are fluted, perhaps to case it with wicker-work
in order that it might be carried about without breaking ;
an *olla* or jar, of the same ware. A kind of pipkin was
also found of this ware in France 15 inches diameter
7 inches high.[1]

The second class of gray pottery is a stone ware much
resembling the modern Staffordshire, and is supposed to
have been made out of clays of the same kind. It is
almost of a stone colour, much heavier than the preceding
class, and sonorous when struck. It is principally used
for amphoræ [2] and mortars ; one remarkable vase of this
ware found at Castor is in shape of a human head.

Some varieties of this ware are filled with quartzose
sand, and covered on the outside with mica.[3]

BLACK WARE.

Brongniart describes a variety of this unglazed pottery, which is not only black on its surface, but the
paste of which is entirely of a grayish black colour, and
often of a fine black, or grayish-red, internally. It has
a coating about a quarter of a *millimeter* thick upon
the surface, but is without any glaze, however shining it
may be. It is distinguished from the Celtic or Gaulish
pottery, which it much resembles, by the fineness of its
paste, the thinness of its pieces, and the perfect manner
in which it is made, having been well turned on the

---

[1] Caumont, Cours. xxviii. 5, p. 217.   fig. 1, 2.
[2] Buckman and Newmarch, p. 80 ;   [3] Caumont, Cours. i. p. 214.
Caumont, Cours. i. p. 215, 216, xxviii.

lathe.[1] This ware varies much in colour, sometimes being almost of a jet black, at others of a bluish black, or even running into an ashy-gray colour. It is generally glazed, but many vessels exhibit no more ornament than a polish upon the surface, given by the potter when the piece was upon the lathe.

This ware is distinguished by its colour, which is sometimes of a jet black, at others of a metallic gray, or even ashy. As it is generally glazed, a fuller description of it will be found under the glazed ware. Sometimes the paste is intermingled with micaceous particles, pebbles, or shells, which gives it a gleamy colour when broken, and it is often covered externally, or frosted with powdered mica. The greater number of vases are evidently native ware, manufactured on the spot by Romans or by Gaulish, British, and German potters in the Roman settlements. The shapes much resemble those of the red ware, and it was chiefly employed for the smaller vases of the table, although a few of larger size are found made of it.

It was principally used for vases for the table, as shown in the following shapes : a shallow cylindrical vase, the *patella*, perhaps the *nigra patella*, or "black plate" of Martial ; the *calix*, or a cup ; the small cup, or a jar ; similar object ; the *ciboria* and the *olla*. The mode of ornamenting these vases is peculiar, and resembles Gaulish rather than Roman work, consisting of zones, hatched bands, and rows of dots, made by moulding little pellets and fixing them in squares and circles, or stamping hemispherical bosses on the body of the vase. Some vases of this ware have a peculiar ornament, made by

[1] Brongniart, i. p. 434.

hollowing small spaces in the sides, and pinching up the clay—giving it the appearance of a series of thorns. Others have engine-turned patterns. The pattern of an urn, from York, is like a series of scales, formed by depressions.

The ornaments indeed are of the rudest character ; consisting of hatched lines, zones, or indented bands, raised dots arranged in squares or parallelograms, series of spurs imitating the pine cones, or rows of thorns, zigzag, and hatched lines, the herring-bone pattern, diagonal and crossing bands.

Four little vessels, found at Binsted, in Essex, illustrate some shapes of this ware. One is a *candelabrum*, or candle-stick ; another, a small vase for oil or vinegar, *acetabulum ;* a third, a jar, *olla ;* two others, small cups, *calices.* They were all found in a sarcophagus. Cups of a thin and finely moulded black ware have been found at the Upchurch marshes. This ware was adapted for useful purposes only ; and by the absence of all floral or animal ornamentations shows a late character and local fabric. It is of the latest period of the Gallo-Roman epoch.

BROWN WARE.

Specimens of brown ware of a very coarse style are often found among other Roman remains of cream-coloured ware, consisting of amphoræ, and other vessels for domestic use. It is, however, much more common in the Celtic and early Etruscan potteries.

Some [1] amphoræ and jugs have their necks decorated

---

[2] Wright, Celt, Roman, and Saxon, p. 223.

with the heads of females moulded upon them, like the bottles of the middle ages. Examples have been found at Richborough.[1] Each is of brown ware, and four and a half inches in diameter.

Many small vases in shape of ollæ or wide-mouthed jars, some with narrow necks and reeded bodies, small *amphoræ*, double-handled bottles, lagenæ, mortars, or pans, and cups or *ciboria* ornamented with tool marks, and lamps of this ware have been found in different parts of England.[2]

[1] R. Smith, Ant. Richborough, p. 74.   [2] Mus. Pract. Geol. Cat. p. 84–91.

CHAPTER V.

GLAZED ROMAN POTTERY.

THE Romans manufactured a glazed ware very distinct in its character from that of the Greeks, and more resembling that of the Etruscans. It must not, however, be supposed that all the lustrous wares of Italy were ornamented with highly finished subjects, as a very large number were entirely covered with a black glaze, which was the great characteristic of the pottery of the best Greek period, and which became more entirely used as the art of vase-painting decayed. On many of the later vases too of Southern Italy and other places, modelled figures in bas-relief were introduced by degrees, an imitation of the metal ware, which was rapidly rising into fashion ; and these, which are entirely glazed with a black lustre, are the nearest approach to the Roman ware.

There are also certain vases found in Etruria and Greece which were apparently made just before the Samian of the time of the Roman Empire. They are of a fine earth of a pale red colour, and have a slight glaze or polish, but their paste is not of the fine lustrous red colour of the so-called Samian. They are, however, made from a mould, and have in bas-relief friezes and other subjects, which imitated the *crustæ* or detachable

No. 196.—Proto-Samian Cup, with an Amazonomachia in relief.   From Athens.

relief ornaments,[1] of the metallic vases, or the *emblemata*, fixed reliefs of the celebrated chased goblets and other vases of the great masters of antiquity.

Some of the vases, too, of the Greek islands, of red ware, with moulded subjects coloured with red paint, are prototypes of the Roman ware.

[1] Cicero in Verrem, vi. 23, 24 ; Juvenal, v. 40 ; Martial, viii. 51-9.

ARETINE WARE.

The Roman ware is of one peculiar kind, being of a bright red, like sealing-wax, and covered, like the Greek lustrous vases, with a silicated alkaline glaze. As most of this ware in Italy has been found at *Arezzo*, the ancient *Aretium*, it will be necessary first to consider its manufacture at that place, where it succeeded the black Etruscan ware found in the sepulchres of the oldest inhabitants.[1]

The potteries of Aretium were in activity during the age of the early Cæsars, probably closing about B. C. 300. The ware is fine, red, and often unglazed, in which case it was formed into hemispherical cups, stamped out of moulds, with the names of makers placed on raised tesseræ on the exterior.[2] Other fragments found at this place resemble the so-called Samian ware. The pottery of Aretium is often mentioned in classical authors. " Oh, Aretine cup, which decorated my father's table, how sound thou wast before the doctor's hand," says Virgil,[3] referring to taking medicine out of it. And Persius subsequently says of the ware of this town, " Behold, he believes himself somebody, because supine with Italian honour, as an ædile, he has broken the unjust measures of Aretium." [4] According to Macrobius, Augustus said to Mæcenas, who was of the Gens Cilnia, and a native

[1] Dennis, ii. 425.
[2] Archæologia, xxvi. p. 254; xxii. p. 8; Dennis, ii. p. 422-428.
[3] " Aretine calix, mensis decorate paternis,
Ante manus medici quam bene sanus eras."—Virgil.
[4] "Sese aliquid credens, Italo quod

honore supinus
Fregerat heminas Areti ædilis iniquas."
—Persius, Sat. i. 144, 145.
Schol. Ann. Cornuti : " Quod meruit dignitatem ædilitiam in aliquo oppido Italiæ fracturus inæquales mensuras, id est minora vasa ex Arretio municipio ubi fiunt Aretina vasa."

of Arezzo,[1] "Fare thee well, oh, honey of families—oh, little honey pot, Etruscan ivory, Aretine gum, diamond of above, pearl of the Tiber, emerald of the Cilnians, jasper of potters, beryll of Porsena, &c.," in which some see an allusion to the red ware of Arretium, his native city. We find the vases of Arretium mentioned by Martial,[2] who flourished from the reign of Domitian to that of Nerva. "Thus," he says in a metaphor, "the vile Champaigne cloak, with its greasy exterior, contaminates the gay scarlet dresses of the city — thus the ware of Aretium violates the splendour of the crystal cup, and thus, as when perchance, on the banks of the Caÿster, a black crow is laughed at when wandering amidst the swans, one of which charmed Leda." Pliny, speaking of this ware, says,[3] "In sacrifices amidst all this wealth libations are not made from myrrhine or crystalline, but from earthenware simpuvia." "The greater part of mankind," says the same author, "uses earthenware. Samian ware is even now used for food. Aretium, in Italy, has also the pre-eminence." Isidorus says,[4] "Earthenware vases are said to have been first invented by Samos, made of clay, and hardened in the fire. Afterwards it was found out how to add a red

---

[1] "Vale, mel gentium, melcule, ebur
　　ex Etruria, laser
Aretinum, adamas supernus, Tiberinum
　　margaritum,
Cilniorum smaragde, jaspis figulorum,
　　berylle
Porsenæ ; carbunculum habeas."—
　　　　　　Sat. ii. c. 4.

[2] "Sic interpositus villo contaminat uncto
Urbica Lingonicus Tyriantina bardocucullus,

Sic Aretinæ violant crystallina testæ,
Sic niger in ripis errat cum forte Caÿstri
Inter Ledæos ridetur corvus olores."
　　　　　　—Martial, i. 54.

"Aretina nimis ne spernas vasa
　　monemus,
Lautus erat Thuscis Porsena fictilibus."
　　　　　　—xiv. 98.

[3] Pliny, N. H. xxxv. c. 12; c. i. c. 46.

[4] Isidorus, xx. 20; A.D. 610.

colour." Aretine vases are so called from a town in Italy, where they are made. Sedulius says of them, "the herbs which are brought up served on the red pottery." These vases are mentioned in a MS. written by S. Ristori, of Aretium, in A. D. 1282, and also by C. Villani, in his History of the World.[1] Alessi, who lived in the time of Leo. X., describes the discovery of red vases of Arezzo about one mile from the city. Vasari[2] states that in A.D. 1484, his grandfather found in the neighbourhood three vaults of an ancient furnace.[3] In A. D. 1734, Gori,[4] who had not seen any of the vases, republished the lists of Alessi. Rossi, who died A. D. 1796, had collected more information.[5] Fabroni[6] found in A. D. 1779, potteries at Cincelli, or Centum Cellae, with the different implements used in the art. The clay of the colour of umber was also found there, and the furnaces formed of bricks. The clay is supposed to have been decanted from vat to vat, and the vats were lined with pottery, and provided with canals for the introduction of water. According to Rossi the vase was first made upon the wheel, and before the clay was quite dry the ornaments and figures were impressed with metallic stamps. The vases were made in moulds, which were oiled, and then had the clay pressed into them. They were com-

[1] Libro della composizione del mondo; Gori, Difesa dell' Alfabeto Etrusco, p. 208, pref.

[2] I. 9, cap. 47.

[3] Fabroni, Storia degli Antichi Vasi fittili Aretini, 8vo, Arezzo, 1841, p. 18 ; Vite dei Pitt. Roma, 1759, t. i. p. 335.

[4] Pref. alla Dif. dell' Alf. Etr. p. 207.

[5] Fabroni, p. 21.

[6] " Trovò le fornaci i trogoli o vasche, e gli utensili dell' arte. Vidde che le fornaci erano construite in quadro sù due braccia toscane di lato con piccolissimi mattoni lunghi ¼ di braccio sopra ⅓ di larghezza. La creta o argilla gli parvi escavata poco piu in basso delle fabriche ed imitante da cruda il colore della terra d'ombra."—Fabroni, p. 22.

pleted upon the wheel, and when the inner part had been
thus perfected, are supposed to have been first baked and
then coated with the slip or glaze, and returned a second
time to the furnace. From one of the moulds in the Rossi
Museum having the name of the potter, Antiochus, the
freedman or slave of P. Cornelius, vases have been made
exactly like the ancient ones. The moulds in which the
vases were fabricated were made of the same clay as the
vases themselves, but less baked, without any glaze, and
about one inch thick. They were composed of separate
parts, so as to take to pieces, and had traces of some fat
or unctuous substance employed to prevent the adhesion
of the paste.[1] A terra-cotta mould, terminating in a
tragic mask was also found, and some instruments. Part
of a potter's wheel was also discovered, and most resembled that in use at present. It is composed of two discs
or tables, both placed horizontally, of unequal diameter,
having a certain distance between them, and their centre
traversed by a vertical pin, which revolved. The wheel
found was apparently part of one of the discs. It was
made of terra-cotta, about three inches thick and eleven
feet in diameter, circular, with a grove all round the
border. Round this vase a kind of leaden tire, held firm
by six cylindrical spokes of the same metal, placed inside
the discs. These cylinders, about half a foot long, one
foot three inches in diameter, came beyond the circumference of the disc, and gave it the appearance of a plate.[2]
There was no mark of any pin in the centre, so that it

---

[1] Fabroni, p. 62, 63. Prof. Buckman   p. 82-85.
& Mr. Newmarch, Remains of Roman   [2] Fabroni, tav. iii. 9, 10; v. 7, 8, 9,
Art in Cirencester, 4to, Cirencester,   p. 64.

must have formed part of the upper disc, called by potters the table, which lies upon a support of under clay, and enables the potter to fix the paste and to form it with the hands during the revolutions of the wheel.[1] The glaze of these vases, both black and red, have been found difficult to analyse. It is not, however, produced by lead, but apparently by a vitreous flux.[2] The vases were baked in furnaces, like those used at present.

GLAZE.

Considerable difference of opinion exists with respect to the varnish of these vases. By some it is stated to be an alkaline glaze,[3] by others a glaze of a metallic nature, while water alone is said to be sufficient to produce the polish. The glaze is not so strong or compact as that of porcelain or majolica, so as to be incapable of infiltration, yet is sufficiently strong to resist the action of wine, vinegar, or oil, although hot, and is not altered by these liquids. It is said to leave traces of having been produced by a brush, which looks as if a slip had been laid on. These vases seem to have been used for the table to hold fruits and liquids, and for medicine, and sacrificial purposes.[4]

FABRIC.

The two collections of Aretine vases at Arezzo are that of the Museo Rossi Bacci, and the public one of the

[1] Fabroni, l. c. 64.
[2] Fabroni, l. c. 66.
[3] Traité, i. p. 414.

[4] Fabroni, l. c. p. 65; Cf. Prof. Buckman & Newmarch, Remains of Roman art in Cirencester, 4to. Cirencester, p. 85.

city. The diacritical marks of this ware are a paste of a red coralline colour, pale when broken, and of a reddish yellow under the fracture, which does not become redder when subject to a red heat, but falls upon friction into an orange red calx. The vases are coated with a very slight glaze, which is levigated and always of a red coral colour, occasionally black, and verging towards azure, sometimes iron grey, or with a bright metallic lustre.[1] They are principally of small size and ornamented with bas-reliefs, of a decorative nature, not mythological, and in accordance with the later subjects of

No. 197.—Patina of Aretine Ware. British Museum.

Roman art. They are generally light. The prevalent form of the vases is that of a tea cup without handles, apparently the calix of Virgil, and these when ornamented

[1] Fabroni, l. c. ii. p. 32, et seq.

with bas-reliefs, have rarely the name of any potter impressed upon them. When a name does occur it is on a tessera, and in bas relief.

Flat circular dishes, patellæ or lances also appear to have emanated from this pottery, together with larger urns, some for cinerary purposes, square tiles, bas-reliefs, and lamps.[1] None of these pieces were, however, of any size, while the smallness of the furnaces prove that large vases could not have been baked in them. The subjects are disposed as friezes, but more often mixed up with architectural ornaments, such as scrolls, egg and tongue borders, and columns with spiral shafts and festoons. The subjects appear to be Hercules and Hylas, Bacchic orgies, Cupids, combats, chaces, dances, candelabra, masks, gladiators, females, horses, dolphins, dogs, goats, serpents, sphinx, lions, and panthers, in a style resembling the Roman art at the best period of the empire.

POTTERS.

Many vases have the potter's name impressed in bas-relief with a metallic stamp in Roman letters, often interlaced in ligatures, as on the consular coins. In the plain ware these are usually inside at the bottom of the vase, but in vases with bas-reliefs they are more often introduced amidst the foliage and ornaments. The letters are often surrounded with a mere square or tessera. Sometimes they are impressed in a human foot, probably in allusion to the treading out of the clay. The inscriptions

---

[1] Fabroni, l. c. 38.

show that the vases were principally made by slaves, who placed their names upon their work, sometimes followed by that of their master, the proprietor of the estate. One person named Publius seems to have employed several slaves. Another, Aulus Titius, calls himself an Aretine potter ; and L. Tettius, stamped *L. Tettii Samia*, proving that this ware had been imitated from the Samian.[1]

Three lists are given by Fabroni, the first of which, consisting of names with prænomens, contains the free citizens, or freedmen, who were proprietors of estates, or who worked the potteries ; the second is that of the slaves whose products were sufficiently good to be impressed upon the ware, or who may have sold it for masters who were too proud to exercise the craft in their own name. The last list contains the inscriptions exactly as they appear on the vases.

Vases of red ware, similar to those found at Arezzo, have been discovered in the vicinity of Modena, having the names of the potters Camurus, Eutychius, L. Gellius, Herennius, Occa, Philadelphus, Sanus, and Villus, and others. This circumstance has given rise to the hypothesis that the so-called Aretine vases were made at Modena.[2] Similar vases are said to have been found at Vulci, bearing the inscription Atrane,[3] and at Cervetri, with the names of the Aretine potters, C. Vibianus Faustus, L. Gellius, Aulus Titius Figulus,[4] and another.

In the Gregorian Museum are three cups and one jug, called in the description of that collection Aretine ware,

[1] Fabroni, p. 41.

[2] Cavedoni, Dichiarazione dei marmi Modenese, 1828 ; Biographia de Cav. Zaumo, 1835, p. 40-41 ; Bull. 1837, p. 10 ; 1838, p. 129-131.

[3] Bull. 1836, p. 171.

[4] Bull. 1830, p. 238 ; 1834, p. 102, 149 ; 1837, p. 108 ; 1839, p. 20.

apparently of the red unglazed terra-cotta ware there found. On the cups are large acanthus leaves, egg and tongue ornaments, goats, and a race of dolphins. On the jug are four bands of fleurettes and festoons, artificial ornaments, and dolphins and anchors repeated. On one cup, with Cupid and other ornaments, is the name of the Roman maker, C. Popilius.[1]

In the Museo Borbonico, at Naples, are several specimens of this red ware, which is found in abundance at Capua, and amidst the ruins of the houses at Pompeii. Some specimens in Sir Woodbine Parish's collection, procured at Naples, were of finer make and ware than those found out of Italy. One had the name of L. Favor.

SAMIAN WARE.

A ware exactly like that of Arezzo, called by some the red Roman ware, and by others Samian, distinguished by its close grain composed of a fine clay, and presenting when broken, edges of an opaque light red colour, whilst the inner and outer surface are quite smooth, and of a brighter and darker red, is found in all places of the ancient world to which the Roman arms or civilisation reached.[2] It is distinguished from the Aretine by its darker tone, stronger glaze, and coarser ornamentation.

Possibly, the whole passage of Pliny,[3] in which he speaks of the earthenware of his day, refers to this

[1] Mus. Etr. Vat. ii. cii.

[2] Buckman & Newmarch, p. 84; Roach Smith, Journ. Brit. Arch. Assoc.

iv. p. 1-20.

[3] N. H. xxxv. 45.

red ware. Thus for dishes he praises the Samian, and the Aretine ware, for cups, that of Surrentum, Asta and Pollentia, Saguntum and Pergamus. Tralles and Mutina had their manufactories. Cos was most esteemed, Hadria produced the hardest ware. That one of these, that of Saguntum, was a red ware, is clear ; that of Cumae was also of the same colour. "The chaste Sibyl has sent thee her own burgess, a red dish of Cuman earth," says Martial.[1] Cups also were made at Allifæ.

That the red ware is found amidst the dense forests of Germany and on the distant shores of Britain, is a remarkable fact in the civilisation of the old world. It was apparently an importation, being exactly identical wherever discovered, and is readily distinguishable from the local pottery.[2] No question has excited more controversy among antiquaries than the place where it was made. Samos, Aretium, Rome, Modena, Ancient Gaul, and Britain [3] (into which, however, it seems to have been imported) have been supposed to be the sites of its manufacture. It belongs to the class of tender lustrous pottery of Brongniart, consisting of a bright red paste like sealing-wax, breaking with a close texture, and covered with a siliceous, or, according to some, a metallic glaze. This glaze is exceedingly thin, transparent, and equally laid upon the whole surface, only slightly augmenting the colour of the clay. The vases made of this ware are generally of small dimensions, and consist of dishes, lances or patinæ, of an oval or flat circular shape, like

---

[1] Epig. xiv. 114.
[2] Brongniart, Traité, i. p. 420, et seq.
[3] Roach Smith, Journ. Brit. Arch. Assoc. iv. p. 1, 20.

modern salvers, of small bowls, apparently for holding
small quantities of viands, perhaps pateræ, and generally
hemispherical or cylindrical, and of little cups either of
globular or of conical shape, probably pocula, and of jugs
or larger vessels.   The ware is generally plain, and impressed with the name of the potter from whose factory
it emanated, and it will be seen from the list of potters'
names, that these were slaves, or at best liberti, and
that many were of Gaulish or British origin.

No. 198.—Ciborium of Red Samian Ware, bearing the name of Divix, a Gaulish potter.

The Samian ware from its peculiar paste was more than
usually brittle.   In the Menæchmus [1] of Plautus, the following dialogue occurs :

" *M.* Knock gently.
" *P.* Are you afraid the doors are Samian."

[1] Menæchmus, I. i. 65.

In another play, the Bacchides,[1] of the same author, the following passage is found :

> " Take care, pr'ythee, lest any heedless one touch that ;
> Thou knowest how soon a Samian vase will break."

The most remarkable fact connected with this ware is the great similarity of its paste in whatever place it may be found, which renders it probable that the ware was made upon one spot, and imported throughout the empire. Brongniart inclines to the idea that the potters did not import their paste prepared, but levigated a colourless clay of the locality, and produced the usual red colour by the introduction of ochre.[2]

PASTE.

The colour of this ware, which was made of a clay like the red ware, was owing to the more perfect oxidation of the iron contained in it, and it was probably baked in open kilns or fire-pans. The glaze or lustre is supposed to be owing to a polish given to it when upon the wheel.[3] The analysis of Brongniart[4] shows that the paste of these vases consists of 56—64 silica, 25—17 alumina, 7—10 ox. iron, 9—2 carb. lime, 2—0 magnesia, 18—2 water, while the glaze consists of 64 silica, 11·0 ox. iron. Dr. Percy's analysis is 54·45—60·67 silica, 22·08—20·96 alumina, 7·31—5·95 peroxide of iron, 9·76—6·77 lime, 1·67—1·22 magnesia, 3·22 potash, and 1·76 soda.[5]

---

[1] Act II. ii. 22, 23.
[2] Brongniart, Traité, i. p. 423.
[3] Buckman and Newmarch, p. 78, 79.
[4] Brongniart, Traité, i. p. 421.
[5] Mus. Pract. Geol. Cat. 8vo. Lond. 1854, p. 59.

The glaze of these vases is stated by the French antiquaries not to be metallic, but produced by some substance laid upon them after they were ready for baking.
The portions not covered with reliefs are stated to have
been polished [1] upon the lathe, and the bas-reliefs themselves were in certain instances retouched with a tool,
which left a furrowed line round them.[2] The colour of
the vases, however, may have been owing to the introduction of an oxide of iron, and the difference of the external colour appears to depend mainly upon the paste.
When heated in the fire, they become a deep claret
colour.[3]

As there are no traces of any pencil being used to
apply the glaze, Brongniart thinks it most probable that
the vases were dipped into a slip which held it in suspension.[4] A similar glaze, however, could probably be obtained by the application of salt thrown into the furnaces
during the baking, in the same way as now practised at
Lambeth for stone ware.

MOULDS.

The pieces of this ware were made upon the wheel by
which the slopes, fillets, mouldings, incised rings, or bands
were produced. Moulds were employed, sometimes of an
entire piece, in which case they were made by punching
the requisite ornaments upon the mould itself from

---

[1] Cf. also on this ware, Grivaud
de la Vincelle, Antiquités decouvertes
dans les jardins du palais du Luxembourg.

[2] Caumont, Cours. p. 206.
[3] Ibid. p. 209.
[4] Brongniart, Traité, i. p. 423.

matrices, or master moulds. Sometimes many separate moulds, representing the same or different subjects, were adjusted together to complete the decoration of the circumference of a cup. The engrailed lines and smaller ornaments were made by means of a circular or revolving mould of terra-cotta or metal,[1] but the larger ones, such as the egg and tongue moulding, were effected by a punch or seal, with a long handle,[2] the part on which the ornament is incised being concave, to correspond with the convex surface of the vase. The same process was adopted for the figures in the central groups,[3] and the more salient parts were separately stamped and placed on the vase while the clay was wet, as is very evident in some reliefs of vases of Aretine ware. Names of potters were also impressed from stamps of terra-cotta or metal.[4] The last mode of fabric consisted in laying upon the general body of the vase some clay in a very viscous state, technically called *barbotine*, either with a pipe or a little spatula in form of a spoon, and with it following out the contours of the branches of olive or laurel, animals with thin limbs,[5] &c. On some specimens an ornament had been modelled with a white paste. Separate figures, *crustæ*, were also made in moulds, and then placed on the body of the vase, one of the finest specimens of which is an Atys, in the York Museum.[6]

---

[1] Brongniart, Traité, i. 424, Pl. xxx. 3, A.

[2] Brongniart, l. c. F. 4. A. B.

[3] Brongniart, i. p. 424, Pl. xxx. F. 2, A.

[4] Ibid. p. 424 ; Musée Céramique, ix, fig. xix.

[5] Brongniart, p. 425; Golbert & Schweighauser, Mem. de la Soc. des Antiq. de France, t. vii. Pl. lxxii. : Caumont, Cours d' Antiq. t. ii. p. 185.

[6] Welbeloved, Antiquities of Yorkshire, Phil. Soc. 1852, p. 50.

Another mode of ornamentation visible on some pieces found in the north of England, consisted in scooping out wreaths, and cutting out fan-shaped patterns in intaglio, with a tool on the clay, while moist, the parts dug out being removed from the plain surface, as shown by the horizontal stripes.[1]

A master mould, formerly in Mr.

No. 199. — Master-Mould of the potter Liber.

Hertz's possession, and presented by him to the British Museum, pyramidal in shape, and convex at the base, has a slight bas-relief of a youth standing full face with some drapery thrown over his left arm. At one side is OFFI LIBERI, "the pottery of Liber," stamped incuse, probably as a preservation against theft or removal from the premises. This die was apparently arranged with others so as to form a pattern, and it was then stamped into the sides of a convex vessel fashioned like one of the cups or dishes, but without the foot, which in some instances appears to have been subsequently added. This original die is of rather a fine terra-cotta, and was found near Mayence. A similar mould, presenting a tragic mask, was found at Arezzo or Aretium.[2] Other moulds in the shape of a hare and of a lion, inscribed with the name of CEREALIS, a well-known maker of red ware, are in the Museum of Sèvres, one, in the shape of a wolf standing, baked almost as hard as stone ware, has on it the name COBENERDVS.[3]

[1] Wellbeloved, Descriptive account of Antiquities of Yorkshire, Phil. Soc. 8vo. York, p, 52, 1, 2.

[2] Fabroni, Tav. v. 4.
[3] Brongniart, Traité. l. c. Museé de Sevres, p. 16.

Some moulds for this purpose of the Roman period
have been found, and the process is of common use at
present. It was particularly desirable in cases where ornaments in high relief were required for the enrichment
of red or black wares. A fragment with a draped figure
from the mould of Liber, already cited, was found at Cirencester.[1] Another mould of a vessel was found near
Mayence. It is
in shape of a
shallow bowl,
with a mould-
ing at the edges
and foot, and
the pattern has
been stamped
out from ma-

No. 200.—Fragment of a Mould found near Mayence.

trices like those already described ; the pattern is coarse,
and represents a series of animals, consisting of a dog or
wolf, boar, and lion pursuing each other. The paste of the
clay when kneaded to a due consistence, was pressed into
and formed a bowl ; the foot was probably afterwards
formed of a separate piece, and added. This matrix vase
was made of a very fine bright red clay, rather light, and
not glazed. In this respect it differs from the mould of
the lamps already mentioned, whose paste was of a bright
yellow colour. It was very porous, rapidly absorbing the
moisture, and so, easily delivering the clay to the potter like
the plaster of Paris moulds now in use. At Arezzo similar
moulds, for other vessels of the Roman red ware, have also
been found. Those of the lamps are mentioned with the

[1] Buckman & Newmarch, p. 92.

lamps.   Besides these moulds, metal dies or punches were
used for stamping intaglio ornaments, such as fleurettes and
other mouldings, on some rare examples of Samian ware.[1]

Dies for stamping the potters' names upon these vases
were discovered at Lezoux,[2] in Auvergne, and in Luxembourg,[3] together with parts of other moulds for festoons
and the tassel pattern,[4] and for making vases.[5]   They
had the names of the potters, Auster and Cobnertus,[6] and
another, with a potter's name, was made of metal.[7]

Modelling tools, styles, punches, and other little instruments of bone or ivory, have been found amidst the
remains of the ancient potteries.[8]

FURNACES.

The mode in which these vases were baked is shown
by furnaces found at Châtelet, in Auvergne, on the banks
of the Rhine, in the vicinity of Strasburg ; at Heilegenberg, near Milz, and also at Ittenweiler.   The furnaces near
Heilegenberg were evidently for the baking of red Roman
ware.   " The flue," says Brongniart, " is a long canal,
with vaulted arch, the mouth of which is 8 feet $2\frac{1}{2}$ inches,
from the space where the flame and heat were concentrated
beneath the laboratory.   Numerous terra-cotta pipes,
of two different diameters, branched off from the upper
part or floor of that chamber, to distribute the heat :
the smaller ware in the outer wall of the laboratory ; the
larger, twelve or fifteen in number, opened under the floor

[1] R. Smith, Ant. Richborough, Pl.
iv. p. 73.
[2] Brongniart, Traité, i. p. 424.
[3] Grivaud de la Vincelle, 1801.
[4] Brongniart, Traité, Pl. xxx. 2, 3, 4.
[5] Roach Smith, Collectanea, vol. i.161.
[6] Brongniart, Musée Ceramique, ix. 19.
[7] Brongniart, Traité, i. p. 424.
[8] Brongniart, Mus. de Sèvres, p. 16.

of the laboratory, to conduct the heat and flame round the pieces which were placed there. The mouths of the pipes were sometimes stopped with terra-cotta stoppers so as to moderate the heat. The upper part, or dome, is never found entire, and is supposed to have been destroyed and replaced by the superincumbent earth. Walls of strong masonry separated and protected the space between the mouth of the flue and the walls of the observatory. The floor of the latter was made of tiles, or large squares of terra-cotta. Fifteen such furnaces were found at Rheinzabern, some round and others square, but all constructed on the same general plan. These furnaces were found at the depth of 2 feet 4 inches, under the ancient soil, and more than 3 feet 3 inches above the modern transported soil. The floor of the laboratory was nearly 3 feet 3 inches below the upper edge of the walls; a kind of tile roof covered it. The brick work was made of masses of clay, 2 feet 4 inches long and 1 foot 4 inches broad and thick. The pieces which supported the floor of the laboratory were in some of these furnaces made of bricks, covered with a coating of clay.[1] The fuel was fir or deal. The pieces placed in the furnace were carried on supports or rests of terra-cotta, in shape of a flattened cylinder, and kept up by pads of a peculiar shape, made by the person who placed the vases in the furnace, by rolling up a piece of clay in shape of a rolling-pin, and squeezing it together. These are the pieces erroneously called hand-bricks. The pieces have no cases, as they were not necessary to prevent adhesion.[2]

---

[1] Brongniart, Traité, l. c. p. 429; Pl. xxx. 7. A. B. C.
[2] Brongniart, i. 449; Shaw, Pottery, 1839, p. 390, note.

ORNAMENTATION.

The scrolls which ornamented the upper part of the bowls made of this ware are of exceedingly elegant device, though clearly architectural in their treatment, and are generally varieties of the tendrils, flowers, leaves, and fruit of the grape or ivy.[1] Sometimes the upper parts of the bowls are ornamented with an egg and tongue moulding, and the scrolls have often figures of little birds introduced into the composition, in arabesque

No. 201.—Vase of Samian Ware ornamented with Arabesques.

style. The animals and other figures consist of isolated groups introduced at intervals into the outer surface of the vase. They are separated by beadings, and are often in niches, formed of pillars with twisted shafts, surmounted by arches, or in medallions. These are clearly intended for representations of statues, and other embellishments of public edifices, as they appeared at the time. Repetition was the object chiefly sought, and as, in the decadence of art, the ornaments occupy much surface in proportion to their importance. They consist of scenic masks, garlands, rosettes, foliage, astragal mouldings above and below, the egg and tongue

[1] Cf. Brongniart, Traité, Pl. xxx. ; Mus. Cer. viii.-ix.

mouldings above, scrolls of flowers, in which birds are pecking the foliage and fruit ; friezes of animals, consisting of lions, goats, hares, rabbits, and deer ; or insects ; among birds, pigeons, eagles, and crows, medallions and other architectural ornaments.[1] The subjects are not arranged on a continuous frieze, but generally consist of one or two friezes, rarely more, repeated several times round the body, and intermingled with the foliage.[2] The subjects consist of the Gods, Cupids, Genii, Venus, Hercules and his exploits, Gladiators, the Circensian games, and erotic representations.[3]

Some of these fragments are clearly as late as the 4th century, as the costume and style of art of the subjects resemble that prevalent at the close of the Roman empire.[4] The subjects are taken from the Roman school of art, from the statues which adorned the Circus, the Forum, the Triumphal Arches, the Thermæ, the Basilicas, and the houses of the wealthy. They resemble in their treatment the reverses of the Roman medallions,[5] except that they bear indications of being entirely influenced by architectural considerations.

USE.

It is evident that the ware was for use and not decoration, its solid character and glaze adapting it for that purpose. Many of the flat dishes were undoubtedly the

---

[1] Brongniart, Traité, Pl. xxx.; Musée Ceramique, Pl. viii. ix.

[2] Caumont, Cours. Pl. xxiii. xxiv. xxv. xxvi. xxvii.; R. Smith, Collectanea, i. p. 165.

[3] Caumont, Cours. ii. p. 200 ; R. Smith,

Collectanea, i. p. 165.

[4] Cf. for example, the fragment found at Hartlip, R. Smith, Collectanea, vol. ii. p. i. p. 12 ; SABINI. M.

[5] Janssen, Inscr. 4to, Lugd. 1842. Tab. xxxi. 230.

lances or paropsides used at entertainments,[1] others are
supposed to have been the mortars used in the kitchen or
at the apothecaries.[2] It is not known to have been employed for cinerary purposes, although often placed in
tombs to contain the objects deposited with the dead.[3]
The observations made upon the Aretine ware apply also
to this. Yet, however common in Rome, it was a comparative luxury in Gaul and Britain, though it is found
in those countries wherever Roman settlements occur.[4]
That it was common at Rome appears from Martial : " If,"
says he, " ye have enough to eat, a few white beans dressed
in oil, upon a red plate, refuse the entertainments of the
wealthy." [5]   The most striking point in the decorations of
these vases is their resemblance in the adoption of arabesque
forms to the mural paintings.   When fractured this ware
was repaired with leaden rivets,[6] which shows the estimation
in which it was held.   It was equivalent to our domestic
porcelain, with a tender paste.

The shapes are few ; all the vases are wide and open-
mouthed, and of small proportions.   Those of the largest
dimensions are the dishes, *paropsides*, *lances*, or *pateræ*,
ornamented with a tendrilled leaf, intended for that of the
ivy or the vine.   These are probably the lances pampi-
natæ, or hederatæ, dishes with grapes, or ivy leaves, such
as Claudius received from Gallienus.   Some rare dishes,
with spouts like the mortaria, and bowls with lion-headed
spouts, are known ; occasionally some of the pateræ have

[1] Martial, Epig. xi. 27.
[2] Brongniart, Traité, i. p. 432.
[3] Ibid.
[4] Caumont, Cours, ii. p. 185.

[5] "Si spumet rubrâ conchis tibi pallida
        testâ,
Lautorum cœnis sæpe negare potes.—
xiii. 7, 1.
[6] Birch, Archæologia, xxx. p. 254.

handles. The small cups are supposed by some to be either *acetabula*, vinegar cups, or *salina*, salt-cellars. The larger cups are the *pocula, cyathi*, or *calices*.[1]

MAKERS' NAMES.

Many of the vases have the makers' names stamped across their centre, or placed upon their sides.[2] The letters are often united in nexus or ligatures. They are always in relief, but the place stamped is depressed, and of a square, circular, or long oval shape ; in a few instances, in that of a human foot, in allusion to the potter's mode of working. They occur inside the plain vases ; those ornamented outside with bas-relief being less frequently stamped with potters' names, which, when they do occur on such vases, are on labels or tesseræ. There are certain philological peculiarities evident upon inspection of these stamps. The double II is used for E, as Riignus and Siixtus for Regnus and Sextus. The ⋏ in the name of Caretus resembles the Celtiberian form, and on one with the name Methillus the ⊗ is used for TH. The words are often in contraction, retrograde, and confused ; and some have supposed that the potters used moveable letters, which is improbable. The names of many potters are Gaulish, apparently of slaves or freedmen. Amongst the names more particularly Gaulish are Advocisus, Beleniccus, Cobnertus, Dagodubnus, Dagomarus, Dagoimnus, Suobnedo, Tasconus, Tascillus. The formula used by the potters was O or OF, OFFIC, for *officina*, or establishment, either before or after the name. M for

---

[1] Buckman & Newmarch, p. 87.   [2] Ibid. p. 93.

manu, "the work," is always placed after the name in the genitive, and F, or FE, for fecit, "he made," probably after names in the nominative. In one instance fecit, "he made," occurs without any potter's name, and in another case the potter, through ignorance or caprice, has impressed the stamp of a Roman oculist, destined for some quack ointment, on the bottom of a cup. Besides these names, a few other inscriptions are found. On a deep poculum of red glazed ware is inscribed, in raised letters, round the outside, BIBE AMICE DE MEO, "Drink, oh friend, from my cup."[1] The idea was probably taken by the potter from the glass cups, which often have similar letters, in complete relief, round their sides.

A list of the potters' names which occur on the Roman earthenware found in Britain has been given by Mr. Roach Smith, in the Archæologia,[2] and in his Collectanea Antiqua.[3] The numerous names found at York are inserted in Mr. Wellbeloved's Eburacum,[4] and others, found at Caerleon, in Mr. Lee's Antiquities of that place.[5]

In some rare instances the potter has scrawled a few illegible words on the mould before the clay was pressed in, and these have been preserved on the vase when baked.[6] Such caprices of the potter are not uncommon, and have been already mentioned in the case of Greek vases. Many Roman tiles and bricks have also had inscriptions and other objects cut upon them before they were baked by idlers in the brick-field. One discovered at Nimeguen,[7]

[1] Mus. Borb. vii. xxix.
[2] Archæologia, xxvii. p. 143.
[3] Smith, Collectanea, i. 150.
[4] p. 128.
[5] p. 10, Pl. iii.
[6] Journ. Brit. Arch. Assoc., ii. 20; Soc. Lux. 4to. 1853; Pl. vi. 4, p. 124.
[7] Janssen, Römisch. Ziegel., 4to. Leyden, 1841.

had the Roman alphabet ; others at Enns, on the Danube, had illegible words and sentences, amongst which can only be read such expressions as the "Emperor Antoninus" and the "Nones of September."[1] A brick in the British Museum, found at Colchester, has Primus or Primulus, and another what may be intended to delineate an edifice. Inscriptions scratched upon Samian ware after it has been baked, chiefly names of its possessors, also occur.

The potters were called *doliarii*, or pot-makers, if they made vessels of unglazed ware and large size,[2] *vascularii*, or vase makers,[3] *fictilarii*,[4] makers of fictile vases, and *figulinarii*, *figuli*, or potters in general. They were generally of servile condition, and are represented wearing only the tunic of the slave.[5] One Gaulish potter, named Casatus Caratius,[6] is, however, represented on a bas-relief, wearing a cloak besides the tunic. He holds in one hand a fluted vase, like those of the black ware.

It would appear almost certain that the ware was an article of export, as stated by Pliny, and that the name of Samian was applied to it in reference to its origin, long after it had ceased to be made in that island.

Traces of manufactories of red pottery and broken moulds and wheels have been found scattered all over Gaul, as near Nancy, at Paris, Nîmes, Lyons, and at Clermont, near Bourdeaux ; but principally at Rheinzabern, and at Heiligenberg, near Strasburg.[7] In Italy

---

[1] Arneth, Hypocaustum, 4to. Wien, 1856, taf. iv.

[2] L. Aurelius Sabinus, *doliarius*, fecit sibi et suis. Grivaud de la Vincelle, xxxiii. 2. In the sepulchral bas-relief are an amphora, olla, and lagena.

[3] Grivaud de la Vincelle, xlvii.

[4] Grivaud de la Vincelle, xlvi.

[5] Grivaud de la Vincelle, xlvi. 1.

[6] Grivaud de la Vincelle, xlvi. 4.

[7] Caumont, ii. p. 211.

the ware has been found from Modena to Pompeii, and
probably extended over many sites in the Peninsula. In
England it has been discovered in great abundance, principally in the south and west of the island.

OTHER GLAZED WARES.

Another kind of the red glazed ware is that used for
lamps, which differs considerably from the Samian. Its
colour is much paler and texture very different from that
of the bowls ; the glaze is of a thin alkaline kind, and
thinly spread over the surface of the ware. The lamps
of this ware are generally found in Italy, and have been
already described in the general account of lamps.

There is a kind of this ware, which is probably the
earliest in point of time, and to which the term Samian
might not be inappropriately applied. The clay is not
uniform in its colour, being gray, black, or yellow, and
the lustre appears as much due to a polish on the lathe as
to a vitrification. The prevalent shape is the cup, either
hemispherical or cylindrical, decorated with figures or
architectural scrolls and ornaments. These so much resemble certain cups of terra-cotta already described, that
they can hardly be separated from them. Such vases have
been found at Melos, and a jug of this style, representing
a sacrifice, was dug up in 1725 at Hadria.[1] Another
variety of this ware, called by some the false Samian, resembles the Samian, but is of an orange, not yellow colour.
The colour too has sometimes a kind of red paint, or

---

[1] Muratori, cxlix.

powdered Samian ware, laid on it externally, in order to deepen it.[1] This ware is often coarse, and ornamented externally with coarse white scrolls, painted with pipeclay on the body. One kind of ware found at Castor is distinguished by its red glaze, which often has a metalloid lustre. The paste is yellowish brown, white, or reddish yellow.[2] In some instances the glaze is lustrous, and shows the colour of the paste. The shapes and ornamentation resemble the black glazed ware. One remarkable jar has a chariot race. The difference of colour assumed by the vases appears partly due to the degree of firing the vases experienced, the paste of some which is black, red, or gray, becoming of a copper hue.[3] A remarkable variety has been found at Boultham, near Lincoln, the site of a local pottery, composed of a light yellow paste, brushed over from the lip downwards with a light yellow wash of a sparkling mica, or dipped in the fluid and inverted to drain off the superfluous fluid. Here the colours consisted of many shades of yellow, brown, purple, and even black, with a metalloid lustre. The shapes and ornaments are the same as those of the Castor black ware, and are sometimes laid on with a slip of pipeclay.[4] These vases are Gallo-Roman, made subsequent to the Samian. Sometimes they have incised inscriptions—dedications to deity, as to the " Genius of Tournay,"[5] on a vase found in France—rarely the names of potters, as " Camaro," on a vase at Lincoln.[6] A remarkable variety has a gray paste

---

[1] As at Comberton, Arch. Journ. vi. 210.

[2] Cat. Mus. Pract. Geol. p. 72-77; Artis, Durobrivæ. Pl. iii. 1, xxx. 4, xlvii. 3, xlix. 4.

[3] Arch. Journ. x. 229.

[4] Arch. Journ. xii. 173.

[5] R. Smith, Collectanea, iii. 193.

[6] Arch. Journ. xii. 174.

baked hard like stone ware, and painted of a yellow mottled colour to imitate marble.

BLACK WARE.

The black ware was made of any tenacious clay in the neighbourhood, and it varies from a dark black to a slate

No. 202.—Cups of Black Ware.

or olive colour. The kilns in which it was baked have been already described, but the phenomenon is differently explained by Professor Buckman,[1] who supposes that the carbon and hydrogen of the smother kiln reduced or rather prevented the iron in the clay changing into a peroxide or the red oxide of iron. Funeral urns were often made of this pottery.

Some varieties of this ware exist like that of the unglazed red. In the first the clay is soft, easily scratched, and covered with a polish or lustre produced by friction on the lathe. From the peculiarities and differences in its paste and embellishments it appears to have been the product of local potteries.[2] The glaze, or coating, may have been produced by water or friction.[3] The paste is fine, and the walls thin and well turned. The paste varies from a kind of gray, or colour like that of the London clay, to a dull black. The vases are mostly small, the ware generally consisting of cups, bottles, and small

[1] Buckman & Newmarch, p. 78. [3] Traité, i. 430.
[2] Artis, Jour. Brit. Arch. Assoc., ii. 166.

amphoræ and jugs, but occasionally of the supposed mortaria. Some of the cups, like those of the red dull ware, have their sides corrugated.

The ornaments which are by far more common than the subjects, are of the most simple nature, consisting of pressed lines and herring-bone patterns ; but the favourite devices are regular clusters of corrugated studs, disposed in squares or bands round the vases, and produced by sticking small pieces on the vase before the clay was baked. Some of these resemble the spines on the blackthorn. In some rare instances the potter has stamped in a series of small square indentations, resembling fleurettes. A great peculiarity of this ware is that it is unaccompanied with the names of potters, nor is it found with coins and other Roman remains.[1] A few vases of this ware are ornamented round the body with rows of little pebbles let into the clay, humble imitation of the cups of the wealthy inlaid with gems.[2] Great quantities of this ware have been found in England, in the Upchurch marshes near Sheerness.[3]

There is a pottery differing from the preceding, by the quality and colour of its paste, which is red with a black glaze. Sometimes, however, it is gray, or even black, but generally not so fine as the first kind. Its grand distinction is its glaze or lustre, which consists of an alkaline earthy silicate, sometimes very black and pure,

[1] For example, a vase was found at Billinghay, near Sleaford, Lincoln, in a cemetery containing twelve skeletons. The heads of eleven were turned to the south, and one to the north ; they were buried two feet deep, with part of a conglomerated quern. Others are de-

scribed by J. Kenrick, Excavations at the Mote Hill, Warrington. 8vo. Warrington, 1853.
[2] The Calix gemmatus. Martial, xiv. 106.
[3] R. Smith, Ant. Richborough, p. 58, Journ. Brit. Arch. Assoc. ii. 138.

but at other times of a green or bluish or slate-coloured tint. Brongniart divides this glaze into two kinds ; one, although thin, being lustrous, but without any metallic reflection,—the other, which seems to be a metallic coating deposited by steam, having a lustre like black lead. This ware was made on the wheel by the same process as the red, and the ornaments were either made by the revolving swivel moulds or else by the usual process.[1] It must be borne in mind that there was a black as well as red Aretine ware, and that plain black lustrous vases continued in Italy till the middle of the Roman empire. A Roman vase of this ware, found at Cumæ, has the subject of Perseus and the Gorgons stamped in intaglio from separate dies, after the vase left the lathe.[2] A hemispherical cup, recently found in the Greek islands,[3] of the proto-Samian class, and of the period of the empire, was made from a mould, has its subject in relief, and is covered with a lustrous black glaze.

Some few of these vases are ornamented with subjects in relief, representing hunting scenes in a low and degenerate style of art, which, from the costume of the figures, may be referred to the last days of the waning empire of Rome, and are clearly later than the red polished glazed ware. The art is apparently Gaulish, and the figures bear striking resemblance to those on the ancient British and Gaulish coins. They are never made from moulds as in the Samian ware, but by the process called barbotine, by depositing on the surface of the vase after it had left the lathe, from a small vessel or tube, masses of semifluid

[1] Brongniart, Traité, i. p. 433.
[2] Mon. 1855. Tav. ii. p. 18.
[3] By Mr. Newton, now in the British Museum.

clay, which were slightly modelled with a tool into the required shape. The glaze and colour are supposed to have been produced by smothering the vases when in the furnace with the smoke of the kiln, and depositing at the same time the carbon on the surface of the heated vases, and thus giving them a black glaze. It has two different glazes, one dark but without any metallic reflections, the other metalloid, like a polish of black lead.

The principal subjects represented on this pottery are hunting scenes,[1] such as dogs chasing stags—deer—hares, —also dolphins, ivy wreaths, and engrailed lines, and engine-turned patterns.[2] In a few instances men with spears are represented, but in a rude and debased style of art. The principal form is the cup of a jar shape, sometimes with deep oval flutings, as on one found at Castor ; but dishes, cups, plates, and mortars, are not found in this ware.

Some of the vases of this ware have ornaments, and sometimes letters painted on them in white slip upon their black ground. They are generally of a small size, and of the nature of bottles or cups, with inscriptions, such as AVE,

No. 203.—Group of Vases of inscribed black glazed ware.

hail ! VIVAS, may you live ; IMPLE, fill ; BIBE, drink ;[3]

---

[1] Journal, Brit. Arch. Assoc. i. p. 5, 7, 8.

[2] Brongniart, Traité, Pl. xxix.

[3] Grivaud de la Vincelle, Antiq. Pl. xxxiii. 48. Janssen, Inscr. Tab. xxviii. 26-29; Gerhard, Berl. ant. Bild. 182.

VINVM, 'wine;' VITA, 'life;' VIVE BIBE MVLTIS;
showing that they were used for purposes purely con-
vivial. Such are the vases found at Étâples near Boulogne,[1]
the ancient Gessoriacum, and at Mesnil.[2]

Some rarer and finer specimens from Bredene, in the
department of Lis, have a moulding round the foot. Great
quantities are found in England, Holland, Belgium, and
France. It is found on the right bank of the Rhine. A
variety of this ware has been lately found at a spot called
Crockhill in the New Forest, together with the kilns in
which it was made, and a heap of potter's sherds, or pieces
spoilt in the baking. The paste was made of the blue
clay of the neighbourhood, covered with an alkaline glaze
of a maroon colour, perhaps the result of imperfect baking;
for the pieces when submitted again to the action of the
fire, decrepitated and split. They were so much vitrified
as to resemble modern stone ware, yet as all of them have
proofs of having been rejected by the potters, it is probable that this was not the proper colour of the ware.
Almost all were of the pinched up fluted shape, and had
no bas-reliefs, having been ornamented with patterns laid
on in white colour. The kilns are supposed to be of the
third century of our era,[3] and the ware was in local use,
for some of it was found at Bittern.

The bottoms of two pots of this Roman ware found at
Lyons showed that it was sometimes made of a very
coarse and gritty paste with many micaceous and calcareous particles distributed through it, breaking with a

---

[1] Roach Smith, Collectanea, I., Pl. iii.
p. 3.
[2] Cochet, Normandie souterraine,
8vo, Paris, 1855, p. 131.

[2] Mr. Akerman, in Archæologia,
xxxv. 91-96; Arch. Journ. March,
1853, p. 8.

coarse fracture of a dark red colour. The ware is covered with rather a thick coat of black glaze also exhibiting the same paste. The bottoms were impressed with a potter's name stamped in circular mouldings and disposed in circles, in characters of the later period of the Empire, and the ornamental grooves were subsequently made. One of these had L CASSIO, perhaps Lucii Cassii officina—"from the factory of L. Cassius;"

No. 204.—Cup of black-glazed Castor ware.

the other had FIRMINVS F(ecit). "Firminus made it." This ware is very different from the Castor ware, and forms a totally distinct class, intermediate between the glazed and plain ware, sprinkled with mica.

SITES.

The distribution of this pottery of Roman manufacture and style, whether of the Samian or other ware, is almost universal over Germany, France, and Eastern Europe, and in the West, extending through Spain and England. In Germany [1] it has been found throughout the country, as at Alsheim, Cassell, Xanten, and Zahlbach. Of the German localities, however, Mayence seems to have been particularly active in its ancient potteries. Details

---

[1] Wagener, Handbuch, 8vo. Weimar, 1842, Pl. 22, 23.

of a still more precise nature are afforded of the different kinds of ware found in France. Thus at the Canal de Bourges in the department of the Cher [1] red Roman ware and that with a black micaceous paste were found; red ware at Esclas [2] near Darney in Vosges, at Limoges in the Haute Vienne,[3] at Aix and Nismes,[4] in Provence, and Languedoc, and at Vienne in Dauphiny; at Paris in the gardens of the Luxembourg, and at St. Geneviève. At Bourdeaux were found the red ware, the black Roman ware and that with white, yellow and red pastes.[5] Large specimens of red ware of an elliptical shape were exhumed east of Thiers near Lezoux, together with moulds, stamps, and the remains of a pottery;[6] as also near Clermont.[7] Amphoræ joined with lead were found at Mont-labathie-Salèon, near Aspres, in the High Alps,[8] Chatelet, between St. Dizier and Joinville in Champagne, the Samian ware with potters' names, dull red ware, that of a yellowish white tint, with a leaden glaze, and others of a black earth with a brown [9] or black lustre.

Roman red ware has also been discovered on the banks of the Seine near Anières at Mount Ganelon, in Oise at Compiègne,[10] near Beauvais,[11] and at Limeray near Dieppe, in Normandy;[12] at Maulevrier near Caudebec in Normandy,

[1] Traité, i. 444.
[2] M. Jollois, Cimitière d'Orléans. Pl. xvi.; Brongniart, l. c.
[3] Brongniart, l. c.
[4] Ménard, Antiq. de Nismes; Brongniart, i. 445.
[5] Brongniart, i. 441; Grivaud de la Vincelle.
[6] Jouannet de Bourdeaux; Antiquités Sépulchrales de la Gironde; Rec.

Académie de Bourdeaux, 1831.
[7] Brongniart, i. 445; Mus. Cer. ix. 1, 8, 13.
[8] Brongniart, i. 445.
[9] Brongniart, i. 408, 445.
[10] Grignon, Bulletin des feuilles faites par l'ordre du roi, 8vo. Paris, 1774.
[11] Brongniart, l. c. 442.
[12] Brongniart, i. 442, Pl. xxxv. 19.

together with coins of Gallienus and Constantine; at
Sarthe near Mans, 2000 pieces, as well as the vitrified
bricks of a furnace, and a cruse, with the name of Tertiolus,
either maker or proprietor, were dug up in throwing
a bridge over the river. They were all broken, some
stamped with the names of Severus, Bassus, Crassus, &c.
At Loiret in the Orleannois, in Brequeruque in the Pays
de Calais, at Noyelles sur Mer[1] in the department of the
Somme, red, black, and yellow Roman ware have also
been found.

Some of the pottery found at Agen resembled the
Samian, but was of a softer paste and exhibited some
local peculiarities. The names of the potters also differed
from those of the usual lists. It has been supposed that
these vases might have been made by potters settled upon
the spot, and it is certain that the Romans, whose villages
must have been decorated by Roman workers in mosaic,
had local potters.

In Italy this ware has been found chiefly at Arezzo, and
also at Hadria, Modena, and other northern sites.
Fine specimens, far surpassing in size and art those of
northern and western Europe, have been discovered at
Capua.[2]

Of Western Europe it now only remains to mention
Spain, in which country numerous specimens of this ware
have been discovered. Saguntum, praised by Pliny[3] for
its calices, or drinking cups, may have been one of the
sites where this pottery was manufactured; Pliny places it

[1] Brongniart, i. 442, 443.
[2] Riccio, Notizie degli scavamenti del suolo dell' antica Capua, 4to. Napoli, 1855, p. 13, Tav. iv. v. viii.
[3] N. H. xxxv. c. 46; Brongniart, i· 455.

in about the third rank.   Martial[1] mentions "a nest of
seven little vases, *septenaria synthesis*, the clayey turning
of the Spanish wheel, polished with the thick glaze of the
Saguntine potter" as part of a dinner set of a person of
moderate circumstances.   In another place he says,
"Nothing is more odious to me than the old cups of Euctus.
I prefer the cymbia made of Saguntine clay."[2]

Saguntum appears to have manufactured boxes, cups,[3]
cymbia, calices,[4] and lagenæ,[5] or bottles.   The actual ware
found at Murviedo[6] is classed under four different kinds,
viz. : 1. The Roman red ware.   2. A cinericious kind.
3. Yellow with certain red spots.   4. Whitish terra-cotta,
unglazed, of the colour of the clay used for bricks and
tiles.   The pieces of the first class were of the usual shape,
and many had the names of the potters.   The same re-
mark applies to those of the second class.   Those of the
third class had only two branches of wild palm stamped
inside ; and those of the last kind had inscriptions incised
upon the tiles and on necks of the amphoræ, some in
Greek, as the name Hermogenes,—in Latin, as "Lucii
Herennii officina,"—others apparently in the Celtiberian
character.

In England the various kinds of Roman red ware are
scattered all over the island, and specimens are every-

[1] "Et crasso figuli polita cœlo,
Septenaria synthesis Sagunti,
Hispanæ luteum rotæ toreuma."
                    —Martial, iv. 46.
[2] "Archetypis vetuli nihil est odio-
        sius Eucti ;
Ficta Saguntino cymbia malo luto."
                    —Martial, viii. 6.
    " Quæ non sollicitus teneat servet-
        que minister

Sume Saguntino pocula ficta luto."
                    —Martial, xiv. 108.
[4] " Calicum tantum Surrentum, Asta,
Pollentia, in Hispania Saguntum."—
Pliny, xxxv. 12.
[5] " Pugna Saguntina fervet commissa
        lagena."—Juv. v. 29.
[6] Valcarcel, Barros Saguntinos, 8vo.
Valencia, 1779.

where turned up with the spade or the plough on all the old Roman sites. The pages of the Archæologia are filled with descriptions of these remains, which have been discovered in abundance on the site of the old city of London, principally near the Bridge,[1] and its vicinity ; [2] at Gloucester ; [3] at Southfleet ; [4] great quantities have also been dug up on the banks of the Medway in the Upchurch Marshes, leading to Sheerness,[5] together with a local fabric of a bluish-black ware.

Roman vases of different wares have also been discovered at Chesterford,[6] at Ickleton near Saffron Walden,[7] at Stanway,[8] at Mount Bures,[9] at Colchester,[10] and at Billericay.[11] A kiln has been found at Ashdon ; [12] false Samian ware at Appleford[13] and Comberton.[14] At Mereworth,[15] Canterbury,[16] East Fairleigh,[17] and Hartlip,[18] Samian and other vases have been exhumed ; but the most remarkable, as well as the earliest discovery of Samian ware, was on the Pan sand, off Margate.[19] Castor ware has been found in the Hoo Marsh, near Rochester.[20] At Richborough [21] all sorts of ware have been discovered. Sussex

[1] Archæologia, xxiv. Pl. xliii. xliv. xxvii. p. 190.

[2] Bermondsey, Journ. Brit. Arch. Assoc. i. 313.

[3] Archæologia, x. Pl. ix. 2, p. 131; Journal, Brit. Assoc. ii. 324.

[4] Archæologia, p. 37.

[5] Journal, Brit. Arch. Assoc. ii. p. 131 ; Roach Smith, Collectanea, Pl. ix. x.

[6] R. C. Neville, Ant. Explor. 8vo. 1847 ; Journal Brit. Arch. Assoc. 173 ; Arch. Journ. xii. 85.

[7] Arch. Journ. vi. 17.

[8] Journ. Brit. Arch. Assoc. ii. 45.

[9] Brongniart Traité, i. 449.

[10] Journ. Brit. Arch. Assoc. ii. 4, vii. 109.

[11] Journ. Brit. Arch. Assoc. iii. 250.

[12] Arch. Journ. x. 21.

[13] Journ. Brit. Arch. Assoc. iii. 328.

[14] Arch. Journ. vi. 210.

[15] Arch. Journ. xi. 404.

[16] Ibid.

[17] Journ. Brit. Arch. Assoc. ii. 4.

[18] R. Smith, Coll. ii. p. 12.

[19] Phil. Trans. xiv. p. 519 ; Shaw, History of Staffordshire Pottery, p. 93 ; Archæologia, v. 282, 290.

[20] Journ. Brit. Arch. Assoc. v. 339.

[21] R. Smith, Ant. Richborough, 8vo. Lond. 1850.

abounds in Roman wares. Samian, and also the glazed maroon ware, having been found at Chichester,[1] Newhaven,[2] and Maresfield.[3] Black unglazed ware has been found at Binstead,[4] and a local black glazed ware with the kilns and potteries in the New Forest.[5] Samian and other wares have been dug up at Dorchester, the Isle of Purbeck,[6] Portland,[7] and Exeter.[8] Similar wares have been found at the Fleam Dyke,[9] and throughout Cambridgeshire. A local fabric of a yellow Castor ware has been discovered at Boultham, near Lincoln ;[10] also at Towcester,[11] Cirencester, and other sites in Gloucestershire. The red and black glazed ware, and the kilns for baking them, and other potteries, have been discovered at Castor,[12] along the banks of the Nen,[13] at Sibson, and the Bedford Purlieus. At Headington [14] numerous mortaria of yellow Castor and other wares, and at Deddington [15] Samian ware has been exhumed. A kiln and a pottery, resembling the German, has been found at Marlborough. Samian and black glazed ware has been excavated at Bath, Samian and other Roman wares at York,[16] and in the north of England, at Caerleon and Carnarvon in Wales ;[17] in fact throughout the whole of the island, and even in the Channel Islands.

In Holland Samian ware has been discovered at

[1] Arch. Journ. xi. 26; Journ. Brit. Arch. Assoc. iv. 158.
[2] Arch. Journ. ix. 263.
[3] Journ. Brit. Arch. Assoc. v. 390.
[4] Arch. Journ. ix. 12.
[5] Arch. Journ. ix. 23, x. 8.
[6] Arch. Journ. vii. 384.
[7] Arch. Journ. x. 61.
[8] Arch. Journ. ix. 9.
[9] Arch. Journ. ix. 229, x. 224, 225.
[10] Arch. Journ. xii. 173.
[11] Journ. Brit. Arch. Assoc. vii. 109.
[12] Journ. Brit. Arch. Assoc. i. 1.
[13] Ibid.
[14] Journ. Brit. Arch. Assoc. vi. 58.
[15] Arch. Journ. viii. 423.
[16] Arch. Journ. vi. 36.
[17] Arch. Journ. vii. 219.

Rossem, Arentsburg,[1] Wijk-bij, Duurstede,[2] and elsewhere. In eastern Europe it is found in quantities along the Danube, Greece, Asia Minor, and the Isles, and at Balaclava, and Kertch, having been carried by commerce beyond the limits of Roman conquests.

ENAMELLED WARE.

There is another kind of pottery found sparingly among Roman remains which has been supposed to be Roman. The paste is generally of a yellow colour, and over this has been laid a thick coat of enamel, of a pale blue, green, yellow, brown, or olive. The shape in which it principally occurs is that of lamps ; but fragments of small vases and jars are also found. It is a later kind of the enamelled ware of the Etruscan sepulchres already described. Very few instances of its discovery in England are known, although some fragments were found in the pits at Ewell, in Surrey, having a glaze produced by lead.[3]

Many vases of this ware have been discovered in Italy, especially at Pompeii and Cervetri. Some amphoræ, measuring 11 inches high ; others in shape of jars, *ollæ ;* wine bottles, *urcei ;* of the wine-skin, *uter ;* small jars, urnæ, and lamps. The larger are ornamented with reliefs, *anaglypha,* or *emblemata,* dispersed at distant intervals on the surface of the vase, and stamped as *crustæ* from separate moulds, and then affused. The smaller

---

[1] Leemans, Romische oudheiden, 8vo. Leyd. 1842.

[2] Jannsen, oudheidkundige Mededeelengen, 8vo, Leyd. 1842.

[3] Archæologia, xxxii. p, 451.

vases, such as lamps, are made entirely in moulds. Their
subjects are Hercules, Bacchus, a goddess sacrificing,
Abundantia, on a lamp is a Gorgon, treated in the usual
coarse style of Roman art. They have been supposed to
be Alexandrian.

There are in the Louvre some remarkable specimens
of Greek glazed ware of the Roman period, found at
Tarsus. The glaze appears to have been produced by
lead ; the colours are green, red, yellow, and blue.[1] The
objects, which are small, were made in moulds like the
Roman red ware. The subjects are various patterns of
leaves and flowers in relief. Amongst the fragments are
portions of a vase with two handles, half of an oscillum
or mask, and some fragments of red ware, like the so-called
Samian, and of finer paste. One of these pieces, inscribed in characters, shows that it was later than the
Antonines. A bottle also in the Museum, ornamented
with masks and other subjects in relief, and of a style
almost mediæval, was found with Roman remains.

---

[1] It reads, [E]MNHCΘHCAN ΦIΛΕTAIPШI "they told, or re- membered Philetærus " . . . but the sense it is difficult to make out.

PART V.

—◆—

CELTIC, TEUTONIC, AND SCANDINAVIAN POTTERY.

CHAPTER I.

Celtic pottery—Paste—Fabric—Ornamentation—Size—Shapes—Sepulchral use—
British—Bascauda—Ornamentation—Triangular patterns—Bosses—Distri-
bution—Scottish—Irish—Type of urns—Ornamentation — Distribution—
Teutonic—Paste—Shapes—Hut vases—Ornamentation and distribution—
Scandinavian pottery—Type—Analogy with Celtic.

CELTIC POTTERY.

It is difficult to draw a line of distinction between the Celtic pottery and the black Gallo-Roman ware, as this was evidently a local ware made upon a Roman type and according to the principles of Roman art. The colour is owing to carbon. Brongniart [1] assigns this ware to the ancient Gauls, while he considers the first to be Gallo-Roman. There are some varieties of this ware which in shape and fabric resemble the German pottery, and are ornamented with zig-zags, salient lines, and reliefs

---

[1] Traité, i. p. 483.

in imitation of letters, arranged in zones or bands. Such pottery has been found at Gisors, in the tumuli of the ancient Gaulish races. It is coarse, of bad texture, very fragile, easily scratched with a knife, the paste either black or gray.

The pieces were often made upon the wheel, the marks of the potter's hands still remaining on the body of the vase ; and where the foot has not been hollowed, indications appear of sawing from the chuck or piece by which it was affixed to the table.[1]   They are rarely found of any considerable size, although some nearly as large as casks have been exhumed in Auvergne,[2] and in the Channel Islands.[3]   Some of these vases were an improved fabric consequent upon the contact of the Celt with a more polished people like the Romans, who by degrees introduced a certain elegance and refinement into the arts of that comparatively barbarous people.

The pottery which had preceded this, and which is found in the barrows or tumuli of the early Celtic race among the remains of stone or bronze weapons, and rude amber and glass beads, is of quite a distinct character, more resembling in its general appearance the urns of the Scandinavians and the vases of other primitive people, above all of the Teutonic tribes, who had but little knowledge of the ceramic art.   The paste consists of the clay found upon the spot, prepared without any irrigation, consequently coarse, and sometimes mixed with small pebbles, which appear to have been added for the sake of holding it compactly together.   It has undergone a

---

[1] Brongniart, Traité, i. p. 485.   [3] Journ. Brit. Arch. Assoc. 1847, p. 309.
[2] Ibid. 8, 11.

baking of a very imperfect kind, the paste being black internally, while at the sides it assumes the natural brown colour of the clay.

The vases are generally of an urn shape, with wide open mouths, and tapering at the feet; the lip is bevelled, and overlaps, thus giving them a peculiar form. As it is impossible, owing to their very great friability, that they could have been of much use for domestic purposes, it is probable that they were expressly made for sepulchral rites. Their style of ornament is of the simplest kind, cords and bands are laid round or down the vase, or the pattern is punctured or incised with a tool, tooth, or pointed piece of stick or bone, for the lower compartment; while the upper appears to have been made by binding a long strip of twisted skin spirally round the urn. The principal ornament is the herring-bone, the same which appears on the torcs, celts, bracelets, and glass beads, and is, perhaps, a representation of the tattooing or the painted marks on the body in use amongst the ancient Gauls and Britons. A few seem to be imitations of wreaths and such other simple ornaments as were placed on Roman ware. These ornaments differ,—each tribe and age probably adopting a different style; and while on most vases they are sparingly introduced, some examples are covered with them in most elaborate style, from the lip to the foot. The size of these vases is by no means inconsiderable, being on an average from 18 to 25 inches in height, and from 13 to 22 inches in diameter; while some measure 32 inches in height and 4 inches in diameter.[1] They are found in the barrows, generally

---

[1] Akerman, Archæological Index, 8vo, London, 1847, pp. 46, 47.

placed with their mouths downwards, like a dish-cover, protecting the ashes of the dead ; beads and rude personal adornments of the Celtic races are found with them, together with bronze, and sometimes iron weapons.

BRITISH POTTERY.

The vases found throughout England and Wales belong to the class above described, and only differ from others by their simpler forms and less elaborate ornamentation. Many small urns and vases have been found in British barrows, sometimes placed inside others, and holding the ashes of children or of the smaller domestic animals. The urns of each tribe, and even period, differ in ornamentation, paste, and shape. Those found in cairns on the Welsh coast have often a striking resemblance to the urns of the Irish Celts. All these vases have large wide mouths ; for the potter, not using a wheel, was obliged to fashion them by the hand, and could not make small necks or mouths by the fingers. They seldom have handles ; one or two vases with such appendages only having been found, but in their place projecting studs with holes bored to admit a cord for suspension. Such vases have been called censers, but more probably were used as pots or lamps in the huts of the Aborigines. Their colour varies from a light yellowish brown to an ashen gray hue ; and their ornaments are principally zig-zag or triangular, hatched, zones, and herring-bone, chiefly placed on the bevelled rim or lip. A few have bosses or knobs in bands around their body, and they are perhaps transitions to the Romano-British and Saxon ware, distinguished by their darker colour, bottle shape, and stamped ornaments. The Romans appear to have termed these vases *bascaudæ*, or baskets. A few other objects, besides vases, were made of this material, such as cylindrical cases to hold vases, and beads, some reeded, apparently in imitation of glass or enamelled beads.

No. 205.—Group of British Vases. The one in the centre is that of Bronwen.

The most important discoveries of these remains are those made in Wiltshire, a county which has produced many monuments of its former Celtic inhabitants. Many urns have been found in the vicinity of Dorchester ;[1]

[1] Archæologia, xxx. Pl. xvii.

others at Heytesbury[1] and Stourton,[2] Barrow Hills,[3] Lake,[4] Upton Level,[5] Everley,[6] Stonehenge,[7] Amesbury,[8] Winterbourne,[9] Fovant,[10] Durrington,[11] and Beckhampton, near Abury.[12] The west of England and Wales have probably produced the most interesting specimens of these urns, which, however, have been found in the South of England ; those of the northern and western parts of the island are most highly ornamented. They have also been found in various places in Sussex, especially in the vicinity of Brighton, in tumuli, on the racecourse ; at Lewes,[13] Storrington Downs,[14] Sullington Warren,[15] Alfriston,[16] and Clayton Hill.[17] In the adjoining county of Hampshire similar urns have been exhumed at Arbor Lowe,[18] at Bakewell,[19] and at Broughton, in the Isle of Wight.[20] In Kent they have been found at Iffin near Canterbury,[21] and at Beedon in Berkshire.[22] Many vases of this class have been discovered at Blandford,[23] Dorsetshire, in the Isle of Purbeck,[24] and at Badbury Camp.[25] They have been found at Broughton[26] and Wolden Newton[27] in Lincolnshire, at Culford,[28] at Felixstowe in Suffolk on the Matlow Hills, in the Fleam

[1] Sir R. Colt Hoare, Anc. Wilt. Pl. ix. viii.
[2] Ibid. Pl. i.
[3] Archæologia, xv. p. 343, xviii.
[4] Sir T. Colt Hoare, Anc. Wilt. pl. xxx.
[5] Ibid., xi.   [6] Ibid., xxii.
[7] Ibid., xvi.   [8] Ibid., xxiii. 4.
[9] Ibid., xiii. 15.   [10] Ibid., xxxiii. 4.
[11] Ibid., xvii.
[12] Horsfield, Hist. Lewes, p. 48, pl. v.
[13] Sussex Archæological Collections, i. p. 55.
[14] Cartwright, Rape of Bramber, p. 128.
[15] Suss. Arch. Coll. ii. 270.

[16] Suss. Arch. Coll. viii. 285.
[17] Journ. Brit. Assoc. Winch., 203.
[18] Ibid., 194.
[19] Arch. Journ., ix. 11.
[20] Journ. Brit. Arch. Assoc., 1856, p. 186.
[21] Arch., xxx. p. 327.
[22] Arch. Journ., vii. 67.
[23] The Barrow diggers, 4to, Lond. 1839, p. 91.
[24] Journ. Brit. Arch. Assoc., vii. 385.
[25] Arch., xvii. 338.
[26] Arch. Journ., viii. 343.
[27] Arch. Journ., vi. 184.
[28] Journ. Brit. Arch. Assoc., ii. 63.

Dyke,[1] Newmarket Heath,[2] and Royston [3] in Cambridge-shire, at Drayton,[4] and at Stow Heath [5] between Tullington and Aylsham in Norfolk.   In the midland counties similar vases have been discovered at Castor,[6] and Brixworth,[7] at Brassington Moor,[8] and Kingston in Derbyshire,[9] at King-ston upon Soar,[10] and at Great Malvern[11] in Worcestershire. In Shropshire these vases have occurred at Bulford,[12] and at Newark, while remarkable examples allied to the Irish urns were found at Port Dafarch,[13] Holyhead, in Anglesea, at Mynnyd Carn Goch in Glamorganshire,[14] and on the Breselu Hills [15] in Pembrokeshire.   One of the most remarkable is the vase which is supposed to have covered the ashes of Bronwen the fair, the daughter of Llyr Llediaith, the aunt of Caractacus, A. D. 50, found in A. D. 1818, on a carnedd or grave on the banks of the Alaw.[16]   In the north of England they have been dis-côvered at Scarborough,[17] York,[18] Bernaldy Moor, near Cleveland [19]; Fylingdale near Whitby ; [20] the Way Hagg, near Hackness ; [21] Furness, in Lancashire ; [22] Jesmond, near Newcastle-on-Tyne ;[23] Black Heddon, in Northumber-land, and elsewhere ; [24] and lastly at L'Ancresse, in Guernsey,[25] and Alderney,[26] amidst the barrows or tumuli

[1] Arch. Journ., ix. 226.
[2] Arch. Journ., iii. 225.
[3] Arch., xxxii. p. 359.
[4] Journ. Brit. Arch. Assoc. v. 154.
[5] Journ. Brit. Arch. Assoc. viii. 59, pl. 9.
[6] Journ. Brit. Arch. Assoc., 1853, 106.
[7] Journ. Brit. Arch. Assoc., iv. 142.
[8] Arch. Journ. i. 248.
[9] Journ. Brit. Arch. Assoc., ii. 62.
[10] Arch. Journ., iii. 154.
[11] Arch. Journ., vii. 67.
[12] Arch. Journ., vi. 319.
[13] Arch. Journ., x. 177.
[14] Arch. Cambr., 1856, 65.
[15] Arch. Journ., x. 177. [16] Ibid. vi. 326.
[17] Journ. Brit. Arch. Assoc., iii. 194, 103, 106, 107 ; Arch., xxx. 458.
[18] Wellbeloved, Descr., p. 8.
[19] Arch. Journ., i. 412.
[20] Arch. Journ., xiii. 95.
[21] Journ. Brit. Arch. Assoc., vi. 1.
[22] Arch. Journ., iii. 68.
[23] Arch. Journ., x. 3.
[24] As at Rombalds Moor. Arch., xxxvii. 306.   [25] Arch. Journ., i. 142, 149.
[26] Clay beads, Journ. Brit. Arch. Assoc. iii. 11.

which formed the graves of the early Celtic population, although in smaller numbers than vases of the different Roman wares.

SCOTTISH POTTERY.

The early pottery of Scotland found in the graves of the ancient inhabitants, principally of those of the so-called bronze period, anterior to, and contemporary with, the Roman conquest of Britain, is exactly like that of the rest of the island.   The vases are of two classes—those feebly baked and made by the hand, and those which appear to have been turned upon the wheel.[1]   The first comprising the urns, or *bascaudæ*, used for covering the ashes of the dead, often measure as much as sixteen inches high, and have the usual bevelled lip ; a few cups, and lamps with small side handles for a cord to sling them, and domestic vases resembling in shape the Roman olla, have been also found.   They are all wide-mouthed, and may have been used for quaffing the Pictish heather ale.   Their ornamentation also is of the simplest kind, consisting of the fern leaf pattern, the zig-zag, and herring-bone.   A few vases are ornamented all over the body as well as lip, and resemble those found in Ireland and upon the Welsh coast. Others have indented patterns.   These vases have been found all over Scotland, at Ronaldshay in Orkney,[2] Craik-raig in Sutherlandshire,[3] Banffshire,[4] Montrose,[5] Kinghorn

---

[1] Wilson, The Archæology and Pre-historic History of Scotland, 8vo, Edinburgh, 1851, p. 281.
[2] Wilson, p. 286.
[3] Ibid., 285.
[4] Arch. Scot., iv. 298, pl. xii.
[5] Wilson, p. 284.

in Fifeshire,[1] at Shealloch near Borthwick, and at Edinburgh ;[2] at Coilsfield,[3] at Banchory[4] and Memsie[5] in Aberdeenshire, and at Whitsome[6] in Berwickshire.

IRISH POTTERY.

The urns discovered in Ireland resemble the British in their form and material, but are often finer in colour, more complex in shape, and more elaborate in ornament ; the whole body of the urn being decorated with punctured marks, lines, zones, zig-zags, and bands. Some urns have a peculiar shape, the upper part, surmounting the jar-shaped body, being in the form of a truncated cone.[7] The prevalence of triangular and hatched ornament is peculiarly Celtic, and appears on the gold objects as well as the urns. In the Irish urns the resemblance to basket-work, in which coloured patterns were worked in, is still more distinct than in the British. The urns generally held or covered the ashes of the dead, but they were sometimes placed around the unburnt body. The most remarkable and beautiful are those found at Cairn Thierna,[8] county Cork, and at Killucken, county Tyrone.[9] Others have been discovered in a cromlech at Phœnix Park, Dublin ;[10] at Knowth, county Meath ;[11] at Powerscourt, county Wicklow ;[12] at Mount Stewart, county

[1] Ibid.
[2] Wilson, p. 290.
[3] Wilson, p. 333.
[4] Wilson, p. 283.
[5] Wilson, p. 287.
[6] New Stat. Arch. Berwick, ii. p. 171.
[7] Cf. the one from Cairn Thierna. Arch. Journ., vi. p. 191.

[8] Ibid., plate.
[9] Journ. Arch. Assoc., i. p. 224 ; Akerman, Arch. Index, pl. ii. 51.
[10] Wakeman, Handbook of Irish Antiquities, p. 5, 155.
[11] Molyneux, Essay on Danish Mounts.
[12] Arch. Journ., vi. p. 192.

Down ;[1] Mayhora, Castle Comar, Kilkenny ;[2] and at Mullingar.[3] They are anterior, and quite free from all traces of Roman civilisation.

GAULISH POTTERY.

The Roman dominion in Gaul has so completely swept away the distinct traces of the Celtic potteries, that it is difficult to point out any which can be referred to the Gauls before the Roman conquest.[4] Such as are found, mixed up with later remains, do not show that peculiarly Celtic type and ornamentation which are seen on the vases of the British isles. A few, however, supposed to be early Celtic, have been found at Fontenay-le-Marmion, in Calvados, near Dieppe, and in Bretagne, made of a black earth, badly prepared, filled with pebbles, breaking with a porous fracture. Their paste is externally of a rusty colour, and black inside. It breaks readily when dry, and can be ground to powder by the finger. Wetted it assumes the hue of decayed bark ; submitted again to the furnace it turns to a brick red colour, but becomes more brittle. These vases are of the rudest shape, and have neither been made in a mould nor turned upon the wheel, but fashioned by the hand, or scooped by rude instruments.[5] It has been supposed that a certain class of pottery, formed of black clay mixed with white pebbles, or ground-up shells, varying in colour from a deep black to a blackish gray or rusty colour, and sometimes glazed

---

[1] Dublin Penny Journal, i. p. 108.
[2] Arch. Journ., viii. 200.
[3] Archæologia, ii. p. 32.

[4] Caumont, Cours, i. p. 255.
[5] Caumont, Bull, Mon., v. 464 ; xiii. 111.

or coated with a carbonaceous black coating, is also of the early Celtic period. The walls of the vases are thicker and the paste more adhesive than the earliest Celtic, while the forms prove an acquaintance with Roman art, and cannot be assigned with certainty to the earlier epoch.[1] They have been found at Abbeville and Portelette.

TEUTONIC POTTERY.

Throughout the whole of Germany various kinds of pottery have been discovered. They are, however, reducible to three great classes. That of the early native population prior to the invasion of the Romans ; that made during the Roman conquest, which although exhibiting local peculiarities of paste and ornamentation, belongs to the Roman wares ; that imported, consisting of red ware made at Arretium, Capua, Modena, and other places in Italy. The two last classes having been already described, there only remains the first which has, unfortunately, not been hitherto carefully discriminated from the others. It must be borne in mind that the Celtic and Anglo-Saxon wares, one class of Teutonic pottery discovered in England, are easily discriminated, the latter being more bottle-shaped, made of a dark paste, with thinner walls, with oblate globular bodies, narrower necks, and having stamped around them a regular band of ornaments, from a die of bone, wood, or metal.

Urns very similar to those of the Celtic potteries have

[1] M. Ravin in M. Boucher de Perthes, Ant. Celt, p. 509.

been found all over Germany, along with the remains of the Teutonic races. They are assignable to an age antecedent to and co-ordinate with the Roman empire, and bear considerable resemblance to those of the Pagan Saxons. They are friable in texture, with punctured patterns, and are grouped round the corpses in the graves of the Teutonic tribes, or are employed to hold their ashes or offerings to the dead.[1]   They are intermediate between the Mexican and early Greek.

The paste of some of these urns is very friable, that of others rings like stone ware when struck by the hand.   It is composed of clay and sand, intermixed with particles of white, yellow, red, or brown mica, which seems to have been introduced either to strengthen the clay or produce a glittering appearance.[2]

The colour of the paste varies according to the localities. The vases at Rossleben and Bottendorf consisted, partly of yellow earth, partly of black, mixed with white quartz pebbles.   Those at Bergen, in Hanover, were of unctuous earth, with a shining blue coating.   Urns of gray or brown paste have been discovered between Cacherin, Gisborn, and Langendorf, in the county of the Wends. In Lauenstein the pottery is gray and well baked.   In Lausitz   and Silesia it is of all varieties of brown, gray, and black colour.   Many of the smaller vases have, as in the Celtic pottery, been modelled by the hand, but the larger urns bear decided marks of having been turned upon the wheel.   Among them are found saucers, plates, cups, goblets with one

---

[1] Keferstein, Keltisch. Altherthum.   [2] Klemm, Handbuch, s. 169.
8vo, Halle, 1846, s. 311—313.

handle, jars, small amphoræ, and bottles. The
handles are generally small, but in some of the jugs
they are as large as
those found under the Ro-
mans. They are rarely
moulded at their edges.
Some few vases are di-
vided with inner vases, as
if used like little boxes ;
others have feet to stand
upon. Their ornaments
are either painted with
colours, or moulded, or
engraved. Generally the

No. 206.—Anglo-Saxon Urn.　From Norfolk.

artist has been content to raise bosses in circles, a series
of lunettes upon the clay of the vase, or bosses pressed
out from within, or studs laid on in separate pieces ;
but in some instances, as in the Etruscan canopi and
Egyptian vases, he has moulded a human head with more
or less skill, but always rudely. Another mode of decoration was that of puncturing or incising the paste.[1] The
ornaments were the hatched lines, bands of points concentric to the axis of the vases, zigzags, screw lines perpendicular to the axis, mæanders, chequers, network lines,
semicircles and dots, diagonals, triangles, lunes, and pen-
tagonal ornaments, all peculiar to the Teutonic pottery.
Some of the ornaments, such as the mæander, are probably
as late as the Roman Empire. The ornaments of other
vases are painted in red and yellow by means of ochreous
earth, and in black by black lead. These are arranged in

[1] Brongniart, Traité, i. 471.

parallel zones or lines.   The vases found in Central
Germany, between the Weser and the Oder, are more
ornamented than those of the North.[1]

The principal shapes are, cups with or without small
handles ; pots resembling the British urns, with bevelled
mouths, found near the Black Elsler, small one-handled
cups like the modern tea-cup ; goblets, of which the most
remarkable are the long-necked double-handled of the
Wends, others in the shape of modern tumblers, flasks,
and bottles ; diotæ or amphoræ with small handles.
Some urns resemble, by their tall necks and bosses, the
Anglo-Saxon, and a remarkable kind of urn has a broad
hemispherical shoulder, and long pointed foot, resembling
those in which olives are still transported.   Some few are
apparently toys, such as the rattles found at Bautzen and
Oschatz, and a bird found at Luben ; others have been
found [2] with human feet, in shape of horns, pierced for
censers, or grouped in threes.   But a scientific classification of the German potteries, according to race and age,
is a research still to be undertaken.

Vast quantities of them have been discovered in the
tumuli of Schkopau, near Merseburg,[3] at the ancient
Suevenhock or Schwenden Hügel (Swedes Hill), the
greater part however broken by rabbits, and in Saxony
between Dresden and Meissen, and near Leipzig, in the
village of Connevitz ; at the mouth of the Black Elsler,
near the Elbe, 800 tumuli have been opened, and various
vases have been found near Gusmandorf, on the right

---

[1] Klemm, Handbuch, s. 171.

[2] Klemm, Handbuch, xii. xiii. xiv.

[3] Brongniart,   i. p.   476 ;   Kruse,

Deutsch alterthum, Hall, 1824, i. p. 73,
Pl. 1.

bank of the Elbe.[1]   At Mecklenburg the vases assume
more of the Scandinavian type.[2]   They have been found
at Kummer, Stolpe, Dobbersten, Spornitz, Marnitz, Lud-
wigslust, Timkenberg, and Stargard.   The vases found in
Western Germany, on the banks of the Rhine, have
moulded lips like the Roman ware, and are apparently
made after Roman types.   They have been found at Schier-
stein and Kemel, and in fact throughout all Germany.

Some remarkable sepulchral urns resembling those of

No. 207.—Group of Hut-shaped Vases, from Halberstadt, Kiekindemark, and
Aschersleben.

the early inhabitants of Alba Longa, already mentioned,
have been found in Germany, and are distinctly Teutonic.
They occur in the sepulchres of the period when bronze
weapons were used, and before the predominance of Roman
art.   One found at Mount Chemnitz, in Thüringen, had a

[1] Brongniart, i. p. 476; Wagner   [2] Schrötter & Lisch, Museum Fride-
in Kruse, Arch., iii. pt. ii. p. 16, et   rico-Franciscum, Leipsig, 1827.
seq. Pl. i. ii.

cylindrical body and conical top, imitating a roof. In
this was a square orifice, representing the door or
window, by which the ashes of the dead were introduced, and the whole then secured by a small door
fastened with a metal pin. A second vase was found
at Roenne ; a third in the island of Bornholm. A
similar urn exhumed at Parchim had a shorter body,
taller roof, and door at the side. Still more remarkable
was another found at Aschersleben, which has its cover
modelled in shape of a tall conical thatched roof, and the
door with its ring still remaining, Another with a taller
body and flatter roof, with a door at the side, was found
at Klus, near Halberstadt.[1]   The larger vases were used
to hold the ashes of the dead, and are sometimes protected by a cover, or stone, or placed in another vase of
coarser fabric.   The others are the household vessels,
which were offered to the dead filled with different viands.
Some of the smaller vases appear to have been toys.

Extraordinary popular superstitions have prevailed
amongst the German peasantry as to the origin and nature
of these vases, which in some districts are considered to
be the work of the elves—in others to grow spontaneously
from the ground like mushrooms—or to be endued with
remarkable properties for the preservation of milk and
other articles of food.[2]   Weights to sink nets, balls, disks,
and little rods of terra-cotta are also found in the graves.

[1] Lisch, ueber die Hausurnen, 8vo,   [2] Keferstein, Kelt. Alt., p. 311.
Schwerin, 1856.

SCANDINAVIAN POTTERY.

Connected with this class, and finishing as it were the series of these remains, is the Scandinavian pottery, which resembles in many particulars that of the Teutonic populations, and is intermediate between the Celtic and the earlier or Pagan Saxon. Its paste is coarse, and much interspersed with calcareous substances and particles of mica.[1] It was made of the local clay and not turned on the lathe, but fashioned with the hand in the lap, a method still retained in Scandinavia.[2] It is probable that it was baked in a way still practised in Scandinavia, namely, by placing the pieces in a hole in the ground, and surrounding them with hay, which is then burnt ; a feeble process, indeed, but yet sufficient for vases only intended to cover the ashes of the dead..[3] The paste is either of a very dark gray, or of a light brown colour. Such at least are those in the Museum at Sèvres. The form is more regular than the Celtic, but not so good as the Roman ; the ornaments are also more distinct, but the baking is feeble.

The prevalent shape is the *olla* or jar, some of which have perforations or little handles at the sides, apparently for cords by which they might be carried. Some rare examples have conical lids. Smaller vases of other shapes are also found. The prevalent ornamentation is the fret or herring-bone, and triangular bands, arranged horizontally or vertically to the axis of the vase. They are found in the oldest tombs of the so-called stone period,[4] and held

[1] Brongniart, Traité, i. p. 480, Pl. xxvi. xxvii. [2] Ibid. [3] Brongniart, Mus. Cer. x. fig. 10, 11.

[4] Worsaae, Primæval Antiquities of Denmark, by W. J. Thoms, 8vo, Lond. 1849, p. 21.

or covered the ashes of the oldest inhabitants of the Cimbric Chersonese.

In the specimens of this ware hitherto published, the shapes bear a resemblance to those found in Greece and Germany rather than in England. Thus, an elegantly formed hemispherical cup, another with two large handles resembling the Greek scyphos, a diota and amphora with tall and narrow cylindrical necks, apparently well turned, have been attributed to the stone period.[1] Such vases were apparently turned on the wheel, and could hardly have been moulded by the hand. The vases of the Bronze period also bear more resemblance to the German than British pottery. The most remarkable shapes are the hut-urn, a kind of amphora, and a tall jar surmounted by a cover.[2] The remains of the Iron Age are contemporary with the Saxon or Christian period, and belong to another branch of the study of the fictile art.

Future researches, more accurate observations, and scientific examination of the remains of the Northern races, will help to class more strictly the pottery of the rude tribes, to assign its ethnological character, and geographical distribution. Amongst those remote from Roman conquest, or those antecedent to the rise of the Empire of the West, may be traced ornaments and types which show the influence of a higher civilisation. The slave's ashes in the *olla* of the Eternal City, those of the unconquered chieftain of the North in his rude urn ; the Etruscan larth's in the model of his house, the

---

[1] Worsaae, Afbildninger, 4to, Kjö-benhavn, 1854, pl. 16.

[2] Ibid., pl. 54.

Teutonic leader's in his hut-shaped urn, the Briton's
ashes covered by the inverted jar, the Roman legionary
laid in his last home roofed with tiles, show one
common idea of sepulture, one universal application of
the potter's art.

Yet time and patience unclose many mysteries. There
are in art, as in literature, certain diacritical signs, which
enable those initiated to fix what appears at first sight to
elude apprehension. Not only each tribe and family use
a separate type of shape and ornamentation, but even
these are in their turn insensibly influenced by time and
external circumstances. Hence the advance and progress
of certain races, as relates to themselves or as compared
with others, are to be seen in their monumental remains.
For the history of those races which have left no written
records, no inscribed memorials, the pottery is an invaluable guide. It may be compared with those fossil remains
by which man attempts to measure the chronology of the
earth, for the pottery of each race bears with it internal
evidence of the stratum of human existence to which it
belongs. Its use is anterior to that of metals; it is as
enduring as brass. All the pottery of the northern races
is of the lowest order with respect to those qualities which
characterise excellence in the potter's art. Their kilns, it
is evident, were of the rudest and feeblest kind; little
care was paid to the preparation of the clay, and the
fashioning was a mere rude modelling with the hand.
The simplest kind of ornamentation delighted the inhabitants of the rude huts of the north. In no instance has
the potter left either his name or other inscription on the
vessels he made; and their age and fabric have to be

searched for in the objects which surround them, or in the character of the locality where they are found. Great doubts will for some time prevail as to their actual age, and even the divisions of time supposed to be marked by the so-called ages of Stone, Bronze, and Iron are not definitely settled. When the potter's art arrives at perfection, it charms by the impress of the art which embellishes it, but the examples in its infancy instruct by the clue it affords to the primitive art of mankind. A due knowledge of the great distinction of the various products of the art of pottery amongst the ancients is essential to a perfect knowledge of the relative antiquity of races and sites. The use of letters is comparatively recent, the glyptic and graphic arts only exist in their later forms as exercised on unperishable materials ; but in every quarter of the world fictile fragments of the earliest efforts lie beneath the soil, fragile but enduring remains of the time when the world was in its youth.

APPENDIX.

No. I. (Vol. I., p. 165.)

MAGISTRATES' NAMES INSCRIBED ON GREEK BRICKS AND TILES.

ΕΓΙ ΑΓΗΣΑΝΔΡΟΥ
... ΑΙΣΧΥΛΙΣΚΟΥ
... ΑΛΚΑΙΟΥ
... ΑΝΔΡΩΝΟΣ
... ΑΓΟΛΛΟΔΩΡΟΥ
... ΑΡΙΣΤΟΚΛΕΟΣ
... ΦΙΛΩΝΙΔΑ
ΟΕΡΟΚΡΑΤ[Ε],
ΟΣ ΑΣΤΥΝ[ΟΜΟΥ]

ΕΓΙ ΑΣΚΛΗΓΙΟΔΩΡΟΥ
... ΒΟΙΣΚΟΥ
... ΒΟΥΒΑΛΟΥ
... ΔΑΜΟΣΤΡΑΤΟΥ
... ΔΑΜΩΝΟΣ
... ΦΑΛΑΚΡΟΥ
ΑΣΤΥΝΟΜΟΥ
ΓΟΣΙΟΣ ΤΟΥ ΑΣΤΥΟΥ
ΜΙΛΤΙΑΔΗΣ

No. II. (Vol. I., p. 186.)

LAMP MAKERS.

ΑΤΥ
ΠΡΟ
ΑΡΥ
ΠΡΟΚ
ΑΒΑCΚΑΝΤΟΥ

ΑΓΥΡΙ
ΓΕΡΜΑΝΙΚΟΥ.... ΙΟν
ΣΕΒΑΣ
ΓΑΙΟΥ
ΔΙΟΚΛΙΤ[ΙΑΝΟΥ]

APPENDIX.

ΣΙΤΤΙΟΥ
ΣΗΤΗΣ
ΚΑΤ
ΚΕΛΕω
ΚΕΛϹΕΙ

ΕΝΓΛΟΙΑ
ΛΑΒΕ ΜΕ ΤΟΝ ΗΛΙΟϹΕ-
ΡΑΠΙΝ
ΙΓΓΑΡΧΟΥ
ΠΡΕΙΜΟΝ

No. III.   (Vol. I. p. 193.)

LIST OF MAGISTRATES' NAMES FOUND ON THE MEDALLIONS OF
RHODIAN AMPHORÆ.

Ænctor	Aristocrates	Damænetus	Menestheus
Æschines	Aristodemos	Damocles	Menestratus
Agastophanes	Aristogenes	Damocrates	Nicasagorus
Agathocles	Aristogiton	Damophilus	Nicomachus
Agoranax	Aristomachus	Demetrius	Nicostratus
Alexander	Ariston	Diocles	Pædippus
Alexiades	Aristopolios	Dionysius	Pausanias
Aleximachus	Aristratus	Dorcylidas	Pecciratus
Anaxander	Arnibius	Eucratidas	Philænius
Anaxibulus	Arylædes	Euphranor	Philocrates
Anaximachus	Astymedes	Evanor	Philodamus
Andrias	Athenodotus	Gorgon	Pisistratus
Andromachus	Atimus	Harpacus	Polyaratus
Andronicus	Autocrates	Harpocrates	Pythodorus
Antipater	Callianax	Heragoras	Pythogenes
Archecrates	Callicrates	Hestiæus	Rhodon
Archelaides	Callias	Hieron	Sicanus
Archembrotus	Clearchus	Hippocrates	Socrates
Archidamus	Cleinostratus	Jason	Sosicles
Archinus	Cleocrates	Laphidas	Sostratus
Aristæus	Cleonymus	Leontidas	Symmachus
Aristagoras	Cleisimbrotidas	Linctor	Thersander
Aristanax	Cratagoras	Lysippus	Thestor
Aristides	Cratidas	Marsyas	Timagoras
Aristocles	Creon	Menedemus	Timocrates

Timarchus	Timotheus	Tisamenes	Xenophon
Timodicus	Timoxenus	Xeno	Zeno
Timorrhodus	Tisagoras	Xenophantus	

For a fuller list, see Böckh. Corpus Inscr. Græc. (Vol. III.. Præf. p. v.—xiv.)

The months are,—Thesmophorius, Diosthyus, Agrianus, Pedageitnius, Badromius, Artamitius, Theudæsius, Dalius, Hyacinthius, Sminthius, Carneius, Panamus, a second Panamus. A Neomenia is also mentioned.

See Trans. Roy. Soc. Lit. iii., p. 38.

No. IV. (Page 195.)

RHODIAN AMPHORÆ, SQUARE LABELS WITH EMBLEMS.

ΑΡΙΣΤΕΙΔΟV
ΚΛΕΑΡΧΟΥ (head of Apollo)
ΚΛΕΟΚΡΑΤΕVΣ
ΚΡΑΤΙΔΑ
ΣVΜΜΑΧΟΥ
ΞΕΝΟΦΩΝΤΟΣ
ΜΕΝΕΣΤΡΑΤΟΥ (head of Medusa)

ΠΡΩΤΟΥ
ΣΟΣΙΚΛΕVΣ
ΦΙΛΟΚΡΑΤΕVΣ
ΑΝΔΡΙΚΟΥ (caduceus)
ΑΝΔΡΟΝΙΚΟΥ
ΑΝΤΙΜΑΧΟΥ
ΑΡΙΣΤΩΝΟΣ
ΚΑΛΛΩΝΟΣ
ΔΑΜΟΚΡΑΤΕVΣ
ΔΡΑΚΟΝΤΙΔΑ
ΕΥΚΛΕΙΤΟΥ
ΗΦΑΙΣΤΙΟΝΟΣ
ΙΕΡΟΚΛΕVΣ

ΙΜΑ
ΜΙΔΑ (bunch of grapes and caduceus)
ΣΩΚΡΑΤΕVΣ (torch and garland)
ΟΛVΜΠΟV
ΜΕΝΟΘΕΜΙΔΟΣ (two cornucopiæ and bipennis)
ΜΕΝΕΣΤΡΑΤΟV (dolphin and anchor)
ΑΜVΝΤΑ (wreath)
ΒΡΟΜΙΟΥ
ΘΕΟΔΩΡΟΥ
ΑΡΙΣΤΑΡΧΟΥ (stars)
ΔΡΑΚΟΝΤΙΔΑ (anchor)
ΠVΘΟΓΕΝΕVΣ (rat)
ΔΑΜΑΤΡΙΟV (caps of Dioscuri)
ΝΙΚΙΑ
ΦΙΛΟΣΤΕΦΑΝΟV (parazonium)
ΦΙΛΟΚΡΑΤΕVΣ

ΓΡΩΤΟΥ
ΣΩΣΙΚΛΕΥΣ
ΗΡΑΚΛΕΙΩΝΟΣ (bunch of grapes)
ΜΕΝΕΚΛΕΥΣ
ΜΙΔΑ
ΘΕΜΙΣΩΝΟΣ
ΑΘΑΝΟΤΟΥ (cornucopiæ)

ΡΟΔΩΝΟΣ
ΔΙΟΔΟΤΟΥ (fish)
ΙΣΙΔΩΡΟΥ (acrostolium)
ΑΡΙΣΤΟΚΡΑΤΕΥΣ (crosses flowered)
ΑΡΙΣΤΕΙΔΑ (head of Apollo)
ΚΛΕΑΡΧΟΥ

And others. See Böchk. Corp. Inscr. Græc. l. c.

No. V. (Vol. I., p. 196.)

NAMES OF CNIDIAN MAGISTRATES.

Agathinus	Callidamas	Eugenes	Philambulus
Alcæus	Cleodotus	Euphragoras	Philinus
Alcidamas	Cleombrotus	Eurilaus	Philombroti-
Alexander	Chrysippus	Heniochus	das
Amyntas	Dædalus	Hermocritus	Poliuchus
Anactagoras	Damocritus	Hipparchus	Protagoras
Anaxander	Democles	Hippolochus	Theodoridas
Apollonidas	Diocles	Maro	Therocrates
Apollonius	Diodotus	Menecrates	Thersander
Archagoras	Diogenes	Menestratus	Theudorus
Aristagathus	Dionysus	Menippus	Theuphides
Aristocles	Eirenidas	Nicasibulus	Timacles
Aristogenes	Eubulus	Nicias	Timoxenus
Ariston	Euclides	Nicidas	Xanthus
Asclepiodorus	Eucrates	Nicippus	Zenas
Athenæus			

The formula on the handles of the amphoræ is ΚΝΙ, ΚΝΙΔΙ, ΚΝΙΔΙΟΝ.

See Trans. R. Soc. Lit. iii. p. 61 ; Böckh. Corp. Inscr., No. 1851—1863 ; and Vol. III., Præf. p. xiv.—xvii.

No. VI. (Vol. I., p. 199.)

NAMES ON HANDLES FOUND AT OLBIA.

LIST OF ASTYNOMI.

Αισχινης
Αισχριων[ο] Αρτεμιδωρου
Απολλοδωρος[ο] Διονυσιου
Απολλωνιος
Ατταλος
Ατταλος Βορυος
Βορυς Διονυσιου
Βορυς Εστιαιου
Γλαυκιας
Διονυσιος
Διονυσιος Αγαθωνος
Διονυσιος Απημαντου
Διονυσιος ο Απημαντου
Διονυσιος ο Διονυσιου
Εκαταιος
Εκαταιος Αρτεμιδωρου
Εστιαιος Βορυος
Εστιαιος Κλεαινετου
Εστιαιος Μιθραδατου
Ευκλης ο Απολλωνιου
Ζηνις ο Απολλοδωρου
Ηρακλειδης
Ηρακλειδης ο Εκαταιου
Ηροκρατης
Θεαγενης ο Νεικανορος
Θεοδωρος

Ικεσιος ο Σωσιος
Ιππων Διονυσιου
Ιρωνυμος ο Ιρωνυμου
Ιστρων ο Απολλωνιδα
Ιφικρατης Νευμηνιου
Καλλισθενης
Μανης
Μαντιθεος ο Πρωταγορι ν
Μνησικλης Αριστωνος
Μνησικλης Πυθου
Ναυτιων
Πολυστρατος
Ποσειδωνιος
Ποσις ο Αστειου
Πρωταγορας ο Κυνισκου
Πτολεμαιος Διοφαντου
Πυθοκλης Καλλισθενους
Πυθοχρηστος
Πυθοχρηστος ο Απολλωνιδου
Πυθοχρηστος Πρωταγορου
Σινωπιων
Τευθρας
Φημιος ο Θυσιλεω
Φιλοκρατης
Χωρηγιων ο Λεωμεδοντος.

No. VII. (Vol. I., p. 201.)

NAMES OF MAGISTRATES.

Αγιης	Διος	Καλλιστρατος	Πυθοκλης
Αισχινης	Επιχαρμος	Κτησων	Σιμαλιων ο Κλει-
Απολλοδωρος	Ερμαιος	Κυρος	ταγορου
Αριστων	Εστιαιος	Μιδας	Σωσιας
Αρτεμιδωρος	Εστιαιος ο Πο-	Μιλτιαδης	Φιλημων
Αστεας	σειδωνιου	Παταικος	Φιλοκρατης
Βιων	Ευκλης	Ποσειδωνιος	Φιλων
Βορυς	Ηφαιστιος	Πρωτος	Φορβας
Γλαυκιας	Θεογειτνος	Πρωτοφανης	Χαβριας
Διονυσιος	Καλλισθενης		

NAMES OF UNCERTAIN ORIGIN.

Adæus	Cephalion	Eucanor	Melanthios
Andragathus	Demarchus	Hieroteles	Psaphon
Castor	Demosthenes	Hicestus	Xophilus

No. VIII. (Vol. I., p. 248.)

ANALYSIS OF GLAZE.

A fragment in the Museum of Sèvres of the black glaze gave the result of 63·0 silica, 20·5 alumina, 4·0 oxide of iron, 9·0 carb. lime, 2·0 magnesia, 2·0 water; that of a Vulcian vase, 55·49 sil., 19·21 alum., 16·55 ox. ir., 7·48 carb. lime, 1·27 magn. The glazes of vases of the Decadence, or so called Campanian, ware, of a phiale, 52·95 sil., 27·15 alum., 12·89 ox. ir., 5·25 carb. lime, 1·76 water; of a large cylix, 55·10 sil., 18·36 alum., 16·54 ox. ir., 9.0 water, 1·0 magn.; of a smaller cylix, 60·0 sil., 13·63 alum., 19·0 ox. ir., 5·91 carb. lime, 2·56 magn.; of another small cylix, 57·50 sil., 18·0 alum., 14·21 ox. ir., 7·73 carb. lime, 2·56 magn.; of a crater, 54·25 sil., 18·91 alum., 15·51 ox. ir., 9·5 carb. lime, 1·83 magn. The analysis of Salvetat gave nearly the same results,—55·88 sil., 18·88 alum., 15·80 ox. ir., 7·48 carb. lime, 1·63 water; and 46·3 sil., 11·9 alum., 16·7 ox. ir., 5·7 carb. lime, 2·30 magn., 17·1 soda. It is supposed to have been a soda glass with an oxide of iron and lime. (Brongniart, Traité, i., p. 550; Cat. Mus. Pract. Geol. p. 35.)

No. IX.   (Vol. II., p. 35, Appendix I.)

LIST OF NAMES ON VASES.

NAMES OF MEN.

Akestorides	Hiketes	Oinokles
Alalkon	Hipparchos	Olympiodoros
Alkibiades	Hippodamos	Onetor
Alkimachos	Hippokritos	Onetorides
Andokides	Hippon	Orthagoras
Antias	Ichias	Panaitios
Antiphon	Isolaos	Pasikles
Argos	Kallias	Pedieus
Aristarchos	Kallikles	Perses
Aristomenes	Kallipides	Phaos
Athenodotos	Kallithes	Pheidon
Batrachos	Karysstos	Philycus
Chærestratos	Kephalos	Polyphrassmon
Charmides	Kephitos	Pythodoros
Charops	Kleitarchus	Pythokles
Choiros	Klymenes	Simax
Cleinias	Krates	Simmiades
Damas	Ktesileos	Solon
Diogenes	Laches	Sostratos
Diokles	Leagros	Stroibos
Dioxippos	Leokrates	Timoxenos
Dorotheos	Lykaon	Tisonides
Epeleios	Lykos	Xenon
Epimedes	Lysippides	NAMES OF WOMEN.
Epidromas	Lysis	Aphrodisia
Epidromos	Megakles	Cheironeia
Erilos	Meletos	Erosanthe
Euaios	Memnon	Glyko
Eunikos	Neokleides	Heras
Euphiletos	Nikesippos	Nelais
Eupoles	Nikias	Oinanthe
Eupar . . . tos	Nikodemos	Pantoxena
Glaukon	Nikolaos	Philomele
Glaukos	Nikon	Phratheinon
Hiketas	Nikostratos	Rhodon
	Nyphes	Stheno

No. X. (Vol. II., p. 249.)

INSCRIPTIONS ON TILES.

The number of inscriptions on these tiles is so great that they would occupy too much space for the Appendix. The principal will be found in Fabretti, Corp. Inscript. c. vii. p. 512-513; Donius Inscr. p. 98; Maffeius, Mus. Veron. p. 109; Boldetti, Osser. sopra i cimiterij di Roma, Vol. I., p. 527-531; A. de Romanis, Le Antiche Camere Esquiline Rom. 1822, Tav. v. p. 45; Schöpflin, Alsat. Illust. T. i. p. 511, Museum, p. 108, Tab. ix.; Hagenbuch, De figlinis in circulo sive in orbem inscriptis in Orellius' Corp. Inscript. Lat., II. p. 37, s. 22; Bellerman, Die Alt. Christl Begrabniss, p. 62; D'Agincourt, Pl. lxxxii., p. 82-88; Janssen, Mus. Lugd. Bat. Inscript. Græc. et Latin. Tab. xxvii., p. 121.

No. XI. (Vol. II., p. 250.)

STAMP OF LEGION.	TITLE.	LOCALITY.
LEG. I.	Adjutrix	Mayence.
I. MIN.	Minervia	Voorburg.
LEG. I. MEN.	Minervia	Nimeguen.
I. PR. MIN.	Prima Minervia	Voorburg.
LEG. I. MR.	Minervia	Augst, Wijk.-bij-Duurstede.
LEG. I. M. ANT.	Minervia Antonina	Voorburg
LEG. II. ITA.	Italica	Enns.
LEG. II.		Enns.
LEG. II. AVG.	Augusta	Caerleon.
LEG. II. AVG. ANT.	Augusta Antonina	Caerleon.
LEG. III. M.	Martia Victrix	Scotland.
LEG. V.		
LEG. V. P. F. M.	Pia Fidelis Macedonica	Cleves, Nimeguen.
LEG. VI. V.	Victrix	Nimeguen, Augst.
LEG. VI. V. P. F.	Victrix Pia Fidelis	Birten.
LEG. VII.		
LEG. VIII. AVG. AR. FE	Augusta Armenia Felix	Niederbieber.
LEG. VIII. AVG.	Augusta	Birten, Mayence.
LEG. IX. VIC.	Victrix	York.
LEG. IX. HISP.	Hispanica	York.
LEG. X. (G.)	Gemina	Caer Rhyn. Nimeguen.
LEG. X. G. P. F.	Gemina Pia Fidelis	Voorburg.
LEG. XI. C. P. F.	Constans Pia Fidelis	Kloten.
LEG. XI. C. P.		Kloten.
LEG. XII. F.	Fulminatrix	Mayence.

STAMP OF LEGION.	TITLE.	LOCALITY.
LEG. XIII. G. M. F.	Gemina Martia Victrix	Mayence, Petronelli.
LEG. XIV.	Transrhenana Germanica	Dormagen, Petronelli.
LEG. XV.		Nimeguen.
LEG. XV. A. P.	Augusta Pia	Petronelli.
LEG. XVI.		Neuss.
LEG. XVII.		
LEG. XVIII. F. P.	Firma Primigenia	Vetera.
LEG. XIX. P.	Primigenia	Xanten.
LEG. XX. PR.	Primigenia	Cleves, Neuss, Nimeguen.
LEG. XX. V. V.	Valeria Victrix	Chester, Nimeguen.
LEG. XXI. R.	Rapax	Mayence, Xanten.
LEG. XXI. S. C. VI.	Secunda Constans Victrix	Kloten.
LEG. XXI. C.		
LEG. XXI. S.		Kloten.
LEG. XXII. P. P. F.	Primigenia Pia Fidelis	Mayence, Xanten.
LEG. XXII. PRI.	Primigenia	Niederbieber.
LEG. XXIII. G.	Gemina	Xanten.
LEG. XXIV.		
LEG. XXV.		
LEG. XXVI.		
LEG. XXVII.		
LEG. XXVII.		
LEG. XXVIII.		
LEG. XXIX.		
LEG. XXX. VAL. S.A.A.	Valeriana Severiana Alexandrina Augusta.	
LEG. XXX. V. V. P. F.	Ulpia Victrix Pia Fidelis	
LEG. XXX. V. V.	Ulpia Victrix	Nimeguen.
LEG. XXX.		Nimeguen, Hooldorn.
LEG. XXX. V. VI.		Nimeguen.
LEG. XXXIX.	Primigenia	Xanten.
LEG. CISRHENANA		

COHORTS.		
PRIMA COH. QV.	Quorquenorum	Nimeguen.
COH. III. VIND.	Vindex	Niederbieber.

VEXILLATIONS.		
VEX. EX. GER. F.	Exercitus Germaniæ Inferioris	
VEX. EX. GERM.	Exercitus Germanicus	Nimeguen.
VEX. LEG. GERM.	Legionis Germanicæ	Nimeguen.
VEX. BRIT.	Britannica	Nimeguen.

EX. GER. INF.	Exercitus Germaniæ Inferioris	Nimeguen.

CL. BR.	Classis Britannica	Lymne, Dover.

KAR.	Carnuntum	Petronelli.
LON.	Londinum	London.
VINDOB.	Vienna	Vienna.

No. XII. (Vol. II., p. 296.)

INSCRIPTIONS ON LAMPS.

A · A ·
A · A · N · N ·
ACE
ACCIANA PVBLI · SATRI
F · CAM ·
A · COCC · FEL ·
AED ·
AELI MAXI
AGATE
AI
AIATO
AIMILI ERONIS
ALEXAN
AMRD
ANNAM
ANI
ANIA
ANISDO
ANTO · AVG ·
ANTON
ANTONINI
ANTONINI · AVG ·
AQVILIN
AQVILINI
AREOLIN
ARI
ARIONIS
ARRE
ATILI · REST ·
ATIMETI
ATTI
ATY
AVF · FRONT
AVG · ANTONINI
AVGNR
AVGNRI
A · VIBI
AVLLI
AVR · XAN
BAGRADI
BALSA
BAS · AVGV
BASSA
BASSIDI
BESTIALIS
CAI · ADIEC ·
C · IVN · DRAC ·
CASSV
CAI · MERCVR
CAES
CAIVS · LVCIVS
  MAVRVS
CAMSAR

CAMVR
CANA · FEL
CANI
CANINIA
CAPITON
CARINIA
CASSI
C · ATILIVES
C · CAESAE
C · CAESAR
C · CISI
C · CLO · SVC ·
C · CLO · SI · O ·
C · CLO · SVC
C · CLODIVS · SVCCVS
C · CORN · VRS ·
C · FAB · IVS
C · FABR ·
C · FABRIS ·
C · FABRVS [?]
C · FAM ·
CHRES
C · ICCI
C · ICCI · VATIC
C · ICCII · VATICAN ·
C · ICCII · VATICANI
C · IV · · EIT ·
CINNAMI
C · IVL · APAAC ·
C · IVL · NIC ·
C · IVL · NICEP ·
C · IVLI · NICI
C · IVL · PHI
C · IVL PHILI ·
C · IVL · SO ·
C · IVL · PHIL
C · IVN · DOMIT
C · IVN · NII
CLO · HE
CLO · HEL
CLO · HELI ·
CL · LVPERCALIS
CLO · L · DIA
CLVNERI ·
C · MARV
C · MEM ·
C · M · EVPO
CN · AP · AP
CN · ATEI ·
COEFI · O
COMITIANS · F
C · OP · REST ·
C · OPPI · REST ·

C · OPPI · RES
COMMODI
COMMODI TERTIA
COR · AV · PAS
CORDI ·
CRACLID ·
C · POM · DIC ·
C · PPE
CRISPIN
C · TER ·
C · TERT ·
C · TESO
C · VICILAR
CVIVRI
C · IAS · AVGV
D · ET · DEI · N
DEO · N · PIS
DIOGENES · F
DOMITIA
DOMITIA D · E · (or, ET)
  D · N
DRAC ·
EG · APRILIS ·
ERACLID ·
EROTIS ·
ERTI · ANC
EX · OFF · HORTENSI ·
EX · OF · PV · ET · TI ·
  AD · PORT · TRIG ·
F ·
FABRI
FABRIC · AGAT
FABRIC · A · MAS
FABRINI ·
F · AEL · ER · AC
FAVSTI ·
FELI ·
FLAV
FLAV · D̂ · P
FLAVI
FLAVIA
FLAVIA D · E ' D · N ·
FLAVIA D · ET · DEI ·
FLAVIA D · ET DEI · N ·
FLAVIA D · ET · D · N ·
FLOREN
FLORENS
FLORENT
FORTIS
FORTIS · N ·
FORTVNI · N ·
FRONTO
GABINIA

G · NVMICII ·
G · P · R · F ·
HERACLIANV
I · ICCI · VATIC
I · M · S · V
INA
INVLISVCO
ION · IV · CI ·
G · V · F
IVLCIRI
IVLIAE NI.·
IVNCA
IVN · ALEXI
IVSTI
IVVIHERM
KV
LABERI
L · CAESAE
L · CAESA · F
L · CAMSAS
L · COELI
L · COELI · F
L · D · P
L · DOMITI · P
L · FARR · AEAE ·
L · FABRI · AEVI
L · FABR
L · FABRIC · MAS
L · FABRIC · MASCL ·
LITOGENES
L · IVLI · RE ·
L · MAMIT
L · MARMI
L · M · C
L · M · MIT ·
L · M · RES
L · M · PHI · O
L · M · SA ·
L · MVRA · M
L · OPPI · RES
L · OREST ·
L · PASISI · O
L · PASISI · R
L · PRI ·
L · SERGI
L · T
LVC · CEI
LVCI

L · MA · ADIEC
LVCIVS · CAECILIVS
SAEVVS
M ·
MARCIAN
MARN
MAXI
MAXIM
MAXIMI
MAXIM · SAC ·
M · ELI
MEMMI
MERA
M · IVL · PHI
M · IVL · PHILIP · COS ·
III
M · IVL · PHILIPPI
M · NOTIVS
MONOS
M · OPPI · OF
M · R · MTO
MVNT · RES
MVNT · REST ·
MVNTRIPI ·
N ·
NATE
NEGIDIVS
NERI
NEREVS
NNA
NNANN ·
NNAELVCI
OF · CHRESTIO ·
OF · IONIS
OF · PAR
ONORATI
OPI
OPPI
OPP · QVART
P · ACCI
PANNICI ·
PASTOR
PAS · AVG
PASISID ·
PONTI
PRIMI
PRISCI

PROB
PROBI
PVBLI
PVB · FABRICII TERTIA
Q · ALLA · D
Q · MAMI · CEL
R ·
RVDIA · SABRI ·
SABINIA ·
SAECVL ·
SAM ·
SAPRI
SAT ·
SERG · PRIM
SEVERI
SEX · EGN · APR ·
STEPANI
STROBILI ·
SVCCESE
SVCCESSIVI
TAXIAPOL
TERTVLLI
T · FLAVI · IANVARI ·
FLORENT ·
TINDA
TINDAR · PLOT · AVG
LIBERTVS ·
TIBERINA · P · C · L
TITI
TITINIA
TRAIANI
TVRICI · SAB
VEICRIS
VIBIAN
VIBIVS
V · MVN · SVC ·
VOVIVS
VRBINVS · F ·
V · SAIA · M
Impressed in labels referring
to subject.
DEO QVI EST MAX-
IMVS
ADIVATE SODALES
ANNVM NOVVM
FAVSTVM FELICEM
MI

No. XIII. (Vol. II., p. 312.)

STAMPS ON THE HANDLES OF ROMAN AMPHORÆ.*

AFRI
APFSC
ARCHEIA
AXII ·
BELLVCI
C., C · F · AI ·
C · I · I; C · I · V · R ·
C · IV
C · V · H
CANINI
CIREXORAS
CORI
CRADOS
DAMAS
DOM ·· S
EIPC
EVI · STERPS
GIAB ·
GORCIA · ·
    ICIOR
IIICA ·· MENSS
IIIMIN
I · O · VII ·
HILARI ··
HOSDAS ·
L :::: EN
L · C · PI
L · ME
L · O · S ·
MIM ·

MOGVED · D
OMR
PAVLLVS
Q · NAND
ROMANI
RVFIAN
RVMAS
S · F · E
SAENNVS
SCALENS
THI · SVV
VALERI ·
VIBIOR
VTRII ·
VISELLI ·
C · ANT · QVIET ·
C · ANTON · QV
C · F · AI
C · IV · R ·
C · MAR · STIL
G · M · T
L · CAN · SEC ·
L · C · SOLL ·
L · CES ·
L · IVN · MELISSAE
L · IVNI MELISSI
L · SER · SENEC ·
L · S · SEX
M · C · C
M · AEM · RUS

MAR
M · EXSONI
M · P · R ·
P · S · A
POR · L · AN ·
P · VENETV
Q · S · P
S · C · L
SEVERI · LVPI
S · VENT · VR ·
F, or FECIT, before the
    name.
GERMARA ·
C · CVF.A
F after the name.
C · AP · F
C · VA ·
EROI ·
[FR]ATERNI
GESCV
OF after the name.
··· EMINC
·· GEBI
·· L · C · F · P · C
·· SANI
SVI
M ·
CARTVNIT
L · V · ROPI
NYMP · M · F · S ·

STAMPS ON MORTARIA.

ALBINVS
AMMIVS ·
ANDREAS
APRILIS
AXII
BRIXSA
CAS ···
CELSANOS ·
CINTVSMVS
DEVA ·
DVBITATVS ·
DOINV ··· DO ·
ENNVSAMI
LICINILLVS
LITVGENI

MALLA
MARINVS
MATVCENVS
MAXI[MVS]
PENEAS
RIDANVS
RIPANI ·
RVCCVS
SABINVS
SAVRANVS ·
SATVRNINVS ·
SECVNDVS
SEXTI
SOLLVS
SVMACI

TANIO
VIALLA
With F, or FECIT, after the
    name.
ALBINVS
BORIEDO ·
CANDIDVS
CATVLVS
LVGVDI ·
MARINVS
MARTINVS ·
MATVSENVS
PAVLVS ·
QVARTVS
QVIETVS

* R. Smith, Collectanea, i. 149—150; Archæol. viii., Janssen, Inscr. p. 12, and following.

SEQVT
SOLLVS
VIBIAN
With M after the name.
RIPANVS
with OF ·
PRIMI
PRASSO
The name only.
A · TEREN · RIPAN
CASSI · C · LEGE

C · ATISIVS · SABINVS
C · ATTIVS MANSINUS
C · HERM
L · CAN · SEC
L · FVRIVS · PRISCVS ·
P · P · R ·
P · R · B
Q · VA · SE ·
Q · VAL · F · VERAN · F
Q · VALERIVS ·

Q · VALERI 5SVNERTI
Q · VALERIVS
VA · SEC · SATVRN
VERANIVS
QVI · VAL ·
SEX · SAT
SEX · VAL ·
TIITVIS · VI
RIPANVS TIBER · F
LVGVDV FACTVS

No. XIV. (Vol. II., p. 362.)

NAMES OF POTTERS OF SAMIAN OR RED WARE.

The accompanying list contains the names stamped on Samian ware in England and on the continent. It does not comprise the Aretine potters. They are given as they have been; many without doubt erroneously; and others as single, which are probably double names. Few are older than the time of Augustus. They are classed according to the formula the potters used, as the same names are found at Augst in Switzerland, at Murviedo in Spain, in London, and in Normandy, and Holland, it is evident that they belong to some renowned pottery, whence they were exported. The principal authorities are the Collectanea of Mr. Roach Smith, the list of Mr. Neville, the Cours of M. Caumont, the Normandie Souterraine of M. Cochet, the Inscriptions of M. Janssen, and the Handbuch of Wagener.

With O, OFF, OFFIC before the potter's name.

ACRISI
ALBI ·
ALBIN ·
CAL ·
CALP ·
CALV ·
CALVI ·
CARAN
CARO ·
CELSI
CEN
GENSO ·
CIRMI ·
COTTO ·
CREM ·

CRES ·
CREST ·
DOM ·
DVDE
FABIN
FACE ·
FEL MA ·
FELICIS
FIRMONIS
FRONTI .
FRONTINI ·
FVSC ·
GER ·
IVCVN ·
IVCVND ·

IVLIA ·
IVLPATR ·
IVSTI
IVVENAL ·
LABI
L · AE ·
L · C · VIRIL
LICINI ·
LOVIRIGO ·
LVCCEI ·
MANA ·
MARAN
MARO ·
MONO
MATE

MEM ·
MINVS
M · LVCCA ·
MO
MODESTI
MOE
MOM
MON
MONO
MONTEI
MONTI
MONTO ·
MONTECI
MURRA
MVRRANI ·
NARIS ·
NATIVIC
NEM
NERI ·

NI., NIGRI ·
NIGRINIANI ·
NITORI ·
NOM ·
PAR ·
PARI ·
PASSI ·
PASSIENI ·
PATRICI ·
PATRIC ·
PATRVCI ·
POLLIO ·
PRIM · , PRIMI ·
PRIMVL ·
PVDEN ·
RICIMI ·
ROS · RVFI
RVFIN
RVL ·

SAB ·
SABIN ·
SARMIT ·
SECV
SEVER
SIIS ·
SIIV ·
SVLPICI
TERT ·
VENMAN
VERINA
VIA ·
VIRILLI ·
L · C · VIRILIS
VIRTVTIS
VITA
VITAL
EX · OF before the name.
HIRVN ·

With O, OFF, or OFFIC after the potter's name.

ABALI ·
ABAN ·
ABARI ·
ACIRAT ·
AVRAP
ADVOCISI ·
ALBAN ·
ALBI ·
AMAND ·
APRILIS ·
APRIS
APRO ·
ATILIAN
AVITOS ·
BASSI
BORILLI ·
BVRDONIS
C · AN · PATR
CASSIA ·

L · C · CELSI ·
CRECIRI ·
M · CRESTI ·
CONTI · CRESTI · ·
DONNA
FELIGIS ·
GERMANI ·
IANVARI
ISE
KALENDI ·
LABIONIS ·
MANSVETI
MARCI
MARTII
MISCI
NASCITI ·
PATERATI
PATERCLINI ·

PATERNI ·
PONTI
REBVRRIS ·
ROMVLI
SACERI ·
SACERVASI
SACIRAP ·
SATERNINI
SCENIGI
SEVERI ·
SEXTI
SIIXTILI ·
SILVI
SOLIMI
SOLEMNI ·
VESTRI
VIRONI ·
VITALI ·

With F, FE, FEC, FECIT after the potter's name.

ACCILINVS
A · CVRIO ·
AEQVIR ·
ALBINVS
ALBVS
AMABILIS
AMMIVS
ANISATVS ·
ARGO
ASSIVS ·
ATILIANVS
ATVSA

AVGELLA
AVLLVS
AVSTVS
BELINICCVS
BIGA
BIO
BITVRIX
BONOXVS
BVODVS
BVODV⸏IVS
BVCCVS
BVRDO

C · ABRILIS
CABRVS
CAIVS
CALMVA
CAMBVS
CAPASIAS
CARVS
CASTVS
CATVS
CASVRIVS
GAVPIN ·
CERIALIS

CERTVS
CIBIS ·
CILLVTIVS
CINTVSMVS
CIRRVS
COCCA
COCVRNV ·
COCVRO
COLLO
COMPRIN
CORNIIRT ·
COSAXTI
COSIA ·
CONSTANS
CRACISA ·
CRAOسNA
CRACVNA
CRIMVS
CROBRO
GVNI · IA
DAGODVBNVS
DAGOMARVS
DESTER ·
DOCILIS
DAGOIMNVS
DOMETOS
DOMITIANVS
DRAPPVS
DRAVCVS
ETVS
FELIX ·
FELIXS ·
FᴇSTVS
GAIVS
GARBVS
GALBINVS
GENITOR
HABILIS
HELVIVS · FI
HELL · ·· S
IABVS
IANVS
ICMRIMO
INPRITV ·
IVSTVS ·
LATINIAN ·
LEO
L · GETVS ·
LICINVS
LOLLIVS
LVCANVS
LVCCEIVS
LVɔIVS
LVTAEVS
MACER
M · ACCIVS
MAGNVS
MAIOR ·

MALLVRO
MANER VS
MARCVS ·
MARTIALIS
MASCVLVS
MESTO
MICCIO
MINVCIVS
MOTIVS ·
MOXIVS
MOXSIVS
MOXSVS
MVISVS
NASSO
NEBBIC
NIGER
NICEPHORVS ·
NISTVS
PASTOR
PASTORINVS
PATER
PATERN ·
PATERCLOS
PATNA
PATRICIANVS
PAVLLVS
SERRVS
QVARTVS
QVINTVS
REGENVS
ROFFVS
ROPPVS
ROPVSI
RVFVS
SACINVS
SALV
SANVCIVS ·
SATTO ·
SATVRNINVS
SECVNDVS
SEDATVS
SENNIVS
SENTRVS
SEVERIANVS
SEXTVS ·
SILVINVS ·
SOLLVS ·
SVOBNEDO
TASCONVS
TAVRICVS
TERTIVS
TOCCA
TOTTIVS
TVLLVS ·
VERTECISA
VERTECISSA
VESPO
VIGTICIVS

VINDVś
VIRILIS
VIRTHVS
VITALIS ·
VITINVS
  With ME FECIT
SEXTVS
  F with a genitive for figuli.
GARANI
CELSIANI
CITSIANI
MAIORIS
MARCI ·
ROMVLI ·
SILVINI ·
  Without F after the name.
ACERO
ACVBIA
ACVTVS
AELIANVS
AGEDILLVS
AGILIS
AGIILITO
AMATOR
AMONVS
AQVIINVS
ARSACVS
ASIATICVS
ATILIANVś
AVGVSTALIS
AVGVSTINVS
AVITVS
BASSVS
BESSVS
BOLDO
BRACTILLO
CABRASIVś
GACAVA
CAPITOLINVS
CAPASIVS ·
CARINVS
CARVSSA
CASTVS
CATIANVS
CAVPIVS
CAVTV
CELSINVS
CELTAS
CENSORINV ·
CERIALIS
CIAMAT ·
CINTVSMV
CINTUCNATUS
CITSIANI
CIRINNA
COBNERTVS
COCVRO
COLLON

COLON
COMICVS
COMITIALIS
COMITIANVS
COMMVNIS
COTTO
CRASSIACVS
CRISPINA
CVCVRO
CVPITVS ·
DAGO ·
DAGODVBNVS ·
DAMONVS
DAVIVS ·
DICETVS
DIGNVS
DIVICATVS
DIVIX
DIVIXTVL ·
DOCCIVS
DOMINAC
DOMITVS
DONATVS
DOVIICCVS
DVRINV
ECVESER .
ELLENIIVS
EPPA
ERCLVS
EROS
EVRVS
FESIVS
FORMOSVS
FORTIS
FRONTINVS
GERMANVS ·
GIAMI
GRACCHVS
HABILIS ·
HILARVS
IACOMIO
IANVARIVS
IASO
ILLVSTACO
IMIVSETGAI
IOENALIS
LASTVCA
LATINIANVS
LATINVS
LIBERTVS
LICINILVS
LICINVS
LINIVSMIX
LITVCAMVS
LOLLIVS
LOSSA
LVCANIVS
LVCANV S

LVPPA
LVTAEVS
MACIRVS
MACRINVS
MAIANVS
MALLIA
MANSINVS
MARCELLINV ·
MARNVS
MARTIALIS
MARTIVS
MASONIVS
MATERNINVS
MATVACV
MATVCENVS
MERCATOR
METHILLVS
MINVVS
MINVTVS
M · NOTIVS
MONTANVS
MOSSVS
MOXIVS
NATALIS
NERTVS
NEQVREC ·
NICEPHOR ·
IVL · NVMIDIC ·
ONATINI ·
PATRICIVS
PATVLVS
PERE ·
PERPET
PERRVS
PETRVLLVS
PRIMVL · PATER
PRIMINVS
PRIMVS
PRVBCVS
PVBLIVS
PVRINX
QVADRATVS
QVARTVS
QVINTVS
RAMVLVS
REBVRRIS
RECMVS
REGALIS
REGVLINVS
REVILINVS
RIIGALIS
RIIGNVS
RVCCATIA
SABELLVS
SABINVS
SARENTIV
SATVRNVS
SENECA

SERRVS
SILVI · PATER
SINATAS
SOLLVS
SVRIVS
SYMPHO ·
TAVRIANVS
TERRVS
TERTIVS
TETT · PRIM ·
TETTVR
TITTIVS
TRINONVS
VENERAND
VENICARVS
VERECVNDVS
VERONISSA
VIBIVS
VICTOR
VICTORINVS
VIRIL ·
VIRILIS ·
VIRTHV
VIRTHVS
VITALIS ·
VILLO ·
VOSIICVNNVS
VMVN · SVC
VNICVS
VRVC

With **M** ·, or **MA**, for *manu*
after the name.

AELIANI ·
AESTIVI ·
AFRICANV
AIISTIVI ·
AISTIVI ·
AETERNI ·
ALBANI ·
ALBILLI ·
ALBINI ·
ANVMI ·
ARACI
ARICI ·
ASCIATICI
ASCILLI ·
ATILIANI ·
ATTICI
AVSTRI
AVENTINI
AVITI
AVINI
BELINICCI
BENICCI
BENNICI
BORILLI ·
BOVTI ·

BRICC ·
CACAS ·
CALVI
CALVINI
CAMTI
CANAI
CARANTINI
CARETI
CARBONIS
CARILLI
CERIAL ·
CHRESTI ·
CINTVSMI
CIRRI ·
CIVRRI ·
COBNERTI ·
COCCIL ·
COCCILI ·
COLLI ·
COMPRINNI
CONGI ·
CONSORTI ·
COSMI ·
CRACI · S ·
CRASIS ·
CRISPINI
CRV
CVCALI
CVCILLI
DAMINI
DAVICI
DECMI
DECVMINI ·
DEM · · · R ·
DIVICATI ·
DIVICI ·
DOCALI ·
DOMNA ·
DONATI ·
FAVI ·
GLVPEI
GENITALIS ·
ILLIANI ·
IVSTI ·
LALLI ·
LIBERTI
LILTANI ·
LIMETII
LOGIRN ·
LOGIRNI ·
LVPEI ·
LVPI ·
LVPINI ·
MACCALI
MACILLI
MACRIANI
MAIORI
MALLI

MALLIACI
MALLICI
MANDVILL
MARCELLI
MARCELLINI
MARCI ·
MARINI ·
MARITI ·
MAROILLI ·
MART(I)ANI ·
MARTIALIS
MARTINI
MATERNINI ·
MAXIMII
MELISSVS
MEMORIS
MERCATOR
MERETI ·
METTI ·
MICCIONIS
MIDI ·
MINVLI
MINVTIVS
MITERNA
MONTI
MOSSI ·
MVXTVLLI ·
MVXIVIII
NERT ·
NOBILIANI
OF · · CIA
OPTATI ·
OSBI
PASSENI ·
PATRICI
PAVLI
PAVLIANI
PAVLLI
PIIRVINCI
POMPEII
POTITIANI ·
POTITINI ·
PRISCILLI ·
PVTRI
QVI · ASSA ·
QVINTINI
REDITI
REGINI.
RIIGALI ·
RIIOGENI
REGVLI ·
ROLOGENI ·
ROPPIRVI ·
ROTTLAI
RVFFI ·
RVFFINI ·
SABINI ·
SACIRO

SACRATI
SACRE
SACRILLI
SANIANI
SANVILLI
SANVITTI ·
SCOTH ·
SECANDI ·
SECVN ·
SECVNDINI
SEDETI ·
SENLIA
SENO
SENON
SEVIRI
SIIGVOI
SIIXTI ·
SILDATIANI ·
SITVSIRI
SORILLI
SVARTI
TASCILI
TASCILLI ·
TAXIL
TERCII
TERTII
TITVRI
TOCCA ·
VEGETI
VENI ·
VERECVNDI ·
VEST ·
VICTORI ·
VIIRI ·
VSAIACN :

With M S, *Manu Sua.*

CAI ·
CENI ·
FVCA ·
SACROT ·
With MANV after the name.
PRISCILLI

Without M · or MA · or F

ABIANI ·
ADIVTORI
ADVOCISI
AEGEDILLI
AITI
ALBVCI
ALBVCIANI
AMATORIS
ANTICVI
A · POL · AVCIR
A · POL · AVSTRI ·
APRONIS
ATEI
BANOLVCCI

BASSI
BASSICI
BELINICCI
BENAVICI
BENNICI
BILICANI
BILICAT·
BLAESI
BOINICCI
BRICCI
BRITANII
BVCIANI
BVRDIVI
CALETINI
CANRVCATI
CARANI
CASSI
CATVLI·
CENSORI·
CENSORINI·
CINNAMI·
CINNVMI
CINTVAGENI·
CINTVSSA·
COSMIANI
CRANI·
CRANIANI
CRESTI
CVTAI·
CVEBRCI
DEOMARTI
DIOGNATI
DIVIXI·
DOMINICI
DONNAVG
DONTIONI
ELVILLI
EPONTI
ERICI·
ERRIMI
FELICIONIS

FOARI
FORTVNI
GENITORIS
GERMANI
GRANANI
GAANIANI
HELINIV··
IABI·
IIIMVI
IOVANTI
ISTVRONIS
IVLIAN·
LENTVLI
LOGIRNI·
LVCCANI
MAIORIS
MALLIACI
MALVNCNI
MAMILIANI
MA[N]SVETI
MARCELLINI
MARCI
MATRIANI
MATVRN
MAXIMI
MAXIMINI
MERCA·
METILI·
MICCIO·
MISSI
NIGRINI·
PASSENI
PASSIENI
P·OPPI·PIN
PP·PATERNI
PATERNVLI
PATRICI
PEREGRINI·
PONTI
PONTIACI

PRIDIANI·
PRIMANI·
PRIMVLI·
PRIMI
PRIMIS
PRIMVLI·
PROTVLI
QVADRATI·
QVE SALVI·
REGINI
REGVILL·
RELATVLI
RIPANI·
RI[T]IOGENI·
RIVICA
RVFINI
SACIANI
SATVRNINI·
SECVNDINI
SENONI
SERVILIS
SEVERI
SILVANI·
SILVINI
SILVI·PATRICI·
STROBILI
SVLPICI·
SVLPICIANI·
TALLINI
TITTILI·
TITVRONIS
VALERI
VASSALI
VERECV.
VERECVNDI
VEROGANDI
VRNNI
XIVI
L·ADN·ADGENI
IVL·NVMIDI·

UNCERTAIN FORMS.

ALSOETIR·
AMIIDV
AQVIT·
AQVITAN
ARDA·C
ARRO
A·SVLPIC
BVTRIV
CACIL·ANTRO
CALV
CASIL·
C·GRATI·
CLO·HEL
COSIR·

COSI·RVFIN
COTON
C·VAL·AB
DOCC
FIRMO
FL·COS·V·
ILLIOMEN
·····RIM
FIMAN·
IVLIA·
IVLIA PATR
LACNO·
LANG·
L·FABR·

GASCE
L·CELI·
LOGIRN
L·RASIN·P·
L·P·RIC
MININ
MR·M·R·R
M·PER·CR·
M·R·M·R·R·
NIBO
PAESTON
PASSIEN
P·CO·
P·COR

PELTA	S · M · R ·	VERECV
PRIMICCO	S · M · T	VINN
Q · V · S ·	TAVRI	VIRTH
· · · R FLAIVII	TEBBIL ·	XVNX
SANTINOV · C	TVRTVNN ·	

A list of incised inscriptions is given, Janssen, loc. cit. p. 159, and following.

OCULIST'S STAMP ON RED SAMIAN WARE.

[Fragment in British Museum.]

C · IVLI CENIS CR   OCOD · AD · ASPE ·

BLACK WARE STAMPS.

CAMAR · O ·   FIRMINVS · F ·
L · CASSI · O   AVGVSTI · F ·

INCISED INSCRIPTIONS.

MEMN · N · SAC · VIII   GENIO TVRNACENSI   DEO · MERCVRIO
VALENTINV · LEG · XXV ·

No. XV.

LIST OF THE PRINCIPAL COLLECTIONS OF ANCIENT POTTERY.

GREAT BRITAIN.

Addington, H. Esq., St. Martin's Lane.
Auldjo, T. Esq., Noel House, Kensington.
Bale, C. S., Esq., 71, Cambridge Terrace, London.
Boileau, Sir J., Bart., 20, Upper Brook Street, London.
British Museum, London.
Cadogan, Earl, 138, Piccadilly, London.
Chichester Museum.
Field, E. W., Esq., Hampstead.
Fitzwilliam Museum, Cambridge.
Forman, W. H., Dyers' Hall Wharf.
Fortnum, E. C., Esq., Stanmore.
Gray, Rev., Hamilton, Bolsover.
Guildhall Museum, London.
Hamilton, Duke of, Hamilton, Scotland.
Henderson, John, Esq., Montague Square.
Hoare, S. R. C.
Iekyll, E., Esq., 2, Grafton St., Bond St.
Lansdowne, Marquis of, Bowood.
Leake, W. M., Esq., Queen Anne Street, London.

Mayer, H., Esq., Liverpool.
Museum of Practical Geology, Jermyn Street, London.
Northwick, Lord, 44, St. James Place.
Northampton, Marquis of, Castle Ashby.
Northumberland, Duke of, Alnwick.
Neville, R. H., Esq., Upper Grosvenor Street, London.
Purnell, H., Esq., Stancombe Park.
Slade, Felix, Esq., Doctors' Commons.
Society of Arts, Adelphi, London.
York, Museum of Philosophical Society.

FRANCE.

Museum of the Louvre, Paris.
Bibliothèque Impériale, Rue Richelieu, Paris.
Boulogne Museum.
M. Fould, Paris.
Count Pourtalès-Gorgier, Paris.
Duc de Luynes, Paris and Dampierre.
Lyons Museum.
M. Panckoucke, Paris.

BELGIUM.
Brussells' Museum.

HOLLAND.
Leyden Museum.

SWITZERLAND.
Berne Museum.

DENMARK.
King's Collection, Copenhagen.
Thorwaldsen Museum, Copenhagen.

RUSSIA.
Hermitage, St. Petersburg.
Odessa Museum.

PRUSSIA.
Berlin Museum.
University of Bonn.

AUSTRIA.
Antiken-Kabinet, Vienna.

KARLSRUHE.
Kunsthalle.

LOMBARDY.
Palagi Collection, Milan.

TUSCANY.
Museum, Florence.

Casuccini Collection, Chiusi.
S. François, Leghorn.
Museo Rossi Bacci, Arezzo.

PAPAL STATES.
Museo Gregoriano, Rome.
S. Campana, Rome.

KINGDOM OF THE TWO SICILIES.
Museo Borbonico, Naples.
Conte di Siracusa, Naples.
Cavaliere St. Angelo, Naples.
S. Barone, Naples.
S. Betti, Naples.
S. Torrusio, Naples.
S. Gargiulo, Naples.
S. Iatta, Ruvo.
S. Fittipaldi, Anzi.
S. Rainone, St. Agata dei Goti.
Museum at Syracuse.
Museum at Palermo.
Principe della Trabbia Palermo.
Giudica Collection, Palazzuolo.

MALTA.
Museum.

INDEX.

M.

W.

THE END.

BRADBURY AND EVANS, PRINTERS, WHITEFRIARS.

CPSIA information can be obtained at www.ICGtesting.com
Printed in the USA
LVOW10s0819220315

431427LV00003B/86/P